THE TRADER'S GUIDE TO EQUITY SPREADS

HOW TO INCREASE RETURNS AND LOWER RISK WITH OPTION STRATEGIES

RANDY FREDERICK

McGraw Hill

New York Chicago San Francisco Lisbon London Madrid Mexico City
Milan New Delhi San Juan Seoul Singapore Sydney Toronto

The McGraw-Hill Companies

1 2 3 4 5 6 7 8 9 0 DOC/DOC 0 9 8 7

ISBN-13: 978-0-07-147811-3

ISBN-10: 0-07-147811-6

This book is printed on acid-free paper.

Library of Congress Cataloging-in-Publication Data

Frederick, Randy.
The trader's guide to equity spreads : how to increase returns and lower risks with option strategies / by Randy Frederick.
p. cm.
Includes bibliographical references and index.
ISBN-13: 978-0-07-147811-3 (hardcover : alk. paper)
ISBN-10: 0-07-147811-6 (alk. paper)
1. Options (Finance) I. Title.
HG6024.A3F73 2007
332.63'2283--dc22
2007010947

To Greg Miller, whose passion for the options business left me some mighty big shoes to fill.

CONTENTS

ACKNOWLEDGMENTS

This book was made possible by the generous support and encouragement of my current employer, CyberTrader, Inc. and The Charles Schwab Corporation.

I would especially like to thank the following people:

Chuck Speiser, who taught me much about options back in 1993 and 1994.

Mark Burke, who despite some reservations gave me my first management opportunity in derivatives.

Tim O'Donnell, who taught me many things relating to options, as well as how to be empathetic when dealing with people, but mostly for being there as a friend for the past 14 years.

Kevin Green, who taught me a great deal about technical analysis and active equities trading.

Butch Jones, whose hands-off style and straightforward approach allowed me much latitude in both defining my ever-changing role and reaching my goals at CyberTrader and Schwab.

Mike Boccio, who has been a constant pleasure to work with, and for helping me navigate through the maze of media and public relations.

Trey Robinson, for relentlessly supporting me in many ways.

All of the various developers and programmers at CyberTrader and Schwab who have been able to piece together the mountain of ideas, drawings, and flowcharts I have provided in order to create one the finest option trading platforms available today.

Most importantly, to my wonderful wife, Kathy, for supporting me throughout my entire career.

DISCLOSURES

The examples in this book are for illustrative purposes only, and are not intended to represent actual trades, situations, people, or outcomes. They are theoretical but intended to be sample representations of possible scenarios that may occur in real life.

To simplify the calculations and highlight the principles and fundamentals, most of the examples in this book do not discuss in great detail the taxes, margin requirements, or commission costs that may be incurred. Commissions, taxes, and transaction costs can be a significant factor when implementing any options strategy, and should be carefully considered before placing any trade. Multiple leg strategies such as spreads involve multiple commission charges. For more details regarding option commissions, margin requirements, or other transaction costs, please consult your broker. Contact a tax advisor for the tax implications involved in these or any option strategies. Before investing you should make your own independent evaluation based on your own circumstances or consult with your investment advisor.

Options carry a high level of risk and are not suitable for all investors. Certain requirements must be met to trade options through most brokers. Prior to buying or selling any option, a person must receive a copy of the Options Clearing Corporation risk disclosure document titled *Characteristics and Risks of Standardized Options.* Copies of this document are available from your broker or by writing CyberTrader, Inc., P.O. Box 202890, Austin, TX 78720. Member NASD/SIPC.

Introduction

The options industry is a dynamic, changing, growing business. From 2003 to 2006, annual industry growth was 16%, 30%, 27%, and 35% respectively. While much of this growth was driven by the advent of the hedge fund industry, just as much was driven by retail investors like you and me. The number of investors who are embracing options as part of their overall investment portfolios is greater than at any time in history. In order to trade options and avoid taking unnecessary risks, it is important to understand the various strategies available to you. While strategies such as buy-writes, sell-writes, collars, and straddles all offer many opportunities for income generation, hedging, or speculation, spreads are by far the most varied and versatile. Spread trading comes in many forms, and this book is intended to introduce you to most of the more common types.

In many ways this book can be viewed as a reference guide, allowing you to jump in at the beginning of nearly any chapter without reading everything up to that point and still learn the strategies discussed. The flow of each chapter is very consistent, starting with a brief explanation of the strategies covered, followed by the calculations you should use to determine important price levels such as the maximum gain, maximum loss, and breakeven points. After that you will see a Quick Overview, which simply illustrates the profit and loss characteristics of the strategy, the sentiment, appropriate usage, risk/reward characteristics, Greeks, and likely outcomes both prior to and at expiration.

Once you cover the Quick Overview you can proceed to the Detail section if you need more information. Throughout the entire book I have included many charts and tables to help illustrate the profit and loss zones for each strategy. In most cases I have also included comparisons of the various spread strategies to simpler strategies to highlight both the similarities and the differences. Additionally, since many option strategies and most spread strategies in particular are established with the original intent of maintaining them through the option's expiration date, I have included explanations and calculations to highlight the possible outcomes at various prices on option expiration date. Most chapters also conclude with a summary of the potential advantages and disadvantages of the strategy discussed.

Often the most difficult part of any option strategy is deciding which strike prices to use. As a result, most chapters include a table to help you decide based on how confident you are in your opinion about the direction of the underlying instrument. This is followed by what is probably one of the most helpful sections: actual stock charts illustrating potentially good candidates for the strategy discussed. The following is a brief summary of each chapter.

Section 1 discusses the pricing and movement of options. This is a section you should read before you read any others. It is essential that you first have a general understanding of how the price of options is calculated and how it relates to the underlying stock, exchange-traded fund (ETF), or index. There are many factors that make up the price of an option, some of which may be surprising to you, but if you ignore them they can cause you to make a bad investment decision or lose money. These various factors can be quantified and measured using values that are commonly referred to as the option "Greeks." While the Greeks can be a bit complicated to the uninitiated, I have attempted to describe them in a number of different ways so that you will understand them even if you have never studied them before.

While not actually a Greek value, volatility is a closely related, extremely important concept with regard to the pricing of options. The first chapter describes the difference between historical volatility and implied volatility as well as the two related concepts of volatility mean reversion and volatility skew.

Today most brokers and even many freely available Internet sites provide pricing models and tools to help you forecast and analyze option prices. In this chapter I have included several illustrations using the Hypothetical Option Pricing Tool and the streaming Greeks displays available in CyberTrader Pro or Schwab's StreetSmart Pro trading software.

Section 2 begins with the most basic of all spreads: two-legged vertical spreads. When discussing simple vertical spreads I have found that it is easiest to categorize them as either bullish or bearish, so we will examine debit call spreads along with credit put spreads and then move into debit put spreads and credit call spreads. Vertical spreads are probably the best place to start if you have never traded spreads before, because they are the easiest to understand. In Chapters 2 and 3 you will find comparisons to simple call and put option trades to help you see how vertical spreads can reduce your risk. You will also find tables to help you select the right strike prices and actual stock charts to use as a guide when you begin searching for vertical spread candidates on the stocks you watch.

Section 3 moves into horizontal or calendar spreads. Horizontal spreads can be a little more complex because they have both a near-term and a longer-term perspective, and that tends to make the profit and loss charts look rather unique. Horizontal spreads are a logical next step once you master the concepts of vertical spreads. In Chapter 4 you will find comparisons to simple call and put option trades to help you see how horizontal spreads can give you more flexibility on your time horizon. As in other chapters, you will find tables to help you select the right strike prices and actual stock charts to use as a guide when you begin searching for horizontal spread candidates on the stocks you watch.

Once you understand both vertical and horizontal spreads, you will be introduced to diagonal spreads, which are a combination of both. Diagonal spreads can be difficult to understand if you are not an experienced spread trader, so Chapter 5 is a chapter you may not want to cover until you are pretty comfortable with vertical and horizontal spreads.

Section 4 covers butterfly spreads. At first glance, butterfly spreads will probably appear much more complex than they really are, simply because they involve three legs rather that two, like the spreads you will have read about in the previous chapters. I believe butterfly spreads are actually easier to understand than diagonal spreads, because they only have a single time horizon. Calculating the net price to enter an order is a little different than with other spreads, but the explanations in Chapter 6 will simplify it for you.

As in other chapters, you will find tables to help you select the right strike prices and actual stock charts to use as a guide when you begin searching for butterfly candidates on the stocks you watch.

Once you understand long and short butterflies, you will be introduced to iron butterflies, which are a little more complex because they involve both calls and puts. At the end of Chapter 7 we will compare traditional butterflies to iron butterflies to help illustrate the differences.

Section 5 covers condor spreads. Condor spreads are very similar to butterfly spreads but may be more appropriate for higher priced stocks. Unlike butterflies, they involve four legs rather that three, but are really not much more complicated to understand, especially since calculating the net price to enter an order is simpler than for butterflies. As in other chapters, you will find tables to help you select the right strike prices and actual stock charts to use as a guide when you begin searching for condor candidates on the stocks you watch.

Once you understand long and short condors, you will be introduced to iron condors, which, like iron butterflies, are a little more complex because they involve both calls and puts. At the end of Chapter 9 we will compare traditional condors to iron condors to help illustrate the differences.

Section 6 consists of a fairly short chapter covering box spreads. Since box spreads only come in two varieties, long and short, and really have very limited use for most investors, I only discuss them in this book to illustrate the versatility of spreads in general. It is unlikely that you will find very many opportunities to use a box spread, because it requires specific pricing anomalies to be profitable. Nonetheless, I believe it is an important concept to learn as you expand your spread education.

Section 7 covers ratio spreads, which, unlike most other strategies, are not really true spreads at all. As a result, the limited risk and reward characteristics of most other spreads are not present. Ratio spreads are not only unique in this regard but also rather complex to understand. While Chapter 11 does include comparisons to standard vertical spreads, I would encourage you to be sure you are comfortable with both vertical and horizontal spreads before you venture out into the world of ratio spreads.

Section 8 covers advanced spreads and is divided into three different chapters: combo spreads, albatross spreads, and ladder spreads.

Each of these has its own unique characteristics and features. As you begin to study these advanced spread concepts, you will notice that many of them are made up of combinations of less complex spreads. You may find that some of these more exotic spreads have limited uses but under the right circumstances may be ideal for the situation. You might even find that you have seen or used these types of spreads before and simply did not know there was a name for them.

Section 9 examines gut spreads but is divided into four separate chapters because there are several types of spreads discussed in earlier chapters that can be converted into gut spreads. What makes a spread a gut spread is simply that in all cases the strike prices of the calls involved in the strategy are lower than the strike prices of the puts. While you could apply this concept to all sorts of different spreads, this section covers only a few of the more common ones.

I sincerely hope you enjoy this book, and since it is unlikely that you will be able to memorize the characteristics of all the different types of spreads covered, I encourage you to keep it handy as a reference guide.

SECTION 1

Valuation

CHAPTER 1

Pricing and Movement

How much is an option worth? It seems like a fairly simple question, but the answer is far from simple. The number crunching that goes into determining an option's price is fairly substantial. Most option market makers use some variation of what is known as a Theoretical Option Pricing Model to determine the prices of the options in which they make markets.

BLACK-SCHOLES MODEL

By far, the best known pricing model is the **Black-Scholes** model. After more than three years of research, university scholars Fisher Black and Myron Scholes first published their model in 1973, only a month after the Chicago Board Options Exchange (CBOE) began trading standardized options. While many option traders initially scoffed at their ideas, this breakthrough turned out to be so substantial that it took nearly a quarter century to be fully appreciated. Though Fisher Black died in 1975, Myron Scholes and Robert Merton, a colleague of theirs who helped improve the formula, were awarded the 1997 Nobel Prize in Economics for their model.

While explaining actual theoretical calculations in detail is beyond the scope of this book, it is important to understand how such prices are calculated and the impact these formulas have in the marketplace. While the Black-Scholes formula appears complicated, it can easily be programmed as a tool in your trading software, and your broker should provide such a tool for you. The original Black-Scholes formula is as follows:

$$\text{Theoretical option price} = PN(D_1) - Se^{-RT}N(D_2)$$

Where:

$$D_1 = \frac{\ln(P/S) + (R + V^2/2)T}{V\sqrt{T}}$$

$D_2 = D_1 - V\sqrt{T}$

$P =$ Current stock price

$S =$ Strike price of the option

$V =$ Stock price volatility, as estimated by the annual standard deviation

$R =$ Risk-free interest rate

$T =$ Time to expiration, as a % of a year

$\ln =$ Natural logarithm

$N(x) =$ Cumulative normal density function

$e =$ Euler's constant for calculating continuously compounded interest (approx. 2.71828)

If you take a look at the components of the Black-Scholes model, you will see that there are five factors:

1. Current stock price
2. Strike price of the option
3. Stock price volatility, as estimated by the annual standard deviation
4. Risk-free interest rate
5. Time to expiration, as a % of a year

What you may notice about these factors is that all but one (stock price volatility) is a known factor. Before you try to calculate the value of an option, you can determine the current price of the underlying stock, the strike price of the option, the risk-free interest rate (usually the 90-day T-bill rate), and the number of days until the option expires. If we further add the dividend yield, as in later pricing models, we have the basic inputs needed to calculate the fair value of an option. Each of these factors will have a positive or negative effect on the value of call or put options, as calculated by the formula. We will examine them individually:

1. The **price of the underlying stock** has a positive effect on call options and a negative effect on put options. In other

words, the higher the underlying stock price, the more value a given call option will have. A call option with a strike price of 30 has more value when the underlying stock is at 40 than it does when the underlying stock is at 35. Remember that prior to expiration, both call and put options will always be worth at least as much as their intrinsic value. A call option with a strike price of 30 has $10 worth of intrinsic value when the stock is at 40, and only $5 worth of intrinsic value when the stock is at 35. By contrast, the higher the underlying stock price, the less value a given put option will have. A put option with a strike price of 40 has $10 worth of intrinsic value when the stock is at 30, and only $5 worth of intrinsic value when the stock is at 35.

2. The **strike price of the option** has a negative effect on call options and a positive effect on put options. In other words, the higher the strike price, the less value a given call option will have. A call option with a strike price of 30 has $10 worth of intrinsic value when the stock is at 40, but a call option with a strike price of 35 has only $5 worth of intrinsic value when the stock is at 40. By contrast, the higher the strike price, the more value a given put option will have. A put option with a strike price of 40 has $10 worth of intrinsic value when the stock price is at 30, but a put option with a strike price of 35 has only $5 worth of intrinsic value when the stock price is at 40.
3. While the future (theoretical) **volatility of the underlying stock** is estimated (based on historical volatility), it has a positive effect on both call options and put options. In other words, the more volatile a stock is expected to be in the future, the more value a given call or put option will have. Consider that an out-of-the-money call option has a much greater likelihood of getting in-the-money on a stock that has historically been very volatile than it does on a stock that has been very stable. Since volatility measures the movement of a stock both up and down, it is a nondirectional measure. As a result, an out-of-the-money put option also has a greater likelihood of getting in-the-money on a stock that has historically been very volatile than it does on a stock that has been very stable. Historically volatile stocks will have a higher implied volatility component in

the pricing model, causing an increase in the value of both puts and calls on that stock. (See **Vega** later in this chapter.)

4. The **risk-free interest rate**, which is usually considered to be the interest rate on the most recently issued 90-day Treasury bill, has a positive effect on call options and a negative effect on put options. This can usually be seen by looking at a put and a call option of the same underlying stock that are both out-of-the-money by the same amount. Typically, the call option will trade at a slightly higher price. The premium of the call price over the put price will be greater as the risk-free interest rate increases. This is primarily caused by the cost of carry. (See **Rho**.)
5. The **time to expiration** has a positive effect on the value of both calls and puts. Quite simply, time value is one of the two components that make up the price of an option. The more time an option has before it expires, the more value it has, because every additional day provides an additional opportunity for the stock price to move up enough for a call option to get in-the-money or down enough for a put option to get in-the-money. (See **Theta**.)
6. The **dividend yield** was added to later modified versions of the Black-Scholes formula, as well as other pricing models. This is an important improvement, because the payment of dividends will have a negative effect on the value of call options and a positive effect on the value of put options. This is because when you own a stock position you are entitled to the dividends paid, whereas when you own a call option, as a substitute for a long stock position, you are not entitled to any dividends. Therefore, the greater the dividend payment, the greater the advantage of owning the stock over owning the call option. By contrast, when you sell stock short, you are required to pay the dividend to the owner of the stock, whereas when you own a put option as a substitute for a short stock position, you do not have an obligation to pay dividends. Therefore, the greater the dividend payment, the greater the advantage of owning the put option over selling the stock short.

While the Black-Scholes formula was quite revolutionary, it was not without limitations. The original formula can be used to calculate a theoretical value (fair value) for an option contract that is European style and pays no dividends. However, since all equity options trading in the United States are American style, many models have evolved from the original Black-Scholes model that are more accurate for American-style options and have the ability to consider the dividend yield of the underlying stock (see Figure 1.1).

COX-ROSS-RUBINSTEIN MODEL

The **Cox-Ross-Rubinstein** binomial model, which is one of the most commonly used models today, takes a different approach to the original Black-Scholes model by dividing the number of days remaining until option expiration date into small intervals of time. The estimated stock price volatility is calculated for each time interval based on the historical volatility of the stock, the number of days remaining until expiration, and the risk-free interest rate. As expiration approaches, the time value of in-the-money options will diminish and the options will approach their intrinsic value. The Cox-Ross-Rubinstein model starts with the value of each option at expiration and calculates the value at specific points by adding back time in small intervals. This allows the model to consider the

FIGURE 1.1

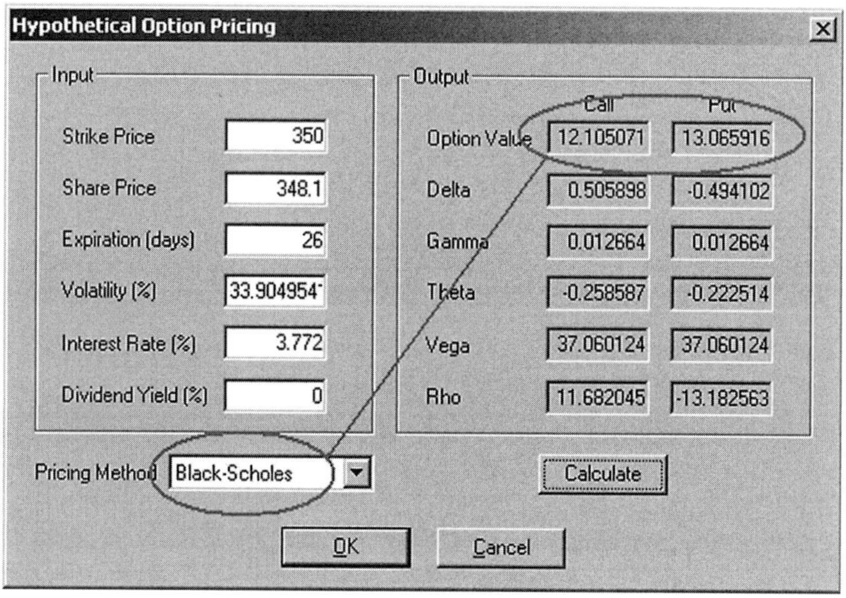

dividend payment at the point at which it is made during the life cycle of the option (see Figure 1.2).

BARONE-ADESI-WHALEY MODEL

The **Barone-Adesi-Whaley** quadratic approximation model uses yet a third approach to solving the same problem (see Figure 1.3).

There are quite a number of different pricing models available today, a detailed explanation of which is beyond the scope of this book. Although the three formulas discussed here take different approaches to reach the same valuation, the outcomes are often very similar. Option experts and mathematicians may disagree about which formula is most accurate, and under what conditions. Probably the best approach to take is to try all three and decide for yourself. Some trading platforms will provide more than one formula so you can do just that. Within the CyberTrader Pro and Schwab's StreetSmart Pro software, for example, a Hypothetical Option Pricing Tool is provided, which allows you to select from any of the three models described here. For most options in near-term months that are near-the-money,

FIGURE 1.2

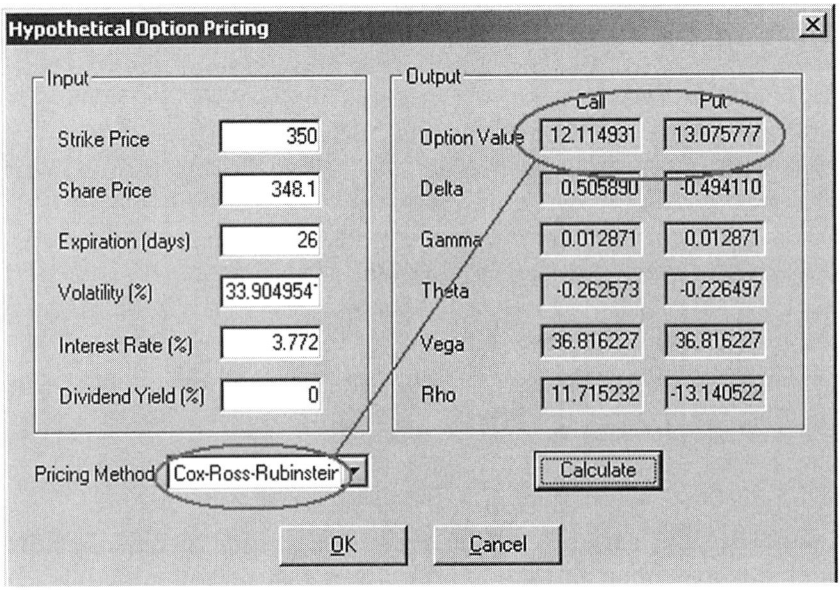

FIGURE 1.3

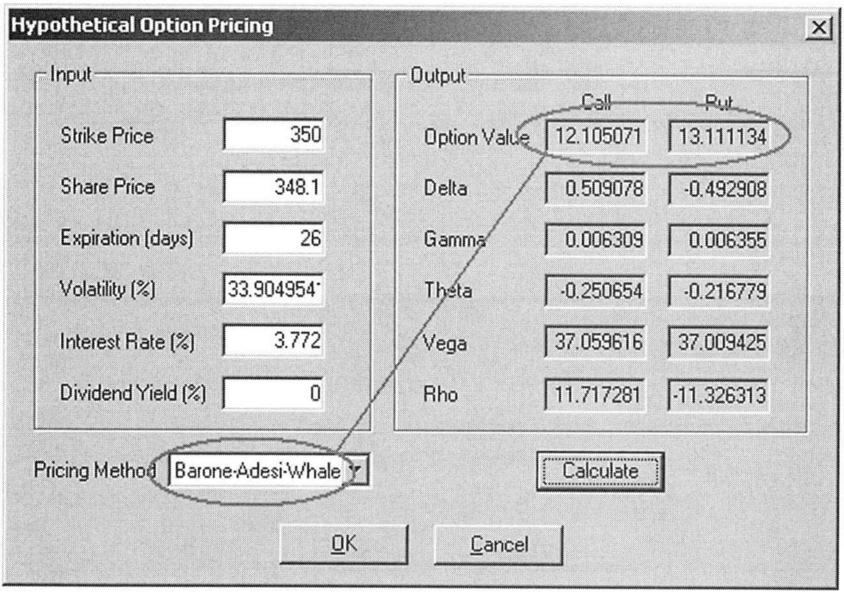

the three models will only vary by a few pennies, as shown in Figures 1.1, 1.2, and 1.3. Since options trade in nickels and dimes, the rounded results will be virtually identical.

However, as you begin to look at options that are either far out-of-the-money or deep in-the-money, and those that have many months until expiration, the differences between the models become more apparent (see example in Figures 1.4 to 1.6).

While these types of tools are certainly valuable, you should never make trading decisions based strictly on how tools like these calculate the value of options. A market maker may have a very valid reason for pricing a particular option higher or lower than a model suggests, so you may not have all the information needed to accurately assess whether an option is actually priced favorably when the models suggests it is. However, a basic understanding of the components that make up the price of an option is critical in becoming a successful trader.

GREEKS

While few people have difficulty with the concept that call options rise with the price of the underlying stock and put options move opposite

FIGURE 1.4

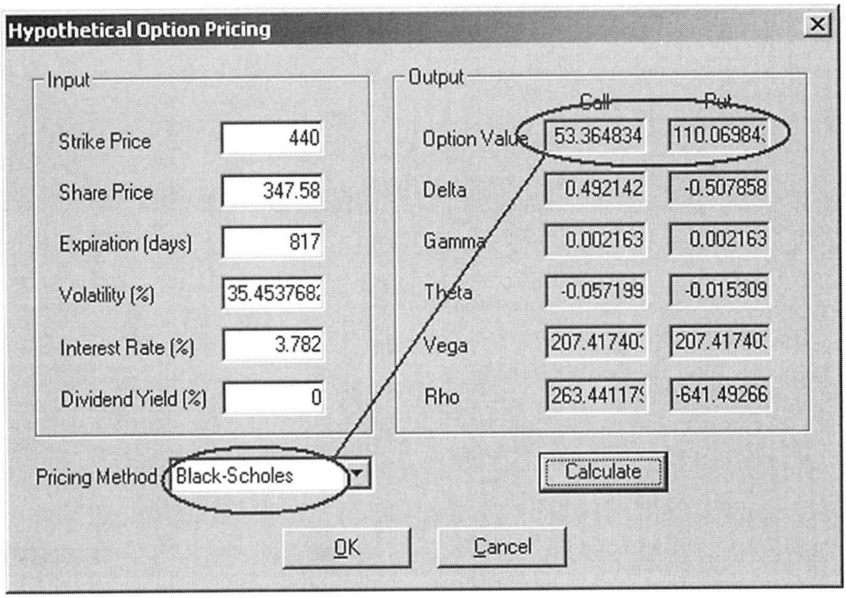

FIGURE 1.5

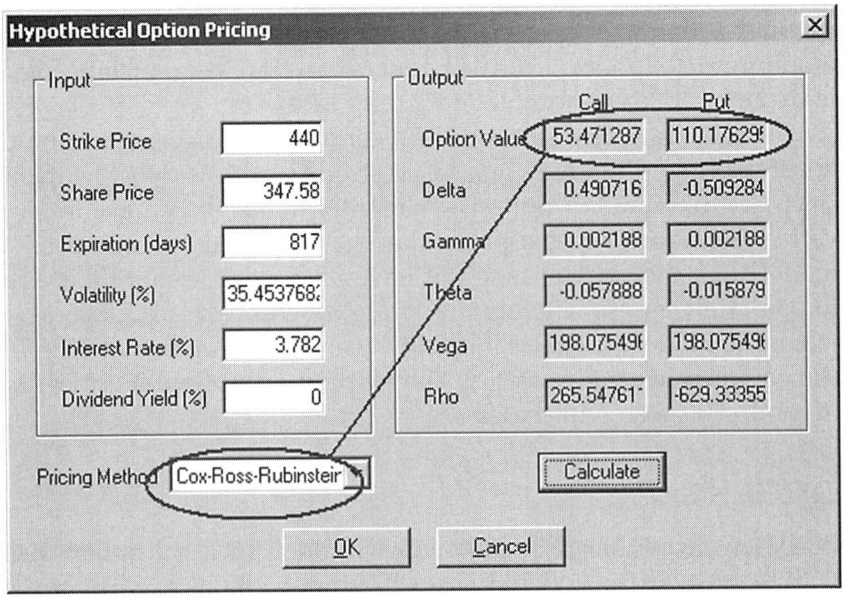

FIGURE 1.6

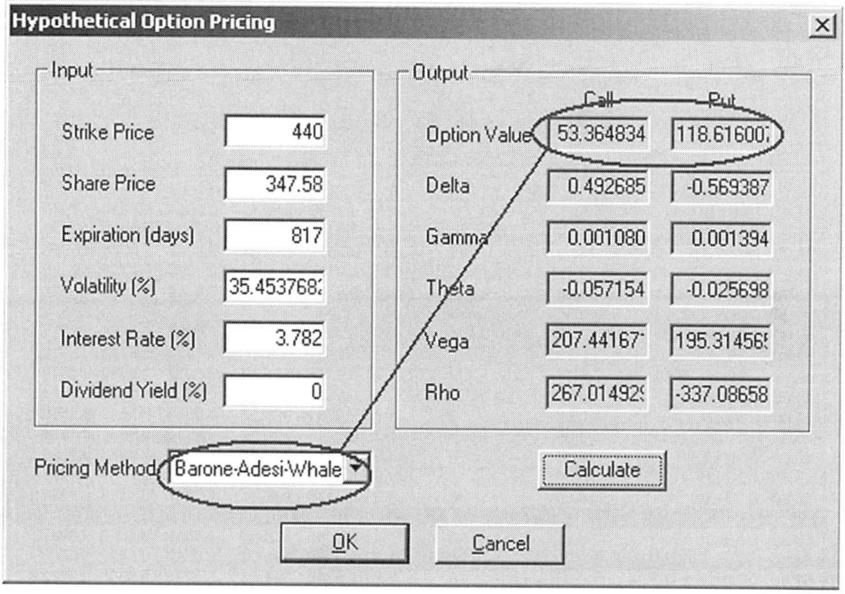

the underlying stock, it is a lack of understanding of how *much* or how *quickly* individual calls and puts move with the underlying stock that often causes investors to lose money. In the same manner, a lack of understanding of the tremendous effect changes in volatility can have on the price of options can also give rise to one of the most frustrating events an investor can experience: being right and still losing money. To be successful trading options, you must have an opinion not only about the direction of the underlying stock but also about how much it will move in the anticipated direction and how quickly it will move in that direction. Profitability with options typically requires you to be right on at least two of these three factors and sometimes on all three. Direction alone will not be profitable if the underlying stock takes too long to move or does not move enough in that direction.

In the same way in which we can calculate the theoretical value of an option contract based on all of the factors that make up these formulas, we can assign a value to the way changes in each of these factors affect the value of the calculation. These values are commonly known as the Greeks.

The Greeks are calculated using a standard pricing model as discussed earlier in this chapter. When the quoted price of a

FIGURE 1.7

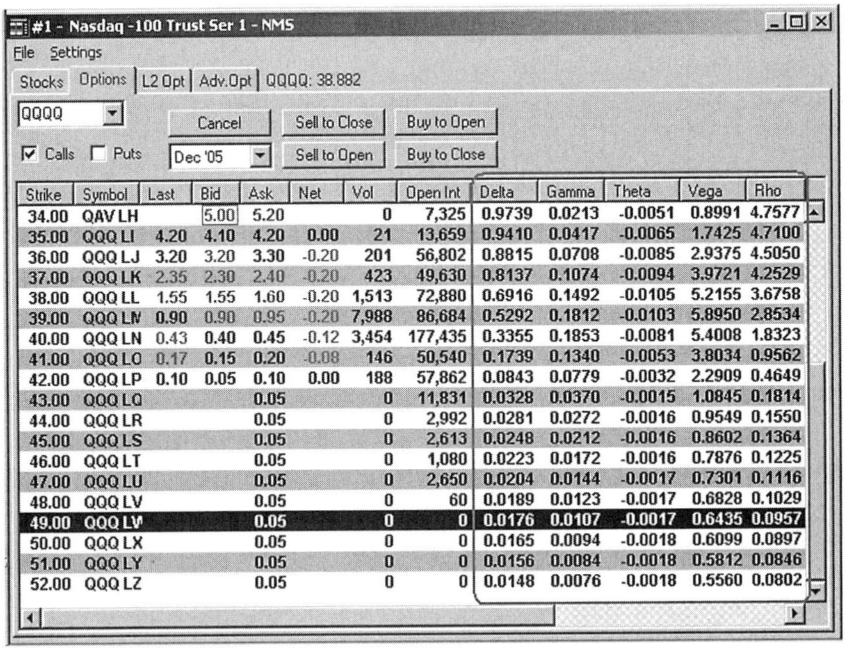

Strike	Symbol	Last	Bid	Ask	Net	Vol	Open Int	Delta	Gamma	Theta	Vega	Rho
34.00	QAV LH		5.00	5.20		0	7,325	0.9739	0.0213	-0.0051	0.8991	4.7577
35.00	QQQ LI	4.20	4.10	4.20	0.00	21	13,659	0.9410	0.0417	-0.0065	1.7425	4.7100
36.00	QQQ LJ	3.20	3.20	3.30	-0.20	201	56,802	0.8815	0.0708	-0.0085	2.9375	4.5050
37.00	QQQ LK	2.35	2.30	2.40	-0.20	423	49,630	0.8137	0.1074	-0.0094	3.9721	4.2529
38.00	QQQ LL	1.55	1.55	1.60	-0.20	1,513	72,880	0.6916	0.1492	-0.0105	5.2155	3.6758
39.00	QQQ LM	0.90	0.90	0.95	-0.20	7,988	86,684	0.5292	0.1812	-0.0103	5.8950	2.8534
40.00	QQQ LN	0.43	0.40	0.45	-0.12	3,454	177,435	0.3355	0.1853	-0.0081	5.4008	1.8323
41.00	QQQ LO	0.17	0.15	0.20	-0.08	146	50,540	0.1739	0.1340	-0.0053	3.8034	0.9562
42.00	QQQ LP	0.10	0.05	0.10	0.00	188	57,862	0.0843	0.0779	-0.0032	2.2909	0.4649
43.00	QQQ LQ			0.05		0	11,831	0.0328	0.0370	-0.0015	1.0845	0.1814
44.00	QQQ LR			0.05		0	2,992	0.0281	0.0272	-0.0016	0.9549	0.1550
45.00	QQQ LS			0.05		0	2,613	0.0248	0.0212	-0.0016	0.8602	0.1364
46.00	QQQ LT			0.05		0	1,080	0.0223	0.0172	-0.0016	0.7876	0.1225
47.00	QQQ LU			0.05		0	2,650	0.0204	0.0144	-0.0017	0.7301	0.1116
48.00	QQQ LV			0.05		0	60	0.0189	0.0123	-0.0017	0.6828	0.1029
49.00	QQQ LW			0.05		0	0	0.0176	0.0107	-0.0017	0.6435	0.0957
50.00	QQQ LX			0.05		0	0	0.0165	0.0094	-0.0018	0.6099	0.0897
51.00	QQQ LY			0.05		0	0	0.0156	0.0084	-0.0018	0.5812	0.0846
52.00	QQQ LZ			0.05		0	0	0.0148	0.0076	-0.0018	0.5560	0.0802

particular option contract is known, the formula can be used to solve for the individual components. Because at least a basic understanding of the Greeks is important in an attempt to become a successful option trader, we will discuss the five main Greeks as shown in the Hypothetical Option Pricing Tool above as well as a couple of other related Greeks. Many trading platforms provide a streaming Greeks display such as the one within CyberTrader Pro and Schwab's StreetSmart Pro (see Figure 1.7).

Beta

Beta (aka the correlation) is the measure of how closely the movement of an individual stock or stock portfolio tracks the movement of the entire stock market. Usually a benchmark such as the S&P 500 (SPX) is used to represent the stock market.

- For example, a stock, or portfolio of stocks, with a beta of .75 will move $0.75 for every $1 movement in the S&P 500.

- This Greek is not typically associated with options, but it is important if you want to use index options to hedge a portfolio of stocks.
- Knowing the beta of a stock or portfolio can help prevent over hedging or under hedging.
- Beta cannot be displayed in the Hypothetical Option Pricing Tool.

Example Assume you had a well-diversified portfolio of blue chip stocks that was closely (but not perfectly) correlated to the S&P 500 index (SPX). Suppose it was .80 correlated (has a beta of .80), which means that if the SPX increases by 18 points from say 1200 to 1218 (about a 1.5% increase), the overall value of your portfolio might increase only 1.2% (1.5% × .80). Since beta affects portfolios in both a positive and a negative direction, you would also only expect a 1.2% drop if the SPX dropped 1.5%. Knowing this, you could use SPX put options to hedge your portfolio in an uncertain market.

Assume you are expecting a possible 10% downturn in the overall market but you do not want to sell off any part of your portfolio. If your portfolio were perfectly correlated to the SPX (had a beta of 1.00), you could expect a 10% drop in the value of your portfolio. Since full-size SPX options have a multiplier of 100, when the SPX is at 1200, each contract has a hedging value of $120,000. This means that if you needed to hedge a portfolio worth $240,000 you would need to purchase two SPX put contracts (if we assume a –1.00 delta on those options) to provide full downside protection. However, to find a put option with a delta of –1.00, you would have to purchase deep in-the-money options, which would be very expensive.

In most cases, you probably would not want to spend the money to buy deep in-the-money options, so instead you purchase options that are at-the-money with a delta value of –.55. If your portfolio was worth $240,000, and it had a perfect beta of 1.00, you could buy four at-the-money put options (with a delta of –.55) and provide full downside protection. However, since you know that your portfolio has a beta of .80, you can provide an adequate hedge by purchasing only three SPX put options with a delta of –.55. Below are the steps in this calculation:

SPX level = 1200

Underlying value = $120,000

10% decline = 1080

New underlying value = $108,000
Decline in value = $12,000
Portfolio value = $240,000
Beta = .80
Decline in portfolio = 8% (.80 × 10%)
New underlying portfolio value = $220,800
Decline in value = $19,200
You choose put options with a –.55 delta.
Downside protection from each contract = –$6,600 ($12,000 × –.55).
Number of contracts needed to fully hedge $19,200 decline = 3
(3 contracts × –.55 delta × $12,000 contract = –$19,800 in protection)

It is important to note that this is not actually a perfect calculation, because in order to simplify the calculations, I intentionally neglected the fact that the –.55 original delta of those options would decrease and approach –1.00 as the market began to decline, because they become deeper in-the-money, thus actually creating more hedge than necessary. You could be more accurate by taking the gamma into account, although this would increase the complexity of the calculation (see **Gamma**).

Delta

Delta (aka the hedge ratio) is the measure of the rate of change in an option's price for a one-dollar change in the price of the underlying stock.

- For example, a delta of .40 means that the option's price will move $0.40 for every $1 move in the price of the underlying stock or index.
- Delta is the first derivative of the price of the option.
- Call options:
  - Call options have a positive delta and can range from 0 to 1.
  - At-the-money options usually have a delta near .50.
  - The delta will increase (and approach 1) as the option gets deeper in-the-money.
  - The delta of in-the-money call options will also approach 1 as expiration approaches.

    - The delta of out-of-the-money call options will approach zero as expiration approaches.
- Put options:
    - Put options have a negative delta and can range from 0 to –1.
    - At-the-money options usually have a delta near –.50.
    - The delta will decrease (and approach –1) as the option gets deeper in-the-money.
    - The delta of in-the-money put options will also approach –1 as expiration approaches.
    - The delta of out-of-the-money put options will approach zero as expiration approaches.
- It is best to think of delta as the % chance that a given option will expire in-the-money.
    - A call option with a .40 delta has a 40% chance of being in-the-money at expiration.
    - A put option with a –.80 delta has an 80% chance of being in-the-money at expiration.

Example Using a Hypothetical Option Pricing Tool like the one shown earlier in this chapter, you can calculate changes in the values of the Greeks based on your anticipation of changes in the underlying stock. This is an ideal way to forecast whether or not the strategy you are considering might be profitable.

Assume you are bullish on a stock, but you have decided to purchase long calls instead of the stock, so you can get more leverage. You use the Hypothetical Option Pricing Tool to check the current value of the option you are considering as well as the delta. Remember that the delta will tell you approximately how much the call option will gain in value if the underlying stock goes up by one point (see Figure 1.8).

Before

- Underlying stock is at 33.76.
- There are 32 days remaining until expiration.
- The value of the call option is approximately 2.04.
- Starting delta is approximately .67 (see also **Gamma**).

You anticipate the stock will go up about 2 points over the course of the next week. You use the Hypothetical Option Pricing Tool to add 2 points to the underlying price and reduce the number of days until expiration by 7 (see Figure 1.9).

FIGURE 1.8

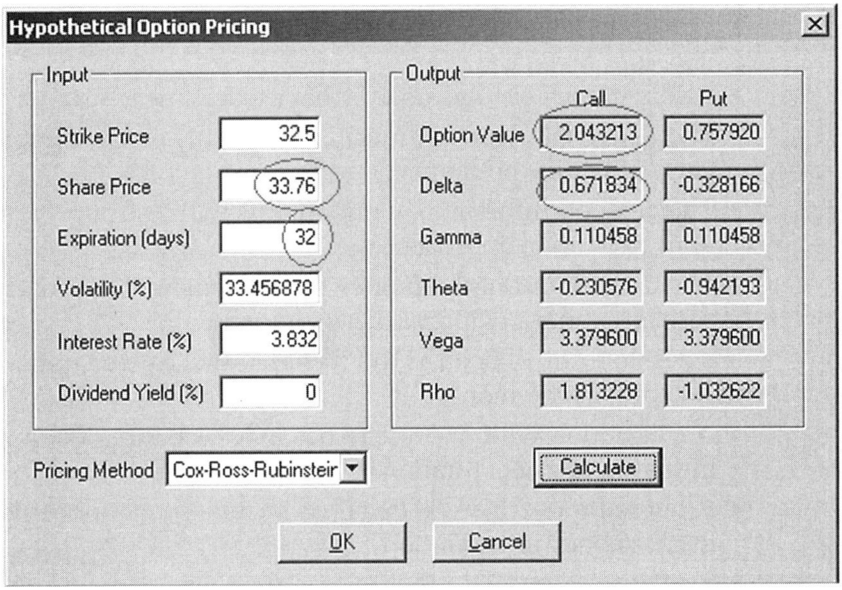

FIGURE 1.9

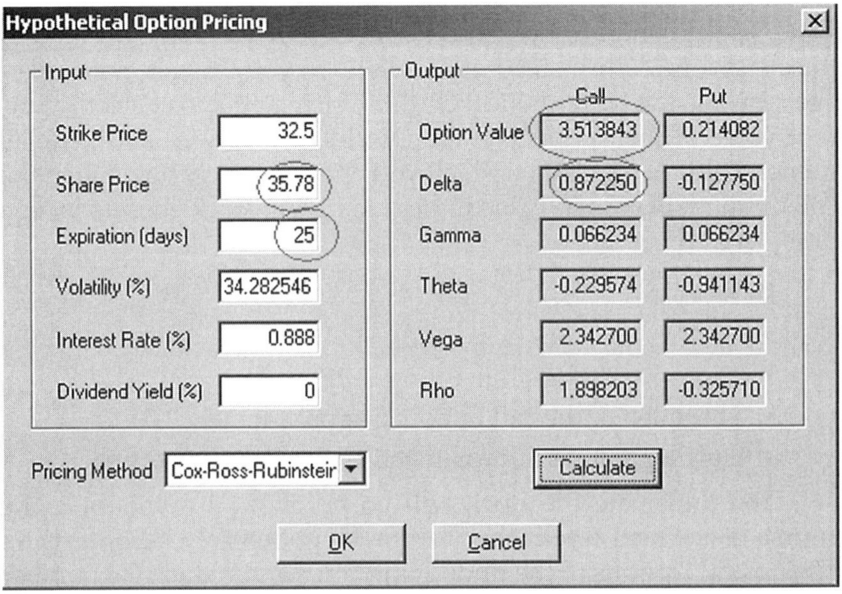

After

- Underlying stock is at 35.78.
- There are 25 days remaining until expiration.
- The value of the call option rises to 3.51.
- The delta has increased by .20 to .87 (see also **Gamma**).

When you recalculate the values, you can see that the call option you are considering should gain about 1.47 if the stock goes up 2 points over the next 7 days.

Gamma

Gamma (aka the speed of change of the hedge ratio or delta) is the measure of the rate of change in an option's delta for a one-dollar change in the price of the underlying stock.

- Gamma is the second derivative of the price of the option.
- Call options and put options both have positive gamma.
- The delta is only accurate at a certain price and time.
- In the delta example, once the stock has moved $1 and the option has subsequently moved $0.40, the delta is no longer .40.
- This $1 move would cause a call option to be more in-the-money, and therefore the delta will move closer to 1.
- The delta might change from .40 to .55.
- This change from .40 to .55 is .15.
- .15 is the gamma of this option.
- Because the option delta cannot exceed 1, the gamma decreases as the option gets further in-the-money.
- **Gamma of the Gamma** (aka the speed of change of the gamma): The measure of the rate of change of an option's gamma for a one-dollar change in the price of the underlying stock.
  - Gamma of the gamma is not displayed in the Hypothetical Option Pricing Tool.
  - In contrast to the delta, the gamma decreases as the delta gets closer to 1.
  - In the example above, the gamma is .15. If the gamma did not decrease, then it would not take long before the delta exceeded 1, which cannot happen, because an option cannot move more than the underlying stock or index.

- For example, assume the stock moves up another point and the option moves up .55 points. At that point, the delta would be recalculated and might be .65.
- Since the delta changed from .55 to .65, the gamma is only .10 now instead of .15 previously.
- The change in the gamma (gamma of the gamma) is therefore .05.

Example As shown in the previous example, not only could you see how the value of the option changes, but also how the value for delta changes. Since delta increases as an option gets deeper in-the-money, in the previous example, you saw the delta change from its starting level of about .67 to .87. Since the delta is only accurate at a specific price and time as the stock moves up in price and the call options get deeper in-the-money, the delta will increase. Since the delta is fairly accurate in predicting only the first one-point move, you can conclude that the option probably increased by .67 on the first point move in the underlying stock. Then the delta increased by the amount of gamma to about .78 (.67 + .11).

On the second point move in the underlying stock, the option increased in price by about .78. The delta was then increased by the amount of the new gamma (probably about .09) to about .87 (.78 + .09). Although we did not forecast a 3 point move in the underlying stock, we can safely predict that if the stock did increase by one more point, the option would probably gain about .87, the new delta would become about .93 (.87 + .06), and the gamma would decrease to about .02 or .03. Notice that to ensure that the delta of this option never exceeds 1.00, the gamma continues to decrease as the option gets deeper in-the-money. This causes the increase in delta to be smaller and smaller with each move in the underlying stock.

Theta

Theta (aka the time decay) is the measure of the rate of change in an option's price for a one-unit change in time to the option's expiration date.

- Typically one unit is considered one day.
- All options have negative theta.
- Since options lose value as expiration approaches, theta estimates how much value the option will lose, each day, if all other factors remain the same.

- Because time value erosion in not linear, theta increases as expiration approaches.
  - The effect of theta is greatest for options that are right at-the-money.
  - Since their price is made up entirely of time value, each one-day move closer to expiration is one less day that option has to move into the money. As time begins to run short, an at-the-money option essentially runs out of time to get into the money, and the price begins to erode very quickly.
  - Out-of-the-money options are affected less by theta since they have less value and can only lose value down to zero.
  - In-the-money options are affected less by theta since their value is partially made up of intrinsic value (in-the-money amount), which is not affected by theta (see Figure 1.10).

FIGURE 1.10

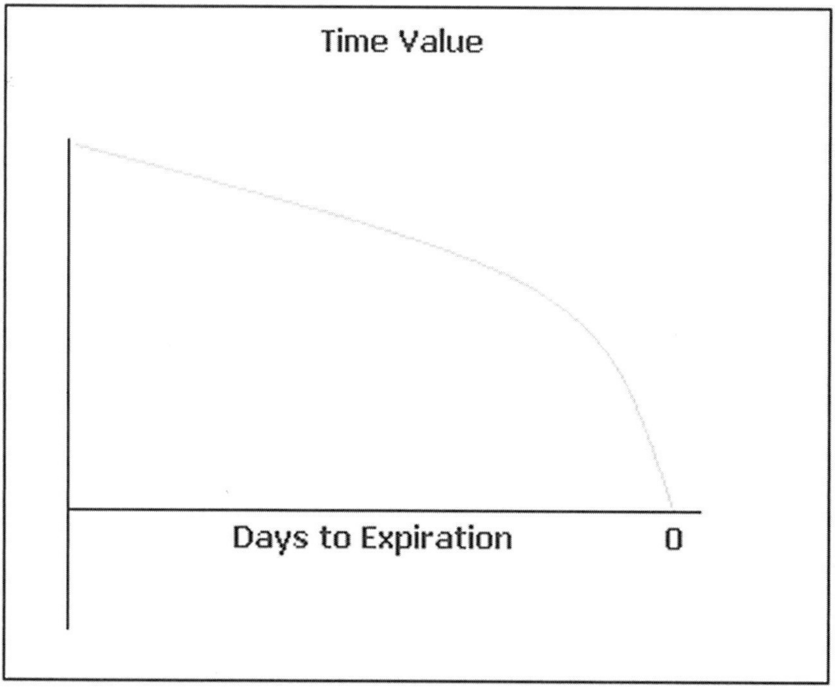

Example Using a Hypothetical Option Pricing Tool again, you can calculate the change in the value of an option as it approaches expiration. As this change gets greater and greater, you are able to see why the time value curve gets steeper.

Figure 1.11 depicts a 60 call option that is just slightly out-of-the-money since the underlying stock is at 59.28. With 60 days until expiration, theta tells us that if the stock does not increase or decrease in price, and assuming no changes in volatility or interest rates, the option will lose approximately \$0.05 by the next day (see Figure 1.11).

Using the Hypothetical Option Pricing Tool, you can calculate the value of the option after 30 days have elapsed. You can now see that the theta has moved from approximately –.047 to –.065. The change in theta from 60 days until expiration to 30 days until expiration is fairly small. Since the change is relatively small, by taking the average theta between 60 days out and 30 days out and multiplying it by the 30 days that have elapsed, you should be able to come close to the amount of value the option has lost. $(-.047 + -.064)/2 \times 30 = -1.67$.

FIGURE 1.11

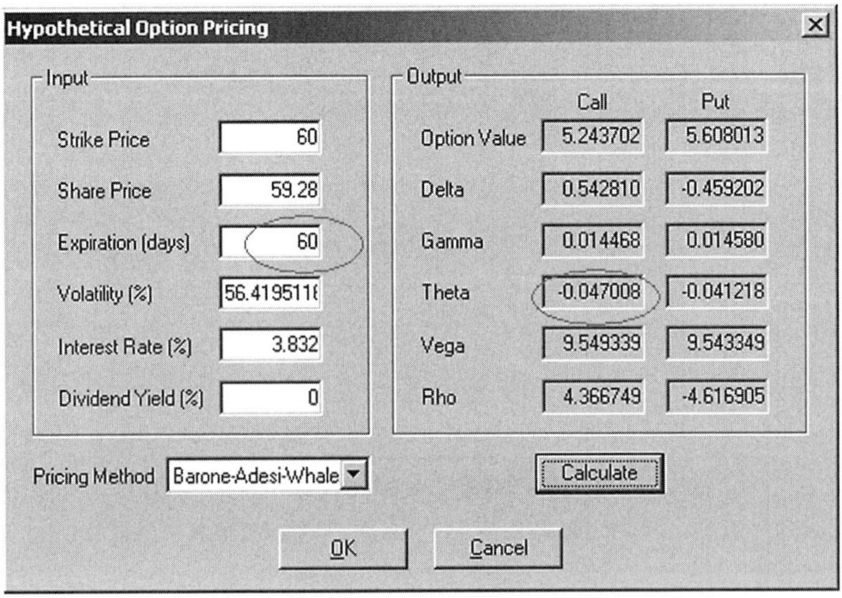

The initial price of the option was 5.24, and 30 days later it decreased to 3.57. (5.24 – 3.57 = 1.67) (see Figure 1.12).

If you reduce the number of days until expiration from 30 to 5, you can see that the theta has become –.137. The first change of 30 days resulted in a daily increase in time erosion of not quite 2 cents per day (–.064 – (–.047) = –.017). However, when you take away the next 25 days, the time erosion increases to more than 7 cents per day (–.136 – (–.064) = –.072) (see Figure 1.13).

As theta changes get greater and greater, it is easy to see why the time value curve gets steeper. This is an important concept to understand if you plan to trade long options. When you trade long options, time value is working against you. In order to combat time erosion, you should try to avoid owning long options during the month in which they expire, when the time erosion curve is the steepest. If you intend to purchase long options and own them for 30 days, it is generally best to buy them with at least 60 days until expiration and then sell them when they still have at least 30 days until expiration. Doing so will minimize the negative effect of theta.

FIGURE 1.12

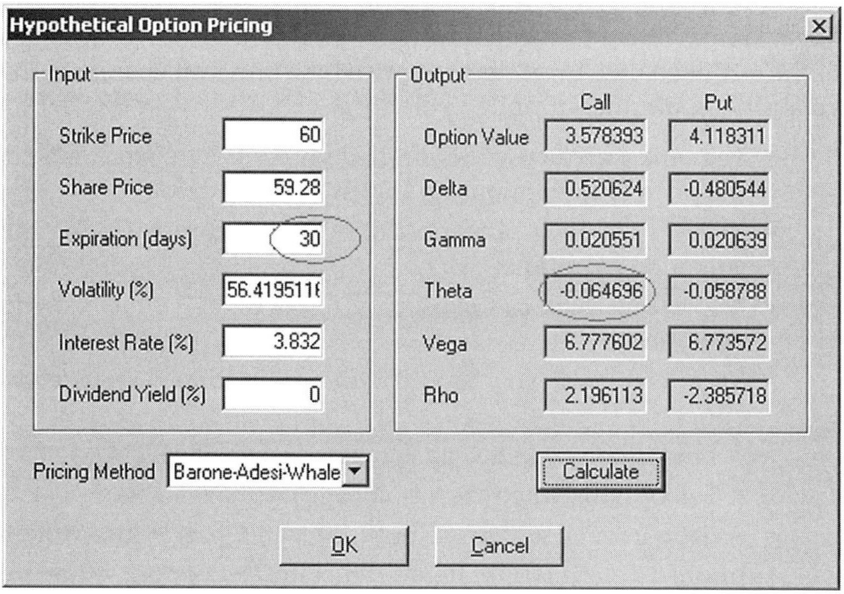

FIGURE 1.13

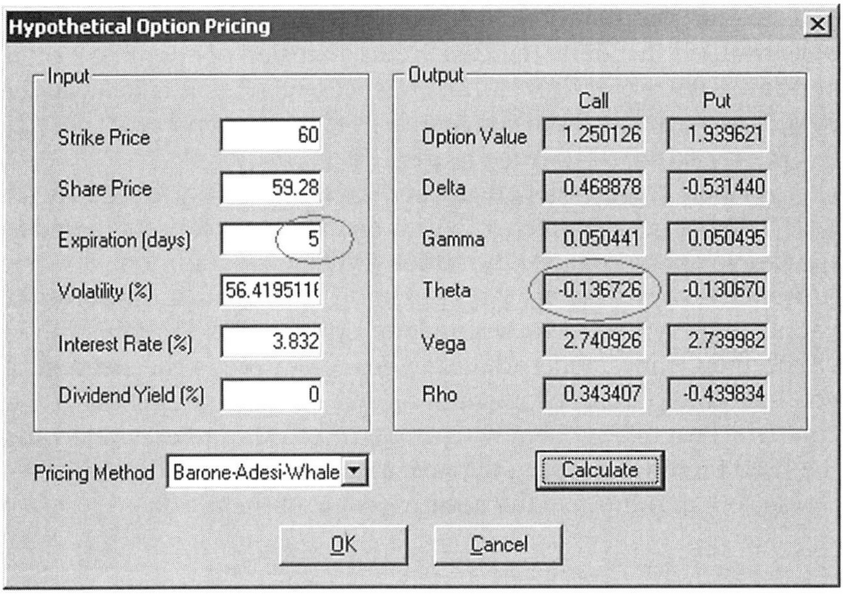

Vega

Vega, kappa, or tau (aka the sensitivity to volatility) is the measure of the rate of change in an option's price for a one-unit change in the volatility assumption (implied volatility).

- Vega measures how the implied volatility of a stock affects the price of the options on that stock.
- Volatility is one of the most important factors affecting the valuation of options.
- Neglecting vega can cause you to "overpay" when buying an option.
- Vega can help you identify the right time to trade an option.
  - Buy options when vega is below "normal" levels.
  - Sell options when vega is above "normal" levels.
- A drop in vega will cause both calls and puts to lose value.
- Implied volatility is generally the lowest on options that are at or close to the money. (See also **Volatility Skew**.)

Example Using a Hypothetical Option Pricing Tool again, you can calculate the change in the value of an option as the implied volatility of that option changes. Changes in implied volatility can have a significant impact on the value of both call and put options (see Figure 1.14).

Assume you believe the current volatility is very low on the underlying stock of a particular call option. You believe that if you buy a long position and volatility goes up (say 10%), you will be able to sell the option at a profit. (See also **Historical Volatility**.)

Since vega is displayed in cents rather than dollars, the vega value of approximately 7.9 indicates that each 1% increase in volatility should result in about \$0.08 of increase in the price of both the calls and puts on this stock. With the Hypothetical Option Pricing Tool, you can calculate the current volatility and then increase the volatility manually by 10% to see how it affects the price of the option (10 × \$0.08 = \$0.80). You should be able to estimate the new price of the option by multiplying the projected volatility increase by the value of vega (see Figure 1.15).

As you can see, a 10% jump in volatility (from 36% to 46%) caused the value of these call options to increase from \$1.67 to \$2.48.

FIGURE 1.14

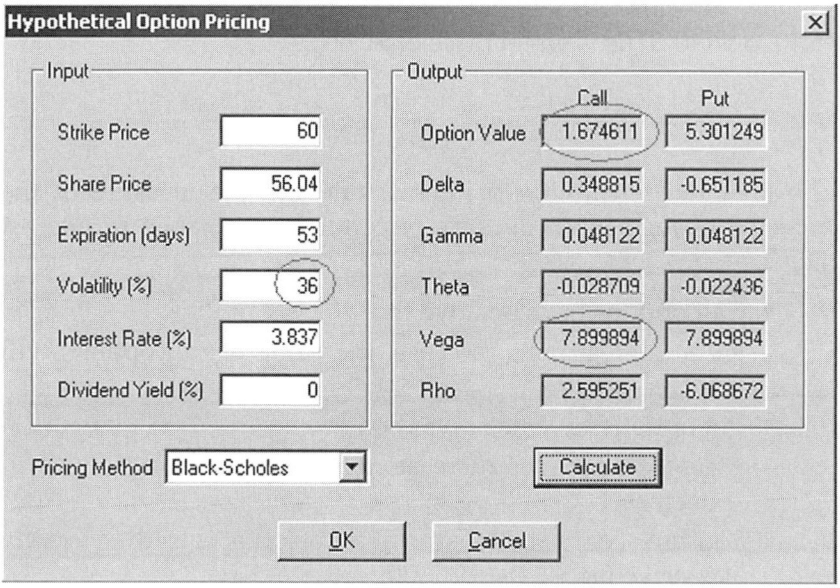

FIGURE 1.15

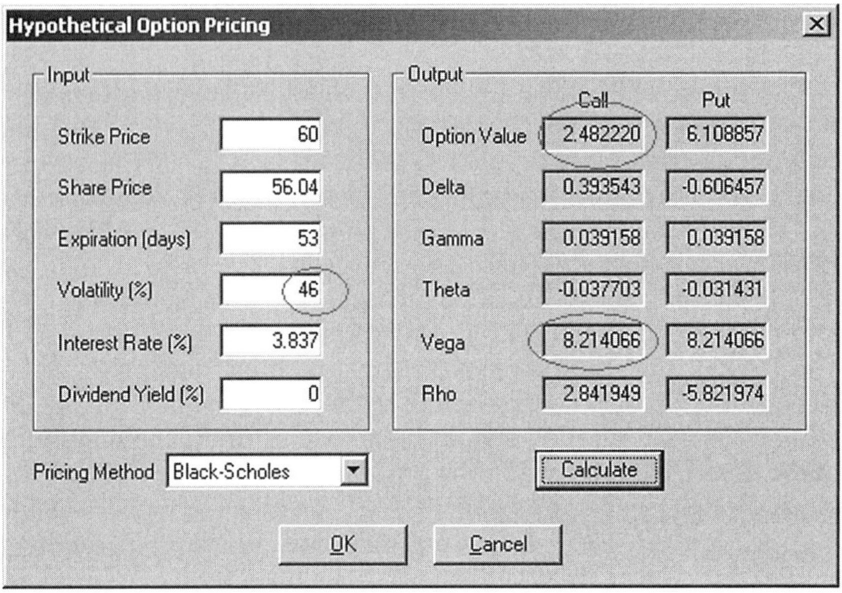

This is an increase of $0.81. Since volatility affects calls and puts equally, you can also see that the value of the puts increased from $5.30 to $6.10. This is an increase of $0.80.

Rho

Rho (aka the sensitivity to interest rates) is the measure of the expected change in an option's price for a 1% change in interest rates.

- Call options have positive rho.
  - As interest rates increase, the value of call options will increase.
- Put options have negative rho.
  - As interest rates increase, the value of put options will decrease.
- You can see this by looking at a stock that is trading exactly at a strike price.

- For example, if a stock is trading at 25, the 25 calls and the 25 puts would both be exactly at-the-money.
- You might see the calls trading at a price of $0.60, while the puts may trade at a price of .50.
- When interest rates are low, the difference will be relatively small.
- This difference is caused by the cost of carry (see also **Cost of Carry**).
- As the risk-free interest rate increases, this difference between puts and calls whose strikes are equidistant from the underlying stock will get wider.
- Rho is generally not a huge factor in the price of a short-term option, but it should be considered if you intend to trade LEAP options or if prevailing interest rates are expected to change over time, such as when the Fed is in a tightening or easing mode for a period of several months.

Cost of Carry Cost of carry is the expenses incurred while a position is being held. It is kind of like opportunity cost, which you may have learned about in high school economics class. If interest rates are high, margin interest expense is also high. Therefore, the advantage of holding call options, as opposed to owning the underlying stock, is greater when interest rates are higher, because the money not invested in the stock can be invested in an interest-bearing account. This causes the value of the call option to increase as interest rates increase.

Short Interest Rebate This effect works in reverse on put options. This is primarily due to the fact that a short stock seller can sometimes be paid a short interest rebate. A long put trader, however, is not entitled to a short interest rebate, and therefore the advantage of owning puts over being short stock is lessened as interest rates increase. The higher the rates, the more short interest rebate is forfeited by the put owner.

Example You believe the Federal Open Market Committee is in a tightening mode, and you anticipate an increase in interest rates of 1% over the next 12 months. You are interested in buying long call LEAPs with 14 months until expiration and you know that this may cause calls to gain value. Since rho is reflected in cents, it is indicating a possible gain of about $0.27 over the year if interest rates increase by 1% (see Figure 1.16).

FIGURE 1.16

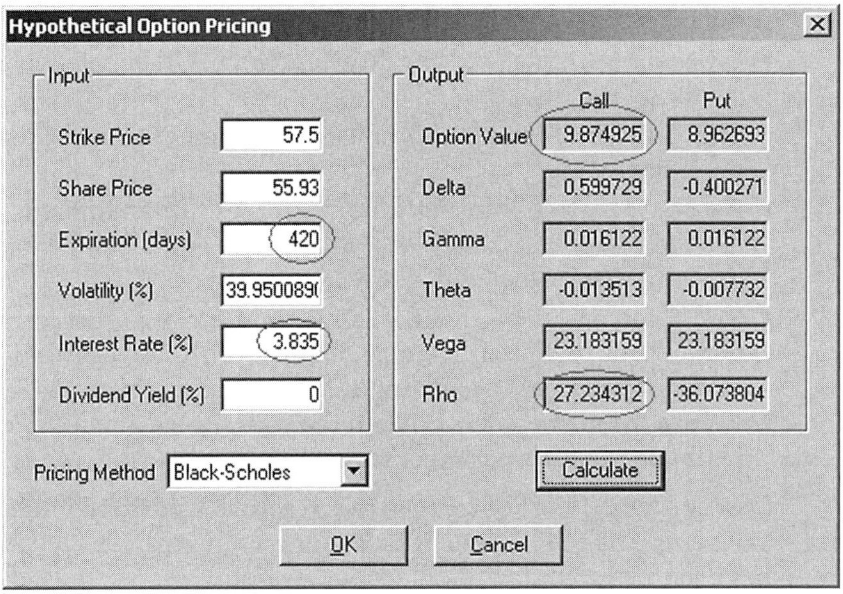

Using the Hypothetical Option Pricing Tool again, you can first simulate a reduction in the time to expiration of 365 days to gain an understanding of the impact of theta over one year, if all other factors remain constant. As you can see, with no other changes, a time elapse of one year will cause these call options to drop from $9.87 to $2.91 for a loss of $6.96. At this price, rho now only indicates a gain of about $0.03 (see Figure 1.17).

To calculate how much an increase in the interest rates will offset this time erosion, you use the tool to increase the interest rate by 1% while simultaneously reducing the time until expiration by 365 days (see Figure 1.18).

As you can see, even on LEAP options, which are more sensitive to interest rate changes than short-term options, a 1% increase in interest rates only adds about $0.03 to the value of this option. This forecast helps you to realize that you would then have to evaluate the merits of this trade without regard to changes in interest rates.

FIGURE 1.17

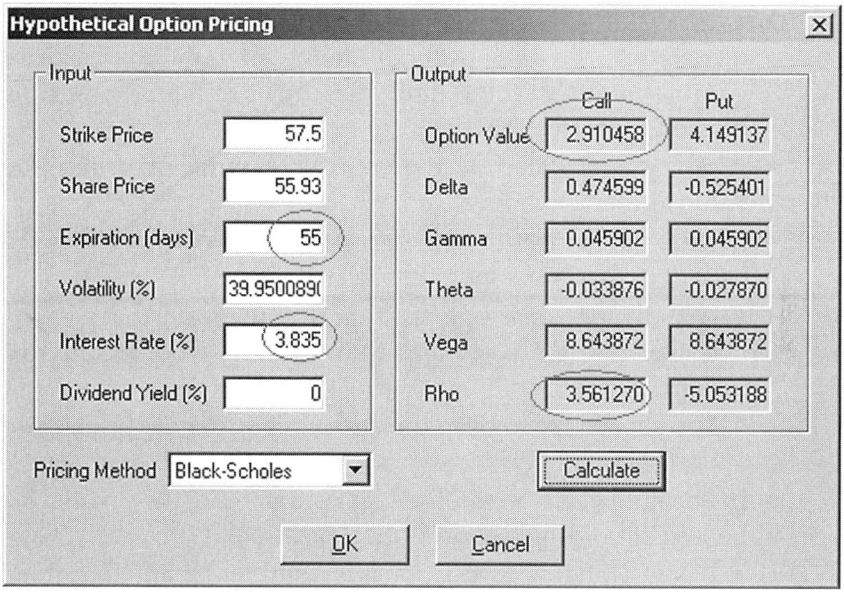

FIGURE 1.18

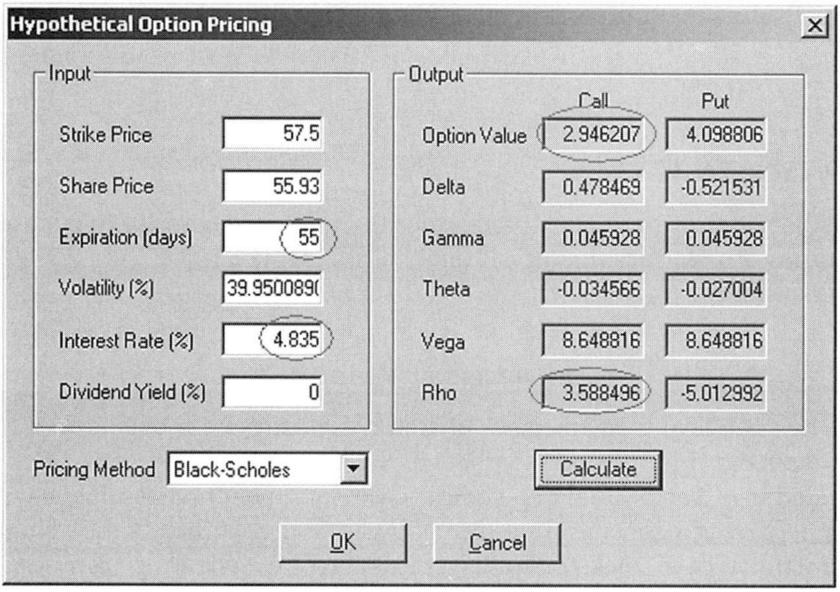

Alpha

Alpha (aka relative benefit) tells you the relative benefit of your gamma versus your theta.

- It compares the daily benefit of being long options (positive gamma) relative to the daily detriment of being long time erosion (negative theta).
- Alpha is calculated as the ratio of gamma over absolute value of theta.
- In absolute value terms, the greater the ratio, the greater the benefit of holding a long option position.
  - A high alpha on a long position simply means that gamma is working for you more than theta is working against you.
  - You should try to keep the alpha of your long option positions above 1.00.
- In absolute value terms, the smaller the ratio, the greater the benefit of holding a short option position.
  - A low alpha on a short position simply means that theta is working for you more than gamma is working against you.
  - You should try to keep the alpha of your short option positions below 1.00.
- Alpha is not displayed in the Hypothetical Option Pricing Tool, but it can easily be calculated as gamma divided by theta.

VOLATILITY

Volatility is a measure of stock price fluctuation. There are two main types of volatility: historical (aka statistical) volatility and implied volatility.

Historical Volatility

The statistical measurement of a stock's past price movement over a specific time period is called its historical volatility. It is calculated using an annualized standard deviation of percent changes in prices over a specific time frame. Historical volatility is the actual volatility of a stock (or index), measured by reviewing how high and how low it has gone over a certain period of time. More specifically, it is the annualized standard deviation of a stock's daily price change, expressed in terms of a percentage, without regard to the direction. If an index moves from 200 to 202 or from 200 to 198, this is a 1% change in volatility. Historical volatility over a given period of time is used to make volatility predictions about the future movements of a particular security. As discussed in the explanation of pricing models earlier in this chapter, the volatility of a stock is a key factor in determining the price of an option. Since volatility is not directional, higher volatility means higher prices on both puts and calls.

Chart studies illustrating the historical volatility of a particular stock or index are available on many trading platforms, such as in CyberTrader Pro and Schwab's StreetSmart Pro software (see Figure 1.19).

Generally, historical volatility studies will allow you to select the period of time over which the historical volatility will be averaged. If you are considering a long-term option strategy, you may want to select a long period of 100–200 days. If you a considering a shorter term strategy, 10 or 20 days may be more appropriate.

FIGURE 1.19

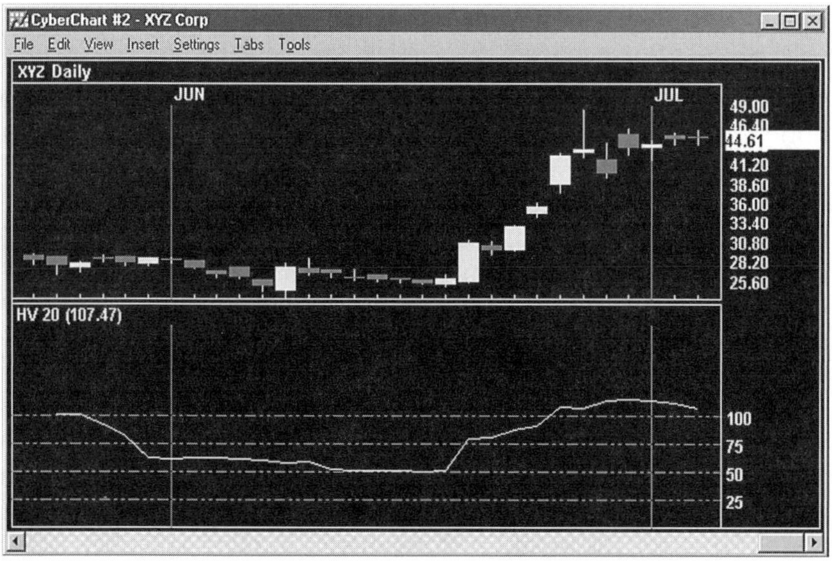

Figure 1.19 illustrates a historical volatility (HV) of 107.47% for the default study period of 20 days. This means that although the chart is displaying approximately 40 days worth of data, the historical volatility of the sample stock averaged over the most recent 20 days was 107.47%. This is an extremely high volatility for a stock, but as you can see, the stock rose from around 25 to around 45 during that period of time.

Volatility Mean Reversion Volatility mean reversion states that the price of a particular stock in any given short time frame can be either erratic or calm. When erratic, it will move to extreme levels either to the upside or the downside or both. However, when temporarily more erratic than normal, it eventually tends to revert back toward its longer term average volatility, meaning volatility will settle back down. Likewise, when a stock becomes temporarily more stable than normal (less volatile), it will eventually revert back toward its longer term average volatility, meaning volatility will pick back up. Since volatility is a *non*directional measure, this theory also holds true in times when volatility is lower than normal or higher than normal.

If you compare the average implied volatility (explained later in this chapter) to the historical volatility of a particular stock or index over a period of time, you should be able to see a pattern of the amount by which the average implied volatility is either below or above the historical volatility. When the gap between the two is wider or narrower than normal, you may be able to take advantage of the mean reversion tendency.

Example Assume you have watched the average implied volatility of XYZ stock over a period of several months. You have noticed that the average implied volatility (as calculated by the option prices) tends to be 5%–7% above the historical volatility. Lately you have noticed that the implied volatility of the options is 15%–17% above the historical volatility. If you subscribe to the mean reversion theory, this may be a time to establish option strategies that benefit from falling volatilities (negative vega). Some of these strategies will be discussed in later chapters.

Implied Volatility

Implied volatility is computed by using an option pricing model such as Black-Scholes, Barone-Adesi-Whaley, or Cox-Ross-Rubinstein and solving for the volatility component. Implied volatility is the theoretical volatility of the underlying stock (or index), based on the quoted price of the options of that particular stock (or index). Since volatility is the only component of a pricing model that is estimated (using the historical volatility), it is possible to work the formula backward and calculate the current volatility estimate being used by the options market maker. It can also help to gauge whether options are relatively cheap or relatively expensive. Rising implied volatility causes option premiums to rise or become more expensive; falling implied volatility results in lower option premiums. Streaming calculations of implied volatility are available on many trading platforms, such as those in the option chain window of CyberTrader Pro and Schwab's StreetSmart Pro software, and any of the three pricing models mentioned above can be selected (see Figure 1.20).

Average Implied Volatility While such calculations only provide the implied volatility of specific option contracts, a reasonable assumption of the average implied volatility for the underlying stock or index can be made by simply averaging the implied volatilities of the two closest month, closest to the money put and call options of any stock or index.

FIGURE 1.20

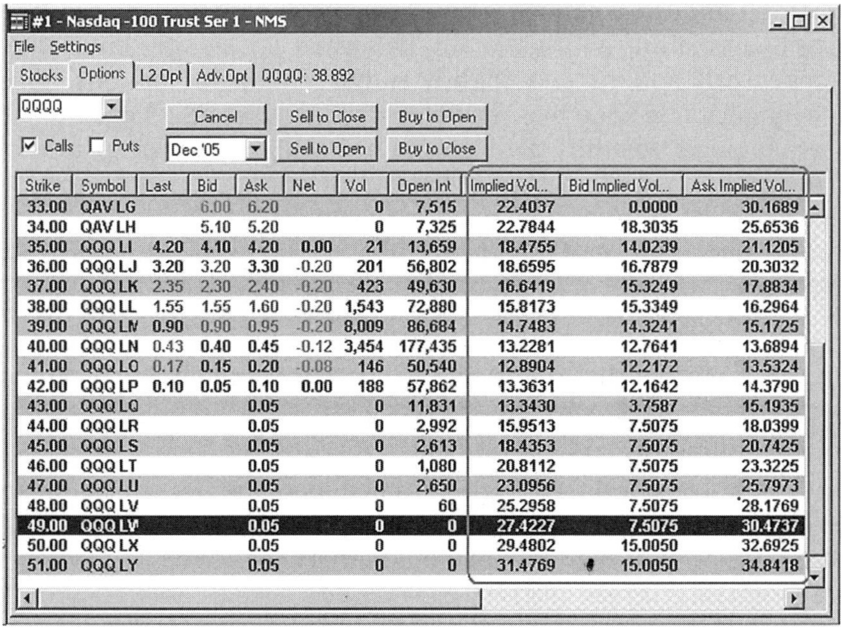

Strike	Symbol	Last	Bid	Ask	Net	Vol	Open Int	Implied Vol...	Bid Implied Vol...	Ask Implied Vol...
33.00	QAV LG		6.00	6.20		0	7,515	22.4037	0.0000	30.1689
34.00	QAV LH		5.10	5.20		0	7,325	22.7844	18.3035	25.6536
35.00	QQQ LI	4.20	4.10	4.20	0.00	21	13,659	18.4755	14.0239	21.1205
36.00	QQQ LJ	3.20	3.20	3.30	-0.20	201	56,802	18.6595	16.7879	20.3032
37.00	QQQ LK	2.35	2.30	2.40	-0.20	423	49,630	16.6419	15.3249	17.8834
38.00	QQQ LL	1.55	1.55	1.60	-0.20	1,543	72,880	15.8173	15.3349	16.2964
39.00	QQQ LM	0.90	0.90	0.95	-0.20	8,009	86,684	14.7483	14.3241	15.1725
40.00	QQQ LN	0.43	0.40	0.45	-0.12	3,454	177,435	13.2281	12.7641	13.6894
41.00	QQQ LO	0.17	0.15	0.20	-0.08	146	50,540	12.8904	12.2172	13.5324
42.00	QQQ LP	0.10	0.05	0.10	0.00	188	57,862	13.3631	12.1642	14.3790
43.00	QQQ LQ			0.05		0	11,831	13.3430	3.7587	15.1935
44.00	QQQ LR			0.05		0	2,992	15.9513	7.5075	18.0399
45.00	QQQ LS			0.05		0	2,613	18.4353	7.5075	20.7425
46.00	QQQ LT			0.05		0	1,080	20.8112	7.5075	23.3225
47.00	QQQ LU			0.05		0	2,650	23.0956	7.5075	25.7973
48.00	QQQ LV			0.05		0	60	25.2958	7.5075	28.1769
49.00	QQQ LW			0.05		0	0	27.4227	7.5075	30.4737
50.00	QQQ LX			0.05		0	0	29.4802	15.0050	32.6925
51.00	QQQ LY			0.05		0	0	31.4769	15.0050	34.8418

As discussed previously, a pricing model formula can be worked in reverse to solve for the implied volatility estimate being used by the options market maker whenever the following information is available:

- The option's expiration date
- The strike price of the option
- The price of the underlying asset
- The annual dividend yield
- The risk-free interest rate
- The option's current price
- The expiration style (American or European)
- Whether the option is a call or put

Using the Black-Scholes model, you would find the implied volatility by adding the current quoted option price for (P) and solving for V. Knowing the implied volatility is generally more useful to an option trader than the theoretical price, since future volatility can be difficult to estimate. When you know the implied volatility being used by the market maker, you are allowing the marketplace to estimate the future volatility for you.

Volatility Skew If you view the implied volatilities of a chain of options on the same underlying stock or index, you may notice that the implied volatility is not the same at each strike price. The implied volatility will generally be lowest for slightly out-of-the-money call options and slightly in-the-money put options. This phenomenon is known as the volatility skew (see also **Vega**).

Implied volatility will generally be higher for deep in-the-money options and way out-of-the-money options. A stock can only have one volatility, so why does this happen?

There are several theories:

- Pricing models assume a lognormal price distribution, which rarely occurs.
- Consider that an option can go up indefinitely, but it cannot go down below zero.
- Intraday market sentiment
  - Consider that high intraday demand for calls on an upward trending stock may push the price of those call options higher than would otherwise occur.

- Availability of underlying stock for hedging
  - Market makers typically do not take directional positions. When option demand is high on stocks that are difficult to hedge in the equity or futures market, the spreads on those options may widen. A higher quoted ask price will raise the implied volatility component of the price model.
- Mean reversion characteristics
  - When a stock becomes more volatile than usual, it often settles back down to its normal volatility level over time.
  - When a stock becomes less volatile than usual, its volatility often picks back up to its normal volatility level over time.
- Supply and demand in the marketplace
  - Consider that the demand is generally highest for options that are closest to the money, while deep in-the-money and far out-of-the-money options trade very infrequently.
  - Volume on a particular option can vary widely from day to day.

FIGURE 1.21

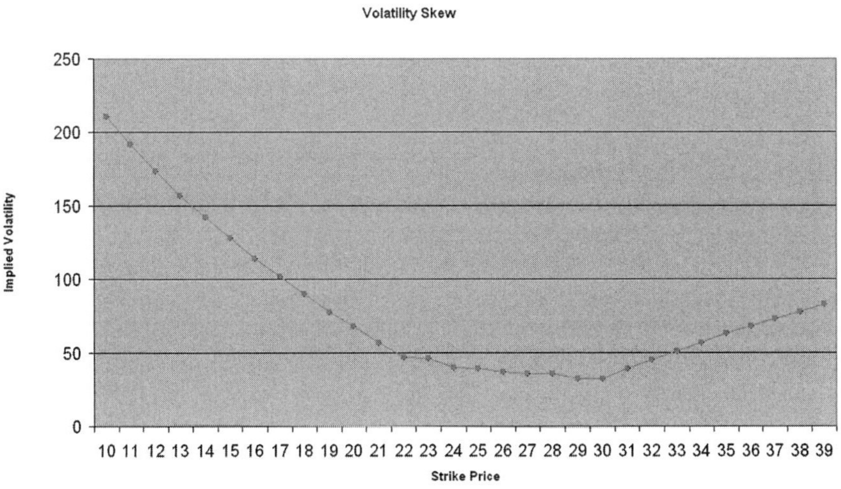

Disagreement still exists regarding the merit of all these theories, but what is important to understand is that volatility skew does exist, and it can sometimes create trading opportunities. If you graph the implied volatility skew of the call options of a particular exchange-traded fund (ETF) that is trading around 28, it will look something like Figure 1.21. Because many ETFs have strike prices at every dollar, they are good examples to use.

If you are a spread trader, this type of information is important because the higher the implied volatility, the more "expensive" the option is, relatively speaking. As a spread trader you should try to structure your spreads so that you buy options with low implied volatility and sell options with high implied volatility. If volatility changes over the life of your spread, the short leg with the higher volatility may work in your favor more than the long leg with the lower volatility works against you. In addition, as expiration approaches, the skew tends to flatten out, causing the short leg with the higher volatility to come down and the long leg with the lower volatility to stay the same or move up, both of which benefit your spread.

SECTION 2

Vertical Spreads

CHAPTER 2

Bullish Spreads

Spreads offer you the opportunity to limit losses in exchange for a limited gain potential. They involve the simultaneous purchase and sale of two options contracts of the same class (puts or calls) on the same underlying security.

VERTICAL SPREADS EXPLANATION

In the case of vertical spreads (also known as price spreads), the expiration month is the same, but the strike price will be different. In many cases, spreads may require that you temporarily establish a long or short stock position. That resulting long or short position will need to be closed out in the market to fully realize the profit potential of the strategy. This is explained in more detail later in this chapter.

Two of the key concepts to understand before you begin trading spreads are how to determine your sentiment (whether you are bullish or bearish) and how to calculate the maximum loss (ML), breakeven points (BE), and maximum gain (MG). These calculations will vary depending upon whether the spread is initially

---

Author's Note: Spreads are very versatile, and with the range of strike prices that are available and the ability to utilize either debit call spreads or credit put spreads, there are many ways to potentially take advantage of charts that are exhibiting signs of varying bullishness.

established as a net debit or net credit and whether or not it is entered using calls or puts. For any credit spread, your broker will also require you to meet an initial margin requirement and maintain funds in your account equal to the maximum loss amount. You can determine your sentiment and calculate the ML, BE, and MG for any vertical spread strategy by applying the following rules:

1. Determine the main leg of the spread.
   a. The main leg is simply the option with the higher premium.
2. Determine whether you are bullish or bearish on the main leg.
   a. Long calls or short puts are bullish.
   b. Long puts or short calls are bearish.
3. Determine whether you are bullish or bearish on the spread.
   a. Your answer to step 2 holds true for the entire spread strategy.
4. Determine whether the spread was entered at a net debit or a net credit.
   a. If the long leg has a higher premium it is a net debit.
   b. If the short leg has a higher premium it is a net credit.
5. Calculate the **ML**.
   a. If the spread is entered at a net debit, the debit is the ML.
   b. If the spread is entered at net credit, the ML is the net of the two strike prices less the credit.
   c. The only exception to a and b occurs in diagonal spreads, discussed in Chapter 5.
6. Calculate the **BE**.
   a. If debit call spread, the BE is the strike price of the main leg + net debit.
   b. If debit put spread, the BE is the strike price of the main leg – net debit.
   c. If credit call spread, the BE is the strike price of the main leg + net credit.
   d. If credit put spread, the BE is the strike price of the main leg – net credit.
   e. * The BE will always be between the two strike prices.

7. Calculate the **MG**.
   a. If the spread is entered at a net credit, the credit is the MG.
   b. If the spread is entered at net debit, the MG is the net of the two strike prices less the debit.

BULLISH SPREADS

The two most basic types of bullish spreads are debit call spreads and credit put spreads. Both are typically used when you are bullish, but they differ somewhat by when and how you can make a profit, or sustain a loss. With bullish spreads, the expiration month is the same, but the strike price of the long option will be lower than the strike price of the short option.

Debit Call Spreads—Quick Overview

A debit call spread is made up of one long call at a lower strike and one short call at a higher strike. Both legs should have the same expiration month. Both sides of this spread are opening transactions, and the number of contracts of the long leg should be the same as the number of the short leg (see Figure 2.1).

At Entry The white line in Figure 2.1 represents what the strategy typically looks like at the point of entry. As expiration approaches, the curve moves toward the black lines, which illustrate the final profit and loss boundaries at expiration.

Direction Neutral to bullish, depending upon the strike prices selected

When to Use You would typically employ a debit call spread in a moderately bullish market, or when you think the market is more likely to rise than fall and you would hope to profit if the underlying stock remains relatively flat or moderately increases until the expiration date of the options. Generally, the more bullish you are, the higher the strike prices you will use.

Risk vs. Reward Limited risk with limited profit potential

Volatility The effect of volatility varies depending upon the strike prices chosen.

FIGURE 2.1

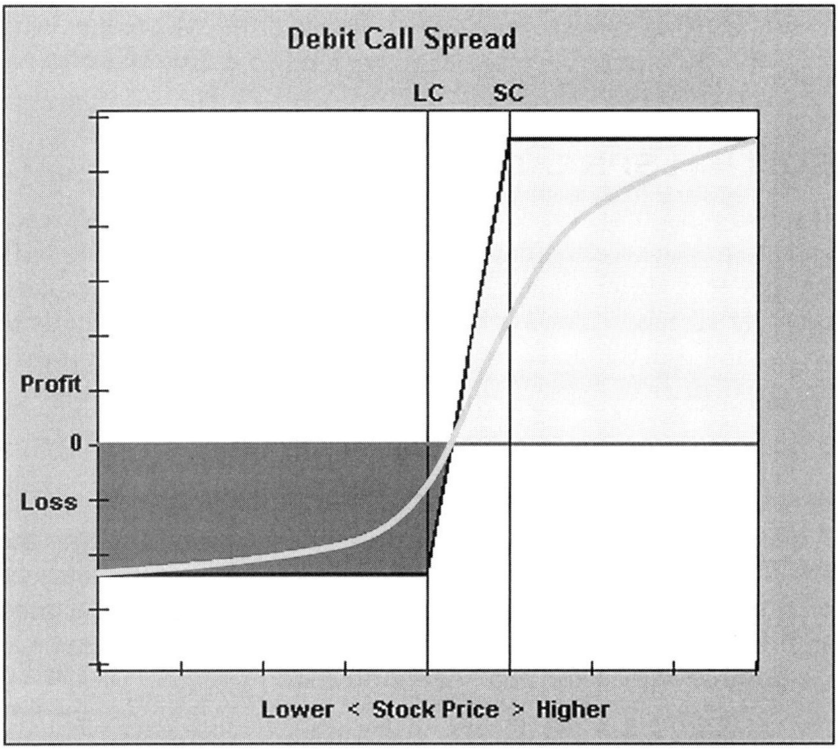

Time Decay The effect of time decay on this strategy varies with the underlying stock's price level in relation to the strike prices. If the stock price is above the strike prices, the effect is positive. If the stock price is between the strike prices, the effect is neutral, and if the stock price is below the strike prices, the effect is negative (see Table 2.1).

Prior to Expiration

- Because the long call has a lower strike price, it will also have a higher delta. As the underlying stock rises in price, the long option will gain value faster than the short option. Likewise, as the underlying stock drops in price, the long option will lose value faster than the short option.
- If the underlying stock rises sharply enough, the spread can often be closed out at a profit prior to expiration. This profit, however, will always be less than the maximum profit possible if held until expiration.

TABLE 2.1

Greeks	In-the-money	At-the-money	Out-of-the-money
Delta	Positive	Positive	Positive
Gamma	Negative	Neutral	Positive
Theta	Positive	Neutral	Negative
Vega	Negative	Neutral	Positive

  - Comparing the early close profit to the maximum potential profit at expiration can help you decide if holding until expiration makes sense.
- If the underlying stock drops sharply enough, the spread can often be closed out at a loss that is less than the maximum loss possible if held until expiration.
  - Comparing the early close loss to the maximum potential loss at expiration can help you decide if holding until expiration makes sense.

At Expiration

- Below the lower strike, both options expire worthless and max loss is sustained.
- Between the lower and upper strike, long stock will be acquired through exercise of the lower strike. The long stock can then be sold in the market. The trade may or may not be profitable.
- Above the higher strike, both options are exercised and/or assigned and max gain is achieved.

Debit Call Spreads—Detail

When you establish a bullish position using a vertical call spread, you will pay a higher premium for the option you purchase than the amount you will receive on the premium from the option sold. As a result, a bullish vertical call spread is always established at a net debit. This type of spread is a common substitute for purchasing long calls outright, as the initial debit is lower and the maximum loss potential is also lower.

Example:

Buy 10 XYZ May 75 Calls @ 2

Sell 10 XYZ May 80 Calls @ .50 for a net debit of 1.50

BE = 76.50 (main position strike price + the debit)

MG = 3.50 (net of strikes – the debit)

ML = 1.50 (debit paid)

This spread is executed for a net cost of $1,500 (2 points premium paid – .50 points premium received × 10 contracts × 100 shares per contract). As shown in Figure 2.2, at expiration you will profit if the market price of XYZ goes above $76.50. You will maximize your profit at $80 or above. You will lose money if the price of XYZ goes below $76.50, and the entire $1,500 will be lost if XYZ declines to $75 or below at expiration.

If, instead of trading a spread, you decided to simply purchase the May 75 calls outright, your total cost would be $2,000, rather than

FIGURE 2.2

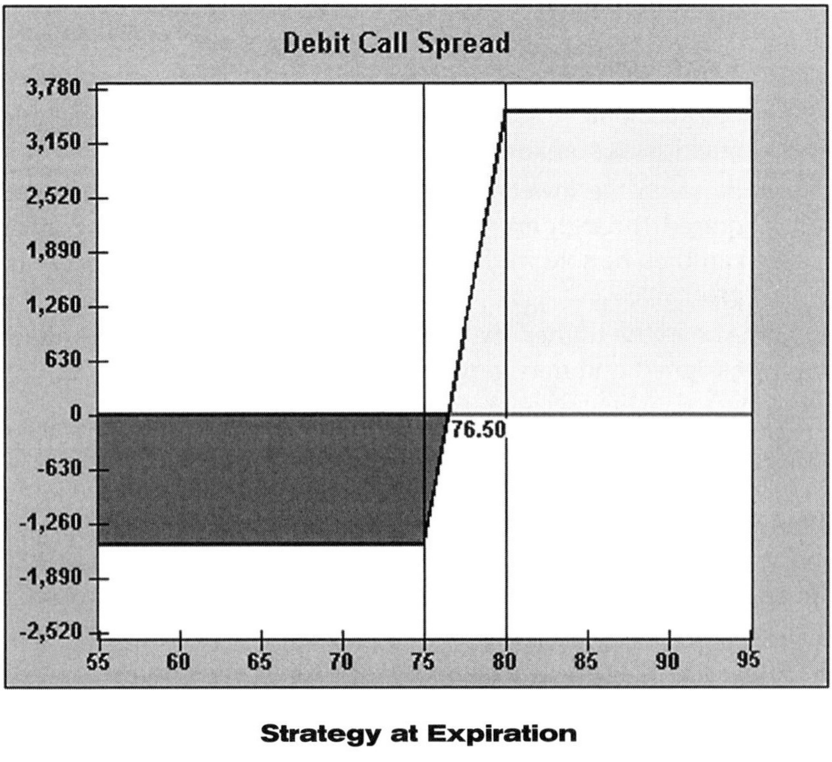

Strategy at Expiration

$1,500. However, the trade-off for reduced risk (in this case $500 of reduced risk) is limited gain potential. If you simply purchased the May 75 calls, your upside potential would be unlimited. In the case of this debit spread, your maximum profit cannot exceed $3,500.

To understand how the profit and loss characteristics of this type of spread work, assume that once you have established this spread, it is held until expiration. There are five different prices that you should examine to draw a clear picture of how this strategy works.

Scenario 1: Assume the stock rallies significantly and closes at 82 on option expiration. If this happens, you will exercise your 75 calls and acquire 1,000 shares of XYZ stock at a cost of $75,000. At the same time, your short 80 calls will be assigned against you, and you will be required to sell your stock for $80,000. The difference between your buy and sell price is $5,000. However, you paid $1,500 initially when the spread was established, so your net profit is $3,500. This will be the case at any price above 80. Therefore, this spread is only advantageous over long calls if XYZ does not exceed 80.50.

Scenario 2: Assume the stock rallies only slightly and closes at 78 on option expiration. If this happens, you will exercise your 75 calls and acquire 1,000 shares of XYZ stock at a cost of $75,000. However, your short 80 calls will expire worthless. The owner of those calls will not exercise if the market price of the stock is below the strike price. You can then sell your shares at the market price of 78 for proceeds of $78,000. In this case, the difference between your buy and sell price is $3,000. However, you paid $1,500 initially when the spread was established, so your net profit is only $1,500. Your profit will vary from $0 to $3,500 at prices from 76.50 up to 80.

Scenario 3: Assume the stock closes at exactly 76.50 on option expiration. If this happens, you will exercise your 75 calls and acquire 1,000 shares of XYZ stock at a cost of $75,000. However, your short 80 calls will expire worthless. You can then sell your shares at the market price of 76.50 for proceeds of $76,500. In this case, the difference between your buy and sell price is $1,500. However, you paid $1,500 initially when the spread was established, so your net profit is $0.

Scenario 4: Assume the stock drops slightly and closes at 76 on option expiration. If this happens, you will exercise your 75 calls and acquire 1,000 shares of XYZ stock at a cost of $75,000. Your short 80 calls will expire worthless. You can then sell your shares at the market price of 76 for proceeds of $76,000. In this case, the difference between your buy and sell price is $1,000. However, you paid $1,500 initially when the spread was established, so your net loss is $500. Your loss will vary from $0 to $1,500 at prices from 76.50 down to 75.

Scenario 5: Assume the stock drops substantially and closes at 73 on option expiration. If this happens, you will not exercise your 75 calls, because the market price is below 75. Your short 80 calls will also expire worthless. In this case, all the options expire worthless, and no stock is bought or sold. However, you paid $1,500 initially when the spread was established, so your net loss is the entire $1,500. This will be the case at any price below 75.

In trying to understand a multi-leg option strategy, sometimes it is helpful to compare it to a more simple strategy and point out the similarities and differences.

Example

Long Calls vs. Debit Call Spread

XYZ = 72

- Long call provides unlimited upside potential and limited risk (see Figure 2.3).
- Debit call spread is created by selling a higher strike call (see Figure 2.4).
- The trade-off is limited upside potential beyond 80.
  - In exchange for a slightly lower initial cost.

Buy 10 XYZ May 75 Calls @ 2

Buy 10 XYZ May 75 Calls @ 2
Sell 10 XYZ May 80 Calls @ .50

FIGURE 2.3 AND 2.4

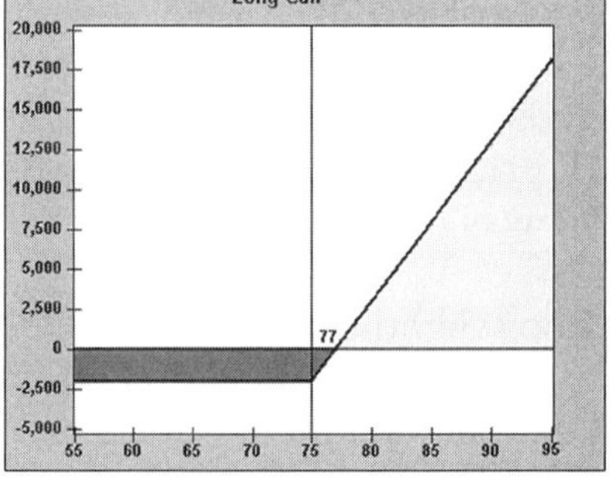

Strategy at Expiration

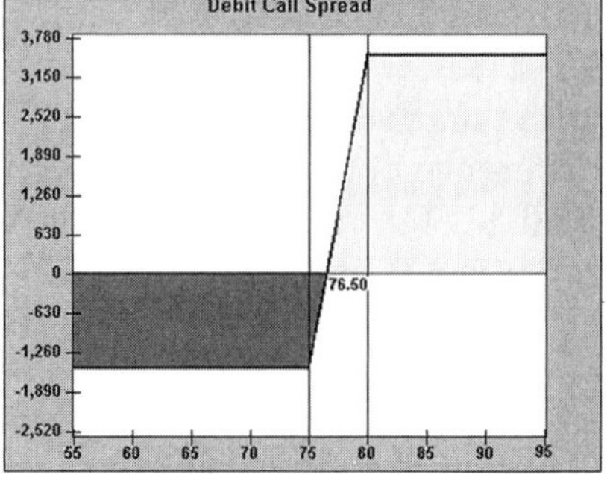

Strategy at Expiration

Long Calls

- May 75 calls purchased outright for a total cost of $2,000.
  - Rather than $1,500 (cost of the spread).
- The trade-off for the increased risk is unlimited gain potential.
  - $500 of increased risk.
- The upside potential for profit is theoretically unlimited as the stock rises.
- In the case of the debit spread, maximum profit cannot exceed $3,500.
- Breakeven is at 77.

Debit Call Spread

- Spread is executed for a net cost of $1,500.
  - 2 points premium paid – .50 points premium received × 10 contracts × 100 shares per contract
- Profitable if the market price of XYZ goes above $76.50 (the breakeven).
- Maximum profit at $80 or above.
- Unprofitable if the price of XYZ is below $76.50.
- Maximum loss of $1,500 if XYZ is $75 or below at expiration.
- Commissions will be higher than for the single call trade.

Advantages of debit call spreads vs. long calls

- Require less capital to enter, since you are taking in some premium from the options that are sold.
- Lower initial cost effectively lowers the breakeven point.

Disadvantages of debit call spreads vs. long calls

- Profit potential is limited.
- May require a higher option trading approval level, depending upon your broker.
- May require a higher minimum account net worth, depending upon your broker.
- Will limit your profits significantly if the underlying stock moves substantially higher.
- Higher commission costs, since two options are traded instead of one.

Credit Put Spreads—Quick Overview

A credit put spread is made up of one long put at the lower strike and one short put at the higher strike. Both legs should have the same expiration month. Both sides of this spread are opening transactions, and the number of contracts of the long leg should be the same as the number of the short leg (see Figure 2.5).

At Entry The white line in Figure 2.5 represents what the strategy typically looks like at the point of entry. As expiration approaches, the curve moves toward the black lines, which illustrate the final profit and loss boundaries at expiration.

Direction Neutral to bullish, depending upon the strike prices selected

FIGURE 2.5

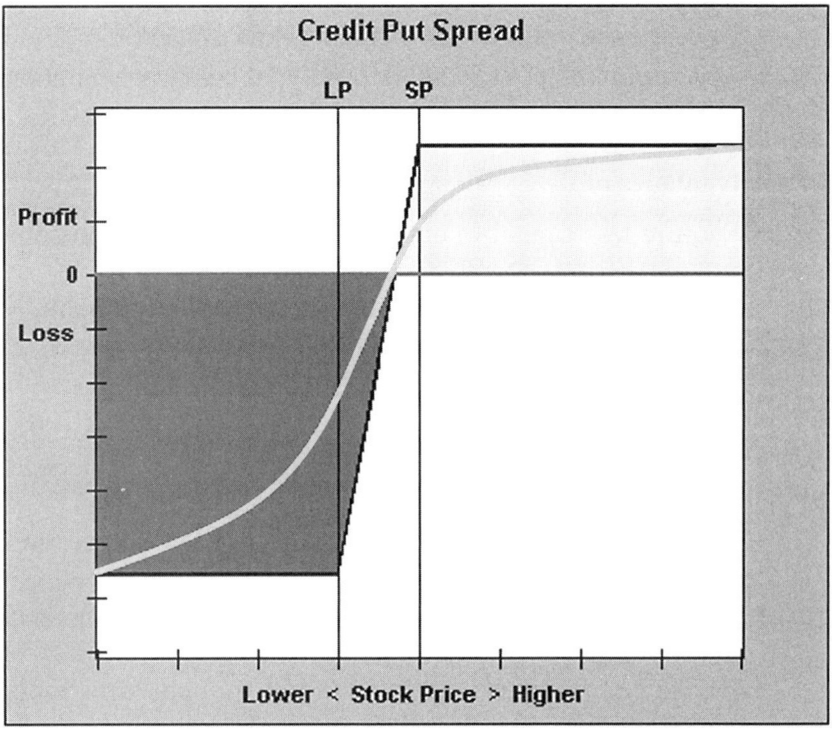

When to Use You would typically employ a credit put spread in a moderately bullish market, or when you think the market is more likely to rise than fall, and you would hope to profit if the underlying stock remains relatively flat or moderately increases until the expiration date of the options. Generally, the more bullish you are, the higher the strike prices you will use.

Risk vs. Reward Limited risk with limited profit potential

Volatility The effect of volatility varies depending upon the strike prices chosen.

Time Decay The effect of time decay on this strategy varies with the underlying stock's price level in relation to the strike prices. If the stock price is above the strike prices, the effect is positive. If the stock price is between the strike prices, the effect is neutral, and if the stock price is below the strike prices, the effect is negative (see Table 2.2).

Prior to Expiration

- Because the short put has a higher strike price, it will also have a higher delta. As the underlying stock rises in price, the short option will lose value faster than the long option. Likewise, as the underlying stock drops in price, the short option will gain value faster than the long option.
- If the underlying stock rises sharply enough, the spread can often be closed out at a profit prior to expiration. This profit, however, will always be less than the maximum profit possible if held until expiration.
  - Comparing the early close profit to the maximum potential profit at expiration can help you decide if holding until expiration makes sense.

TABLE 2.2

Greeks	In-the-money	At-the-money	Out-of-the-money
Delta	Positive	Positive	Positive
Gamma	Positive	Neutral	Negative
Theta	Negative	Neutral	Positive
Vega	Positive	Neutral	Negative

- If the underlying stock drops sharply enough, the spread can often be closed out at a loss that is less than the maximum loss possible if held until expiration.
  - Comparing the early close loss to the maximum potential loss at expiration can help you decide if holding until expiration makes sense.

At Expiration

- Below the lower strike, both options are exercised and/or assigned and max loss is sustained.
- Between the lower and upper strike, long stock will be acquired through assignment of the upper strike. The long stock can then be sold in the market. The trade may or may not be profitable.
- Above the higher strike, both options expire worthless and max gain is achieved.

Credit Put Spreads—Detail

When you establish a bullish position using a vertical put spread, you will pay a lower premium for the option you purchase than the amount you will receive on the premium from the option sold. As a result, a bullish vertical put spread is always established at a net credit. This type of spread is a common substitute for selling uncovered (naked) puts outright; though the initial credit is lower, the maximum loss potential is also lower.

Example

Buy 10 XYZ May 65 Puts @ .50

Sell 10 XYZ May 70 Puts @ 2 for a net credit of 1.50

BE = 68.50 (main position strike price – the credit)

MG = 1.50 (credit received)

ML = 3.50 (net of strikes – the credit)

This spread is executed for a net credit of $1,500 (2 points premium received – .50 points premium paid × 10 contracts × 100 shares per contract). As shown in Figure 2.6, at expiration you will profit if the market price of XYZ goes above $68.50. You will maximize your profit ($1,500) at $70 or above. You will lose money if the price of XYZ goes below $68.50, and you could lose up to a maximum of $3,500 if XYZ declines to $65 or below at expiration.

FIGURE 2.6

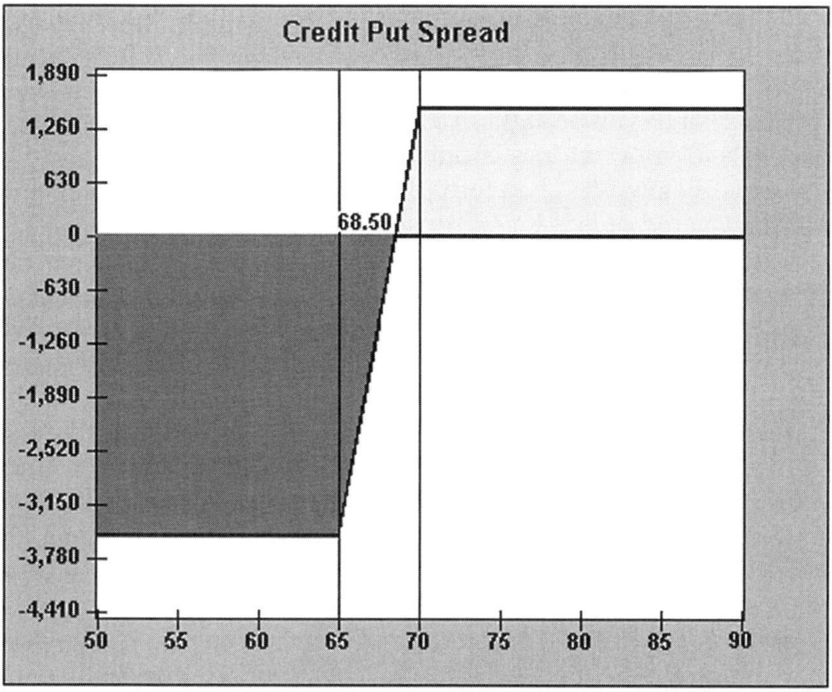

Strategy at Expiration

If instead of trading a spread, you simply sold the May 70 puts uncovered, you would have initially brought in $2,000, rather than $1,500. However, the trade-off for reduced profit potential (in this case only $500 of reduced profit potential) is the ability to have significantly limited risk. If you simply sold the May 70 puts uncovered, your loss potential would essentially be $68,000 ($70,000 loss on the stock, less $2,000 premium received on the sale of the puts), if XYZ were to drop all the way to zero. In the case of this credit spread, your maximum loss cannot exceed $3,500. This maximum loss is the difference between the strike prices on the two options minus the amount you were credited when the position was established.

To understand how the profit and loss characteristics of this type of spread work, assume that once you have established this spread, it is held until expiration. There are five different prices that you should examine to draw a clear picture of how this strategy works.

Scenario 1: Assume the stock drops significantly and closes at 62 on option expiration. If this happens, you will exercise your 65 puts and sell short 1,000 shares of XYZ stock for net proceeds of $65,000. At the same time, your short 70 puts will be assigned, and you will be required to buy back your short position to close for $70,000. The difference between your buy and sell price is –$5,000. However, since you brought in $1,500 initially when the spread was established, your net loss is only –$3,500. This will be the case at any price below 65. Therefore, this spread is only advantageous over uncovered puts if XYZ drops below 64.50.

Scenario 2: Assume the stock drops only slightly and closes at 67 on option expiration. If this happens, you will not exercise your 65 puts, because they are out-of-the-money. However, your short 70 puts will be assigned, and you will be required to buy 1,000 shares of XYZ at a cost of $70,000. You can then sell your shares at the market price of 67 for net proceeds of $67,000. In this case, the difference between your buy and sell price is –$3,000. However, since you brought in $1,500 initially when the spread was established, your net loss is only –$1,500. Your loss will vary from $0 to –$3,500 at prices from 68.50 down to 65.

Scenario 3: Assume the stock closes at exactly 68.50 on option expiration. If this happens, you will not exercise your 65 puts, because they are out-of-the-money. However, your short 70 puts will be assigned and you will be required to buy 1,000 shares of XYZ at a cost of $70,000. You can then sell your shares at the market price of 68.50 for net proceeds of $68,500. In this case, the difference between your buy and sell price is –$1,500. However, since you brought in $1,500 initially when the spread was established, your net loss is actually $0.

Scenario 4: Assume the stock rises only slightly and closes at 69 on option expiration. If this happens, you will not exercise your 65 puts, because they are out-of-the-money. However, your short 70 puts will be assigned, and you will be required to buy 1,000 shares of XYZ at a cost of $70,000. You can then sell your shares at the market price of 69 for net proceeds of $69,000. In this case, the difference between your buy and sell price is –$1,000. However, since you brought in $1,500 initially when the spread was established, your net gain is actually $500. Your gain will vary from $0 to $1,500 at prices from 68.50 up to 70.

Scenario 5: Assume the stock rises substantially and closes at 72 on option expiration. If this happens, you will not exercise your 65 puts, because they are out-of-the-money. Your short 70 puts will also not be assigned, because they are out-of-the-money. In this case, all of the options expire worthless and no stock is bought or sold. However, since you initially brought in $1,500 when the spread was established, your net gain is the entire $1,500. This maximum profit of $1,500 will occur at all prices above 70.

Though the examples above all deal with the outcome of these strategies at expiration, you are not required to hold a spread until expiration. If the underlying instrument moves enough, you may be able to close out the spread position at a net profit prior to expiration. Once established, spreads should be reviewed occasionally to determine if holding them until expiration is still warranted.

In trying to understand a multi-leg option strategy, sometimes it is helpful to compare it to a more simple strategy and point out the similarities and differences.

Example

Uncovered Puts vs. Credit Put Spread

XYZ = 72

- Uncovered put provides limited upside potential, with downside risk all the way to zero (see Figure 2.7).
- Credit put spread created by buying another further out-of-the-money put (see Figure 2.8).
- Risk is now limited to the downside.
    - Which is the trade-off for slightly lower initial credit.

FIGURE 2.7 AND 2.8

Sell 10 XYZ May 70 Puts @ 2

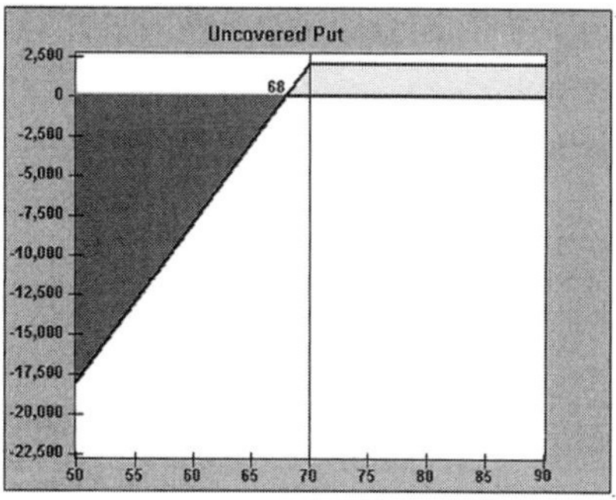

Strategy at Expiration

Buy 10 XYZ May 65 Puts @ .50
Sell 10 XYZ May 70 Puts @ 2

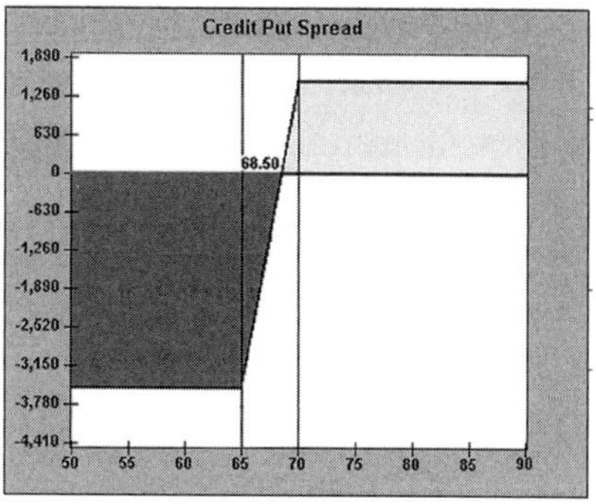

Strategy at Expiration

Uncovered Puts

- Uncovered (naked) puts sold for an initial credit of $2,000.
  - Rather than $1,500 (the initial credit on the spread).
- The trade-off for increased profit potential is significantly higher risk.
  - $500 of increased profit potential.
- The maximum loss potential would be $68,000 if the stock falls to zero.
  - $70,000 loss on the stock, less $2,000 premium received on the sale of the puts.
- Risk on this position is to the downside where XYZ can drop all the way to zero.
  - In the case of the credit spread, the maximum loss cannot exceed $3,500.
- Maximum potential gain is $2,000.
- Breakeven is at 68.

Credit Put Spread

- Spread is executed for a net credit of $1,500.
  - 2 points premium received – .50 points premium paid × 10 contracts × 100 shares per contract
- Profitable if the market price of XYZ is above $68.50 (the breakeven).
- Maximum profit at $70 or above.
- Unprofitable if the price of XYZ is below $68.50.
- Maximum loss of $3,500 if XYZ declines to $65 or below at expiration.
  - Maximum loss is the difference between the strike prices on the two options minus the initial credit when the position was established.
- Commissions will be higher than for the single put trade.

Advantages of credit put spreads vs. uncovered puts

- Substantially lower risk if the stock moves dramatically against you.
- The risk margin requirement for credit spreads is generally lower than for uncovered options.

- It is not possible to lose more money than the risk margin requirement that is held in your account at the time the position is established.
- Uncovered options will require a higher options trading approval level.
- Uncovered options will require a higher minimum account net worth.

Disadvantages of credit put spreads vs. uncovered puts

- Your profit potential will be reduced by the amount spent on the long option leg of the spread.
- Higher commission costs, since two options are traded instead of one.

Characteristics

Many option traders, when first introduced to spreads, have little trouble understanding the risk/reward characteristics but often have difficulty deciding which strike prices to use and how wide to make the spreads. Which strike prices you use and whether or not those strike prices are in, at, or out-of-the-money will affect the magnitude of the underlying move needed to reach profitability and will also determine whether or not the spread can be profitable if the underlying stock remains unchanged.

Table 2.3 illustrates how to properly structure a bullish spread to match your level of bullishness. For example, if you are extremely bullish, you may want to consider an out-of-the-money (OOTM) debit call spread or an in-the-money (ITM) credit put spread. Keep in mind that both will generally require a bullish move of extreme magnitude in the underlying stock in order to reach profitability. By contrast, if you are neutral to only slightly bullish, you may want to consider an ITM debit call spread or an OOTM credit put spread, both of which can sometimes be profitable with little or no movement in the underlying stock. As with most option strategies, the greater the underlying move needed, the higher the profit potential, but also the less likely it is that a profit will be made. Similarly, if you structure your spread so that profitability is possible with no movement in the underlying stock, a profit, if earned, will likely be very small.

TABLE 2.3

Bull Spread Strategy	<<< Direction >>>				<<< Magnitude >>>		
	Bullish	**Neutral**	**Breakout**	**Bearish**	**Extreme**	**Moderate**	**Slight**
Debit call spread OOTM	X				X		
Debit call spread ATM	X					X	
Debit call spread ITM	X	X					X
Credit put spread OOTM	X	X					X
Credit put spread ATM	X					X	
Credit put spread ITM	X				X		

Understanding Table 2.3 will help you identify possible bull spread candidates. Figures 2.9 and 2.10 are sample charts using simple technical analysis where bull spreads might be appropriate. Keep in mind that these examples do not include commission charges, which may be significant and will impact the profit or loss.

In Figure 2.9, you have identified XYZ stock, which appears to be bouncing off a support line. As a result, you are expecting a continued upward move.

If you are only slightly bullish, you may want to consider the following debit call spread. As with all spreads, you can calculate the breakeven (BE), maximum gain (MG), and maximum loss (ML) before you actually enter the trade. The maximum loss (ML) on a debit spread will always be the amount of the initial net debit.

Example 1A

Buy 10 XYZ Jun 50 Calls @ 3.35
Sell 10 XYZ Jun 55 Calls @ .45
Debit = 2.90
BE = 52.90 (main position strike price + debit amount)
MG = 2.10 (net of strikes – the debit)
ML = 2.90 (net debit paid)

FIGURE 2.9

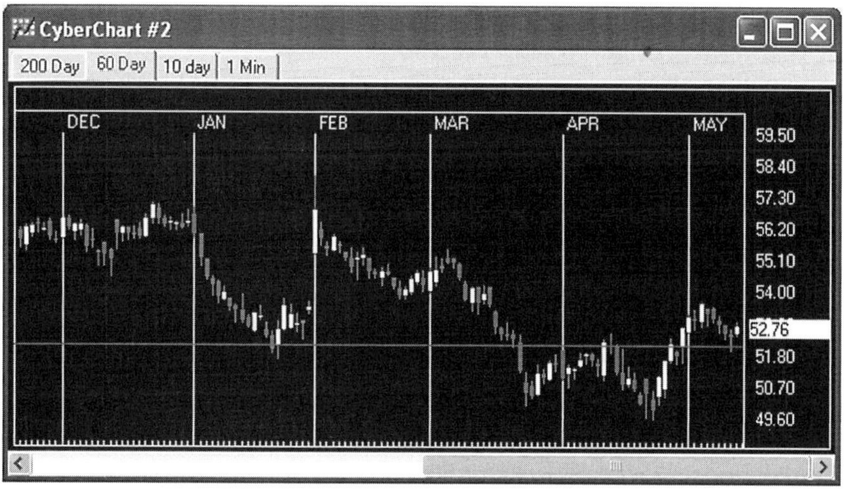

Total cost of this trade = $2,900 (debit × # of spreads × option multiplier) or (2.90 × 10 × 100)

This example would be considered at-the-money, since the long option is in-the-money and the short option is out-of-the-money. Since Figure 2.9 presents data in early May, these options have about five weeks until expiration. By calculating the breakeven before you enter the trade, you can see that with a breakeven price of 52.90, XYZ only needs to increase in price by $0.14 or more by expiration to be profitable. The maximum profit of $2,100 will be reached if XYZ is above 55 (the higher strike price) at expiration, since both options will be exercised and the net between the two is $5,000. Subtract $5,000 from the initial cost of $2,900 to arrive at the net profit. Losses will be incurred if XYZ closes below 52.90 at expiration, with the maximum loss of $2,900 occurring at any price below 50 (where both options expire worthless). When that occurs, the initial cost is completely lost.

If you are very bullish, you may want to consider the following credit put spread. In this example, you would receive a credit at the time the spread is established, but you can still calculate the breakeven (BE), maximum gain (MG) and maximum loss (ML) before the trade is entered. The maximum gain (MG) on a credit spread will always be the amount of the initial credit. In addition, a credit spread has a margin requirement that is equal to the maximum loss, but the initial credit can be applied against it.

Example 1B

Buy 10 XYZ Jun 55 Puts @ 3.00

Sell 10 XYZ Jun 60 Puts @ 7.60

Credit = 4.60

BE = 55.40 (main position strike price – the credit)

MG = 4.60 (credit received)

ML = .40 (net of strikes – the credit)

Total margin requirements of this trade = $400 ([net of strikes – the credit] × # of spreads × option multiplier) or ([60 – 55 – 4.60] × 10 × 100)

This example would be considered in-the-money, since both put options are in-the-money. Since Figure 2.9 presents data as of around May 9, these options have about five weeks until expiration. By calculating the breakeven before you enter the trade, you can see that with a breakeven price of 55.40, XYZ needs to increase considerably in price by $2.64 or more by expiration to be profitable. The maximum profit of $4,600 will be reached if XYZ is above 60 (the higher strike price) at expiration, since both options will expire worthless and the entire initial credit will be retained. Losses will be incurred if XYZ closes below 55.40 at expiration, with the maximum loss of $400 occurring at any price below 55 (where both options are exercised). When that occurs, the initial credit will be completely lost. Subtract the initial credit of $4,600 from the net loss between the two strike prices of $5,000 to arrive at the maximum loss of $400.

Figure 2.10 is a second chart using simple technical analysis where bull spreads might also be appropriate. In Figure 2.10, you have identified XYZ stock, which appears to have just broken through an upside resistance line. As a result, you are expecting a continued upward move.

If you are only slightly bullish, you may want to consider the following debit call spread.

Example 2A

Buy 10 XYZ Jun 40 Calls @ 4.40

Sell 10 XYZ Jun 45 Calls @ .40

Debit = 4.00

BE = 44.00 (main position strike price + debit amount)

FIGURE 2.10

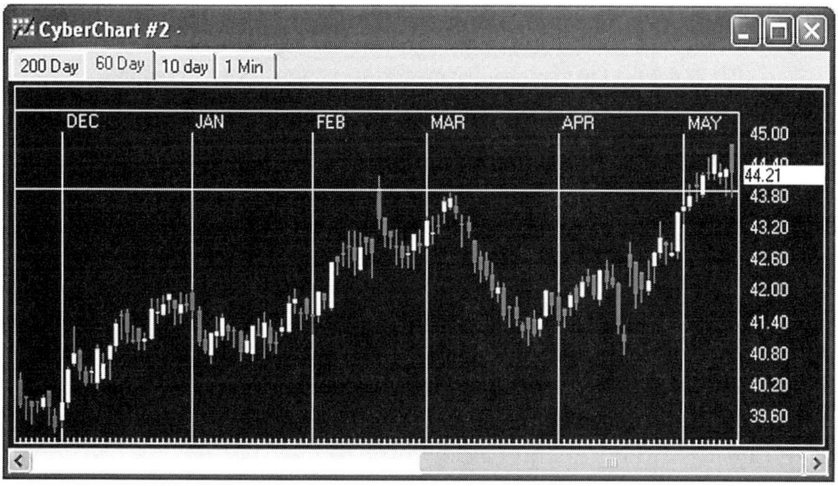

MG = 1.00 (net of strikes – the debit)

ML = 4.00 (net debit paid)

Total cost of this trade = $4,000 (DR × # of spreads × option multiplier) or (4.00 × 10 × 100)

This example could be considered at- or in-the-money, since the long option is in-the-money and the short option is just slightly out-of-the-money. Since Figure 2.10 presents data as of around May 9, these options have about five weeks until expiration. By calculating the breakeven before you enter the trade, you can see that with a breakeven price of 44.00, XYZ can actually drop in price by up to $0.21 or less by expiration and still be profitable. The maximum profit of $1,000 will be reached if XYZ is above 45 (the higher strike price) at expiration, since both options will be exercised and the net between the two is $5,000. Subtract $5,000 from the initial cost of $4,000 to arrive at the net profit. Losses will be incurred if XYZ closes below 44.00 at expiration, with the maximum loss of $4,000 occurring at any price below 40 (where both options expire worthless). When that occurs, the initial cost is completely lost.

If you are moderately bullish, you may want to consider the following credit put spread.

Example 2B

Buy 10 XYZ Jun 42.50 Puts @ .30

Sell 10 XYZ Jun 47.50 Puts @ 3.40

Credit = 3.10

BE = 44.40 (main position strike price – the credit)

MG = 3.10 (credit received)

ML = 1.90 (net of strikes – the credit)

Total margin requirements of this trade = $1,900 ([net of strikes – the credit] × # of spreads × option multiplier) or ([47.50 – 42.50 – 3.10] × 10 × 100)

This example would be considered at-the-money since the long option is out-of-the-money and the short option is in-the-money. Since Figure 2.10 presents data as of around May 9, these options have about five weeks until expiration. By calculating the break-even before you enter the trade, you can see that with a breakeven price of 44.40, XYZ only needs to increase in price by $0.19 or more by expiration to be profitable. The maximum profit of $3,100 will be reached if XYZ is above 47.50 (the higher strike price) at expiration, since both options will expire worthless and the entire initial credit will be retained. Losses will be incurred if XYZ closes below 44.40 at expiration, with the maximum loss of $1,900 occurring at any price below 42.50 (where both options are exercised). When that occurs, the initial credit will be completely lost. Subtract the initial credit of $3,100 from the net loss between the two strike prices of $5,000 to arrive at the maximum loss of $1,900.

CHAPTER 3

Bearish Spreads

Spreads offer you the opportunity to limit losses in exchange for a limited gain potential. They involve the simultaneous purchase and sale of two options contracts of the same class (puts or calls) on the same underlying security.

VERTICAL SPREADS EXPLANATION

In the case of vertical spreads (also known as price spreads), the expiration month is the same, but the strike price will be different. In many cases, spreads may require that you temporarily establish a long or short stock position. That resulting long or short position will need to be closed out in the market to fully realize the profit potential of the strategy. This is explained in more detail later in this chapter.

Two of the key concepts to understand before you begin trading spreads are how to determine your sentiment (whether you are bullish or bearish) and how to calculate the maximum loss (ML), breakeven points (BE), and maximum gain (MG). These calcula-

---

Author's Note: Spreads are very versatile, and with the range of strike prices that are available and the ability to utilize either debit put spreads or credit call spreads, there are many ways to potentially take advantage of charts that are exhibiting signs of varying bearishness.

tions will vary depending upon whether the spread is initially established as a net debit or net credit and whether or not it is entered using calls or puts. For any credit spread, your broker will also require you to meet an initial margin requirement and maintain funds in your account equal to the maximum loss amount. You can determine your sentiment and calculate the ML, BE, and MG for any vertical spread strategy by applying the following rules:

1. Determine the main leg of the spread.
   a. The main leg is simply the option with the higher premium.
2. Determine whether you are bullish or bearish on the main leg.
   a. Long calls or short puts are bullish.
   b. Long puts or short calls are bearish.
3. Determine whether you are bullish or bearish on the spread.
   a. Your answer to step 2 holds true for the entire spread strategy.
4. Determine whether the spread was entered at a net debit or a net credit.
   a. If the long leg has a higher premium it is a net debit.
   b. If the short leg has a higher premium it is a net credit.
5. Calculate the **ML.**
   a. If the spread is entered at net debit, the debit is the ML.
   b. If the spread is entered at net credit, the ML is the net of the two strike prices less the credit.
   c. The only exception to this rule occurs in diagonal spreads, discussed in Chapter 5.
6. Calculate the **BE**.
   a. If debit call spread, the BE is the strike price of the main leg + net debit.
   b. If debit put spread, the BE is the strike price of the main leg – net debit.
   c. If credit call spread, the BE is the strike price of the main leg + net credit.
   d. If credit put spread, the BE is the strike price of the main leg – net credit.
   e. * The BE will always be between the two strike prices.
7. Calculate the **MG**.
   a. If the spread is entered at a net credit, the credit is the MG.

b. If the spread is entered at net debit, the MG is the net of the two strike prices less the debit.

BEARISH SPREADS

The two most basic types of bearish spreads are debit put spreads and credit call spreads. Both are typically used when you are bearish, but they differ somewhat by when and how you can make a profit, or sustain a loss. With bearish spreads, the expiration month is the same, but the strike price of the long option will be higher than the strike price of the short option.

Debit Put Spreads—Quick Overview

A debit put spread is made up of one short put at the lower strike and one long put at the higher strike. Both legs should have the same expiration month. Both sides of this spread are opening trans-

FIGURE 3.1

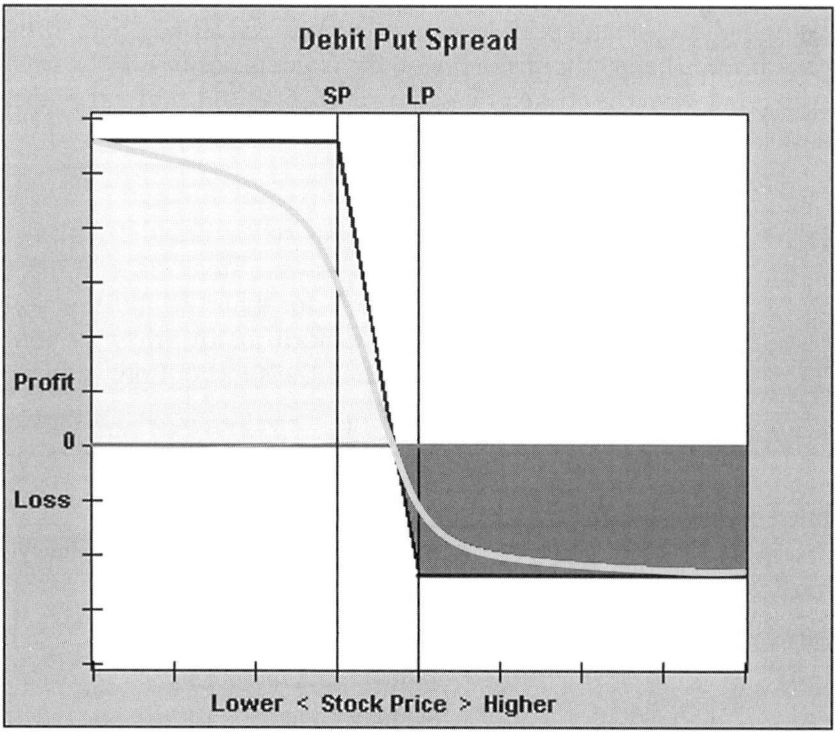

actions, and the number of contracts of the long leg should be the same as the number of the short leg (see Figure 3.1).

At Entry The white line in Figure 3.1 represents what the strategy typically looks like at the point of entry. As expiration approaches, the curve moves toward the black lines, which illustrate the final profit and loss boundaries at expiration.

Direction Neutral to bearish, depending upon the strike prices selected

When to Use You would typically employ a debit put spread in a moderately bearish market, or when you think the market is more likely to fall than rise, and you would hope to profit if the underlying stock remains relatively flat or moderately decreases until the expiration date of the options. Generally, the more bearish you are, the lower the strike prices you will use.

Risk vs. Reward Limited risk with limited profit potential

Volatility The effect of volatility varies depending upon the strike prices chosen.

Time Decay The effect of time decay on this strategy varies with the underlying stock's price level in relation to the strike prices. If the stock price is below the strike prices, the effect is positive. If the stock price is between the strike prices, the effect is neutral, and if the stock price is above the strike prices, the effect is negative (see Table 3.1).

Prior to Expiration

- Because the long put has a higher strike price, it will also have a higher delta. As the underlying stock rises in price, the long option will lose value faster than the short option. Likewise, as the underlying stock drops in price, the long option will gain value faster than the short option.

TABLE 3.1

Greeks	In-the-money	At-the-money	Out-of-the-money
Delta	Negative	Negative	Negative
Gamma	Negative	Neutral	Positive
Theta	Positive	Neutral	Negative
Vega	Negative	Neutral	Positive

- If the underlying stock drops sharply enough, the spread can often be closed out at a profit prior to expiration. This profit, however, will always be less than the maximum profit possible if held until expiration.
  - Comparing the early close profit to the maximum potential profit at expiration can help you decide if holding until expiration makes sense.
- If the underlying stock rises sharply enough, the spread can often be closed out at a loss that is less than the maximum loss possible if held until expiration.
  - Comparing the early close loss to the maximum potential loss at expiration can help you decide if holding until expiration makes sense.

At Expiration

- Below the lower strike, both options are exercised and/or assigned and max gain is achieved.
- Between the lower and upper strike, a short stock position will be established through exercise of the lower strike. The short stock can then be closed out in the market. The trade may or may not be profitable.
- Above the higher strike, both options expire worthless and the max loss is sustained.

Debit Put Spreads—Detail

When you establish a bearish position using a vertical put spread, you will pay a higher premium for the option you purchase than the amount you will receive on the premium from the option sold. As a result, a bearish vertical put spread is always established at a net debit. This type of spread is a common substitute for purchasing long puts outright, as the initial debit is lower and the maximum loss potential is also lower.

Example:

Buy 10 XYZ May 70 Puts @ 2

Sell 10 XYZ May 65 Puts @ .50 for a net debit of 1.50

BE = 68.50 (main position strike price – the debit)

MG = 3.50 (net of strikes – the debit)

ML = 1.50 (debit paid)

This spread is executed for a net cost of $1,500 (2 points premium paid – .50 points premium received × 10 contracts × 100 shares per contract). As shown in Figure 3.2, you will profit if the market price of XYZ goes below $68.50. You will maximize your profit at $65. You will lose money if the price of XYZ goes above $68.50, and the entire $1,500 will be lost if XYZ rises above $70 at expiration.

If you purchased the May 70 puts outright, your total cost would be $2,000, rather than $1,500. However, the trade-off for reduced risk (in this case $500 of reduced risk) is limited gain potential. If you simply purchased the May 70 puts, your profit potential on the downside grows until the stock reaches 0. In the case of this debit spread, your maximum profit cannot exceed $3,500.

To understand how the profit and loss characteristics of this type of spread work, assume that once you have established this

FIGURE 3.2

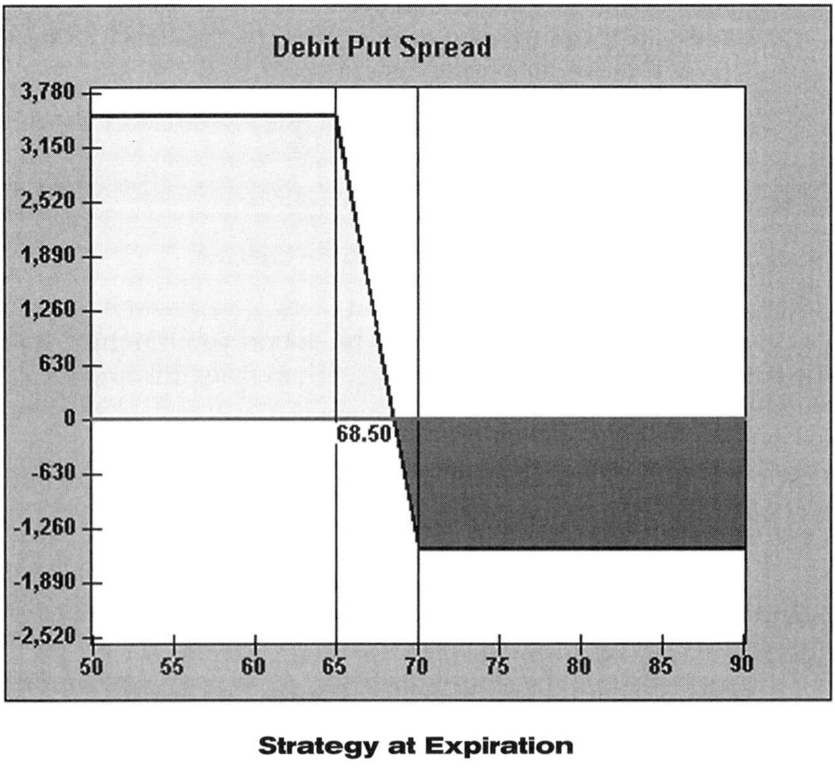

spread, it is held until expiration. There are five different prices that you should examine to draw a clear picture of how this strategy works.

Scenario 1: Assume the stock drops significantly and closes at 63 on option expiration. If this happens, you will exercise your 70 puts and sell short 1,000 shares of XYZ for proceeds of $70,000. At the same time, your short 65 puts will be assigned against you and you will be required to purchase 1,000 shares of XYZ at a cost of $65,000. The difference between your buy and sell price is $5,000. However, you paid $1,500 initially when the spread was established, so your net profit is $3,500. This will be the case at any price below 65. Therefore, this spread is only advantageous over long puts if XYZ does *not* drop below 65.

Scenario 2: Assume the stock drops only slightly and closes at 67 on option expiration. If this happens, you will exercise your 70 puts and sell short 1,000 shares of XYZ for proceeds of $70,000. However, your short 65 puts will expire worthless. The owner of those puts will not exercise if the market price of the stock is above the strike price. You can now buy back your short shares at the market price of 67 at a cost of $67,000. In this case, the difference between your buy and sell price is $3,000. However, you paid $1,500 initially when the spread was established, so your net profit is only $1,500. Your profit will vary from $0 to $3,500 at prices from 68.50 down to 65.

Scenario 3: Assume the stock closes at exactly 68.50 on option expiration. If this happens, you will exercise your 70 puts and sell short 1,000 shares of XYZ for proceeds of $70,000. However, your short 65 calls will expire worthless. You can now buy back your shares at the market price of 68.50 at a cost of $68,500. In this case, the difference between your buy and sell price is $1,500. However, you paid $1,500 initially when the spread was established so your net profit is $0.

Scenario 4: Assume the stock rises slightly and closes at 69 on option expiration. If this happens, you will exercise your 70 puts and sell short 1,000 shares of XYZ for proceeds of $70,000. However, your short 65 puts will expire worthless. You can now buy back your short shares at the market price of 69 at a cost of $69,000. In this case, the difference between your buy and sell price is $1,000. However, you paid $1,500 initially when the spread was established, so your net loss is $500. Your loss will vary from $0 to $1,500 at prices from 68.50 up to 70.

Scenario 5: Assume the stock rises substantially and closes at 72 on option expiration. If this happens, you will not exercise your 70 puts, because the market price is above 70. Your short 65 puts will also expire worthless. In this case, all the options expire worthless, and no stock is bought or sold. However, you paid $1,500 initially when the spread was established, so your net loss is the entire $1,500. This will be the case at any price above 70.

In trying to understand a multi-leg option strategy, sometimes it is helpful to compare it to a more simple strategy and point out the similarities and differences.

Example

Long Puts vs. Debit Put Spread

XYZ = 72

- Long put provides downside potential to zero and limited risk (see Figure 3.3).
- Debit put spread is created by selling a lower strike put (see Figure 3.4).
- The trade-off is limited profit potential below 65.
  - In exchange for a slightly lower initial cost.

Buy 10 XYZ May 70 Puts @ 2

Buy 10 XYZ May 70 Puts @ 2
Sell 10 XYZ May 65 Puts @ .50

FIGURE 3.3 AND 3.4

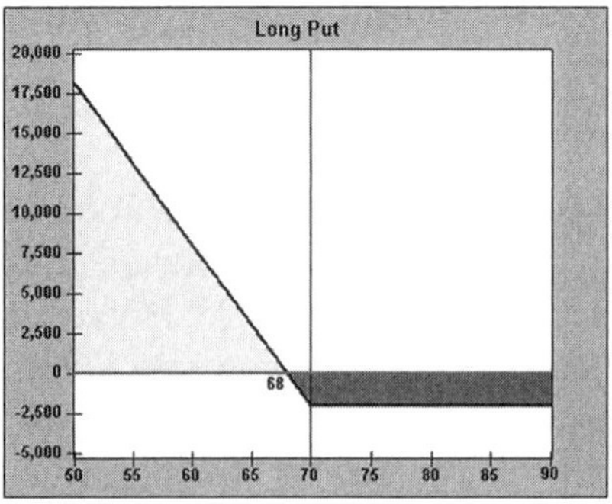

Strategy at Expiration

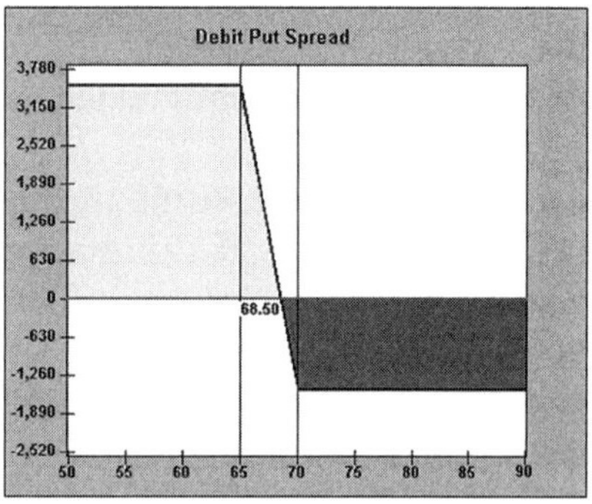

Strategy at Expiration

Long Puts

- May 70 puts purchased outright for a total cost of $2,000.
  - Rather than $1,500 (the cost of the spread).
- The trade-off for increased risk is greatly increased gain potential.
  - $500 of increased risk.
- Profit potential is on the downside until the stock reaches 0.
- In the case of the debit spread, maximum profit cannot exceed $3,500.
- Breakeven is at 68.

Debit Put Spread

- Spread is executed for a net cost of $1,500.
  - 2 points premium paid – .50 points premium received × 10 contracts × 100 shares per contract
- Profitable if the market price of XYZ goes below $68.50 (the breakeven).
- Maximum profit at $65 or below.
- Unprofitable if the price of XYZ is above $68.50.
- Maximum loss of $1,500 if XYZ is $70 or above at expiration.
- Commissions will be higher than for the single put trade.

Advantages of debit put spreads vs. long puts

- Require less capital to enter, since you are taking in some premium from the options that are sold.
- Lower initial cost effectively lowers the breakeven point.

Disadvantages of debit put spreads vs. long puts

- Profit potential is limited.
- May require a higher option trading approval level, depending upon your broker.
- May require a higher minimum account net worth, depending upon your broker.
- Will limit your profits significantly if the underlying stock moves substantially lower.

- Higher commission costs, since two options are traded instead of one.

Credit Call Spreads—Quick Overview

A credit call spread is made up of one short call at the lower strike and one long call at the higher strike. Both legs should have the same expiration month. Both sides of this spread are opening transactions, and the number of contracts of the long leg should be the same as the number of the short leg (see Figure 3.5).

At Entry The white line in Figure 3.5 represents what the strategy typically looks like at the point of entry. As expiration approaches, the curve moves toward the black lines, which illustrate the final profit and loss boundaries at expiration.

FIGURE 3.5

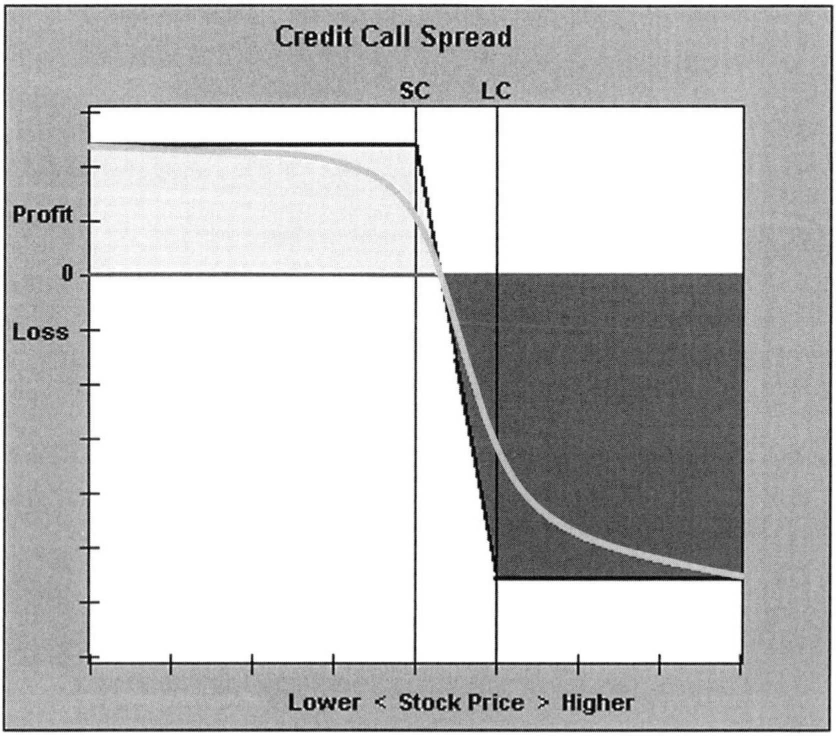

Direction Neutral to bearish, depending upon the strike prices selected

When to Use You would typically employ a credit call spread in a moderately bearish market, or when you think the market is more likely to fall than rise, and you would hope to profit if the underlying stock remains relatively flat or moderately decreases until the expiration date of the options. Generally, the more bearish you are, the lower the strike prices you will use.

Risk vs. Reward Limited risk with limited profit potential

Volatility The effect of volatility varies depending upon the strike prices chosen.

Time Decay The effect of time decay on this strategy varies with the underlying stock's price level in relation to the strike prices. If the stock price is below the strike prices, the effect is positive. If the stock price is between the strike prices, the effect is neutral, and if the stock price is above the strike prices, the effect is negative (see Table 3.2).

Prior to Expiration

- Because the short call has a lower strike price, it will also have a higher delta. As the underlying stock rises in price, the short option will gain value faster than the long option. Likewise, as the underlying stock drops in price, the short option will lose value faster than the long option.
- If the underlying stock drops sharply enough, the spread can often be closed out at a profit prior to expiration. This profit, however, will always be less than the maximum profit possible if held until expiration.

TABLE 3.2

Greeks	In-the-money	At-the-money	Out-of-the-money
Delta	Positive	Positive	Positive
Gamma	Positive	Neutral	Negative
Theta	Negative	Neutral	Positive
Vega	Positive	Neutral	Negative

    - Comparing the early close profit to the maximum potential profit at expiration can help you decide if holding until expiration makes sense.
- If the underlying stock rises sharply enough, the spread can often be closed out at a loss that is less than the maximum loss possible if held until expiration.
    - Comparing the early close loss to the maximum potential loss at expiration can help you decide if holding until expiration makes sense.

At Expiration

- Below the lower strike, both options expire worthless and max gain is achieved.
- Between the lower and upper strike, short stock will be established through assignment of the lower strike. The short stock can then be closed out in the market. The trade may or may not be profitable.
- Above the higher strike, both options are exercised and/or assigned and max loss is sustained.

Credit Call Spreads—Detail

When you establish a bearish position using a vertical call spread, you will pay a lower premium for the option you purchase than the amount you will receive on the premium from the option sold. As a result, a bearish vertical call spread is always established at a net credit. This type of spread is a common substitute for selling uncovered (naked) calls outright; though the initial credit is lower, the maximum loss potential is also lower.

Example:

Buy 10 XYZ May 80 Calls @ .50

Sell 10 XYZ May 75 Calls @ 2 for a net credit of 1.50

BE = 76.50 (main position strike price + the credit)

MG = 1.50 (credit received)

ML = 3.50 (net of strikes – the credit)

This spread is executed for a net credit of $1,500 (2 points premium received – .50 points premium paid × 10 contracts × 100 shares per contract). As shown in Figure 3.6, you will profit if the market price of XYZ goes below $76.50. You will maximize your

FIGURE 3.6

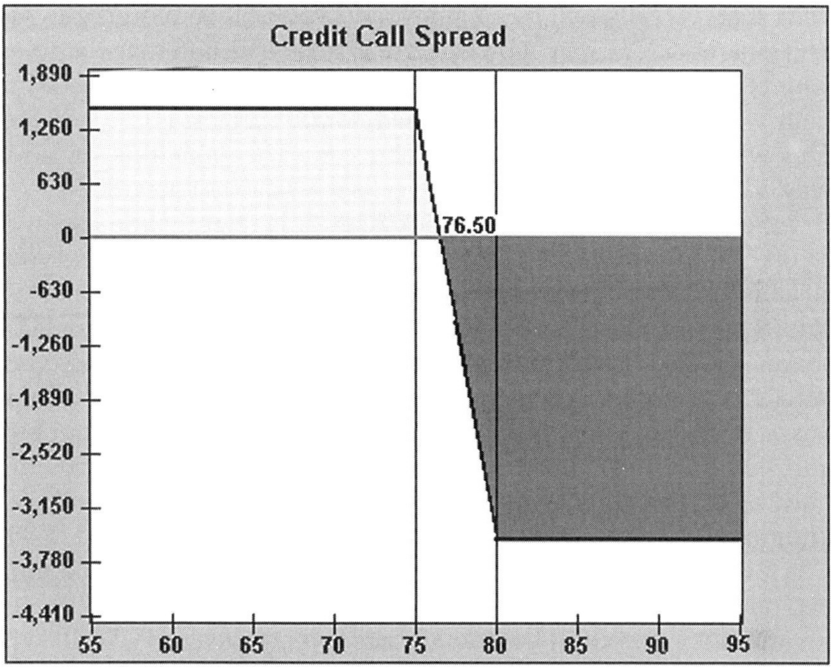

Strategy at Expiration

profit at $75. You will lose money if the price of XYZ goes above $76.50, and you could lose up to a maximum of $3,500 if XYZ rises to $80 or above at expiration.

If you sold the May 75 calls uncovered, you would have initially brought in $2,000, rather than $1,500. However, the trade-off for reduced profit potential (in this case only $500 of reduced profit potential) is the ability to have significantly limited risk. If you simply sold the May 75 calls uncovered, your loss potential would be virtually unlimited, if XYZ were to rise substantially. In the case of this credit spread, your maximum loss cannot exceed $3,500. This maximum loss is the difference between the strike prices on the two options minus the amount you were credited when the position was established.

To understand how the profit and loss characteristics of this type of spread work, assume that once you have established this spread, it is held until expiration. There are five different prices that you should examine to draw a clear picture of how this strategy works.

Scenario 1: Assume the stock rises significantly and closes at 83 on option expiration. If this happens, you will exercise your 80 calls and acquire 1,000 shares of XYZ at a cost of –$80,000. At the same time, your short 75 calls will be assigned, and you will be required to sell 1,000 shares of XYZ for net proceeds of $75,000. The difference between your buy and sell price is –$5,000. However, you brought in $1,500 initially when the spread was established, so your net loss is only –$3,500. This will be the case at any price above 80. Therefore, this spread is only advantageous over uncovered calls if XYZ rises above 80.50

Scenario 2: Assume the stock rises only slightly and closes at 78 on option expiration. If this happens, you will not exercise your 80 calls, because they are out-of-the-money. However, your short 75 calls will be assigned, and you will be required to sell short 1,000 shares of XYZ for net proceeds of $75,000. You can then close out your short position buy purchasing 1,000 shares of XYZ at the market price of 78 at a cost of –$78,000. The difference between your buy and sell price is –$3,000. However, since you brought in $1,500 initially when the spread was established, your net loss is only –$1,500. Your loss will vary from $0 to –$3,500 at prices from 76.50 up to 80.

Scenario 3: Assume the stock closes at exactly 76.50 on option expiration. If this happens, you will not exercise your 80 calls, because they are out-of-the-money. However, your short 75 calls will be assigned, and you will be required to sell short 1,000 shares of XYZ for net proceeds of $75,000. You can then close out your short position buy purchasing 1,000 shares of XYZ at a cost of –$76,500. The difference between your buy and sell price is –$1,500. However, since you brought in $1,500 initially when the spread was established, your net loss is actually $0.

Scenario 4: Assume the stock drops only slightly and closes at 76 on option expiration. If this happens, you will not exercise your 80 calls, because they are out-of-the-money. However, your short 75 calls will be assigned, and you will be required to sell short 1,000 shares of XYZ for net proceeds of $75,000. You can then close out your short position buy purchasing 1,000 shares of XYZ at a cost of –$76,000. The difference between your buy and sell price is –$1,000. However, since you brought in $1,500 initially when the spread was established, you actually have a net *gain* of $500. Your gain will vary from $0 to $1,500 at prices from 76.50 down to 75.

Scenario 5: Assume the stock drops substantially and closes at 73 on option expiration. If this happens, you will not exercise your 80 calls, because they are out-of-the-money. Your short 75 calls will also not be assigned, because they are out-of-the-money. In this case, all of the options expire worthless and no stock is bought or sold. However, since you initially brought in $1,500 when the spread was established, your net gain is the entire $1,500. This maximum profit of $1,500 will occur at all prices below 75.

Though the examples above all deal with the outcome of these strategies at expiration, you are not required to hold a spread until expiration. If the underlying instrument moves enough, you may be able to close out the spread position at a net profit prior to expiration. Once established, spreads should be reviewed occasionally to determine if holding them until expiration is still warranted.

In trying to understand a multi-leg option strategy, sometimes it is helpful to compare it to a more simple strategy and point out the similarities and differences.

Example

Uncovered Calls vs. Credit Call Spread

XYZ = 72

- Uncovered call provides limited downside potential with unlimited upside risk (see Figure 3.7).
- Credit call spread created by buying another further out-of-the-money call (see Figure 3.8).
- Risk is now limited to the upside.
  - Which is the trade-off for a slightly lower initial credit.

Sell 10 XYZ May 75 Calls @ 2

Buy 10 XYZ May 80 Calls @ .50
Sell 10 XYZ May 75 Calls @ 2

FIGURE 3.7 AND 3.8

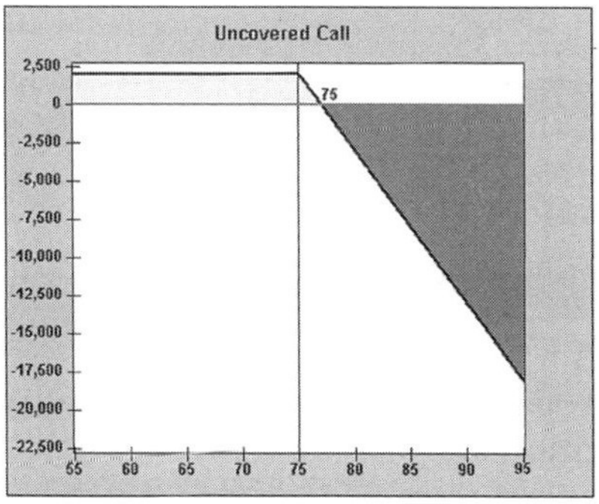

Strategy at Expiration

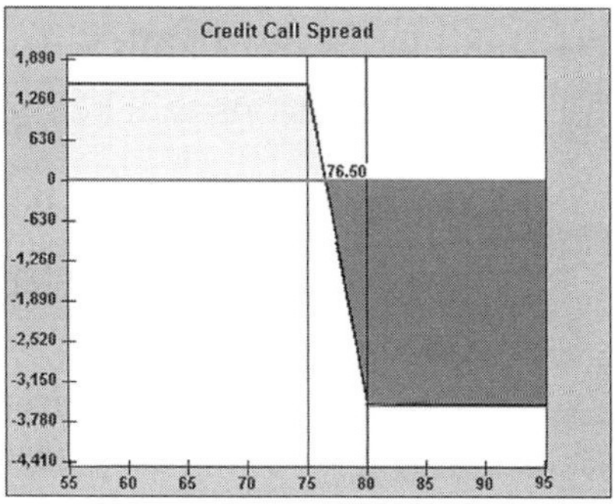

Strategy at Expiration

Uncovered Calls

- Uncovered (naked) calls sold for an initial credit of $2,000.
  - Rather than $1,500 (the initial credit on the spread).
- The trade-off for increased profit potential is significantly higher risk.
  - $500 of increased profit potential.
- Loss potential would be virtually unlimited.
  - Unlimited loss on the stock, less $2,000 premium received on sale of the calls.
- Risk on this position can increase indefinitely as XYZ rises.
  - In the case of the credit spread, maximum loss cannot exceed $3,500.
- Maximum potential gain is $2,000.
- Breakeven is at 75.

Credit Call Spread

- Spread is executed for a net credit of $1,500.
  - 2 points premium received – .50 points premium paid × 10 contracts × 100 shares per contract
- Profitable if the market price of XYZ is below $76.50 (the breakeven).
- Maximum profit at $75 or below.
- Unprofitable if the price of XYZ is above $76.50.
- Maximum loss of $3,500 if XYZ rises to $80 or above at expiration.
  - Maximum loss is the difference between the strike prices on the two options minus the initial credit when the position was established.
- Commissions will be higher than for the single call trade.

Advantages of credit call spreads vs. uncovered calls

- Substantially lower risk if the stock moves dramatically against you.
- The risk margin requirement for credit spreads is generally lower than for uncovered options.

- It is not possible to lose more money than the risk margin requirement that is held in the account at the time the position is established.
- Uncovered options will require a higher options trading approval level.
- Uncovered options will require a higher minimum account net worth.

Disadvantages of credit call spreads vs. uncovered calls

- Your profit potential will be reduced by the amount spent on the long option leg of the spread.
- Higher commission costs, since two options are traded instead of one.

Characteristics

Many option traders, when first introduced to spreads, have little trouble understanding the risk/reward characteristics but often have difficulty deciding which strike prices to use and how wide to make the spreads. Which strike prices you use and whether or not those strike prices are in, at, or out-of-the-money will affect the magnitude of the underlying move needed to reach profitability and will also determine whether or not the spread can be profitable if the underlying stock remains unchanged.

Table 3.3 illustrates how to properly structure a bearish spread to match your level of bearishness. For example, if you are extremely bearish, you may want to consider an out-of-the-money (OOTM) debit put spread or an in-the-money (ITM) credit call spread. Keep in mind that both will generally require a bearish move of extreme magnitude in the underlying stock in order to reach profitability. By contrast, if you are neutral to only slightly bearish, you may want to consider an ITM debit put spread or an OOTM credit call spread, both of which can sometimes be profitable with little or no movement in the underlying stock. As with most option strategies, the greater the underlying move needed, the higher the profit potential, but also the less likely it is that a profit will be made. Similarly, if you structure your spread so that profitability is possible with no movement in the underlying stock, a profit, if earned, will likely be very small.

TABLE 3.3

Bear Spread Strategy	<<< Direction >>>				<<< Magnitude >>>		
	Bearish	**Neutral**	**Breakout**	**Bearish**	**Extreme**	**Moderate**	**Slight**
Debit put spread OOTM				X	X		
Debit put spread ATM				X		X	
Debit put spreadITM		X		X			X
Credit call spread OOTM		X		X			X
Credit call spread ATM				X		X	
Credit call spread ITM				X	X		

Understanding Table 3.3 will help you identify possible bear spread candidates. Figures 3.9 and 3.10 are sample charts using simple technical analysis where bear spreads might be appropriate. Keep in mind that these examples do not include commission charges, which may be significant and will impact the profit or loss.

In Figure 3.9, you have identified XYZ stock, which appears to be hitting some upside resistance. As a result, you are expecting a possible downward move.

If you are only slightly bearish, you may want to consider the following debit put spread. As with all spreads, you can calculate the max gain (MG), max loss (ML), and breakeven (BE) before you actually enter the trade. The maximum loss (ML) on a debit spread will always be the amount of the initial debit.

Example 1A

Buy 10 XYZ Jun 27.50 Puts @ 2.60

Sell 10 XYZ Jun 25 Puts @ .65

Debit = 1.95

BE = 25.55 (main position strike price – debit amount)

MG = .55 (net of strikes – the debit)

ML = 1.95 (net debit paid)

FIGURE 3.9

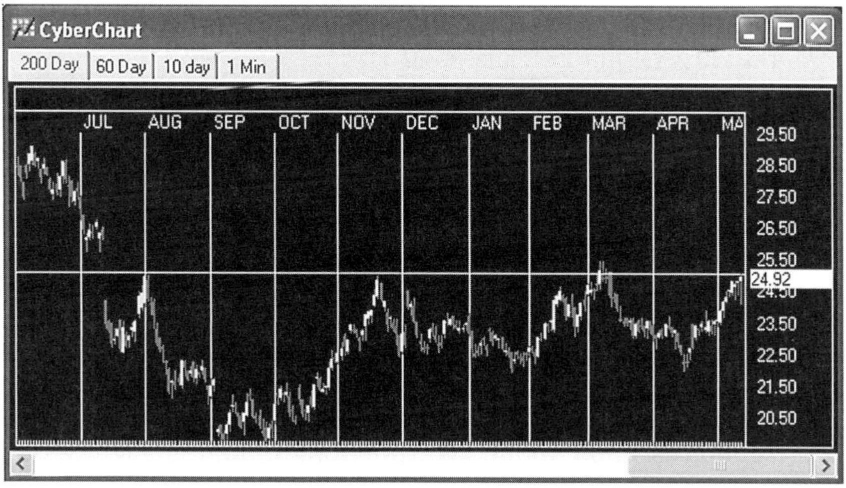

Total cost of this trade = \$1,950 (debit × # of spreads × option multiplier) or (1.95 × 10 × 100)

This example would be considered in-the-money, since the long option is in-the-money and the short option is slightly in-the-money. Since Figure 3.9 presents data as of around May 9, these options have about five weeks until expiration. By calculating the breakeven before you enter the trade, you can see that with a breakeven price of 25.55, XYZ can actually move against you by as much as \$0.63 by expiration and still be profitable. The maximum profit of \$550 will be reached if XYZ is below 25 (the lower strike price) at expiration, since both options will be exercised and the net between the two is \$2,500. Subtract \$2,500 from the initial cost of \$1,950 to arrive at the net profit. Losses will be incurred if XYZ closes above 25.55 at expiration, with the maximum loss of \$1,950 occurring at any price above 27.50 (where both options expire worthless). When that occurs, the initial cost is completely lost.

If you are very bearish, you may want to consider the following credit call spread. In this example, you would receive a credit at the time the spread is established, but you can still calculate the maximum gain (MG), maximum loss (ML), and breakeven (BE) before the trade is entered. The maximum gain (MG) on a credit spread will always be the amount of the initial credit. In addition, a credit spread has a margin requirement that is equal to the maximum loss, but the initial credit can be applied against it.

Example 1B

Buy 10 XYZ Jun 25 Calls @ .70

Sell 10 XYZ Jun 22.50 Calls @ 2.55

Credit = 1.85

BE = 24.35 (main position strike price + credit amount)

MG = 1.85 (credit received)

ML = .65 (net of strikes – the credit)

Total margin requirements of this trade = $650 ([net of strikes – the credit] × # of spreads × option multiplier) or ([25 – 22.50 – 1.85] × 10 × 100)

This example would be considered at-the-money, since the short option is in-the-money and the long option is slightly out-of-the-money. Since Figure 3.9 presents data as of early May, these options have about five weeks until expiration. By calculating the breakeven before you enter the trade, you can see that with a breakeven price of 24.35, XYZ needs to decrease in price by at least $0.57 or more by expiration to be profitable. The maximum profit of $1,850 will be reached if XYZ is below 22.50 (the lower strike price) at expiration, since both options will expire worthless and the entire initial credit will be retained. Losses will be incurred if XYZ closes above 24.35 at expiration, with the maximum loss of $650 occurring at any price above 25 (where both options are exercised). When that occurs, the initial credit will be completely lost. Subtract the initial credit of $1,850 from the net loss between the two strike prices of $2,500 to arrive at the maximum loss of $650.

Figure 3.10 is a second chart using simple technical analysis where bear spreads might also be appropriate. In Figure 3.10, you have identified XYZ stock, which appears to have just fallen through a downside support line. As a result, you are expecting a continued downward move.

If you are only slightly bearish, you may want to consider the following debit put spread.

Example 2A

Buy 10 XYZ Jun 17.50 Puts @ 2.85

Sell 10 XYZ Jun 15 Puts @ .70

Debit = 2.15

FIGURE 3.10

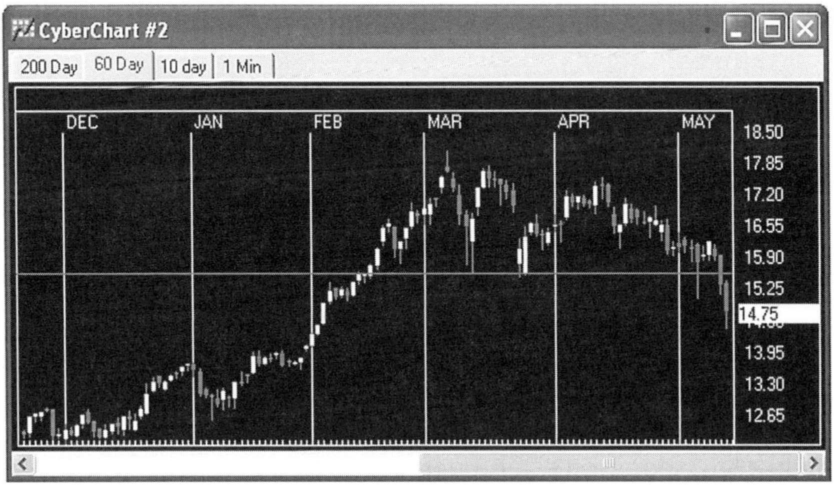

BE = 15.35 (main position strike price – debit amount)

MG = .35 (net of strikes – the debit)

ML = 2.15 (net debit paid)

Total cost of this trade = $2,150 (debit × # of spreads × option multiplier) or (2.15 × 10 × 100)

This example would be considered in-the-money, since the long option is in-the-money and the short option is slightly in-the-money. Since Figure 3.10 presents data as of around May 9, these options have about five weeks until expiration. By calculating the breakeven before you enter the trade, you can see that with a breakeven price of 15.35, XYZ can actually rise in price by up to $0.60 by expiration and still be profitable. The maximum profit of $350 will be reached if XYZ is below 15 (the lower strike price) at expiration, since both options will be exercised and the net between the two is $2,500. Subtract $2,500 from the initial cost of $2,150 to arrive at the net profit. Losses will be incurred if XYZ closes above 15.35 at expiration with the maximum loss of $2,150 occurring at any price above 17.50 (where both options expire worthless). When that occurs, the initial cost is completely lost.

If you are very bearish, you may want to consider the following credit call spread.

Example 2B

Buy 10 XYZ Jun 17.50 Calls @ .15

Sell 10 XYZ Jun 12.50 Calls @ 2.40

Credit = 2.25

BE = 14.75 (main position strike price + the credit)

MG = 2.25 (credit received)

ML = 2.75 (net of strikes – the credit)

Total margin requirements of this trade = \$2,750 ([net of strikes – the credit] × # of spreads × option multiplier) or ([17.50 – 12.50 – 2.25] × 10 × 100)

This example would be considered at-the-money, since the long option is out-of-the-money and the short option is in-the-money. Since Figure 3.10 presents data as of around May 9, these options have about five weeks until expiration. By calculating the breakeven before you enter the trade, you can see that with a break-even price of 14.75, XYZ can remain unchanged by expiration and still be profitable. The maximum profit of \$2,250 will be reached if XYZ is below 12.50 (the lower strike price) at expiration, since both options will expire worthless and the entire initial credit will be retained. Losses will be incurred if XYZ closes above 14.75 at expiration, with the maximum loss of \$2,750 occurring at any price above 17.50 (where both options are exercised). When that occurs, the initial credit will be completely lost. Subtract the initial credit of \$2,250 from the net loss between the two strike prices of \$5,000 to arrive at the maximum loss of \$2,750.

SECTION 3

Horizontal Spreads

CHAPTER 4

Calendar Spreads

Spreads offer you the opportunity to limit losses in exchange for a limited gain potential. They involve the simultaneous purchase and sale of two options contracts of the same class (puts or calls) on the same underlying security.

HORIZONTAL SPREADS EXPLANATION

In the case of horizontal spreads (also known as calendar spreads or time spreads), the strike price is the same, but the expiration month will be different. For calendar spreads, the long leg has to expire later than the short leg, or the strategy cannot be classified as a spread. If the long leg expires before the short leg, the two options will be considered unrelated long and short options. In many cases, spreads may require that you temporarily establish a long or short stock position. That resulting long or short position will need to be closed out in the market to fully realize the profit potential of the strategy. This is explained in more detail later in this chapter.

Author's Note: Spreads are very versatile, and with the range of strike prices that are available and the ability to utilize either calendar call spreads or calendar put spreads, there are many ways to potentially take advantage of charts that are exhibiting signs of short-term neutrality with longer-term bullishness or bearishness.

Two of the key concepts to understand before you begin trading spreads are how to determine your sentiment (whether you are bullish or bearish) and how to calculate the maximum loss (ML), breakeven points (BE), and maximum gain (MG). These calculations will vary depending upon whether the spread is initially established as a net debit or net credit and whether or not it is entered using calls or puts. For any credit spread, your broker will also require you to meet an initial margin requirement and maintain funds in your account equal to the maximum loss amount. Since a calendar spread is always a debit spread, there is never a margin requirement beyond the debit needed to enter the trade.

A calendar spread has both a short-term and a longer-term sentiment that can be determined. While the short-term MG and BE are impossible to determine exactly, you can calculate your longer-term ML, BE, and MG for any calendar spread strategy by applying the following rules:

Short-Term

1. Determine the short leg of the spread.
   a. The short leg is the option with the nearer expiration date.
2. Determine whether you are bullish, bearish, or neutral on the short leg.
   a. Short puts are bullish if they are in-the-money.
      i. Neutral if out-of-the-money.
   b. Short calls are bearish if they are in-the-money.
      i. Neutral if out-of-the-money.
3. Determine whether you are short-term bullish, bearish, or neutral on the spread.
   a. Your answer to step 2 holds true for the entire spread strategy in the short term.
4. Determine whether the spread was entered at a net debit or a net credit.
   a. If the strike prices of the two options are the same, it will always be a net debit.
   b. * If the strike prices of the two options are different, see diagonal spreads in Chapter 5.
5. Calculate the short-term **ML**.
   a. If the spread is entered at net debit, the debit is the ML.
   b. The only exception to this rule occurs in diagonal spreads discussed in Chapter 5

6. Calculate the short-term **BE**.
   a. If debit call spread, the BE is the strike price + net debit – remaining long-term call time value.
   b. If debit put spread, the BE is the strike price – net debit + remaining long-term put time value.
7. Calculate the short-term **MG.**
   a. The MG is the remaining time value in the long-term option less the initial debit paid.

Long-Term

1. Determine the long leg of the spread.
   a. The long leg is the option with the later expiration date.
2. Determine whether you are bullish or bearish on the long leg.
   a. Long calls are bullish.
   b. Long puts are bearish.
3. Determine whether you are longer-term bullish or bearish on the spread.
   a. Your answer to step 2 holds true for the entire spread strategy.
4. Determine whether the spread was entered at a net debit or a net credit.
   a. If the strike prices of the two options are the same, it will always be a net debit.
   b. If the strike prices of the two options are different, see diagonal spreads in Chapter 5.
5. Calculate the long-term **ML**.
   a. If the spread is entered at net debit, the debit is the ML.
   b. The only exception to this rule occurs in diagonal spreads, discussed in Chapter 5.
6. Calculate the long-term **BE**.
   a. If debit call spread, the BE is the strike price + net debit.
   b. If debit put spread, the BE is the strike price – net debit.
7. Calculate the long-term **MG**.
   a. If debit call spread, the MG is unlimited after the short option expires.
   b. If debit put spread, the MG is the strike price of the long option less the debit.

TYPES OF CALENDAR SPREADS

There are basically two types of calendar spreads: calendar call spreads and calendar put spreads. Both are typically used to establish both a short-term and a longer-term sentiment. The short-term sentiment is your sentiment from the moment you establish the spread until the expiration date of the short option. The longer-term sentiment is your sentiment from the moment the short option expires until the expiration date of the long option. Typically, the near-term sentiment is neutral (if the short option is out-of-the-money) and the longer-term sentiment is either bullish or bearish.

Calendar Call Spreads—Quick Overview

A calendar call spread is made up of one long call in a distant month and one short call in a nearer month. Both legs should have the same strike price. Both sides of this spread are opening transactions, and the number of contracts of the long leg should be the same as the number of the short leg (see Figure 4.1).

At Entry The white line in Figure 4.1 represents what the strategy typically looks like at the point of entry. As expiration approaches, the curve moves toward the black lines, which illustrate the final profit and loss boundaries at expiration.

Direction Short-term neutral to moderately bullish, longer-term bullish depending upon the strike prices selected

When to Use You would typically employ a calendar call spread in a neutral to moderately bullish market, when you think the market will become more bullish. You hope to profit if the underlying stock remains below the strike price until the expiration date of the short-term option but rises above the strike price by the expiration date of the longer-term option. Generally, the more bullish you are, the higher the strike prices you will use.

Risk vs. Reward Limited risk with limited profit potential

Volatility The effect of volatility is generally favorable.

Time Decay The effect of time decay on this strategy is favorable, as the near-term call will lose time value at a faster rate than the longer-term call (see Table 4.1).

FIGURE 4.1

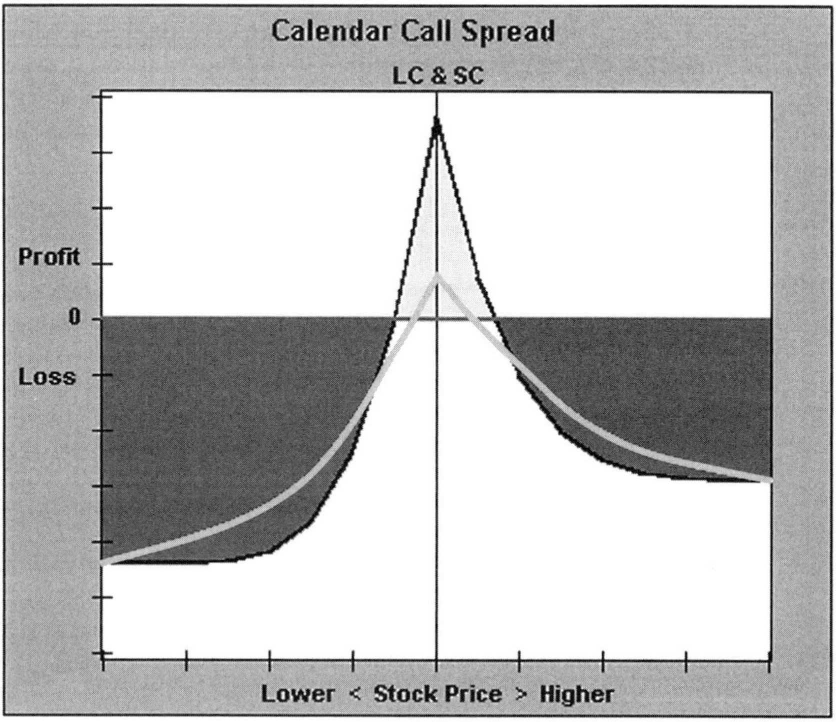

Prior to Near-Term Expiration

- Because the short option is near expiration, it is in the steepest part of the time erosion curve, which causes the short option to lose time value faster than the long option.

TABLE 4.1

Greeks	Near-term	Longer-term
Delta	Neutral	Positive
Gamma	Neutral	Positive
Theta	Positive	Negative
Vega	Positive	Positive

  - As a result, with little or no movement in the underlying stock price, the spread can often be closed out at a profit prior to expiration, once time value has eroded sufficiently.
- Similarly, if the underlying stock rises or drops sharply enough, the spread can often be closed out at a loss that is less than the maximum loss possible if held until expiration, because time value will erode the value of the near-term option more quickly.
  - Comparing the early close loss to the maximum potential loss at expiration can help you decide if holding until expiration makes sense.

At Near-Term Expiration

- Below the near-term strike, the near-term call expires worthless and the near-term call premium is retained.
- At the near-term strike, the near-term call expires worthless and the near-term call premium is retained.
- Above the near-term strike, a short stock position will be established through assignment of the near-term call. The short stock can then be closed out in the market. The longer-term call may be sold to offset all or part of the loss on the stock position. The trade may or may not be profitable.

Prior to Long-Term Expiration

- Once the short-term option has expired, you are left with a long call option. At that point, your upside profit potential is unlimited.
- If the underlying stock rises sufficiently to cause the value of the remaining long call to exceed the initial debit of the original calendar spread, the long call can be sold at a profit.
- With little or no movement in the underlying stock, time value erosion will begin to take its toll on the long option. Unless you are still bullish, you may want to consider closing the long option before the month in which it expires.

At Long-Term Expiration (assuming near-term call expired worthless)

- Below the long-term strike, the long-term call will expire worthless and the max loss is sustained.
- At the long-term strike, the long-term call will expire worthless and the max loss is sustained.

- Above the long-term strike, long stock will be acquired through exercise of the long-term call. The long stock can then be sold in the market. The trade may or may not be profitable.

Calendar Call Spreads—Detail

When you establish a calendar call spread, you will pay a higher premium for the long-term option purchased than the amount you will receive on the premium from the short-term option sold. As a result, a calendar call spread is always established at a net debit. This type of spread is intended to profit from the fact that time decay erodes the price of the short-term option faster than the long-term option.

Example:

Buy 10 XYZ Aug 55 Calls @ 3.00
Sell 10 XYZ Jun 55 Calls @ 1.60 for a net debit of 1.40
Long-term BE = 56.40 (strike price + debit amount)
MG = Unlimited (after June expiration)
ML = 1.40 (net debit paid)

This spread is executed for a net cost of $1,400 (3.00 points premium paid – 1.60 points premium received × 10 contracts × 100 shares per contract). As shown in Figure 4.2, at near-term expiration, you will profit if the market price of XYZ is between approximately $53 and $58. You will maximize your profit at $55. You will lose money if the price of XYZ goes below approximately $53 or above $58. Most of your $1,400 will be lost if XYZ increases or declines substantially by the near-term expiration.

If, instead of trading a spread, you decided to simply purchase the August 55 calls outright, your total cost would be $3,000, rather than $1,400. Your long-term breakeven would still be 58, but you would only profit above 58, rather than between 53 and 58. If you simply purchased the August 55 calls, your upside potential is unlimited immediately, rather than only after the short-term expiration.

A calendar call spread should be closely watched as the near-term expiration approaches, and then evaluated again after the near-term expiration. If the short-term call has expired and you are still bullish, you may decide to retain the long-term call option. If you are neutral or bearish, the long-term call should be sold. To understand how the profit and loss characteristics of this type of spread work, assume that once you have established this spread, it is held until the

FIGURE 4.2

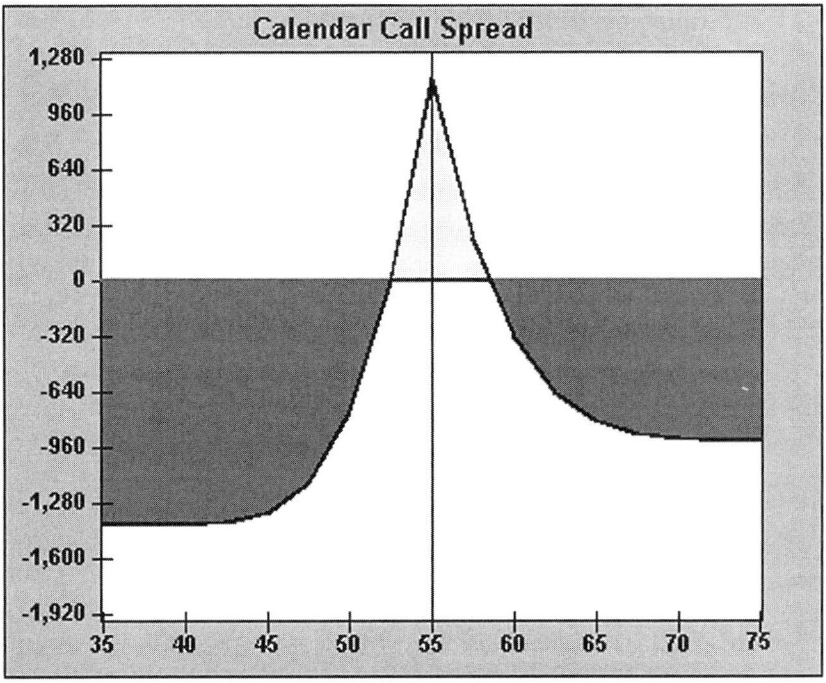

Strategy at Expiration

near-term expiration. There are five different prices that you should examine to draw a clearer picture of how this strategy works.

Scenario 1: Assume the stock rallies significantly and closes at 59 by the June option expiration. If this happens, you will be assigned on your June 55 calls and you will be short 1,000 shares of XYZ stock for net proceeds of $55,000. At that time, you would buy back your short shares at the market price of 59 for a net cost of –$59,000. The difference between your buy and sell price is –$4,000. However, your August calls will be worth at least 4.00 (+ approximately 1.00 point time value) and could be sold for approximately $5,000. Since you paid –$1,400 initially when the spread was established, your net loss would be approximately –$400. At prices higher than 59 at the June expiration, this loss will continue to increase up to a maximum of close to –$1,400 at very high prices. Although exact time values are difficult to predict, all prices above approximately 58 at the June expiration will probably result in a loss. Therefore, this spread is only advantageous if you expect XYZ *not* to exceed approximately 58 by the June expiration.

Scenario 2: Assume the stock rallies only slightly and closes at 58 by the June option expiration. If this happens, you will be assigned on your June 55 calls and you will be short 1,000 shares of XYZ stock for net proceeds of $55,000. At that time, you would buy back your short shares at the market price of 58 for a net cost of –$58,000. The difference between your buy and sell price is –$3,000. However, your August calls will be worth at least 3.00 (+ approximately 1.40 points time value) and could be sold for approximately $4,400. Since you paid –$1,400 initially when the spread was established, your net loss would actually be $0.

Scenario 3: Assume the stock closes at exactly 55 by the June option expiration. If this happens, your June 55 calls will expire worthless. However, your August calls will be worth approximately 2.50 points time value and could be sold for approximately $2,500. Since you paid –$1,400 initially when the spread was established, your net gain would be approximately $1,100.

Scenario 4: Assume the stock drops slightly and closes at 53 by the June option expiration. If this happens, your June 55 calls will expire worthless. However, your August calls will be worth approximately 1.40 points time value and could be sold for approximately $1,400. Since you paid –$1,400 initially when the spread was established, your net return would be approximately $0.

Scenario 5: Assume the stock drops substantially and closes at 51 by the June option expiration. If this happens, your June 55 calls will expire worthless. However, your August calls will be worth approximately .80 points time value and could be sold for approximately $800. Since you paid –$1,400 initially when the spread was established, your net loss would be approximately –$600.

Example

Long Calls vs. Calendar Call Spread

XYZ = 55

- Long-term call provides unlimited upside potential and limited risk of 3 points (see Figure 4.3).
- Calendar call spread is created by selling a close-term call (see Figure 4.4).
- The trade-off is limited profit potential in the near term.
  - In exchange for a lower initial cost.

Buy 10 XYZ Aug 55 Calls @ 3

Buy 10 XYZ Aug 55 Calls @ 3
Sell 10 XYZ Jun 55 Calls @ 1.60

FIGURE 4.3 AND 4.4

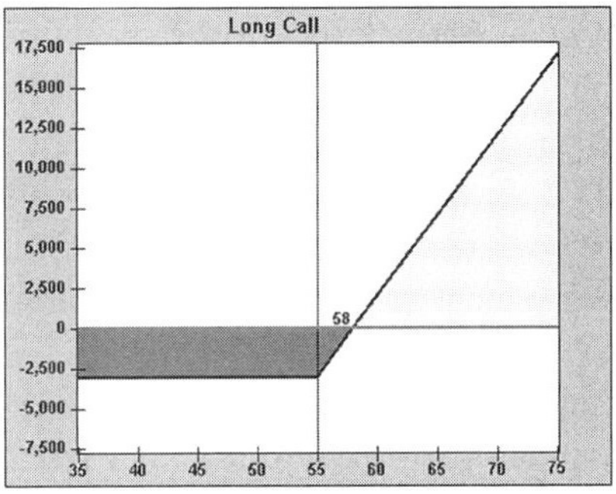

Strategy at Expiration

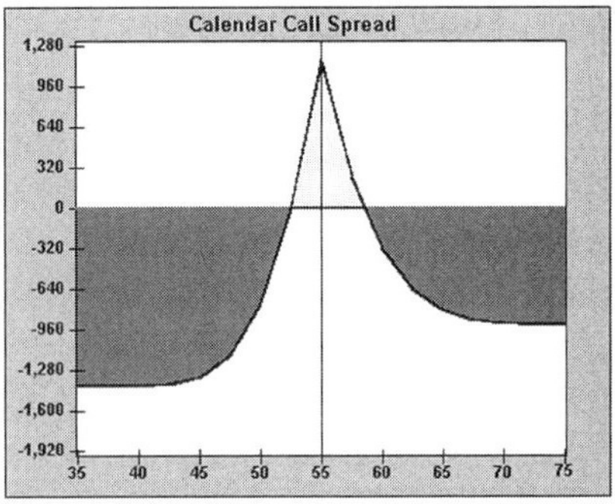

Strategy at Expiration

Long Calls

- August 55 calls purchased outright for a total cost of $3,000.
  - Rather than $1,400 (cost of the spread).
- The trade-off for the increased risk is unlimited gain potential.
  - $1,600 of increased risk.
- The upside potential for profit is theoretically unlimited as the stock rises.
  - In the case of the calendar spread, maximum profit cannot exceed approximately $1,100 in the short term.
- Breakeven is at 58.
- Maximum loss of $3,000 if XYZ is below 55 at August expiration.

Calendar Call Spread

- Spread is executed for a net cost of $1,400.
  - 3 points premium paid – 1.60 points premium received × 10 contracts × 100 shares per contract
- Profitable if the market price of XYZ stays between approximately 53 and 58 in the short term (the breakeven points).
  - Profitable above $56.40 in the long term.
- Maximum profit at $55 in the short term.
  - Unlimited in the long term.

- Unprofitable if the price of XYZ is above $58 or below $53 in the short term.
  - Unprofitable if XYZ is below $56.40 in the long term.
- Maximum loss of $1,400 if XYZ is very high or very low at the short-term expiration.
  - Maximum loss of $1,400 if XYZ is below $55 in the long term.
- Commissions will be higher than for the single call trade.

Advantages of calendar call spreads vs. long calls

- Require less capital to enter, since you are taking in some premium from the options that are sold.
- Lower initial cost effectively lowers the breakeven point.

Disadvantages of calendar call spreads vs. long calls

- Profit potential is limited in the short term.
- May require a higher option trading approval level, depending upon your broker.
- May require a higher minimum account net worth, depending upon your broker.
- Will limit your profits significantly if the underlying stock moves substantially higher or lower in the short term.
- Higher commission costs, since two options are traded instead of one.

Calendar Put Spreads—Quick Overview

A calendar put spread is made up of one long put in a distant month and one short put in a nearer month. Both legs should have the same strike price. Both sides of this spread are opening transactions, and the number of contracts of the long leg should be the same as the number of the short leg (see Figure 4.5).

At Entry The white line in Figure 4.5 represents what the strategy typically looks like at the point of entry. As expiration approaches, the curve moves toward the black lines, which illustrate the final profit and loss boundaries at expiration.

Direction Short-term neutral to moderately bearish, longer-term bearish depending upon the strike prices selected

FIGURE 4.5

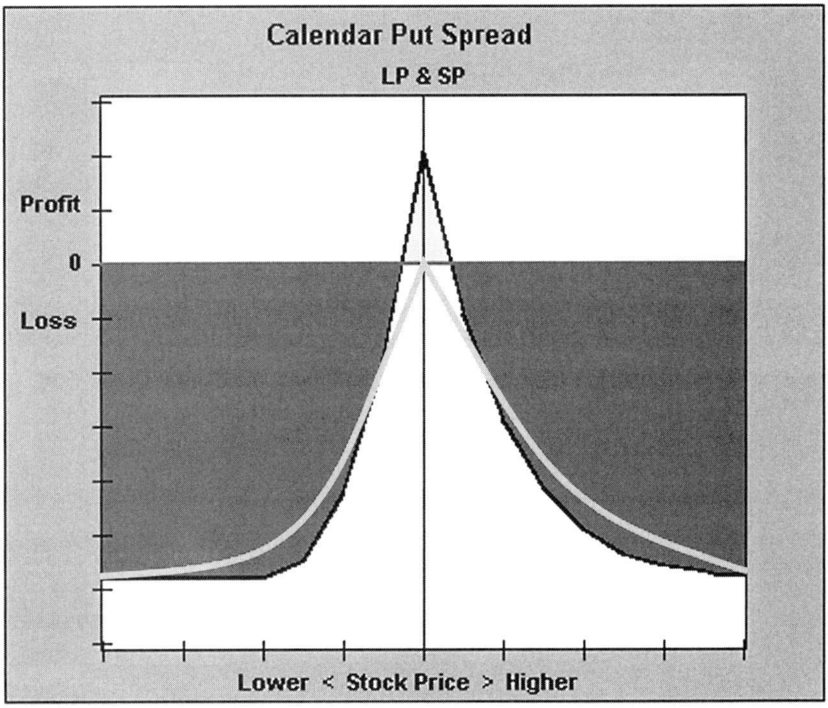

When to Use You would typically employ a calendar put spread in a neutral to moderately bearish market, when you think the market will become more bearish. You hope to profit if the underlying stock remains above the strike price until the expiration date of the short-term option but drops below the strike price by the expiration date of the longer-term option. Generally, the more bearish you are, the lower the strike prices you will use.

Risk vs. Reward Limited risk with limited profit potential

Volatility The effect of volatility is generally favorable.

Time Decay The effect of time decay on this strategy is favorable, as the near-term put will lose time value at a faster rate than the longer-term put (see Table 4.2).

Prior to Near-Term Expiration

- Because the short option is near expiration, it is in the steepest part of the time erosion curve, which causes

TABLE 4.2

Greeks	Near-term	Longer-term
Delta	Neutral	Positive
Gamma	Neutral	Positive
Theta	Positive	Negative
Vega	Positive	Positive

the short option to lose time value faster than the long option.

- As a result, with little or no movement in the underlying stock price, the spread can often be closed out at a profit prior to expiration, once time value has eroded sufficiently.

- Similarly, if the underlying stock rises or drops sharply enough, the spread can often be closed out at a loss that is less than the maximum loss possible if held until expiration, because time value will erode the value of the near-term option more quickly.
  - Comparing the early close loss to the maximum potential loss at expiration can help you decide if holding until expiration makes sense.

At Near-Term Expiration

- Above the near-term strike, the near-term put expires worthless and the near-term put premium is retained.
- At the near-term strike, the near-term put expires worthless and the near-term put premium is retained.
- Below the near-term strike, a long stock position will be established through assignment of the near-term put. The long stock can then be closed out in the market. The longer-term put is sold to offset all or part of the loss on the stock position. The trade may or may not be profitable.

Prior to Long-Term Expiration

- Once the short-term option has expired, you are left with a long put option. At that point, your downside profit potential is significant.

- If the underlying stock drops sufficiently to cause the value of the remaining long put to exceed the initial debit of the original calendar spread, the long put can be sold at a profit.
- With little or no movement in the underlying stock, time value erosion will begin to take its toll on the long option. Unless you are still bearish, you may want to consider closing the long option before the month in which it expires.

At Long-Term Expiration (assuming near-term put expired worthless)

- Above the long-term strike, the long-term put will expire worthless and max loss is sustained.
- At the long-term strike, the long-term put will expire worthless and max loss is sustained.
- Below the long-term strike, a short stock position will be established through exercise of the long-term put. The short stock position can then be closed out in the market. The trade may or may not be profitable.

Calendar Put Spreads—Detail

When you establish a calendar put spread, you will pay a higher premium for the long-term option purchased than the amount you will receive on the premium from the short-term option sold. As a result, a calendar put spread is always established at a net debit. This type of spread is intended to profit from the fact that time decay erodes the price of the short-term option faster than the long-term option.

Example

Buy 10 XYZ Aug 30 Put @ 2.80

Sell 10 XYZ Jun 30 Put @ 1.00 for a net debit of 1.80

Long-term BE = 28.20 (strike price – debit amount)

MG = 28.20 (after June expiration)

ML = 1.80 (net debit paid)

This spread is executed for a net cost of $1,800 (2.80 points premium paid – 1.00 points premium received × 10 contracts × 100 shares per contract). Although exact time values are difficult to predict, in this example, as seen in Figure 4.6, at near-term expiration you will profit if the market price of XYZ is between approximately $28.20 and $32.20. This assumes the time value on the August puts at the June expiration is approximately 1.80. You will maximize your profit at $30. You will lose money if the price of XYZ goes below approximately $28.20 or above $32.20. Most of your $1,800 will be lost if XYZ increases or declines substantially by the near-term expiration.

If, instead of trading a spread, you decided to simply purchase the August 30 puts outright, your total cost would be $2,800, rather than $1,800. Your long-term breakeven would be 27.20, but you would only profit below 27.20, rather than between 28.20 and 32.20. If you simply purchased the August 30 puts, your downside potential is 27.20 immediately, rather than only after the short-term expiration.

A calendar put spread should be closely watched as the near-term expiration approaches, and then evaluated again after the near-term expiration. If the short-term put has expired and you are

FIGURE 4.6

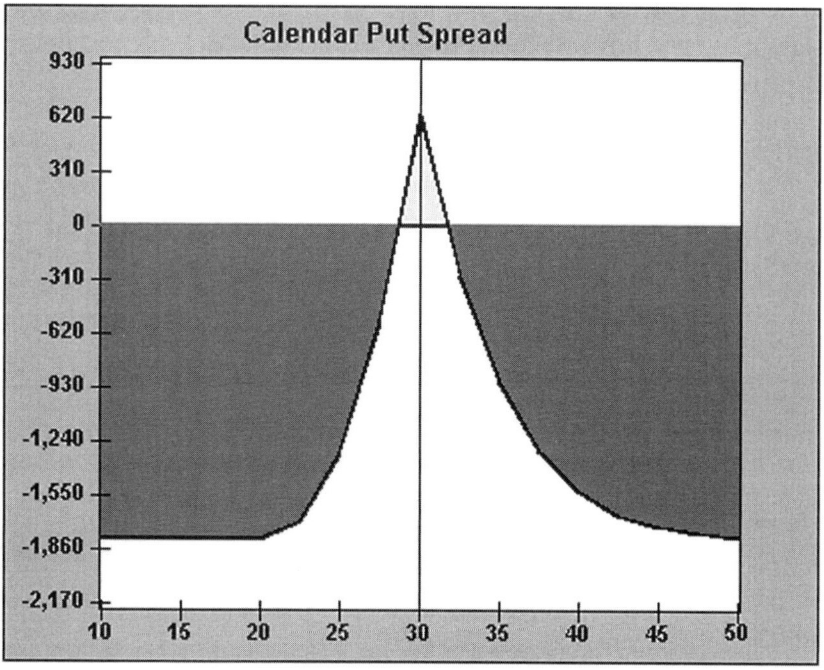

Strategy at Expiration

still bearish, you may decide to retain the long-term put option. If you are neutral or bullish, the long-term put should be sold. To understand how the profit and loss characteristics of this type of spread work, assume that once you have established this spread, it is held until the near-term expiration. There are five different prices that you should examine to draw a clear picture of how this strategy works.

Scenario 1: Assume the stock drops significantly and closes at 26 by the June option expiration. If this happens, you will be assigned on your June 30 puts and you will be long 1,000 shares of XYZ stock at a net cost of –$30,000. At that time, you would sell your long stock at the market price of 26 for net proceeds of $26,000. The difference between your buy and sell price is –$4,000. However, your August puts will be worth at least 4.00 (+ approximately .80 time value) and could be sold for approximately $4,800. Since you paid –$1,800 initially when the spread was established, your net loss would be approximately –$1,000. At prices lower than 26 at the June expiration, this loss will continue to increase up to a maximum of close to –$1,800 at very low prices. Although exact time values are difficult to predict, all prices below approximately 28.20 at the June expiration will probably result in a loss. Therefore, this spread is only advantageous if you expect XYZ *not* to drop below approximately 28.20 by the June expiration.

Scenario 2: Assume the stock drops only slightly and closes at 28.20 by the June option expiration. If this happens, you will be assigned on your June 30 puts and you will be long 1,000 shares of XYZ stock at a net cost of $30,000. At that time, you would sell your long stock at the market price of 28.20 for net proceeds of $28,200. The difference between your buy and sell price is –$1,800. However, your August puts will be worth at least 1.80 (+ approximately 1.80 time value) and could be sold for approximately $3,600. Since you paid –$1,800 initially when the spread was established, your net return would be approximately $0.

Scenario 3: Assume the stock closes at exactly 30 by the June option expiration. If this happens, your June 30 puts will expire worthless. However, your August puts will be worth approximately 2.40 points time value and could be sold for approximately $2,400. Since you paid –$1,800 initially when the spread was established, your net gain would be approximately $600.

Scenario 4: Assume the stock increases slightly and closes at 32.20 by the June option expiration. If this happens, your June 30 puts will expire worthless. However, your August puts will be worth approximately 1.80 points time value and could be sold for approximately $1,800. Since you paid –$1,800 initially when the spread was established, your net return would be approximately $0.

Scenario 5: Assume the stock increases substantially and closes at 34 by the June option expiration. If this happens, your June 30 puts will expire worthless. However, your August puts will be worth approximately 1.00 points time value and could be sold for approximately $1,000. Since you paid –$1,800 initially when the spread was established, your net loss would be approximately –$800.

Example

Long Puts vs. Calendar Put Spread

XYZ = 30

- Long-term put provides substantial downside potential and limited risk of 2.80 points (see Figure 4.7).
- Calendar put spread is created by selling a close-term put (see Figure 4.8).
- The trade-off is limited profit potential in the near term.
  - In exchange for a lower initial cost.

Buy 10 XYZ Aug 30 Puts @ 2.80

Buy 10 XYZ Aug 30 Puts @ 2.80
Sell 10 XYZ Jun 30 Puts @ 1.00

FIGURE 4.7 AND 4.8

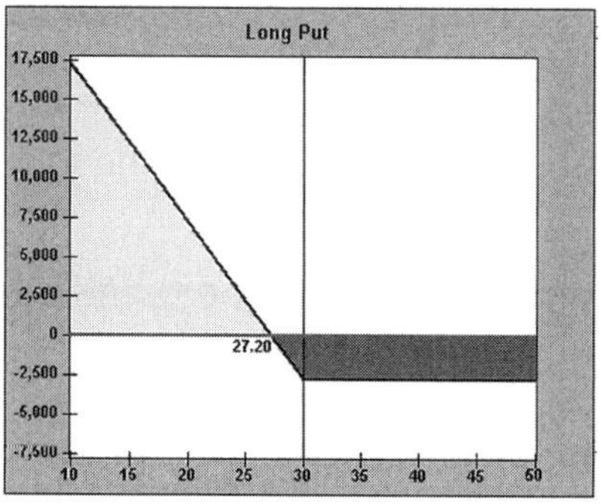

Strategy at Expiration

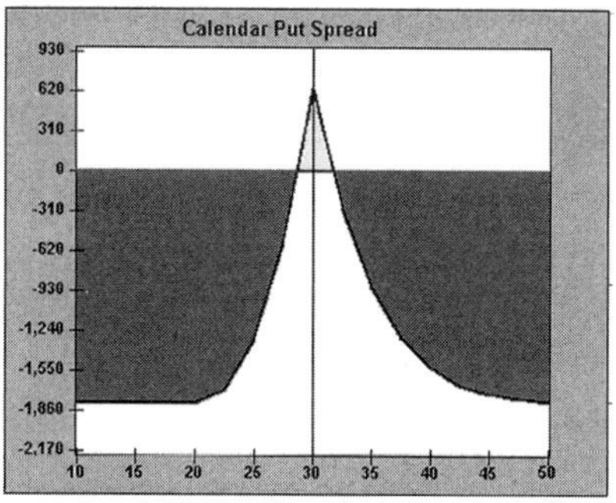

Strategy at Expiration

Long Puts

- August 30 puts purchased outright for a total cost of $2,800.
  - Rather than $1,800 (cost of the spread).
- The trade-off for the increased risk is significant gain potential.
  - $1,000 of increased risk.
- The downside potential for profit is up to $27,200 as the stock drops.
  - In the case of the calendar spread, maximum profit cannot exceed approximately $600 in the short term.
- Breakeven is at 27.20.
- Maximum loss of $2,800 if XYZ is above 30 at August expiration.

Calendar Put Spread

- Spread is executed for a net cost of $1,800.
  - 2.80 points premium paid – 1.00 points premium received × 10 contracts × 100 shares per contract
- Profitable if the market price of XYZ stays between approximately 28.20 and 32.20 in the short term (the breakeven points).
  - Profitable below $28.20 in the long term.
- Maximum profit at $30 in the short term.
  - At $0 in the long term.
- Unprofitable if the price of XYZ is below $28.20 or above $32.20 in the short term.
  - Unprofitable if XYZ is above $28.20 in the long term.
- Maximum loss of $1,800 if XYZ is very high or very low at the short-term expiration.
  - Maximum loss of $1,800 if XYZ is above $30 in the long term.
- Commissions will be higher than for the single put trade.

Advantages of calendar put spreads vs. long puts

- Require less capital to enter, since you are taking in some premium from the options that are sold.

- Lower initial cost effectively raises the breakeven point.

Disadvantages of calendar put spreads vs. long puts

- Profit potential is limited in the short term.
- May require a higher option trading approval level, depending upon your broker.
- May require a higher minimum account net worth, depending upon your broker.
- Will limit your profits significantly if the underlying stock moves substantially higher or lower in the short term.
- Higher commission costs, since two options are traded instead of one.

Characteristics

While the risk/reward characteristics of calendar spreads are a little more challenging, since you have both short term and longer term to be concerned with, it is equally important to understand how to select your strike prices. Which strike prices you use and whether or not those strike prices are in, at, or out-of-the-money will affect the magnitude of the underlying move needed to reach profitability and will also determine whether or not the spread can be profitable if the underlying stock remains unchanged. An important thing to keep in mind is that once the short-term option expires, the spread dissolves and the long-term option is simply considered long.

Table 4.3 illustrates how to properly structure a calendar spread to match your level of bullishness or bearishness in the short term (ST) and long term (LT). For example, if you are extremely bullish in the long term and slightly bullish in the short term, you may want to consider an out-of-the-money (OOTM) call spread. If you are extremely bearish in the long term and slightly bearish in the short term, you may want to consider an out-of-the-money (OOTM) put spread. Keep in mind that both will generally require a move of extreme magnitude in the underlying stock in order to reach profitability. By contrast, if you are only slightly bullish or slightly bearish in the long term, you may want to consider an in-the-money (ITM) spread, which can sometimes be profitable with little or no movement in the underlying stock. Keep in mind that in-the-money trades will typically have the exact opposite sentiment in the short term as in the long term. As with most option strategies, the greater the underlying move needed, the higher the profit potential, but also the less likely it is that a profit will be made. Similarly, if you structure your spread so that profitability is possible with no movement in the underlying stock, a profit, if earned, will likely be very small.

Understanding Table 4.3 will help you identify possible calendar spread candidates. Figures 4.9 and 4.10 are sample charts using simple technical analysis where calendar spreads might be appropriate. Keep in mind that these examples do not include commission charges, which may be significant and will impact the profit or loss.

In Figure 4.9, you have identified XYZ stock, which appears to be in a long-term uptrend but is experiencing some short-term weakness. As a result, you are expecting only minor gains in the near term but a continued upward move in the coming months.

If you are very bullish, you may want to consider the following calendar call spread. With calendar spreads, you can calculate the long-term max gain (MG), max loss (ML), and one of the breakevens (BE) before you actually enter the trade. The maximum loss (ML) on a debit spread will always be the amount of the initial debit.

TABLE 4.3

Calendar Spread Strategy	**<< Direction >>**				**<< Magnitude >>**		
	Bullish	**Neutral**	**Breakout**	**Bearish**	**Extreme**	**Moderate**	**Slight**
Calendar call spread OOTM	X				X LT		X ST
Calendar call spread ATM	X LT	X ST				X	
Calendar call spread ITM	X ST			X ST			X
Calendar put spread OOTM				X	X LT		X ST
Calendar put spread ATM		X ST		X LT		X	
Calendar put spread ITM	X ST			X LT			X

FIGURE 4.9

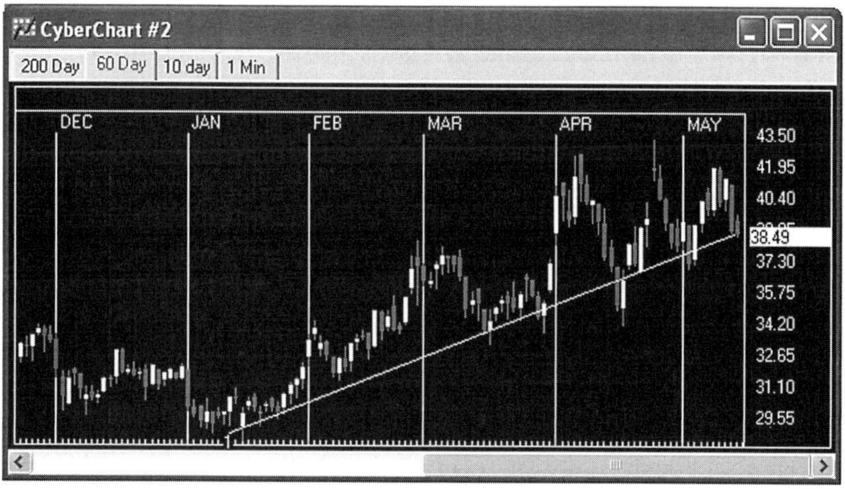

Example 1

Buy 10 XYZ Aug 40 Calls @ 3.00

Sell 10 XYZ Jun 40 Calls @ 1.40

Debit = 1.60

BE = 41.60 (strike price + debit amount)

MG = Undefined in the short term (occurs at 40) (unlimited after June expiration)

ML = 1.60 (net debit paid)

Total cost of this trade = $1,600 (debit × # of spreads × option multiplier) or (1.60 × 10 × 100)

This example would be considered out-of-the-money, since the stock price is below the strike price. Since Figure 4.9 presents data as of around May 9, the June options have about five weeks until expiration. By calculating the breakeven before you enter the trade, you can see that with an upper breakeven price of 41.60, you would want XYZ to stay below 40 until the June expiration and then rise above 41.60 by the August expiration to be profitable. The exact maximum profit in the near term will be the difference between the price of the August calls on the June expiration and the initial debit amount. This will occur if XYZ is at exactly 40 on the June expiration. The long-term maximum profit is unlimited. Losses will be incurred if XYZ moves sharply higher or lower by the June expiration. After the June expiration, losses will be incurred if XYZ does not exceed 41.60 by the August expiration. The long-term maximum loss occurs if XYZ does not exceed 40 by the August expiration. When that occurs, the August calls will expire worthless and the initial debit paid is completely lost.

In Figure 4.10, you have identified XYZ stock, which appears to be in a long-term downtrend but is experiencing some short-term strength. As a result, you are expecting only minor declines in the near term but a continued downward move in the coming months.

If you are very bearish, you may want to consider the following calendar put spread. With calendar spreads, you can calculate the long-term max gain (MG), max loss (ML), and one of the breakevens (BE) before you actually enter the trade. The maximum loss (ML) on a debit spread will always be the amount of the initial debit.

Example 2

Buy 10 XYZ Sep 40 Puts @ 1.30
Sell 10 XYZ Jun 40 Puts @ .30

FIGURE 4.10

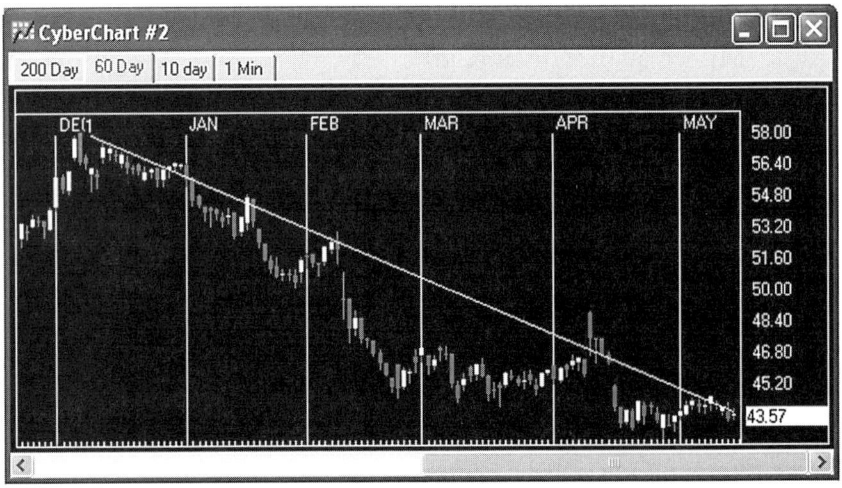

Debit = 1.00

BE = 39.00 (strike price – debit amount)

MG = Undefined in the short term (occurs at 40) (39.00 after June expiration)

ML = 1.00 (net debit paid)

Total cost of this trade = $1,000 (debit × # of spreads × option multiplier) or (1.00 × 10 × 100)

This example would be considered out-of-the-money, since the stock price is above the strike price. Since Figure 4.10 presents data as of around May 9, the June options have about five weeks until expiration. By calculating the breakeven before you enter the trade, you can see that with a lower breakeven price of 39, you would want XYZ to stay above 40 until the June expiration and then drop below 39 by the September expiration to be profitable. The exact maximum profit in the near term will be the difference between the price of the September puts on the June expiration and the initial debit amount. This will occur if XYZ is at exactly 40 on the June expiration. The long-term maximum profit is 39 points. Losses will be incurred if XYZ moves sharply higher or lower by the June expiration. After the June expiration, losses will be incurred if XYZ does not drop below 39 by the September expiration. The long-term maximum loss occurs if XYZ does not drop below 40 by the September expiration. When that occurs, the September puts will expire worthless and the initial debit paid is completely lost.

CHAPTER 5

Diagonal Spreads

Spreads offer you the opportunity to limit losses in exchange for a limited gain potential. They involve the simultaneous purchase and sale of two options contracts of the same class (puts or calls) on the same underlying security.

DIAGONAL SPREADS EXPLANATION

In the case of diagonal spreads, both the strike price *and* the expiration month will be different. For diagonal spreads, the long leg has to expire later than the short leg, or the strategy cannot be classified as a spread. If the long leg expires before the short leg, the two options will be considered unrelated long and short options. In many cases, spreads may require that you temporarily establish a long or short stock position. That resulting long or short position will need to be closed out in the market to fully realize the profit potential of the strategy. This is explained in more detail later in this chapter.

Two of the key concepts to understand before you begin trading spreads are how to determine your sentiment (whether you are

---

Author's Note: Spreads are very versatile, and with the range of strike prices that are available and the ability to utilize puts or calls, different strike prices, and different expiration months, the possibilities are virtually unlimited. The examples in this chapter are intended to illustrate a few of the many ways to potentially take advantage of charts that are exhibiting signs of short-term neutrality with longer-term bullishness or bearishness.

bullish or bearish) and how to calculate maximum loss (ML), break-even points (BE), and the maximum gain (MG). These calculations will vary depending upon whether the spread is initially established as a net debit or net credit and whether or not it is entered using calls or puts. For any credit spread, your broker will also require you to meet an initial margin requirement and maintain funds in your account equal to the maximum loss amount.

Because a diagonal spread is both a horizontal and a vertical spread, for margin purposes, it must be classified as either a debit spread or a credit spread. Unlike vertical spreads, it is not possible to determine whether it is a debit spread or a credit spread based strictly on whether it is entered at a net debit or a net credit. In the case of diagonal spreads, it is sometimes possible to enter a credit spread at a net debit. This will happen if the time premium on the long-term option is great enough to offset the amount by which the long-option is farther out-of-the-money than the short-term option. The more months between the two options, the greater the likelihood this will occur. However, even when entered at a net debit, your broker may still require a margin deposit, because the strategy is technically a credit spread.

A diagonal spread has both a short-term and a longer-term sentiment that can be determined. While the short-term MG and BE are impossible to determine exactly, you can calculate your longer-term ML, BE, and MG for any diagonal spread strategy by applying the following rules:

Short-Term

1. Determine the short leg of the spread.
   a. The short leg is the option with the nearer expiration date.
2. Determine whether you are bullish, bearish, or neutral on the short leg.
   a. Short puts are bullish if they are in-the-money.
      i. Neutral if out-of-the-money.
   b. Short calls are bearish if they are in-the-money.
      i. Neutral if out-of-the-money.
3. Determine whether you are short-term bullish, bearish, or neutral on the spread.
   a. Your answer to step 2 holds true for the entire spread strategy in the short term.

4. Determine whether the spread is a debit spread or a credit spread.
   a. For diagonal spreads, this is *not* determined by whether it is entered as a net debit or net credit.
   b. If entered at a net credit, it is *always* a credit spread.
   c. If entered at a net debit, it *may be* a debit spread or a credit spread.
      i. If it is a call spread and the long strike price is lower, it is a debit spread.
      ii. If it is a put spread and the long strike price is higher, it is a debit spread.
      iii. If it is a call spread and the long strike price is higher, it is a credit spread.
      iv. If it is a put spread and the long strike price is lower, it is a credit spread.
5. Calculate the short-term **ML**.
   a. If the spread is a debit spread, the debit is the ML.
   b. If the spread is a credit spread, the ML is the net of the two strike prices – the credit (or + the debit).
6. Calculate the short-term **BE**.
   a. If debit call spread, the BE is the strike price of the long leg + net debit – remaining long-term call time value.
   b. If debit put spread, the BE is the strike price of the long leg – net debit + remaining long-term put time value.
   c. If credit call spread, the BE is the strike price of the short leg + net credit (or – debit).
   d. If credit put spread, the BE is the strike price of the short leg – net credit (or + debit).
7. Calculate the short-term **MG**.
   a. If the spread is entered at a net debit, the MG is the remaining time value in the long-term option – the initial debit paid.
   b. If the spread is entered at a net credit, the MG is the remaining time value in the long-term option + the initial credit received.

Long-Term

1. Determine the long leg of the spread.
   a. The long leg is the option with the later expiration date.

2. Determine whether you are bullish or bearish on the long leg.
   a. Long calls are bullish.
   b. Long puts are bearish.
3. Determine whether you are longer-term bullish or bearish on the spread.
   a. Your answer to step 2 holds true for the entire spread strategy.
4. Determine whether the spread is a debit spread or a credit spread.
   a. See step 4 under **Short-Term**.
5. Determine the long-term **ML**.
   a. If the spread is a debit spread, the debit is the ML.
   b. If the spread is a credit spread, the ML is the difference between the strikes – the net credit (or + the debit).
6. Calculate the long-term **BE**.
   a. If call spread, the BE is the long strike price + net debit (or – credit).
   b. If put spread, the BE is the long strike price – net debit (or + credit).
7. Calculate the long-term **MG**.
   a. If call spread, the MG is unlimited after the short option expires.
   b. If put spread, the MG is the strike price of the long option – the debit (or + the credit).

TYPES OF DIAGONAL SPREADS

There are basically two types of diagonal spreads, diagonal call spreads and diagonal put spreads. Both are typically used to establish both a short-term and a longer-term sentiment. The short-term sentiment is your sentiment from the moment you establish the spread until the expiration date of the short option. The longer-term sentiment is your sentiment from the moment the short option expires until the expiration date of the long option. Typically, the near-term sentiment is neutral (if the short option is out-of-the-money) and the longer-term sentiment is either bullish or bearish.

Diagonal Call Spreads—Quick Overview

A diagonal call spread is made up of one long call in a distant month and one short call in a nearer month. Both legs should have different strike prices, so this spread could be entered at a net debit or a net credit. Both sides of this spread are opening transactions, and the number of contracts of the long leg should be the same as the number of the short leg (see Figure 5.1).

At Entry The white line in Figure 5.1 represents what the strategy typically looks like at the point of entry. As expiration approaches, the curve moves toward the black lines, which illustrate the final profit and loss boundaries at expiration.

Direction Short-term neutral to moderately bullish, longer-term bullish depending upon the strike prices selected

FIGURE 5.1

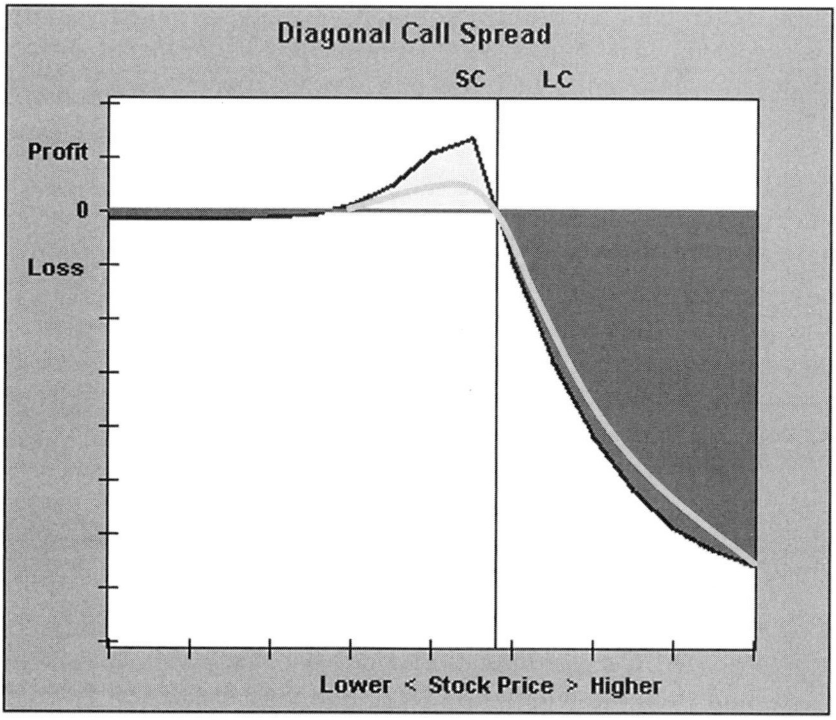

TABLE 5.1

Greeks	Near-term	Longer-term
Delta	Neutral	Positive
Gamma	Neutral	Positive
Theta	Positive	Negative
Vega	Positive	Positive

When to Use You would typically employ a diagonal call spread in a neutral to moderately bullish market, when you think the market will become more bullish. You hope to profit if the underlying stock remains below the strike price until the expiration date of the short-term option but rises above the strike price by the expiration date of the longer-term option. Generally, the more bullish you are, the higher the strike prices you will use. A diagonal call spread is a reasonable substitute for a calendar call spread when you want to reduce your overall cost basis and your long-term sentiment is more bullish than your short-term sentiment. A diagonal call spread can also be used when your long-term sentiment is less bullish than your short-term sentiment, which will increase your overall cost basis.

Risk vs. Reward Limited risk with limited profit potential

Volatility The effect of volatility is generally favorable.

Time Decay The effect of time decay on this strategy is favorable, as the near-term call will lose time value at a faster rate than the longer-term call (see Table 5.1).

Prior to Near-Term Expiration

- Because the short option is near expiration, it is in the steepest part of the time erosion curve, which causes the short option to lose time value more quickly than the long option.
  - As a result, with little or no movement in the underlying stock price, the spread can often be closed out at a profit prior to expiration, once time value has eroded sufficiently.
- Similarly, if the underlying stock rises sharply enough, the spread can often be closed out at a loss that is less than the maximum loss possible if held until expiration, because time value will erode the value of the near-term option more quickly.

- Comparing the early close loss to the maximum potential loss at expiration can help you decide if holding until expiration makes sense.

At Near-Term Expiration

- Below the near-term strike, the near-term call expires worthless and the near-term call premium is retained.
- At the near-term strike, the near-term call expires worthless and the near-term call premium is retained.
- Above the near-term strike, a short stock position will be established through assignment of the near-term call. The short stock can then be closed out in the market. The longer-term call is sold to offset all or part of the loss on the stock position. The trade may or may not be profitable.

Prior to Long-Term Expiration

- Once the short-term option has expired, you are left with a long call option. At that point your upside profit potential is unlimited.
- If the underlying stock rises sufficiently to cause the value of the remaining long call to exceed the initial debit of the original calendar spread, the long call can be sold at a profit.
  - If the original spread was entered at a credit and any value exists in the long option once the short option has expired, the long option can be sold at a profit.
- With little or no movement in the underlying stock, time value erosion will begin to take its toll on the long option. Unless you are still bullish, you may want to consider closing the long option before the month in which it expires.

At Long-Term Expiration (assuming near-term call expired worthless)

- Below the long-term strike, the long-term call will expire worthless and max loss is sustained.
- At the long-term strike, the long-term call will expire worthless and max loss is sustained.
- Above the long-term strike, long stock will be acquired through exercise of the long-term call. The long stock can then be sold in the market. The trade may or may not be profitable.

Diagonal Call Spreads—Detail

When you establish a diagonal call spread, the premium for the long-term call option may be higher or lower than the premium on the short-term call, depending upon the long-term call strike price and time premium. As a result, a diagonal call spread may be either a debit spread or a credit spread and may be established at either a net debit or a net credit. This type of spread is intended to potentially profit from the fact that time decay erodes the price of the short-term option faster than the long-term option. Since a diagonal call spread is both a vertical and a horizontal spread, it is also appropriate for taking a more or less bullish approach in the long term.

Example

Buy 10 XYZ Jan 60 Calls @ 1.20

Sell 10 XYZ Nov 55 Calls @ 1.10 for a net debit of .10

Long-term BE = 54.90 (short position strike price + the credit [or – debit])

MG = Unlimited (after November expiration)

ML = 5.10 (net of strikes – the credit [or + debit])

This spread is executed for a net cost of $100 (1.20 points premium paid – 1.10 points premium received × 10 contracts × 100 shares per contract). As shown in Figure 5.2, at near-term expiration you will profit if the market price of XYZ is between approximately $49 and $56. You will maximize your profit at $55. You will sustain a small loss if the price of XYZ goes below approximately $49, and a much larger loss if XYZ goes above $56. Most of your $5,100 potential maximum loss will be incurred if XYZ increases substantially by the near-term expiration.

If, instead of trading a spread, you decided to simply purchase the January 60 calls outright, your total cost would be $1,200, rather than $100. Your breakeven would be 61.20 instead of 60.10, but you would only profit above 60.10, rather than between 49 and 56. If you simply purchased the January 60 calls, your upside potential is unlimited immediately, rather than only after the short-term expiration.

A diagonal call spread should be closely watched as the near-term expiration approaches, and then evaluated again after the near-term expiration. If the short-term call has expired and you are still bullish, you may decide to retain the long-term call option. If you are neutral or bearish, the long-term call should be sold. To understand how the profit and loss characteristics of this type of spread work,

FIGURE 5.2

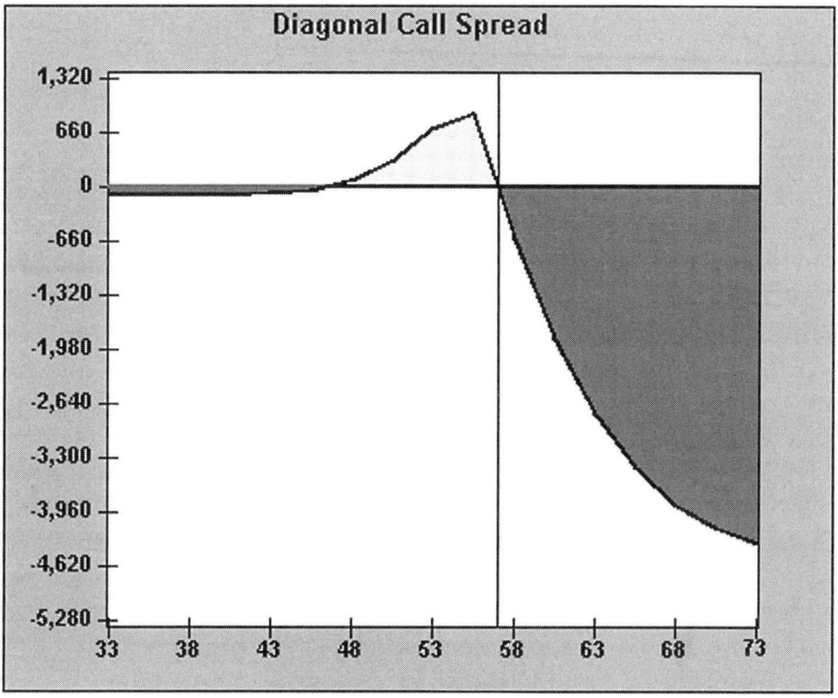

Strategy at Expiration

assume that once you have established this spread, it is held until the near-term expiration. There are five different prices that you should examine to draw a clearer picture of how this strategy works.

Scenario 1: Assume the stock rallies significantly and closes at 59 by the November option expiration. If this happens, you will be assigned on your November 55 calls and you will be short 1,000 shares of XYZ stock for net proceeds of $55,000. At that time, you would buy back your short shares at the market price of 59 for a net cost of –$59,000. The difference between your buy and sell price is –$4,000. However, your January calls will be worth about 2.30 points in time value, and could be sold for approximately $2,300. Since you paid –$100 initially when the spread was established, your net loss would be approximately –$1,800. This loss will continue to increase at all prices above approximately 56, up to a maximum of –$5,100. Therefore, this spread is only advantageous if you expect XYZ *not* to exceed approximately 56 by the November expiration.

Scenario 2: Assume the stock rallies only slightly and closes at 56 by the November option expiration. If this happens, you will be assigned on your November 55 calls and you will be short 1,000 shares of XYZ stock for net proceeds of $55,000. At that time, you would buy back your short shares at the market price of 56 for a net cost of –$56,000. The difference between your buy and sell price is –$1,000. However, your January calls will be worth at least 1.10 points in time value, and could be sold for approximately $1,100. Since you paid –$100 initially when the spread was established, your net return would be approximately $0.

Scenario 3: Assume the stock closes at exactly 55 by the November option expiration. If this happens, your November 55 calls will expire worthless. However, your January calls will be worth approximately .80 points time value and could be sold for approximately $800. Since you paid –$100 initially when the spread was established, your net gain would be approximately $700.

Scenario 4: Assume the stock drops slightly and closes at 52 by the November option expiration. If this happens, your November 55 calls will expire worthless. However, your January calls will be worth approximately .30 points time value and could be sold for approximately $300. Since you paid –$100 initially when the spread was established, your net gain would be approximately $200.

Scenario 5: Assume the stock drops substantially and closes at 45 by the November option expiration. If this happens, your November 55 calls will expire worthless, and your January calls will probably be worthless. Since you paid –$100 initially when the spread was established, your net loss would be approximately –$100.

Example

Long Calls vs. Diagonal Call Spread

XYZ = 55

- Long-term call provides unlimited upside potential and limited risk of 1.20 points (see Figure 5.3).
- Diagonal call spread is created by selling a close-term call at-the-money (see Figure 5.4).
- The trade-off is limited profit potential in the near term.
    - In exchange for a lower initial cost.

	Buy 10 XYZ Jan 60 Calls @ 1.20
Buy 10 XYZ Jan 60 Calls @ 1.20	Sell 10 XYZ Nov 55 Calls @ 1.10

FIGURE 5.3 AND 5.4

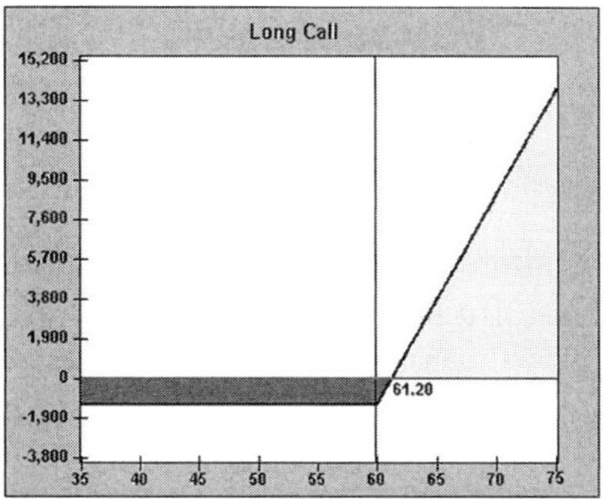

Strategy at Expiration

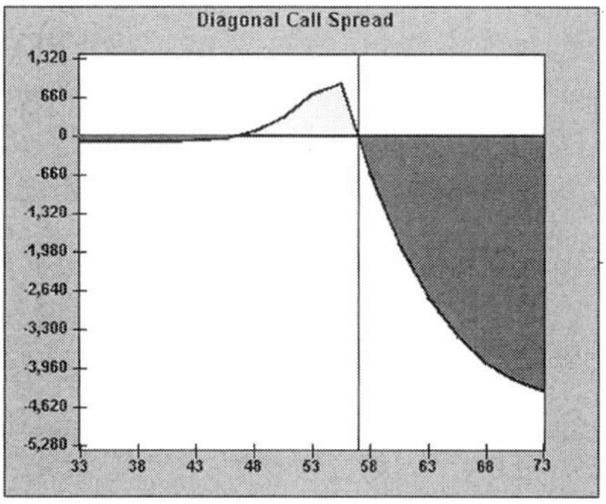

Strategy at Expiration

Long Calls

- January 60 calls purchased outright for a total cost of $1,200.
  - Rather than $100 (cost of the spread).
- The trade-off for the increased risk is unlimited gain potential.
  - $1,100 of increased risk.
- The upside potential for profit is theoretically unlimited as the stock rises.
  - In the case of the diagonal spread, maximum profit cannot exceed approximately $700 in the short term.
- Breakeven is at 61.20.

Diagonal Call Spread

- Spread is executed for a net cost of $100.
  - 1.20 points premium paid – 1.10 points premium received × 10 contracts × 100 shares per contract
- Profitable if the market price of XYZ stays between approximately 49 and 56 in the short term (the breakeven points).
  - Profitable above $60.10 in the long term.
- Maximum profit at $55 in the short term.
  - Unlimited in the long term.
- Unprofitable if the price of XYZ is above $56 or below $49 in the short term.

    - Unprofitable if XYZ is below $60.10 in the long term.
- Maximum loss of $5,100 if XYZ is at a very high price at the short-term expiration.
    - Maximum loss of $100 if XYZ is below $60 in the long term.
- Commissions will be higher than for the single call trade.

Advantages of diagonal call spreads vs. long calls

- Require less capital to enter, since you are taking in some premium from the options that are sold.
- Lower initial cost effectively lowers the breakeven point.

Disadvantages of diagonal call spreads vs. long calls

- Profit potential is limited in the short term.
- May require a higher option trading approval level, depending upon your broker.
- May require a higher minimum account net worth, depending upon your broker.
- May limit your potential profits significantly if the underlying stock moves substantially higher in the short term.
- Higher commission costs, since two options are traded instead of one.

Diagonal Put Spreads—Quick Overview

A diagonal put spread is made up of one long put in a distant month and one short put in a nearer month. Both legs should have different strike prices, so this spread could be entered at a net debit or a net credit. Both sides of this spread are opening transactions, and the number of contracts of the long leg should be the same as the number of the short leg (see Figure 5.5).

At Entry The white line in Figure 5.5 represents what the strategy typically looks like at the point of entry. As expiration approaches, the curve moves toward the black lines, which illustrate the final profit and loss boundaries at expiration.

Direction Short-term neutral to moderately bearish, longer-term bearish depending upon the strike prices selected

When to Use You would typically employ a diagonal put spread in a neutral to moderately bearish market, when you think the market will become more bearish. You hope to profit if the underlying

FIGURE 5.5

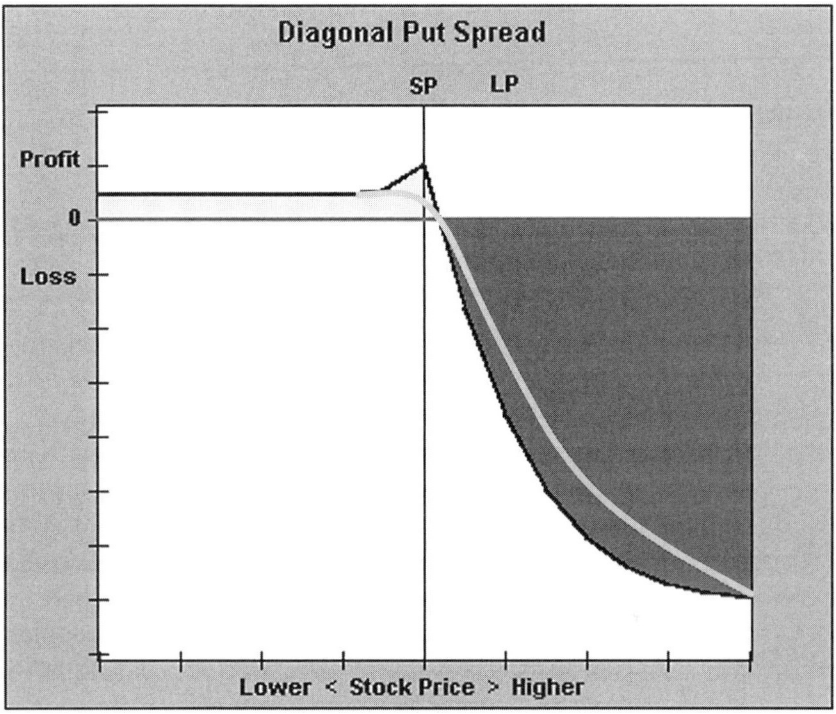

stock remains above the strike price until the expiration date of the short-term option but drops below the strike price by the expiration date of the longer-term option. Generally, the more bearish you are, the lower the strike prices you will use. A diagonal put spread is a reasonable substitute for a calendar put spread when you want to reduce your overall cost basis and your long-term sentiment is more bearish than your short-term sentiment. A diagonal put spread can also be used when your long-term sentiment is less bearish than your short-term sentiment, which will increase your overall cost basis.

Risk vs. Reward Limited risk with limited profit potential

Volatility The effect of volatility is generally favorable.

Time Decay The effect of time decay on this strategy is favorable, as the near-term put will lose time value at a faster rate than the longer-term put (see Table 5.2).

TABLE 5.2

Greeks	Near-term	Longer-term
Delta	Neutral	Positive
Gamma	Neutral	Positive
Theta	Positive	Negative
Vega	Positive	Positive

Prior to Near-Term Expiration

- Because the short option is near expiration, it is in the steepest part of the time erosion curve, which causes the short option to lose time value more quickly than the long option.
  - As a result, with little or no movement in the underlying stock price, the spread can often be closed out at a profit prior to expiration, once time value has eroded sufficiently.
- Similarly, if the underlying stock rises sharply enough, the spread can often be closed out at a loss that is less than the maximum loss possible if held until expiration, because time value will erode the value of the near-term option more quickly.
  - Comparing the early close loss to the maximum potential loss at expiration can help you decide if holding until expiration makes sense.

At Near-Term Expiration

- Above the near-term strike, the near-term put expires worthless and the near-term put premium is retained.
- At the near-term strike, the near-term put expires worthless and the near-term put premium is retained.
- Below the near-term strike, a long stock position will be established through assignment of the near-term put. The long stock can then be closed out in the market. The longer-term put is sold to offset all or part of the loss on the stock position. The trade may or may not be profitable.

Prior to Long-Term Expiration

- Once the short-term option has expired, you are left with a long put option. At that point, your downside profit potential is significant.

- If the underlying stock drops sufficiently to cause the value of the remaining long put to exceed the initial debit of the original calendar spread, the long put can be sold at a profit.
  - If the original spread was entered at a credit and any value exists in the long option once the short option has expired, the long option can be sold at a profit.
- With little or no movement in the underlying stock, time value erosion will begin to take its toll on the long option. Unless you are still bearish, you may want to consider closing the long option before the month in which it expires.

At Long-Term Expiration (assuming near-term put expired worthless)

- Above the long-term strike, the long-term put will expire worthless and max loss is sustained.
- At the long-term strike, the long-term put will expire worthless and max loss is sustained.
- Below the long-term strike, a short stock position will be established through exercise of the long-term put. The short stock position can then be closed out in the market. The trade may or may not be profitable.

Diagonal Put Spreads—Detail

When you establish a diagonal put spread, the premium for the long-term put option may be higher or lower than the premium on the short-term put, depending upon the long-term put strike price and time premium. As a result, a diagonal put spread may be either a debit spread or a credit spread and may be established at either a net debit or a net credit. This type of spread is intended to profit from the fact that time decay erodes the price of the short-term option faster than the long-term option. Since a diagonal put spread is both a vertical and a horizontal spread, it is also appropriate for taking a more or less bearish approach in the long term.

Example

Buy 10 XYZ Feb 35 Puts @ 5.50
Sell 10 XYZ Nov 30 Puts @ .80
  Debit = 4.70

Long term BE = 30.30 (long position strike price – debit [or + credit])

MG = 30.30 (after November expiration)

ML = 4.70 (net debit paid)

This spread is executed for a net cost of $4,700 (5.50 points premium paid – .80 points premium received × 10 contracts × 100 shares per contract). As shown in Figure 5.6, at near-term expiration you will profit if the market price of XYZ is below approximately $31.00. You will maximize your profit at $30. You will lose money if the price of XYZ goes above approximately $32.20. Most of your $4,700 will be lost if XYZ increases substantially by the near-term expiration.

Strategy at Near-Term Expiration If, instead of trading a spread, you decided to simply purchase the Feb 35 puts outright, your total cost would be $5,500, rather than $4,700. Your breakeven would be 29.50, and you would only profit below 29.50, rather than

FIGURE 5.6

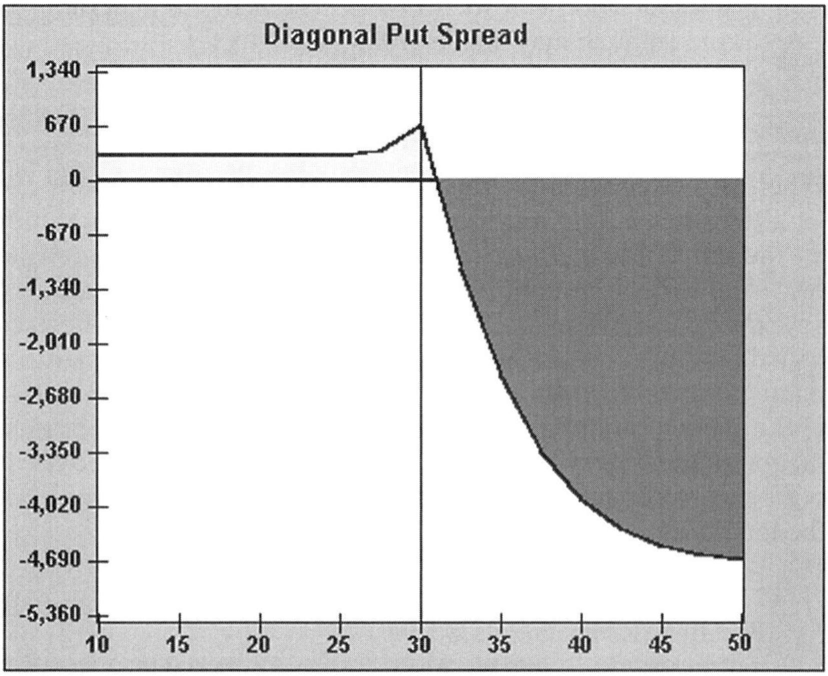

Strategy at Expiration

below approximately 31. If you simply purchased the February 35 puts, your downside potential is 29.50 immediately, rather than only after the short-term expiration.

A diagonal put spread should be closely watched as the near-term expiration approaches, and then evaluated again after the near-term expiration. If the short-term put has expired and you are still bearish, you may decide to retain the long-term put option. If you are neutral or bullish, the long-term put should be sold. To understand how the profit and loss characteristics of this type of spread work, assume that once you have established this spread, it is held until the near-term expiration. There are five different prices that you should examine to draw a clear picture of how this strategy works.

Scenario 1: Assume the stock drops significantly and closes at 25 by the November option expiration. If this happens, you will be assigned on your November 30 puts and you will be long 1,000 shares of XYZ stock at a net cost of –$30,000. At that time, you would sell your long stock at the market price of 25 for net proceeds of $25,000. The difference between your buy and sell price is –$5,000. However, your February puts will be worth at least 10 (+ approximately .00 time value) and could be sold for approximately $10,000. Since you paid –$4,700 initially when the spread was established, your net gain would be approximately $300. This gain will remain at this level for all prices down to 0. Therefore, this spread is slightly advantageous if you expect XYZ to drop before the November expiration.

Scenario 2: Assume the stock drops only slightly and closes at 29 by the November option expiration. If this happens, you will be assigned on your November 30 puts and you will be long 1,000 shares of XYZ stock at a net cost of $30,000. At that time, you would sell your long stock at the market price of 29 for net proceeds of $29,000. The difference between your buy and sell price is –$1,000. However, your February puts will be worth at least 6.00 (+ approximately .20 time value) and could be sold for approximately $6,200. Since you paid –$4,700 initially when the spread was established, your net gain would be about $500.

Scenario 3: Assume the stock closes at exactly 30 by the November option expiration. If this happens, your November 30 puts will expire worthless. However, your February puts will be worth at least 5.00 points (+ approximately .40 points time value) and could be sold for approximately $5,400. Since you paid –$4,700 initially when the spread was established, your net gain would be approximately $700.

Scenario 4: Assume the stock increases slightly and closes at 31 by the November option expiration. If this happens, your November 30 puts will expire worthless. However, your February puts will be worth at least 4.00 (+ approximately .70 points time value) and could be sold for approximately $4,700. Since you paid –$4,700 initially when the spread was established, your net return would be approximately $0.

Scenario 5: Assume the stock increases substantially and closes at 35 by the November option expiration. If this happens, your November 30 puts will expire worthless. However, your February puts will be worth approximately 2.20 points time value and could be sold for approximately $2,200. Since you paid –$4,700 initially when the spread was established, your net loss would be approximately –$2,500.

Example

Long Puts vs. Diagonal Put Spread

XYZ = 30

- Long-term put provides substantial downside potential and limited risk of 5.50 points (see Figure 5.7).
- Diagonal put spread is created by selling a close-term put (see Figure 5.8).
- The trade-off is limited profit potential in the near term.
  - In exchange for a lower initial cost.

Buy 10 XYZ Feb 35 Puts @ 5.50

Buy 10 XYZ Feb 35 Puts @ 5.50
Sell 10 XYZ Nov 30 Puts @ .80

FIGURE 5.7 AND 5.8

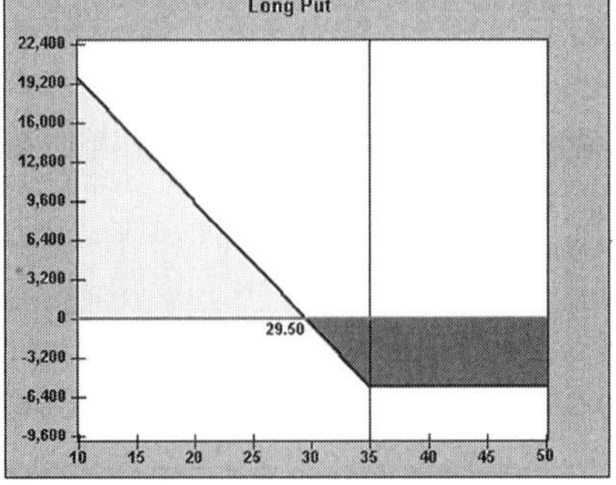

Strategy at Expiration

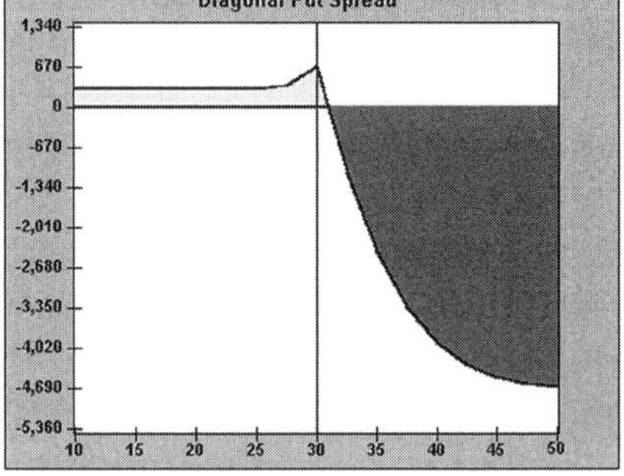

Strategy at Expiration

Long Puts

- February 35 puts purchased outright for a total cost of $5,500.
  - Rather than $4,700 (cost of the spread).
- The trade-off for the increased risk is significant gain potential.
  - $800 of increased risk.
- The downside potential for profit is up to $29,500 as the stock drops.
  - In the case of the diagonal spread, maximum profit cannot exceed approximately $700 in the short term.
- Breakeven is at 29.50.
- Commissions will be lower for the single put trade.

Diagonal Put Spread

- Spread is executed for a net cost of $4,700.
  - 5.50 points premium paid – .80 points premium received × 10 contracts × 100 shares per contract
- Profitable if the market price of XYZ stays below approximately 31 in the short term.
  - Profitable below $30.30 in the long term.
- Maximum profit at $700 in the short term.
  - At $0 in the long term.
- Unprofitable if the price of XYZ is above $31 in the short term.
  - Unprofitable if XYZ is above $30.30 in the long term.
- Maximum loss of $4,700 if XYZ is very high at the short-term expiration.
  - Maximum loss of $4,700 if XYZ is above $35 in the long term.
- Commissions will be higher than for the single put trade.

Advantages of diagonal put spreads vs. long puts

- Require less capital to enter, since you are taking in some premium from the options that are sold.
- Lower initial cost effectively raises the breakeven point.

Disadvantages of diagonal put spreads vs. long puts

- Profit potential is limited in the short term.
- May require a higher option trading approval level, depending upon your broker.

- May require a higher minimum account net worth, depending upon your broker.
- Will limit your profits significantly if the underlying stock moves substantially lower in the short term.
- Higher commission costs, since two options are traded instead of one.

Characteristics

While the risk/reward characteristics of diagonal spreads are a little more challenging, since you have both short term and longer term to be concerned with, it is equally important to understand how to select your strike prices. Which strike prices you use and whether or not those strike prices are in, at, or out-of-the-money will affect the magnitude of the underlying move needed to reach profitability and will also determine whether or not the spread can be profitable if the underlying stock remains unchanged. An important thing to keep in mind is that once the short-term option expires, the spread dissolves and the long-term option is simply considered long.

Table 5.3 illustrates how to properly structure a diagonal spread to match your level of bullishness or bearishness in the short term (ST) and long term (LT). Since diagonal spreads are similar to calendar spreads, the same chart can be used, with these additional pieces of information:

- If the distant month is farther out-of-the-money than the near month, the diagonal spread will be less expensive than the calendar spread.
- If the distant month is farther in-the-money than the near month, the diagonal spread will be more expensive than the calendar spread.
- Diagonal spreads can be entered at a credit or a debit, depending upon the strike prices.
- The direction and magnitude of diagonals can vary depending on prices, strikes, and months.

For example, if you are extremely bullish in the long term and slightly bullish in the short term, you may want to consider an out-of-the-money (OOTM) call spread. If you are extremely bearish in the long term and slightly bearish in the short term, you may want to consider an out-of-the-money (OOTM) put spread. Keep in mind that both will generally require a move of extreme magnitude in the underlying stock in order to reach profitability. By contrast, if you are only slightly bullish or slightly bearish in the long term, you may want to consider an in-the-money (ITM) spread, which can sometimes be profitable with little or no movement in the underlying stock. Keep in mind that in-the-money trades will typically have the exact opposite sentiment in the short term as in the long term. As with most option strategies, the greater the underlying move needed, the higher the profit potential, but also the less likely it is that a profit will be made. Similarly, if you structure your spread so that profitability is possible with no movement in the underlying stock, a profit, if earned, will likely be very small.

Understanding Table 5.3 will help you identify possible diagonal spread candidates. Figures 5.9 and 5.10 are sample charts using simple technical analysis where diagonal spreads might be appropriate. Keep in mind that these examples do not include commission charges, which may be significant and will impact the profit or loss.

In Figure 5.9, you have identified XYZ stock, which appears to be in a long-term uptrend but is experiencing some short-term weakness. As a result, you are expecting only minor gains in the near term but a continued upward move in the coming months.

TABLE 5.3

Diagonal Spread Strategy	<< Direction >>				<< Magnitude >>		
	Bullish	Neutral	Breakout	Bearish	Extreme	Moderate	Slight
Diagonal call spread OOTM	X				X LT		X ST
Diagonal call spread ATM	X LT	X ST				X	
Diagonal call spread ITM	X LT			X ST			X
Diagonal put spread OOTM				X	X LT		X ST
Diagonal put spread ATM		X ST		X LT		X	
Diagonal put spread ITM	X ST			X LT			X

FIGURE 5.9

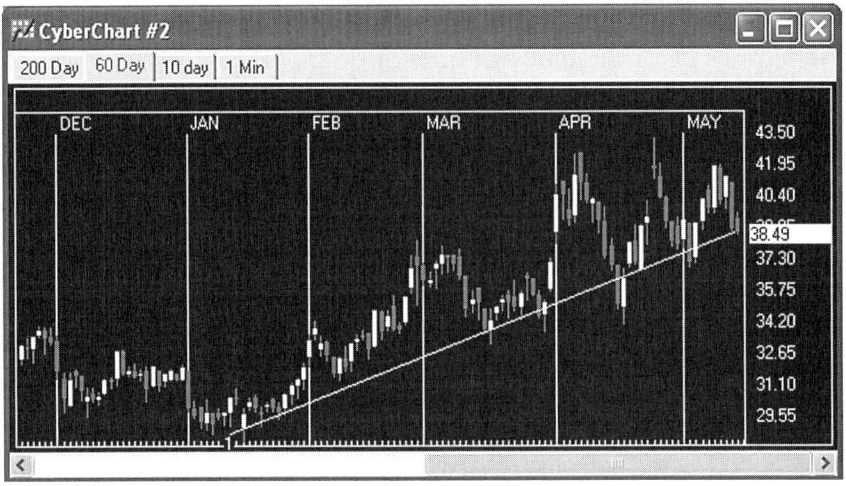

If you are very bullish, you may want to consider the following diagonal call spread. With diagonal spreads, you can calculate the long-term max gain (MG), max loss (ML), and one of the breakevens (BE) before you actually enter the trade. The short-term maximum gain (MG) on a diagonal credit spread will always be the amount of the initial credit.

Example 1

Buy 10 XYZ Aug 45 Calls @ 1.40

Sell 10 XYZ Jun 40 Calls @ 1.45

Credit = .05

BE = 44.95 (long position strike price – credit [or + debit])

MG = .05 + time value of the long calls (short term) (unlimited after June expiration)

ML = 4.95 (net of strikes – the credit [or + debit])

Total credit from this trade = $50 (credit × # of spreads × option multiplier) or (.05 × 10 × 100)

This example would be considered out-of-the-money, since the stock price is below the strike prices. Since Figure 5.9 presents data as of around May 9, the June options have about five weeks until expiration. By calculating the breakeven before you enter the trade, you can see that with an upper breakeven price of 44.95, you would want XYZ to stay below 40 until the June expiration and then rise above 44.95 by the August expiration to be profitable. The exact maximum profit in the near term will be the sum of the price of the August calls on the June expiration and the initial credit amount. This will occur if XYZ is at exactly 40 on the June expiration. The long-term maximum profit is unlimited. Losses will be incurred if XYZ moves sharply higher by the June expiration. After the June expiration, losses will be incurred if XYZ does not exceed 44.95 by the August expiration. The maximum loss at the June expiration occurs if the stock is greater than 45 and you are assigned on the June 40 calls. In this case you would have to exercise the August 45 calls or sell them and buy back your short position in XYZ. The long-term maximum loss occurs if XYZ stays below 40 in the near term and does not exceed 45 by the August expiration. When that occurs, the August calls will expire worthless and only the initial credit received is retained.

In Figure 5.10, you have identified XYZ stock, which appears to be in a long-term downtrend but is experiencing some short-term strength. As a result, you are expecting only minor declines in the near term but a continued downward move in the coming months.

If you are only slightly bearish, you may want to consider the following diagonal put spread. With diagonal spreads, you can calculate the long-term max gain (MG), max loss (ML), and one of the

FIGURE 5.10

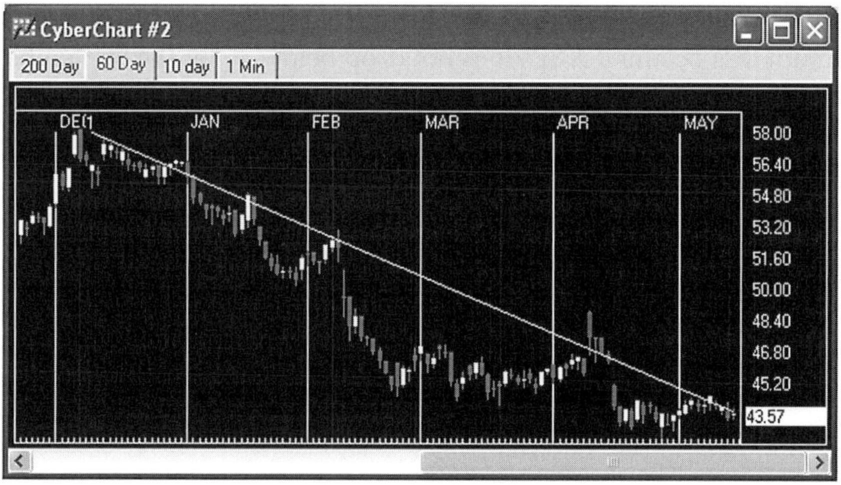

breakevens (BE) before you actually enter the trade. The maximum loss (ML) on a debit spread will always be the amount of the initial debit.

Example 2

Buy 10 XYZ Sep 45 Puts @ 3.30

Sell 10 XYZ Jun 40 Puts @ .30

Debit = 3.00

BE = 42.00 (long position strike price – debit [or + credit])

MG = 2.00 (short term); 42.00 (after June expiration)

ML = 3.00 (net debit paid)

Total cost of this trade = $3,000 (debit × # of spreads × option multiplier) or (3.00 × 10 × 100)

This example would be considered at-the-money, since the stock price is between the strike prices. Since Figure 5.10 presents data as of around May 9, the June options have about five weeks until expiration. By calculating the breakeven before you enter the trade, you can see that with a lower breakeven price of 42, you would want XYZ to stay above 40 until the June expiration and then stay below 45 by the September expiration to be profitable. The exact maximum profit in the near term will be the difference between the price of the September puts on the June expiration and the initial debit amount. This will occur if XYZ is at exactly 40 on the June expiration. The long-term maximum profit is 42 points. Losses will be incurred if XYZ moves sharply higher by the June expiration. After the June expiration, losses will be incurred if XYZ does not stay below 42 by the September expiration. The long-term maximum loss occurs if XYZ does not drop below 45 by the September expiration. When that occurs, the September puts will expire worthless and the initial debit paid is completely lost.

SECTION 4

Butterfly Spreads

CHAPTER 6

Standard Butterfly Spreads

Butterfly spreads offer you the opportunity to limit losses in exchange for a limited gain potential. They involve the simultaneous purchase and sale of options contracts of the same class (puts or calls), in the same expiration month, on the same underlying security, but there are three different strike prices involved.

BUTTERFLY SPREADS EXPLANATION

In many cases, butterfly spreads may require that you temporarily establish a long or short stock position. That resulting long or short position will need to be closed out in the market to fully realize the profit potential of the strategy. This is explained in more detail later in this chapter.

Two of the key concepts to understand before you begin trading butterfly spreads are how to determine your sentiment (whether you are breakout or neutral) and how to calculate the maximum loss (ML), maximum gain (MG), and breakeven points (BE). These calculations will vary depending upon whether the spread is initially established as a net debit or net credit and whether or not it is entered using calls or puts. Because of the unique profit and loss characteristics of butterfly spreads, the amount of the initial margin requirement is likely to be determined more by your broker than by industry regulations. In some cases you may be required to maintain funds in your account that exceed your maximum possible loss.

You can determine your sentiment and calculate the ML, MG, and BE for any butterfly strategy by applying the following rules:

1. Arrange your butterfly spread from lowest to highest strike price.
   a. Leg 1 is the contract with the lowest strike price, regardless of whether it is a put or a call.
   b. Leg 2 is the middle strike price, and the quantity should always be 2 × leg 1.
   c. Leg 3 is the highest strike price, and the quantity should be equal to leg 1.
2. Determine whether your sentiment is neutral or breakout on the spread.
   a. If legs 1 and 3 are buys and leg 2 is a sell, you are neutral.
      i. This is considered a long butterfly.
   b. If legs 1 and 3 are sells and leg 2 is a buy, you are breakout.
      i. This is considered a short butterfly.
3. Determine whether the spread was entered at a net debit or a net credit.
   a. A long butterfly is entered at a net debit.
   b. A short butterfly is entered at a net credit.
4. Calculate the **ML**.
   a. If long butterfly, the debit is the ML.
      i. The ML will occur at any price above the leg 3 strike price.
      ii. The ML will occur at any price below the leg 1 strike price.
   b. If short butterfly, the ML is lower strike – middle strike + the initial credit.
      i. The ML occurs at the middle strike price.
5. Calculate the **MG**.
   a. If long butterfly, the MG is the middle strike – lowest strike – debit.
      i. The MG occurs only at the middle strike price.
   b. If short butterfly, the MG is the initial credit received.
      i. The MG occurs above the highest strike price or below the lowest strike price.
6. Calculate the **BE**.

a. If long butterfly, the upper BE is the middle strike price + MG.
b. If long butterfly, the lower BE is the middle strike price – MG.
c. If short butterfly, the upper BE is the middle strike price + ML.
d. If short butterfly, the lower BE is the middle strike price – ML.

LONG BUTTERFLY SPREADS

The two most basic types of long butterfly spreads are long call butterflies and long put butterflies. Both are typically used when you have a neutral sentiment, but they sometimes differ by the amount of the initial debit you must pay to establish them. In both cases, you will buy the lowest strike price, sell twice as many of the middle strike price, and buy the highest strike price in a quantity equal to the first strike price. Since the outcome at expiration is virtually identical, often the decision whether to establish a long call butterfly or a long put butterfly can be made strictly on price alone. The amount of the initial debit may be 10 or 20 cents lower for one versus the other, and you can simply choose the lower one.

Calculate Your Limit Price

A butterfly spread is also a type of ratio spread. An important thing to learn about ratio spreads is how to specify a net debit or credit when entering an order. With a normal spread, you simply net the prices of the legs together. With a ratio spread, that will not work. In the example below, the first step is to reduce the ratio spread to the smallest common fraction. You do this by dividing by the greatest common factor. Then you would figure out the market price (also called the natural) by multiplying the number of contracts by the price and then netting the two legs together.

Example

Buy 9 XYZ May 60 Calls @ 3

Sell 18 XYZ May 65 Calls @ .75

Buy 9 XYZ May 70 Calls @ .10

9×18×9 reduces to 1×2×1 (all butterflies must reduce to 1×2×1)

Then:

1 × –3.00 = –3.00
2 × +.75 = +1.50
1 × –.10 = –.10

The natural or market price = 1.60 debit for each 1×2×1 spread. Since you divided by 9 to reduce the ratio, you know that there are 9 (1×2×1) spreads.

To calculate the total cost of this trade, you would multiply the net price by the number of spreads times the option multiplier: –1.60 × 9 × 100 = –$1,440.

Another way to approach this is to start with the amount you want to spend (or receive if entered for a credit) and work backward to determine your entry price. This method may be helpful if you are trying to reach a specific profit percentage target.

Example If you want to enter the following trade:

ZYX = 34

and you only have $1,335 available to spend

Buy 5 ZYXAG quoting 5.70–6
Sell 10 ZYXAH quoting 2–2.20
Buy 5 ZYXAI quoting .65–.70

Step 1 Reduce the 5×10×5 fraction to 1×2×1

Step 2 Multiply the buy sides by the ask and net them against the sell side times the bid:

1 × –6.00 = –6.00
2 × +2.00 = +4.00
1 × –.70 = –.70

Net debit at the market price would be –2.70. You know there are 5 spreads (since you divided by 5 to reduce the ratio), so the cost of the trade at the market would be $1,350. Since you only have $1,335 to spend, you must find a net debit (less than 2.70) that will cost no more than $1,335.

Figure this out with the following steps:

1. Divide 1,335 by 100 (the options multiplier) = 13.35.
2. Divide 13.35 by the number of spreads (5) = 2.67.
3. Convert 2.67 to the next lower nickel or dime increment.

a. Dime if all options are priced > 3, or nickel if at least one is < 3.

4. This spread could be entered at 2.65.
5. Calculate the total cost as 2.65 × 5 spreads × 100 = $1,325

Long Call Butterfly—Quick Overview

A long call butterfly is made up of one long call at the lowest strike, two short calls at the middle strike, and one long call at the highest strike, with the same strike price interval between all legs. All legs should also have the same expiration month. All sides of this spread are opening transactions, and the ratio of the second leg is always twice the number of contracts of the first and third legs. This strategy is actually made up of one debit call spread and one credit call spread combined together as a single strategy (see Figure 6.1).

At Entry The white line in Figure 6.1 represents what the strategy typically looks like at the point of entry. As expiration

FIGURE 6.1

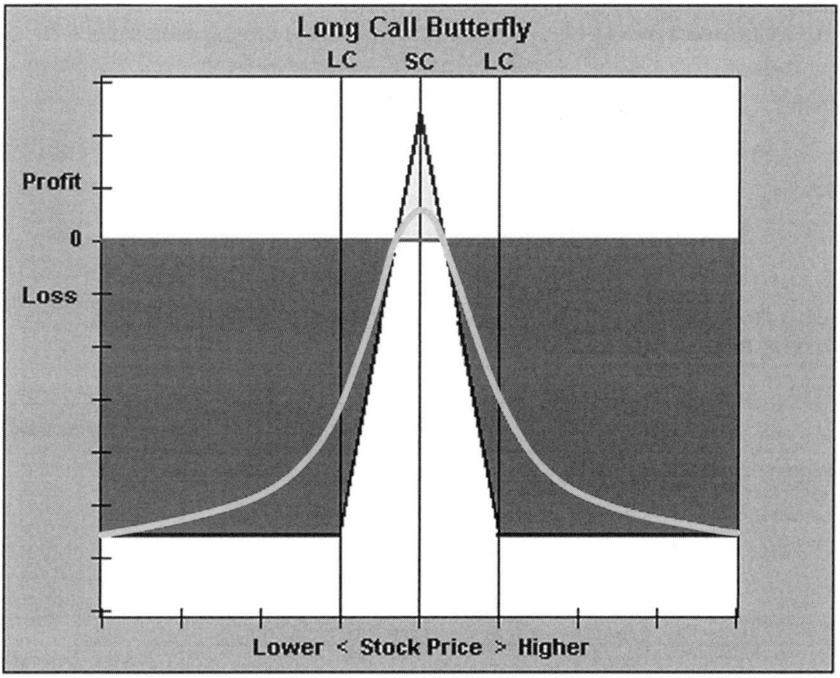

approaches, the curve moves toward the black lines, which illustrate the final profit and loss boundaries at expiration.

Direction Neutral with a bullish or bearish bias, depending upon the strike prices selected

When to Use You would typically employ a long call butterfly in neutral markets and would hope to profit if the underlying stock remains relatively flat until the expiration date of the options. Generally, the middle strike price should be about the same as the underlying stock price at the time of entry. If you are moderately bullish, higher strike prices should be used (stock slightly below the middle strike), and if you are moderately bearish, lower strike prices should be used (stock slightly above the middle strike).

Risk vs. Reward Limited risk with limited profit potential

Volatility The effect of volatility varies depending upon the strike prices chosen. This strategy generally benefits moderately from volatility decreases.

Time Decay The effect of time decay on this strategy varies with the underlying stock's price level in relation to the strike prices. If the stock price is between the outer strike prices, the effect is positive. If the stock price is above the upper strike price or below the lower strike price, the effect is negative (see Table 6.1).

Prior to Expiration

- Because the highest strike options have little value to begin with and the lowest strike options are in-the-money and

TABLE 6.1

Greeks	Below-the-money	At-the-money	Above-the-money
Delta	Positive	Neutral	Negative
Gamma	Negative	Negative	Negative
Theta	Negative	Positive	Negative
Vega	Positive	Negative	Positive

have a relatively small time value component, the middle strike options will lose time value more quickly than either of the long options.

  - As a result, with little or no movement in the underlying stock price, the spread can often be closed out at a profit prior to expiration, once time value has eroded sufficiently.
  - However, because of the large number of commissions involved, this strategy is typically held until expiration if the stock has remained relatively stable.

- Similarly, if the underlying stock rises or drops sharply enough, the spread can often be closed out at a loss that is less than the maximum loss possible if held until expiration, because time value will erode the value of the middle strike options more quickly.
  - Comparing the early close loss to the maximum potential loss at expiration can help you decide if holding until expiration makes sense.

At Expiration

- Below the lowest strike, all options expire worthless and max loss is sustained.
- Between the lowest and middle strikes, long stock will be acquired through exercise of the lowest strike. The long stock can then be sold in the market. The trade may or may not be profitable.
- Between the middle and highest strikes, short stock will be obtained through the exercise of the lowest strike and assignment on the two middle strikes. The short stock position can then be covered in the market. The trade may or may not be profitable.
- Above the highest strike, all options are exercised and/or assigned and max loss is sustained.

Long Call Butterfly—Detail

When you establish a long call butterfly, the combined cost of the first and third legs will exceed the amount you receive on the second leg. As a result, a long call butterfly is established at a net debit. This type of strategy is intended to take advantage of a stock that is moving sideways and is therefore considered a neutral strategy.

Example

Buy to open 10 XYZ Dec 55 Calls @ 6.00

Sell to open 20 XYZ Dec 60 Calls @ 1.50

Buy to open 10 XYZ Dec 65 Calls @ .50

Debit (DR) = –3.50 (–1st leg + [2 × 2nd leg] – 3rd leg)

Lower Breakeven (BE) = 58.50 (2nd strike – MG)

Upper Breakeven (BE) = 61.50 (2nd strike + MG)

Max Gain (MG) = 1.50 (2nd strike – 1st strike – debit) (occurs at 2nd strike)

Max Loss (ML) = –3.50 (debit paid) (occurs beyond the outside strike prices)

When you set up an order like this, most butterfly order entry systems automatically calculate the market price of this 10/20/10 spread. To do so manually, reduce the spread by its greatest common factor of 10 to 1/2/1. Then multiply each leg by the market price using the ask price on the legs you are buying and the bid price on the leg you are selling:

1 × –6.00 = –6.00

2 × +1.50 = +3.00

1 × –.50 = –.50

Net = –3.50 × 10 spreads × 100 shares per contract = ($3,500) total initial debt

Figure 6.2 depicts the profit/loss zones of this example, including the breakeven points at the option expiration date.

As you can see, the maximum gain on this strategy, which occurs only at a price of exactly 60 at expiration, is $1,500. There are two breakeven points at 58.50 and 61.50. All prices below 58.50 or above 61.50 result in a loss. The maximum loss on the upside or downside is –$3,500. To get a better feel for the profit and loss zones, see the following sample prices at expiration.

XYZ at 55 or below at expiration:	
Initial debt:	($3,500)
All options expire worthless:	-0-
Net loss of 3.50 × 10 spreads:	**= ($3,500)**

FIGURE 6.2

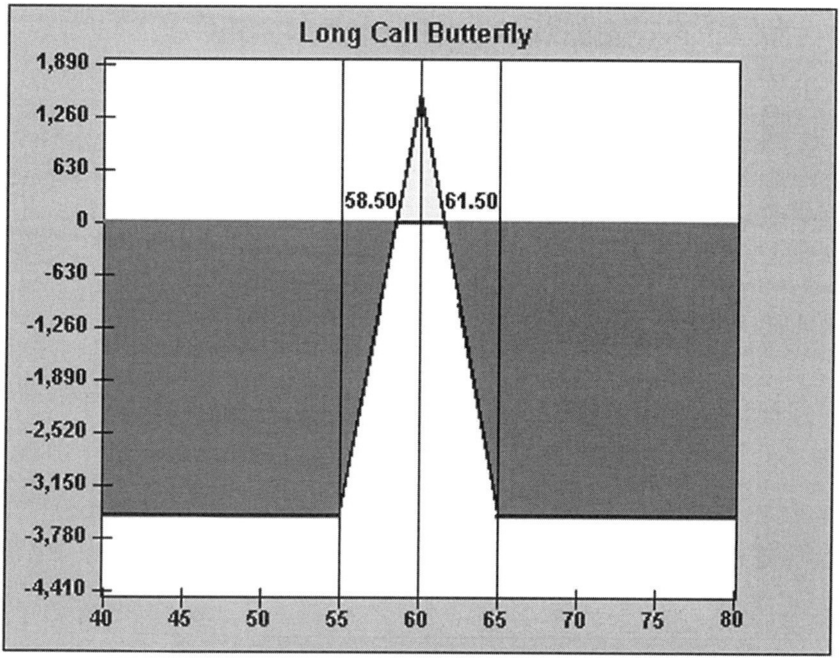

Strategy at Expiration

XYZ at 58.50 at expiration:	
Initial debt:	($3,500)
Exercise 55 calls & acquire 1,000 shares:	($55,000)
Sell 1,000 shares @ market:	$58,500
60 and 65 calls expire worthless:	-0-
Net profit/loss:	= $**0**

XYZ at 60 at expiration:	
Initial debt:	($3,500)
Exercise 55 calls & acquire 1,000 shares:	($55,000)
1,000 shares sold @ market:	$60,000
60 and 65 calls expire worthless:	-0-
Net profit/loss:	= **$1,500**

XYZ at 61.50 at expiration:	
Initial debt:	($3,500)

Exercise 55 calls & acquire 1,000 shares:	($55,000)
Called away on 2,000 shares at 60:	$120,000
1,000 short shares bought back @ market:	($61,500)
65 calls expire worthless:	-0-
Net profit/loss:	= **$0**

XYZ at 65 at expiration:

Initial debt:	($3,500)
Exercise 55 calls & acquire 1,000 shares:	($55,000)
Called away on 2,000 shares at 60:	$120,000
1,000 short shares bought back @ market:	($65,000)
65 calls expire worthless:	-0-
Net profit/loss:	= **($3,500)**

XYZ above 65 at expiration:

Initial debt:	($3,500)
Exercise 55 calls & acquire 1,000 shares:	($55,000)
Called away on 2,000 shares at 60:	$120,000

FIGURE 6.3

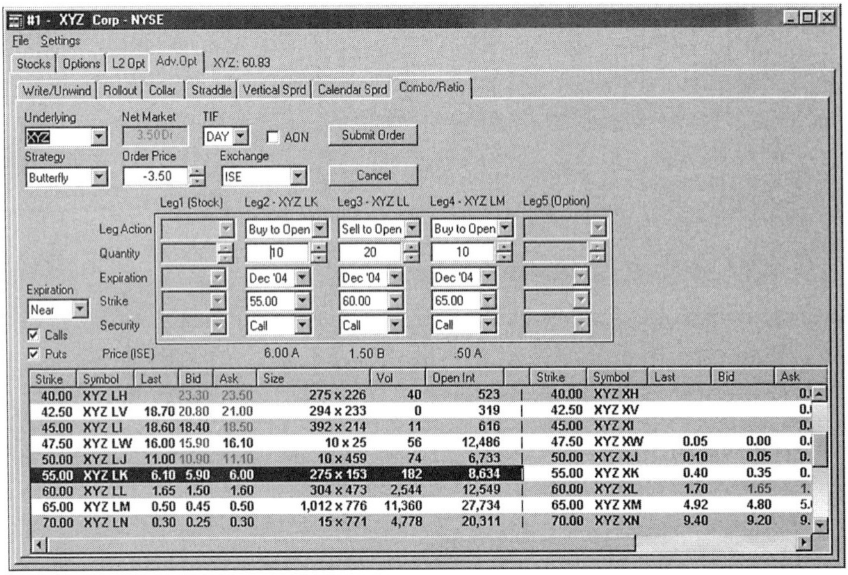

Exercise 65 calls & acquire 1,000 shares:	($65,000)
Net profit/loss:	= **($3,500)**

Figure 6.3 is the butterfly order entry screen within the CyberTrader Pro software that shows the sample trade above. This should help you visualize how this type of order is typically entered.

Long Put Butterfly—Quick Overview

A long put butterfly is made up of one long put at the lowest strike, two short puts at the middle strike, and one long put at the highest strike, with the same strike price interval between all legs. All legs should also have the same expiration month. All sides of this spread are opening transactions, and the ratio of the second leg is always twice the number of contracts of the first and third legs. This strategy is actually made up of one debit put spread and one credit put spread combined together as a single strategy (see Figure 6.4).

FIGURE 6.4

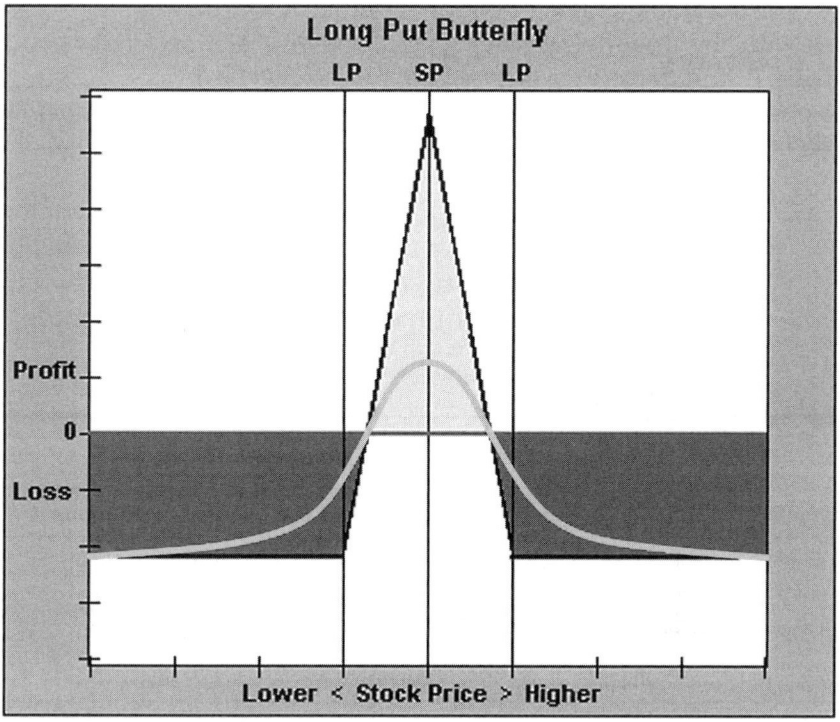

At Entry The white line in Figure 6.4 represents what the strategy typically looks like at the point of entry. As expiration approaches, the curve moves toward the black lines, which illustrate the final profit and loss boundaries at expiration.

Direction Neutral with a bullish or bearish bias, depending upon the strike prices selected

When to Use You would typically employ a long put butterfly in neutral markets and would hope to profit if the underlying stock remains relatively flat until the expiration date of the options. Generally, the middle strike price should be about the same as the underlying stock price at the time of entry. If you are moderately bullish, higher strike prices should be used (stock slightly below the middle strike), and if you are moderately bearish, lower strike prices should be used (stock slightly above the middle strike).

Risk vs. Reward Limited risk with limited profit potential

Volatility The effect of volatility varies depending upon the strike prices chosen. This strategy generally benefits moderately from volatility decreases.

Time Decay The effect of time decay on this strategy varies with the underlying stock's price level in relation to the strike prices. If the stock price is between the outer strike prices, the effect is positive. If the stock price is above the upper strike price or below the lower strike price, the effect is negative (see Table 6.2).

Prior to Expiration

- Because the lowest strike options have little value to begin with and the highest strike options are in-the-money and have a relatively small time value component, the middle

TABLE 6.2

Greeks	Below-the-money	At-the-money	Above-the-money
Delta	Positive	Neutral	Negative
Gamma	Negative	Negative	Negative
Theta	Negative	Positive	Negative
Vega	Positive	Negative	Positive

strike options will lose time value more quickly than either of the long options.

- As a result, with little or no movement in the underlying stock price, the spread can often be closed out at a profit prior to expiration, once time value has eroded sufficiently.
- However, because of the large number of commissions involved, this strategy is typically held until expiration if the stock has remained relatively stable.

- Similarly, if the underlying stock rises or drops sharply enough, the spread can often be closed out at a loss that is less than the maximum loss possible if held until expiration, because time value will erode the value of the middle strike options more quickly.
  - Comparing the early close loss to the maximum potential loss at expiration can help you decide if holding until expiration makes sense.

At Expiration

- Above the highest strike, all options expire worthless and max loss is sustained.
- Between the highest and middle strikes, short stock will be acquired through exercise of the highest strike. The short stock position can then be closed out in the market. The trade may or may not be profitable.
- Between the middle and lowest strikes, long stock will be obtained through the exercise of the highest strike and assignment on the two middle strikes. The long stock position can then be closed out in the market. The trade may or may not be profitable.
- Below the lowest strike, all options are exercised and/or assigned and max loss is sustained.

Long Put Butterfly—Detail

When you establish a long put butterfly, the combined cost of the first and third legs will exceed the amount you receive on the second leg. As a result, a long put butterfly is established at a net debit. This type of strategy is intended to take advantage of a stock that is moving sideways and is therefore considered a neutral strategy.

Example

Buy to open 5 XYZ Dec 55 Puts @ 1.00
Sell to open 10 XYZ Dec 60 Puts @ 2.80
Buy to open 5 XYZ Dec 65 Puts @ 6.00

Debit (DR) = –1.40 (–1st leg + [2 × 2nd leg] – 3rd leg)
Lower Breakeven (BE) = 56.40 (2nd strike – MG)
Upper Breakeven (BE) = 63.60 (2nd strike + MG)
Max Gain (MG) = 3.60 (2nd strike – 1st strike – debit) (occurs at 2nd strike)
Max Loss (ML) = –1.40 (debit paid) (occurs beyond the outside strike prices)

When you set up an order like this, most butterfly order entry systems automatically calculate the market price of this 5/10/5 spread. To do so manually, reduce the spread by its greatest common factor of 5 to 1/2/1. Then multiply each leg by the market price using the ask price on the legs you are buying and the bid price on the leg you are selling:

1 × –1.00 = –1.00
2 × +2.80 = +5.60
1 × –6.00 = –6.00
Net = –1.40 × 5 spreads × 100 shares per contract = ($700) total initial debt

Figure 6.5 depicts the profit/loss zones of this example, including the breakeven points at the option expiration date.

As you can see, the maximum gain on this strategy, which occurs only at a price of exactly 60 at expiration, is $1,800. There are two breakeven points at 56.40 and 63.60. All prices below 56.40 or above 63.60 result in a loss. The maximum loss on the upside or downside is –$700. To get a better feel for the profit and loss zones, see the following sample prices at expiration.

XYZ at 65 or above at expiration:

Initial debt:	($700)
All options expire worthless:	-0-
Net loss of 1.40 × 5 spreads:	**= ($700)**

XYZ at 63.60 at expiration:

Initial debt:	($700)

FIGURE 6.5

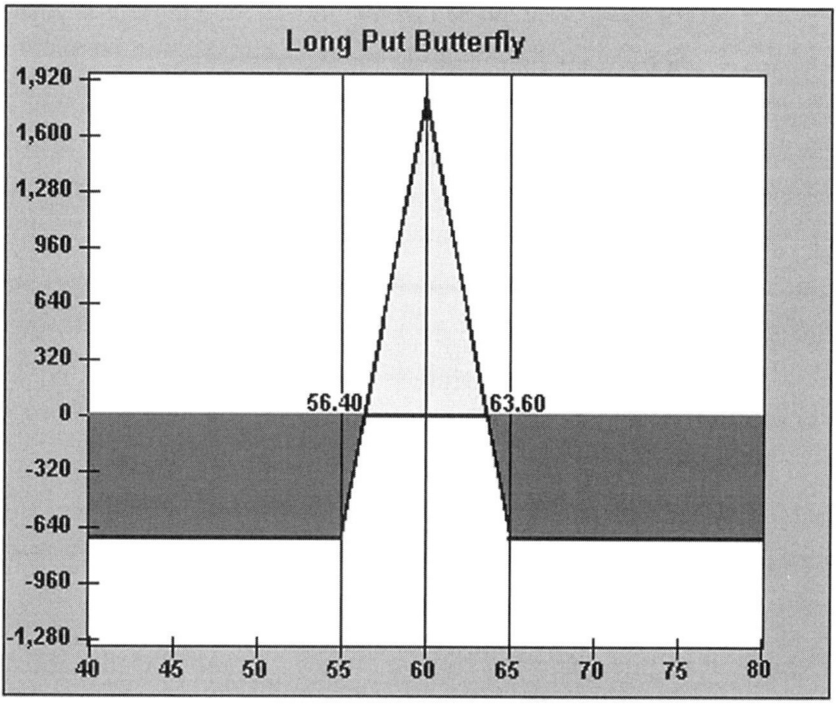

Strategy at Expiration

Exercise 65 puts to sell short 500 shares:	$32,500
Buy back 500 shares @ market:	($31,800)
60 and 55 puts expire worthless:	-0-
Net profit/loss:	= **$0**

XYZ at 60 at expiration:

Initial debt:	($700)
Exercise 65 puts to sell short 500 shares:	$32,500
Buy back 500 shares @ market:	($30,000)
60 and 55 puts expire worthless:	-0-
Net profit/loss:	= **$1,800**

XYZ at 56.40 at expiration:

Initial debt:	($700)
Exercise 65 puts to sell short 500 shares:	$32,500

Assigned on 60 puts to buy 1,000 shares:	($60,000)
500 long shares sold @ market:	$28,200
55 puts expire worthless:	-0-
Net profit/loss:	= **$0**

XYZ at 55 at expiration:

Initial debt:	($700)
Exercise 65 puts to sell short 500 shares:	$32,500
Assigned on 60 puts to buy 1,000 shares:	($60,000)
500 long shares sold @ market:	$27,500
55 puts expire worthless:	-0-
Net profit/loss:	= **($700)**

XYZ below 55 at expiration:

Initial debt:	($700)
Exercise 65 puts to sell short 500 shares:	$32,500
Assigned on 60 puts to buy 1,000 shares:	($60,000)
Exercise 55 puts to sell 500 shares:	$27,500
Net profit/loss:	= **($700)**

Figure 6.6 is the butterfly order entry screen within the CyberTrader Pro software that shows the sample trade above. This should help you visualize how this type of order is typically entered.

Characteristics

While a long butterfly is primarily a neutral strategy, it is possible to put a slightly bullish or bearish bias on it depending upon which strike prices you use. If you are completely neutral, you would want the stock to be as close to the middle strike price as possible at the time the butterfly is established. This would be an around-the-money (RTM) butterfly.

Table 6.3 illustrates how to properly structure a long butterfly spread to match your level of bullishness or bearishness. For example, if you are slightly bullish, you may want to consider a long call butterfly that is above-the-money (ABTM) or a long put butterfly that is below-the-money (BTM). By contrast, if you are slightly bearish, you may want to consider a long call butterfly that is below-the-money (BTM) or a long put butterfly that is above-the-money (ABTM).

FIGURE 6.6

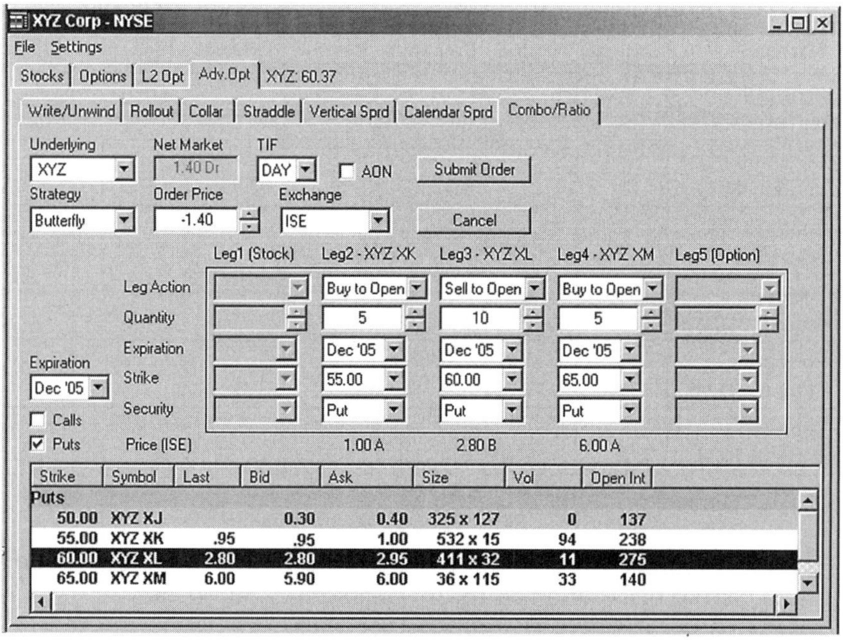

Remember, to maximize your profit, you want the stock to be as close to the middle strike price as possible on option expiration day.

Since your best chance of a profitable trade comes from a stock that stays within a certain range, you need to have a way of identifying which stocks might do this. Common sense would indicate that a stock most likely to stay range-bound in the near future might be one that has been range-bound for an extended period of time in the recent past. Therefore, when you are researching stocks, you can usually find good butterfly candidates by looking for stocks with the following criteria:

- In a 5–15 point channel for about 6–8 weeks or more.
- Currently trading in about the middle of that channel.
- No expected news or events coming up that might cause them to move out of that channel or cause a sharp increase in volatility.
  - Such as earnings or merger and acquisition news.

TABLE 6.3

	<< Direction >>				<< Magnitude >>		
Strategy	**Bullish**	**Neutral**	**Breakout**	**Bearish**	**Extreme**	**Moderate**	**Slight**
Long call butterfly ABTM	X						X
Long call butterfly RTM		X			X		
Long call butterfly BTM				X			X
Long put butterfly ABTM				X			X
Long put butterfly RTM		X			X		
Long put butterfly BTM	X						X

- Currently trading at a price that is near a standard option strike price, such as 15, 20, 22.50, 25, 27.50, 30, etc.

While these criteria might sound overly restrictive, you may be surprised how many good candidates you will find with only a little research. Once you have identified a potential butterfly through this process, it is often very helpful to view what the strategy might look like by drawing the important price levels on a chart. This will help you visualize where you may be profitable and how much the stock must break out in order for your strategy to be unprofitable. First, calculate the key price levels on a sample 2.5 point long call butterfly, so you will know where to draw the lines.

Example 1A

Buy 10 XYZ Feb 40 Calls @ 2.90
Sell 20 XYZ Feb 42.50 Calls @ 1.20
Buy 10 XYZ Feb 45 Calls @ .45

DR (Debit) = .95 (–2.90 + [2 × 1.20] – .45)
MG (Maximum Gain) = 1.55 (2nd strike – 1st strike – debit) (occurs at 2nd strike)

ML (Maximum Loss) = .95 (debit paid) (occurs at outside strike prices)

Upper BE (Breakeven) = 44.05 (2nd strike + MG)

Lower BE (Breakeven) = 40.95 (2nd strike – MG)

Total cost of this trade = $950 (DR × # of spreads × option multiplier) or (.95 × 10 × 100)

Once you have calculated the key price levels, you can draw them on a chart. The lines you will want to show on the chart are the outside strike prices of 40 and 45 (max loss levels) and the upper and lower breakeven levels of 40.95 and 44.05. On CyberTrader Pro or Schwab's StreetSmart Pro software, you can do this using the support line tool (red line) for the outer maximum loss lines and the resistance line tool (green line) for the breakeven thresholds, as illustrated in Figure 6.7.

The upper and lower red lines represent the outer strike (maximum loss) levels. The inner green lines represent the breakeven levels.

To ensure that the risk/reward characteristics of the butterfly you are considering are favorable, it is advisable to also calculate

FIGURE 6.7

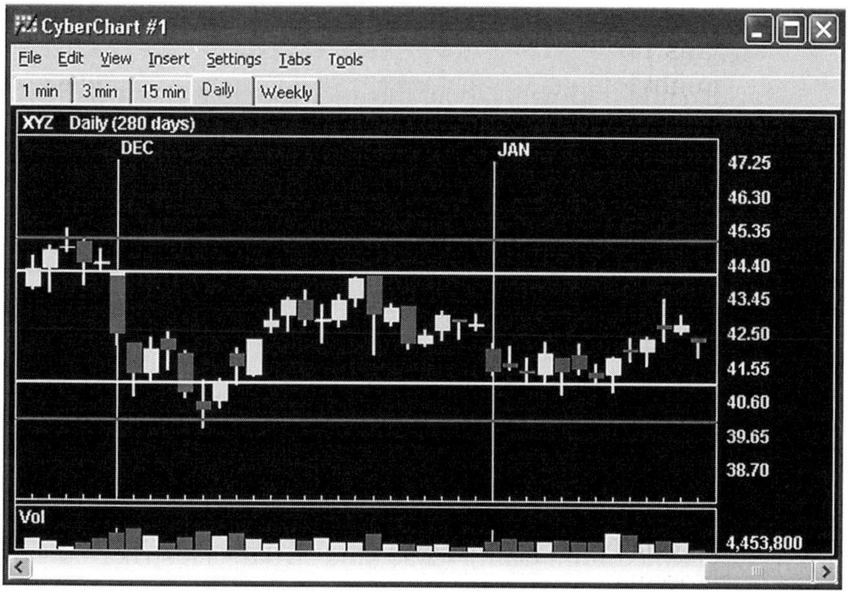

the MG/ML ratio and look for a value of at least 75%. In the example above, the MG/ML would be 1.55/.95 = 163%; this means the maximum potential profit is 163% of the maximum potential loss. Since Figure 6.7 presents data as of mid-January, the February butterfly you are considering has about 29 days until expiration. If XYZ is between 40.95 and 44.05 at the February option expiration, this trade may be profitable. The maximum profit will be reached if XYZ is at exactly 42.50 at expiration. Losses will be incurred if XYZ closes above 44.05 at expiration, with the maximum loss of $950 occurring at any price above 45. Likewise, losses will be incurred if XYZ closes below 40.95 at expiration, with the maximum loss of $950 also occurring at any price below 40.

As with most butterfly spreads, it is very unlikely that the stock will close *exactly* at the maximum profit price of 42.50. However, with a profit zone of 3.10 points (44.05 – 40.95), this candidate has a little room for normal market fluctuation. If the trade ends up profitable, the rate of return can be calculated by dividing the amount of the eventual gain ($0 up to $1,550) by the amount invested ($950). Thus your rate of return will be somewhere between 0% and 163%.

Example 1B illustrates a 5 point long call butterfly candidate with different profit and loss characteristics.

ZYX has the following characteristics:

- In a 10 point channel between about 50 and 60 for about six weeks
- Currently trading in about the middle of that channel (54.92)
- No expected news or events (such as an earnings report) coming up that might cause it to move out of that channel or cause a sharp increase in volatility
- Currently trading at a price that is near the standard option strike price of 55

Example 1B

Buy 5 ZYX Apr 50 Calls @ 5.40
Sell 10 ZYX Apr 55 Calls @ 1.45
Buy 5 ZYX Apr 60 Calls @ .20

DR (Debit) = 2.70 (–5.40 + [2 × 1.45] – .20)

MG (Maximum Gain) = 2.30 (2nd strike – 1st strike – debit) (occurs at 2nd strike)

ML (Maximum Loss) = 2.70 (debit paid) (occurs at outside strike prices)
Upper BE (Breakeven) = 57.30 (2nd strike + MG)
Lower BE (Breakeven) = 52.70 (2nd strike – MG)
Total cost of this trade = $1,350 (DR × # of spreads × option multiplier) or (2.70 × 5 × 100)

To ensure that the risk/reward characteristics of this butterfly are favorable, you calculate the MG/ML ratio and look for a value of at least 75%. In this example, the MG/ML would be 2.30/2.70 = 85%; this means the maximum potential profit is 85% of the maximum potential loss.

The lines you will want to show on the chart are the outside strike prices of 50 and 60 (represented by the red lines) and the upper and lower breakeven levels of 52.70 and 57.30 (represented by the green lines). Using the support and resistance line tools creates a chart as illustrated in Figure 6.8.

The upper and lower red lines represent the outer strike (max loss) levels. The inner green lines represent the breakeven levels.

FIGURE 6.8

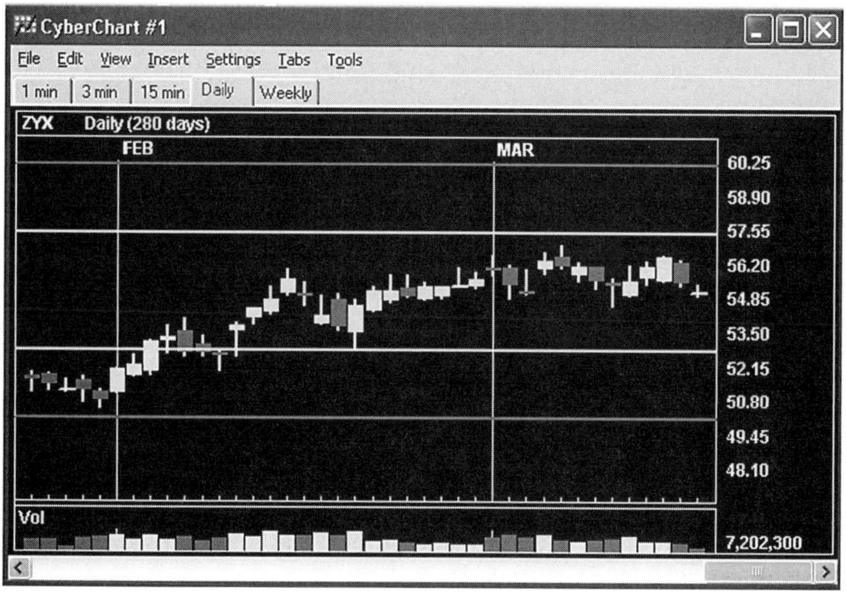

Since Figure 6.8 presents data as of around March 17, the April butterfly you are considering has about 28 days until expiration. If ZYX is between 52.70 and 57.30 at the April option expiration, this trade may be profitable. The maximum profit will be reached if ZYX is at exactly 55 at expiration. Losses will be incurred if ZYX closes above 57.30 at expiration, with the maximum loss of $1,350 occurring at any price above 60. Likewise, losses will be incurred if ZYX closes below 52.70 at expiration, with the maximum loss of $1,350 also occurring at any price below 50.

It is very unlikely that the stock will close *exactly* at the maximum profit price of 55. However, with a profit zone of 4.60 points (57.30 – 52.70), this candidate has a fair amount of room for normal market fluctuation, and a good chance of ending up profitable. If the trade is profitable, the profit will be between $0 and $1,150, with a rate of return somewhere between 0% and 85%.

While entering a three-legged order may seem complicated, there are a number of reasons why it makes sense to enter a butterfly as a single order, rather than two separate spreads.

Advantages

- Since you can specify a single price for the whole strategy, the market can fluctuate while your order is open, and there are number of different prices among the three options that will work out to your specified net debit.
- Since all three legs are part of the same order, they must execute in an equal 1×2×1 ratio or not at all.

Disadvantages

- Most of the option exchanges handle these orders manually, which could result is slower fill reports than you are used to on simpler orders.
- As of year-end 2005, only the International Securities Exchange (ISE) had the ability to execute butterflies in a fully electronic manner.

SHORT BUTTERFLY SPREADS

The two most basic types of short butterfly spreads are short call butterflies and short put butterflies. Both are typically used when you have a breakout sentiment, but they sometimes differ by the amount of the initial credit you can receive to establish them. In both cases, you will sell the lowest strike price, buy twice as many of the middle strike price, and sell the highest strike price in a quantity equal to the first strike price.

Any stock that you might consider a good candidate for a long straddle is probably a good candidate for a short butterfly. While a long straddle will generally only be profitable with a significant move in either direction, a short butterfly, by contrast, requires less movement, since a potential profit beyond a certain level in both directions is sold for a small premium. This premium lowers the maximum loss, since it moves the breakeven points closer to the starting point, requiring less movement to reach the potential profit zone.

Since the outcome at expiration is virtually identical, often the decision whether to establish a short call butterfly or a short put butterfly can be made strictly on price alone. The amount of the initial credit may be 10 or 20 cents higher for one versus the other, and you can simply choose the higher one.

Short Call Butterfly—Quick Overview

A short call butterfly is made up of one short call at the lowest strike, two long calls at the middle strike, and one short call at the highest strike, with the same strike price interval between all legs. All legs should also have the same expiration month. All sides of this spread are opening transactions, and the ratio of the second leg is always twice the number of contracts of the first and third legs. This strategy is actually made up of one debit call spread and one credit call spread combined together as a single strategy (see Figure 6.9).

At Entry The white line in Figure 6.9 represents what the strategy typically looks like at the point of entry. As expiration approaches, the curve moves toward the black lines, which illustrate the final profit and loss boundaries at expiration.

Direction Breakout with a bullish or bearish bias, depending upon the strike prices selected

When to Use You would typically employ a short call butterfly in uncertain markets and would hope to profit if the underlying stock breaks out either higher or lower than the current price by the expiration date of the options. Generally, the middle strike price should be about the same as the underlying stock price at the time of entry. If you are moderately bullish, higher strike prices

FIGURE 6.9

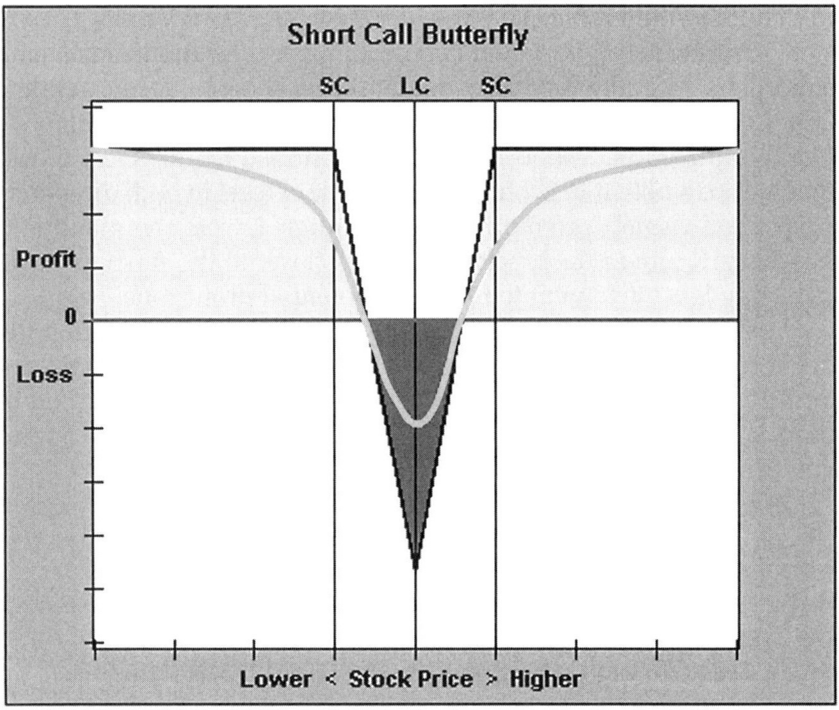

should be used (stock slightly below the middle strike), and if you are moderately bearish, lower strike prices should be used (stock slightly above the middle strike).

Risk vs. Reward Limited risk with limited profit potential

Volatility The effect of volatility varies depending upon the strike prices chosen. This strategy generally benefits moderately when volatility increases. Volatility benefit will be the greatest near the middle strike price.

Time Decay The effect of time decay on this strategy varies with the underlying stock's price level in relation to the strike prices. If the stock price is between the outer strike prices, the effect is negative. If the stock price is above the upper strike price or below the lower strike price, the effect is positive (see Table 6.4).

TABLE 6.4

Greeks	Below-the-money	At-the-money	Above-the-money
Delta	Positive	Neutral	Negative
Gamma	Positive	Positive	Positive
Theta	Positive	Negative	Positive
Vega	Positive	Positive	Positive

Prior to Expiration

- Because the highest strike options have little value to begin with and the lowest strike options are in-the-money and have a relatively small time value component, the middle strike options will lose time value more quickly than either of the short options.
    - As a result, with little or no movement in the underlying stock price, the spread can often be closed out at a loss that is less than the maximum loss possible if held until expiration, because time value will erode the value of the middle strike options more quickly.
- Similarly, if the underlying stock rises or drops sharply enough, the spread can often be closed out at a gain that is less than the maximum gain possible if held until expiration.
    - Comparing the early close gain to the maximum potential gain at expiration can help you decide if holding until expiration makes sense.
    - However, because of the large number of commissions involved, this strategy is typically held until expiration if the stock has begun to move higher or lower.

At Expiration

- Below the lowest strike, all options expire worthless and max gain is achieved.
- Between the lowest and middle strikes, short stock will be acquired through assignment of the lowest strike. The short

stock position can then be closed in the market. The trade may or may not be profitable.

- Between the middle and highest strikes, long stock will be obtained through the assignment of the lowest strike and exercise of the two middle strikes. The long stock may then be closed in the market. The trade may or may not be profitable.
- Above the highest strike, all options are exercised and/or assigned and max gain is achieved.

Short Call Butterfly—Detail

When you establish a short call butterfly, the combined credit from the first and third legs will be greater than the amount you spend on the second leg. As a result, a short call butterfly is established at a net credit. This type of strategy is intended to take advantage of a stock that is expected to rise or drop sharply and is therefore considered a breakout strategy.

Example

Sell to open 10 XYZ Dec 40 Calls @ 6.10

Buy to open 20 XYZ Dec 45 Calls @ 2.20

Sell to open 10 XYZ Dec 50 Calls @ .30

Credit (CR) = 2.00 (1st leg – [2 × 2nd leg] + 3rd leg)

Upper Breakeven (BE) = 48 (2nd strike + ML)

Lower Breakeven (BE) = 42 (2nd strike – ML)

Max Gain (MG) = 2.00 (credit received) (occurs beyond the outside strike prices)

Max Loss (ML) = 3.00 (1st strike – 2nd strike + credit) (occurs at 2nd strike)

When you set up an order like this, most butterfly order entry systems automatically calculate the market price of this 10/20/10 spread. To do so manually, reduce the spread by its greatest common factor of 10 to 1/2/1. Then multiply each leg by the market price, using the ask price on the leg you are buying and the bid price on the legs you are selling:

$1 \times +6.10 = +6.10$

$2 \times -2.20 = -4.40$

$1 \times +.30 = +.30$

Net = +2.00 × 10 spreads × 100 shares per contract = \$2,000 total initial credit

Figure 6.10 depicts the profit/loss zones of this example, including the breakeven points at the option expiration date.

As you can see, the maximum gain on this strategy, which occurs only above or below the outer strike prices at expiration, is \$2,000. There are two breakeven points at 42 and 48. All prices between 42 and 48 result in a loss. The maximum loss is –\$3,000 and occurs only at the middle strike price of 45. To get a better feel for the profit and loss zones, see the following sample prices at expiration.

XYZ at 40 or below at expiration:

Initial credit:	\$2,000
All options expire worthless:	-0-
Net gain of 2.00 × 10 spreads:	= **\$2,000**

FIGURE 6.10

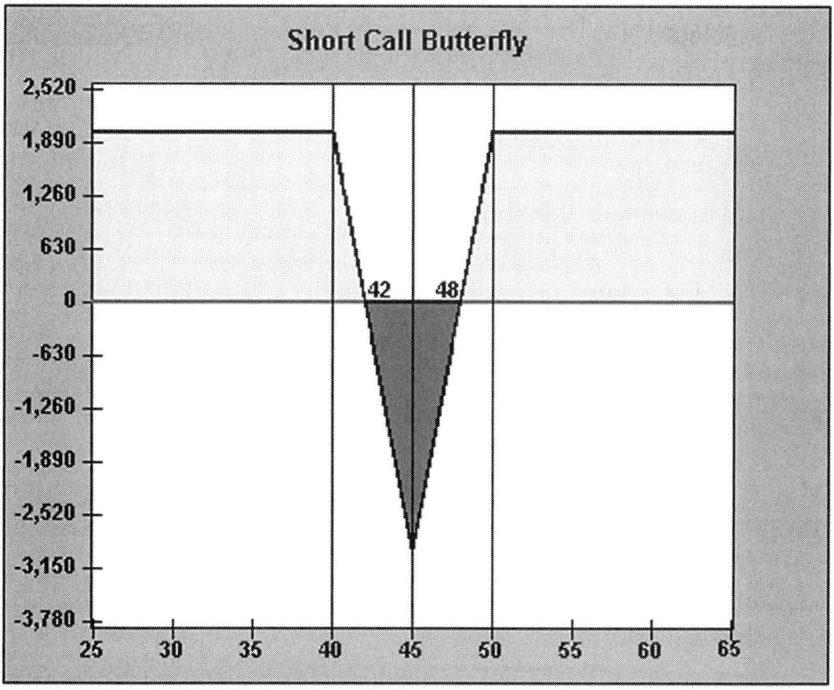

Strategy at Expiration

XYZ at 42 at expiration:

Initial credit:	$2,000
Called away on 1,000 shares @ 40:	$40,000
Buy back 1,000 shares @ market:	($42,000)
45 and 50 calls expire worthless:	-0-
Net profit/loss:	= **$0**

XYZ at 45 at expiration:

Initial credit:	$2,000
Called away on 1,000 shares @ 40:	$40,000
Buy back 1,000 shares @ market:	($45,000)
45 and 50 calls expire worthless:	-0-
Net profit/loss:	= **($3,000)**

XYZ at 48 at expiration:

Initial credit:	$2,000
Called away on 1,000 shares @ 40:	$40,000
Exercise calls and acquire 2,000 shares:	($90,000)
Sell 1,000 shares @ market:	$48,000
50 calls expire worthless:	-0-
Net profit/loss:	= **$0**

XYZ at 50 at expiration:

Initial credit:	$2,000
Called away on 1,000 shares @ 40:	$40,000
Exercise calls and acquire 2,000 shares:	($90,000)
Sell 1,000 shares @ market:	$50,000
50 calls expire worthless:	-0-
Net profit/loss:	= **$2,000**

XYZ above 50 at expiration:

Initial credit:	$2,000
Called away on 1,000 shares @ 40:	$40,000
Exercise calls and acquire 2,000 shares:	($90,000)
Called away on 1,000 shares @ 50:	$50,000
Net profit/loss:	= **$2,000**

Figure 6.11 is the butterfly order entry screen within the CyberTrader Pro software that shows the sample trade above. This should help you visualize how this type of order is typically entered.

Short Put Butterfly—Quick Overview

A short put butterfly is made up of one short put at the lowest strike, two long puts at the middle strike, and one short put at the highest strike, with the same strike price interval between all legs. All legs should also have the same expiration month. All sides of this spread are opening transactions, and the ratio of the second leg is always twice the number of contracts of the first and third legs. This strategy is actually made up of one debit put spread and one credit put spread combined together as a single strategy (see Figure 6.12).

FIGURE 6.11

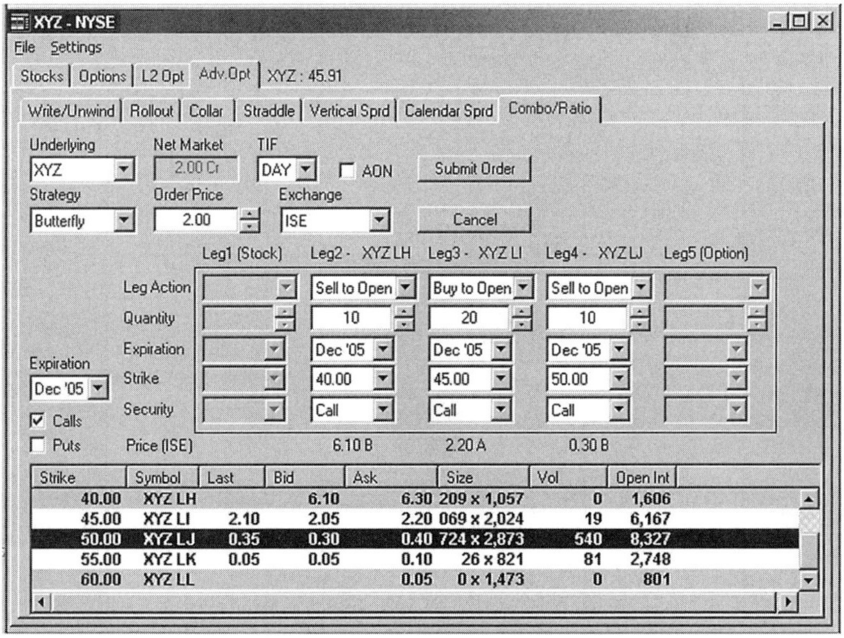

At Entry The white line in Figure 6.12 represents what the strategy typically looks like at the point of entry. As expiration approaches, the curve moves toward the black lines, which illustrate the final profit and loss boundaries at expiration.

Direction Breakout with a bullish or bearish bias, depending upon the strike prices selected

When to Use You would typically employ a short put butterfly in uncertain markets and would hope to profit if the underlying stock breaks out either higher or lower than the current price by the expiration date of the options. Generally, the middle strike price should be about the same as the underlying stock price at the time of entry. If you are moderately bullish, higher strike prices should be used (stock slightly below the middle strike), and if your

FIGURE 6.12

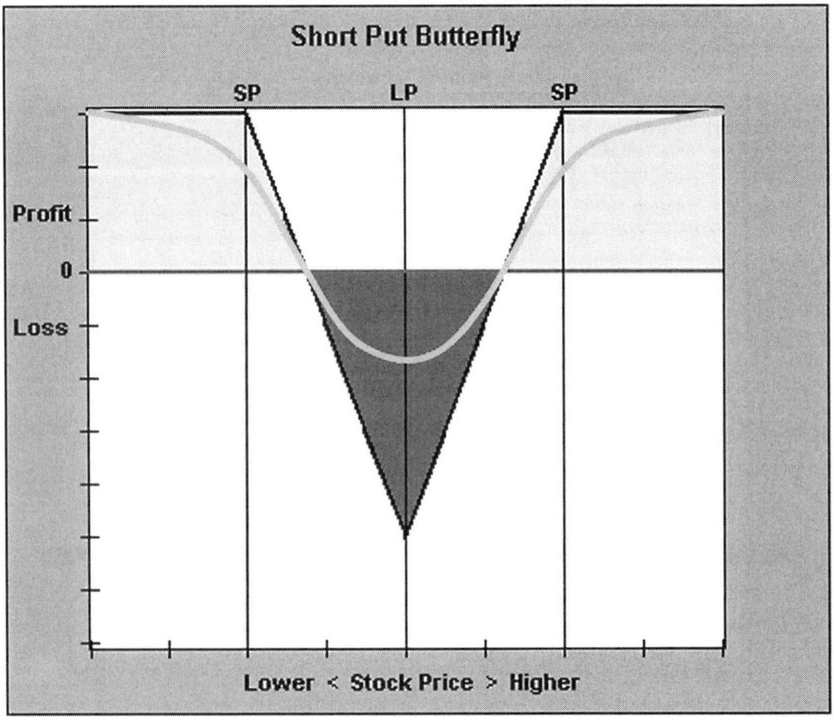

are moderately bearish, lower strike prices should be used (stock slightly above the middle strike).

Risk vs. Reward Limited risk with limited profit potential

Volatility The effect of volatility varies depending upon the strike prices chosen. This strategy generally benefits moderately when volatility increases. Volatility benefit will be the greatest near the middle strike price.

Time Decay The effect of time decay on this strategy varies with the underlying stock's price level in relation to the strike prices. If the stock price is between the outer strike prices, the effect is negative. If the stock price is above the upper strike price or below the lower strike price, the effect is positive (see Table 6.5).

Prior to Expiration

- Because the lowest strike options have little value to begin with and the highest strike options are in-the-money and have a relatively small time value component, the middle strike options will lose time value more quickly than either of the short options.
  - As a result, with little or no movement in the underlying stock price, the spread can often be closed out at a loss that is less than the maximum loss possible if held until expiration, because time value will erode the value of the middle strike options more quickly.
- Similarly, if the underlying stock rises or drops sharply enough, the spread can often be closed out at a gain that is less than the maximum gain possible if held until expiration.

TABLE 6.5

Greeks	Below-the-money	At-the-money	Above-the-money
Delta	Negative	Neutral	Positive
Gamma	Positive	Positive	Positive
Theta	Positive	Negative	Positive
Vega	Positive	Positive	Positive

- Comparing the early close gain to the maximum potential gain at expiration can help you decide if holding until expiration makes sense.
- However, because of the large number of commissions involved, this strategy is typically held until expiration if the stock has begun to move higher or lower.

At Expiration

- Below the lowest strike, all options are exercised and/or assigned and max gain is achieved.
- Between the lowest and middle strikes, long stock will be acquired through assignment of the lowest strike. The long stock position can then be closed in the market. The trade may or may not be profitable.
- Between the middle and highest strikes, short stock will be obtained through the assignment of the lowest strike and exercise of the two middle strikes. The short stock may then be closed in the market. The trade may or may not be profitable.
- Above the highest strike, all options expire worthless and max gain is achieved.

Short Put Butterfly—Detail

When you establish a short put butterfly, the combined credit from the first and third legs will be greater than the amount you spend on the second leg. As a result, a short put butterfly is established at a net credit. This type of strategy is intended to take advantage of a stock that is expected to rise or drop sharply and is therefore considered a breakout strategy.

Example

Sell to open 2 XYZ Nov 105 Puts @ .50
Buy to open 4 XYZ Nov 115 Puts @ 2.80
Sell to open 2 XYZ Nov 125 Puts @ 8.60

Credit (CR) = 3.50 (1st leg – [2 × 2nd leg] + 3rd leg)
Upper Breakeven (BE) = 121.50 (2nd strike + ML)
Lower Breakeven (BE) = 108.50 (2nd strike – ML)
Max Gain (MG) = 3.50 (credit received) (occurs beyond the outside strike prices)

Max Loss (ML) = 6.50 (1st strike – 2nd strike + credit)
(occurs at 2nd strike)

When you set up an order like this, most butterfly order entry systems automatically calculate the market price of this 2/4/2 spread. To do so manually, reduce the spread by its greatest common factor of 2 to 1/2/1. Then multiply each leg by the market price, using the ask price on the leg you are buying and the bid price on the legs you are selling:

1 × +.50 = +.50

2 × –2.80 = –5.60

1 × +8.60 = +8.60

Net = +3.50 × 2 spreads × 100 shares per contract = $700 total initial credit

Figure 6.13 depicts the profit/loss zones of this example, including the breakeven points at the option expiration date.

Strategy at Expiration As you can see, the maximum gain on this strategy, which occurs only above or below the outer strike prices at expiration, is $700. There are two breakeven points at 108.50 and 121.50. All prices between 108.50 and 121.50 result in a loss. The maximum loss is –$1,300 and occurs only at the middle strike price of 115. To get a better feel for the profit and loss zones, see the following sample prices at expiration.

XYZ at or above 125 at expiration:

Initial credit:	$700
All options expire worthless:	-0-
Net gain of 3.50 × 2 spreads:	= **$700**

XYZ at 121.50 at expiration:

Initial credit:	$700
Assigned on 200 shares @ 125:	($25,000)
Sell 200 shares @ market:	$24,300
115 and 105 puts expire worthless:	-0-
Net profit/loss:	= **$0**

XYZ at 115 at expiration:

Initial credit:	$700
Assigned on 200 shares @ 125:	($25,000)
Sell 200 shares @ market:	$23,000

FIGURE 6.13

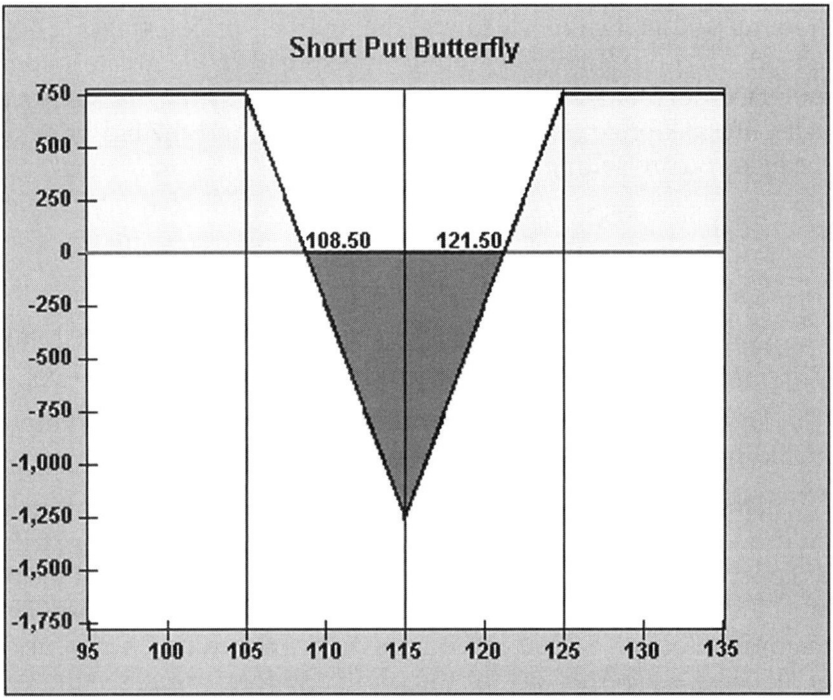

Strategy at Expiration

115 and 105 puts expire worthless:	-0-
Net profit/loss:	= **($1,300)**

XYZ at 108.50 at expiration:

Initial credit:	$700
Assigned on 200 shares @ 125:	($25,000)
Exercise 115 puts & sell 400 shares:	$46,000
Buy back 200 shares @ market:	($21,700)
105 puts expire worthless:	-0-
Net profit/loss:	= $**0**

XYZ at 105 at expiration:

Initial credit:	$700
Assigned on 200 shares @ 125:	($25,000)

Exercise 115 puts & sell 400 shares:	$46,000
105 puts expire worthless:	-0-
Buy back 200 shares @ market:	($21,000)
Net profit/loss:	**= $700**

XYZ below 105 at expiration:

Initial credit:	$700
Assigned on 200 shares @ 125:	($25,000)
Exercise 115 puts & sell 400 shares:	$46,000
Assigned on 200 shares @ 105:	($21,000)
Net profit/loss:	**= $700**

Figure 6.14 is the butterfly order entry screen within the CyberTrader Pro software that shows the sample trade above. This should help you visualize how this type of order is typically entered.

FIGURE 6.14

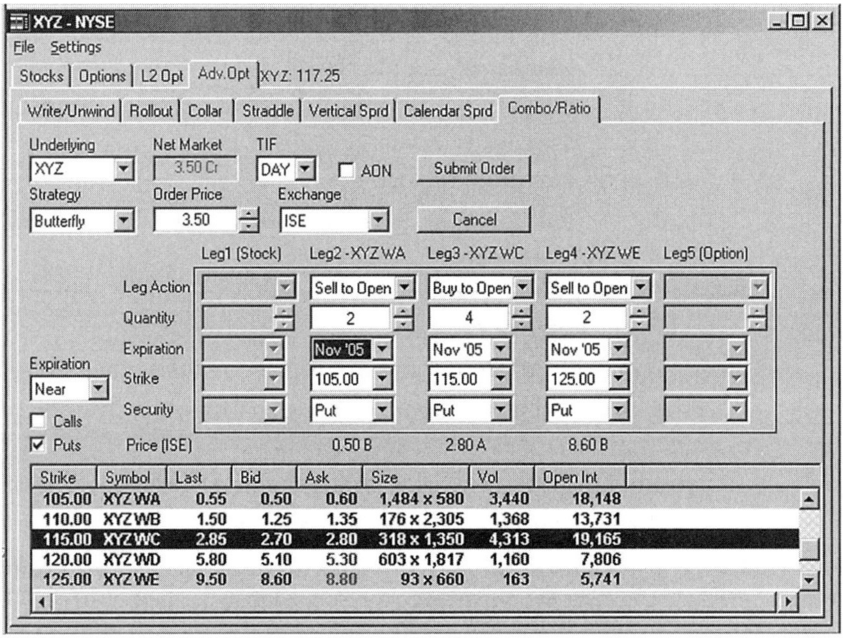

Characteristics

While a short butterfly is primarily a breakout strategy, it is possible to put a slightly bullish or bearish bias on it, depending upon which strike prices you use. If you are completely neutral, you would want the stock to be as close to the middle strike price as possible at the time the butterfly is established. Doing so will typically give you the largest initial credit and provide an equal chance of the stock going higher or lower into the profit ranges of your strategy. This would be an around-the-money (RTM) butterfly.

Table 6.6 illustrates how to properly structure a short butterfly spread to match your level of bullishness or bearishness. For example, if you are slightly bullish, you may want to consider a short call butterfly that is below-the-money (BTM) or a short put butterfly that is above-the-money (ABTM). By contrast, if you are slightly bearish, you may want to consider a short call butterfly that is above-the-money (ABTM) or a short put butterfly that is below-the-money (BTM). Remember, to maximize your potential profit, you want the stock above the highest strike price or below the lowest strike price on option expiration day.

Since your best chance of a profitable trade comes from a stock that breaks out of a certain range, you need to have a way of identifying which stocks might do this. Therefore, when you are researching stocks, you can usually find good short butterfly candidates by looking for stocks with the following criteria:

- Expecting a sharp move in either direction due to pending news.
  - Such as an earnings report.
- Typically a volatile stock, but has recently been less volatile than normal.
  - The theory of volatility mean reversion would anticipate a pickup in volatility.
- Recent consolidation around a support or resistance level.
  - After consolidation, stocks typically break out higher or lower.
- Currently trading at a price that is near a standard option strike price, such as 15, 20, 22.50, 25, 27.50, 30, etc.

While these criteria might sound overly restrictive, you may be surprised how many good candidates you will find with only

TABLE 6.6

Strategy	<< Direction >>				<< Magnitude >>		
	Bullish	Neutral	Breakout	Bearish	Extreme	Moderate	Slight
Short call butterfly ABTM				X		X	
Short call butterfly RTM			X			X	
Short call butterfly BTM	X					X	
Short put butterfly ABTM	X					X	
Short put butterfly RTM			X			X	
Short put butterfly BTM				X		X	

a little research. Once you have identified a potential short butterfly through this process, it is often very helpful to view what the strategy might look like by drawing the important price levels on a chart. This will help you visualize where you will be unprofitable and how much the stock must break out in order for your strategy to be profitable. Using the sample 5 point short call butterfly discussed previously in this chapter, review the key price levels so you will know where to draw the lines on the chart.

Example 2A

Sell to open 10 XYZ Dec 40 Calls @ 6.10
Buy to open 20 XYZ Dec 45 Calls @ 2.20
Sell to open 10 XYZ Dec 50 Calls @ .30

Credit (CR) = 2.00 (1st leg – [2 × 2nd leg] + 3rd leg)
Upper Breakeven (BE) = 48 (2nd strike + ML)
Lower Breakeven (BE) = 42 (2nd strike – ML)
Max Gain (MG) = 2.00 (credit received) (occurs beyond the outside strike prices)
Max Loss (ML) = 3.00 (1st strike – 2nd strike + credit) (occurs at 2nd strike)

Total credit from this trade = \$2,000 (CR × # of spreads × option multiplier) or (2.00 × 10 × 100)

Once you have calculated the key price levels, you can draw them on a chart. The lines you will want to show on the chart are the outside strike prices of 40 and 50 (max gain levels) and the upper and lower breakeven levels of 42 and 48. On CyberTrader Pro or Schwab's StreetSmart Pro software, you can do this using the support line tool (red line) for the outer BE lines, and the resistance line tool (green line) for the MG thresholds as illustrated in Figure 6.15.

The upper and lower green lines represent the outer strike (max gain) levels. The inner red lines represent the breakeven levels. To be profitable, XYZ must be outside the red lines by December option expiration.

Since Figure 6.15 presents data as of around October 31, the December short call butterfly you are considering has about 46 days until expiration. If XYZ is below 42 or above 48 at the December option expiration, this trade will be profitable. The maximum profit will be reached if XYZ is below 40 or above 50 at expiration. Losses will be incurred if XYZ closes between 42 and 48 at expiration, with the maximum loss of \$3,000 occurring at 45.

FIGURE 6.15

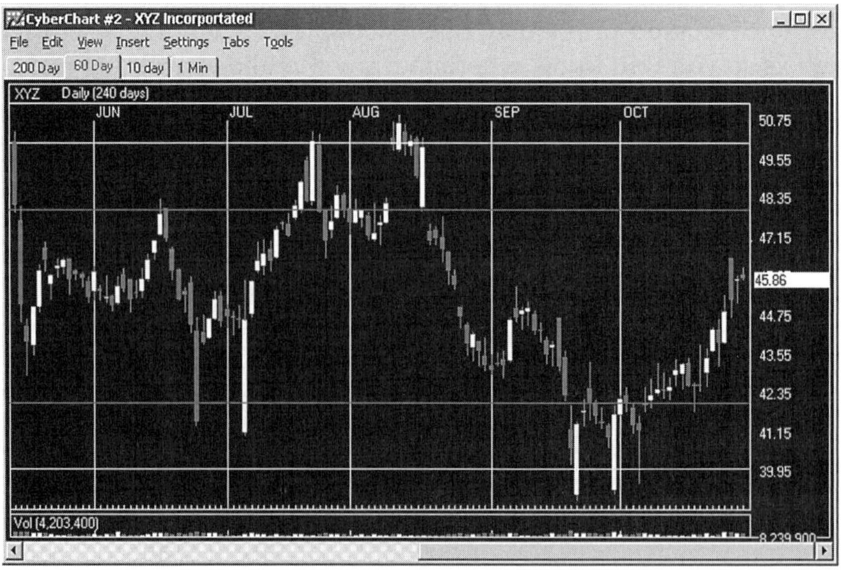

As with most short butterfly spreads, it is very unlikely that the stock will close *exactly* at the maximum loss price of 45. Though this chart shows a stock that has been very volatile, with a loss zone of 6 points (42–48), this stock needs to move up at least 2.14 points or down at least 3.86 points to be profitable. Your broker will also require you to hold a margin deposit equal to the maximum loss amount of $3,000 in your account, to cover any possible losses.

Example 2B

Sell to open 2 XYZ Nov 105 Puts @ .50
Buy to open 4 XYZ Nov 115 Puts @ 2.80
Sell to open 2 XYZ Nov 125 Puts @ 8.60

Credit (CR) = 3.50 (1st leg – [2 × 2nd leg] + 3rd leg)
Upper Breakeven (BE) = 121.50 (2nd strike + ML)
Lower Breakeven (BE) = 108.50 (2nd strike – ML)
Max Gain (MG) = 3.50 (credit received) (occurs beyond the outside strike prices)
Max Loss (ML) = 6.50 (1st strike – 2nd strike + credit) (occurs at 2nd strike)
Total credit from this trade = $700 (CR × # of spreads × option multiplier) or (3.50 × 2 × 100)

Using the sample 10 point short put butterfly discussed previously, review the key price levels so you will know where to draw the lines on the chart.

Once you have calculated the key price levels, you can draw them on a chart. The lines you will want to show on the chart are the outside strike prices of 105 and 125 (maximum gain levels) and the upper and lower breakeven levels of 108.50 and 121.50. On CyberTrader Pro or Schwab's StreetSmart Pro software, you can do this using the support line tool (red line) for the outer BE lines and the resistance line tool (green line) for the MG thresholds as illustrated in Figure 6.16.

The upper and lower green lines represent the outer strike (max gain) levels. The inner red lines represent the breakeven levels. To be profitable, XYZ must be outside the red lines by December option expiration.

Since Figure 6.16 presents data as of around October 31, the November short put butterfly you are considering has about 46 days until expiration. If XYZ is below 108.50 or above 121.50 at the November option expiration, this trade will be profitable. The maximum profit will be reached if XYZ is below 105 or above 125 at expiration.

FIGURE 6.16

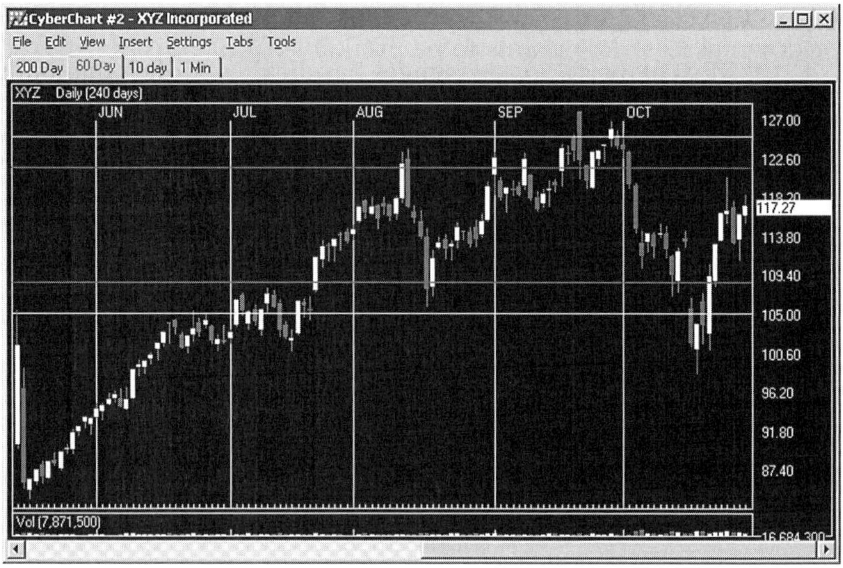

Losses will be incurred if XYZ closes between 108.50 and 121.50 at expiration, with the maximum loss of $1,300 occurring at 115.

As with most short butterfly spreads, it is very unlikely that the stock will close *exactly* at the maximum loss price of 115. Though this chart shows a stock that has been very volatile, with a loss zone of 13 points (108.50–121.50), this stock needs to move up at least 4.23 points or down at least 8.77 points to be profitable. Your broker will also require you to hold a margin deposit equal to the maximum loss amount of $1,300 in your account, to cover any possible losses.

While entering a three-legged order may seem complicated, there are a number of reasons why it makes sense to enter a butterfly as a single order rather than two separate spreads.

Advantages

- Since you can specify a single price for the whole strategy, the market can fluctuate while your order is open, and there are a number of different prices among the three options that will work out to your specified net debit.

- Since all three legs are part of the same order, they must execute in an equal 1×2×1 ratio or not at all.

Disadvantages

- Most of the option exchanges handle these orders manually, which could result is slower fill reports than you are used to on simpler orders.
- As of year-end 2005, only the International Securities Exchange (ISE) had the ability to execute butterflies in a fully electronic manner.

CHAPTER 7

Iron Butterfly Spreads

Standard butterfly spreads offer you the opportunity to limit losses in exchange for a limited gain potential. They involve the simultaneous purchase and sale of options contracts of the same class (puts or calls), in the same expiration month, on the same underlying security, at three different strike prices. By contrast, iron butterflies involve buying and selling of both puts *and* calls at three different strike prices in the same expiration month, on the same underlying security.

IRON BUTTERFLY SPREADS EXPLANATION

In many cases, butterfly spreads may require that you temporarily establish a long or short stock position. That resulting long or short position will need to be closed out in the market to fully realize the profit potential of the strategy. This is explained in more detail later in this chapter.

Two of the key concepts to understand before you begin trading butterfly spreads are how to determine your sentiment (whether you are breakout or neutral) and how to calculate the maximum loss (ML), maximum gain (MG), and breakeven points (BE). With iron butterflies, these calculations will vary depending upon whether the spread is initially established as a net debit or net credit. Because of the unique profit and loss characteristics of iron butterfly spreads, the amount of the initial margin requirement and the maintenance margin requirement is likely to be determined more by your broker than by industry regulations. In some cases you may be required to maintain funds in your account that exceed your maximum possible loss. You can determine your sentiment and calculate the ML, MG, and BE for any iron butterfly strategy by applying the following rules:

1. Arrange your iron butterfly spread from lowest to highest strike price.
   a. Leg 1 is the put contract with the lowest strike price.
   b. Leg 2 is the put contract with the next highest strike price.
   c. Leg 3 is the call contract with the same strike price as leg 2.
   d. Leg 4 is the call contract with the highest strike price.
2. Determine whether your sentiment is neutral or breakout on the spread.
   a. If legs 1 and 4 are buys, you are neutral.
      i. This is considered a long iron butterfly.
   b. If legs 1 and 4 are sells, you are breakout.
      i. This is considered a short iron butterfly.
3. Determine whether the spread was entered at a net debit or a net credit.
   a. A long iron butterfly is entered at a net credit.
   b. A short iron butterfly is entered at a net debit.
4. Calculate the **ML**.
   a. If long iron butterfly, the ML is lower strike - middle strike + the initial credit.
      i. The ML will occur at any price above the leg 4 strike price.
      ii. The ML will occur at any price below the leg 1 strike price.
   b. If short iron butterfly, the debit is the ML.
      i. The ML occurs at the middle strike price.
5. Calculate the **MG**.
   a. If long iron butterfly, the MG is the initial credit received.
      i. The MG occurs only at the middle strike price.
   b. If short iron butterfly, the MG is the middle strike – lowest strike – debit.

   i. The MG occurs above the highest strike price or below the lowest strike price.
6. Calculate the **BE**.
   a. If long iron butterfly, the upper BE is the middle strike price + MG.
   b. If long iron butterfly, the lower BE is the middle strike price – MG.
   c. If short iron butterfly, the upper BE is the middle strike price + ML.
   d. If short iron butterfly, the lower BE is the middle strike price – ML.

TYPES OF IRON BUTTERFLY SPREADS

The are only two types of iron butterfly spreads, long iron butterflies and short iron butterflies. Long iron butterflies are used when you have a neutral sentiment, and short iron butterflies are used when you have a breakout sentiment. They also differ by whether you pay an initial debit or receive an initial credit when you establish them. Unlike standard long and short butterflies, iron butterflies involve buying and selling of both puts and calls, and they have four legs instead of just three. Since a long iron butterfly has profit and loss characteristics that are very similar to a long butterfly, which one you choose may be based primarily on whether you would rather receive a credit initially or pay a debit up front. If you are considering a long iron butterfly, it is a good idea to calculate the breakeven points for both the long iron butterfly and the long butterfly to ensure that you trade the one that is most beneficial. This comparison will be made in more detail later in this chapter.

Long Iron Butterfly—Quick Overview

A long iron butterfly is made up of one long put at the lowest strike, one short put at the middle strike, one short call at the same middle strike, and one long call at the highest strike, with the same strike price interval between all legs. All legs should also have the same expiration month. All sides of this spread are opening transactions, and the ratio of all the legs is always 1/1/1/1. This strategy is actually made up of one credit put spread and one credit call spread combined together as a single strategy (see Figure 7.1).

FIGURE 7.1

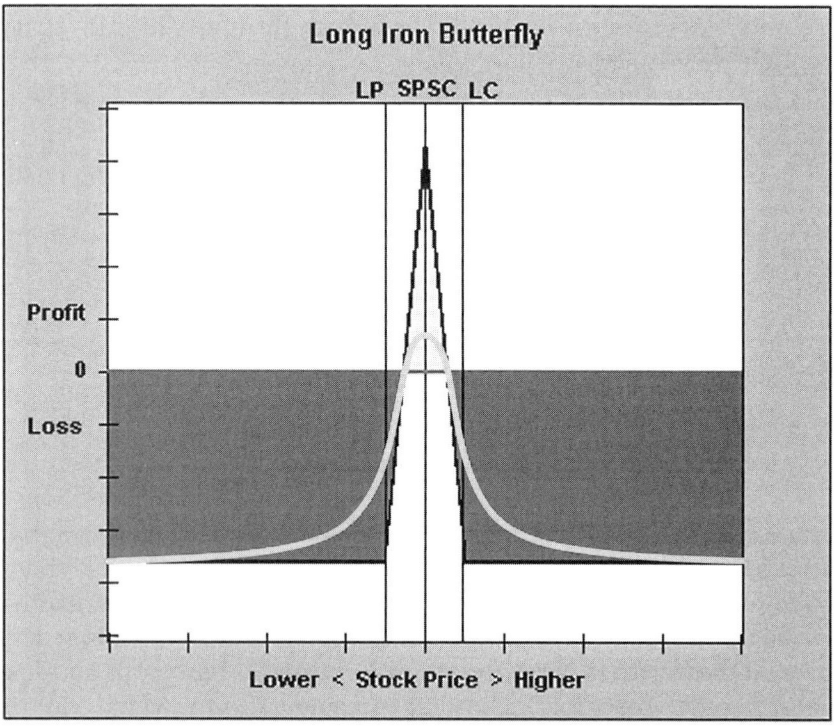

At Entry The white line in Figure 7.1 represents what the strategy typically looks like at the point of entry. As expiration approaches, the curve moves toward the black lines, which illustrate the final profit and loss boundaries at expiration.

Direction Neutral

When to Use You would typically employ a long iron butterfly in neutral markets and would hope to profit if the underlying stock remains relatively flat until the expiration date of the options. Generally, the middle strike price should be about the same as the underlying stock price at the time of entry. If you are moderately bullish or bearish, you could use strike prices that are slightly higher or lower, but this strategy generally works best when you stay closest to the middle.

Risk vs. Reward Limited risk with limited profit potential

Volatility The effect of volatility is negative. This strategy benefits from volatility decreases.

Time Decay The effect of time decay on this strategy varies with the underlying stock's price level in relation to the strike prices. If the stock price is between the outer strike prices, the effect is positive. If the stock price is above the upper strike price or below the lower strike price, the effect is negative (see Table 7.1).

Prior to Expiration

- Because the highest and lowest strike options have little value to begin with, the middle strike options will lose time value more quickly than either of the long options.
  - As a result, with little or no movement in the underlying stock price, the spread can often be closed out at a profit prior to expiration, once time value has eroded sufficiently.
  - However, because of the large number of commissions involved, this strategy is typically held until expiration if the stock has remained relatively stable.
- Similarly, if the underlying stock rises or drops sharply enough, the spread can often be closed out at a loss that is less than the maximum loss possible if held until expiration, because time value will erode the value of the middle strike options more quickly.
  - Comparing the early close loss to the maximum potential loss at expiration can help you decide if holding until expiration makes sense.

TABLE 7.1

Greeks	Below-the-money	At-the-money	Above-the-money
Delta	Positive	Neutral	Negative
Gamma	Negative	Negative	Negative
Theta	Negative	Positive	Negative
Vega	Positive	Negative	Positive

At Expiration

- Below the lowest strike, the short puts will be assigned, the long puts will be exercised, and max loss is sustained.
- Between the lowest and middle strikes, long stock will be acquired through assignment of the short puts. The long stock can then be sold in the market. The trade may or may not be profitable.
- Between the middle and highest strikes, short stock will be acquired through assignment of the short calls. The short stock position can then be closed out in the market. The trade may or may not be profitable.
- Above the highest strike, the short calls are assigned, the long calls are exercised, and max loss is sustained.

Long Iron Butterfly—Detail

When you establish a long iron butterfly, the combined credit from the second and third legs will exceed the combined cost of the first and fourth legs. As a result, a long iron butterfly is established at a net credit. This type of strategy is intended to take advantage of a stock that is moving sideways and is therefore considered a neutral strategy.

Example

Buy to open 10 XYZ Jan 22.50 Puts @ .10
Sell to open 10 XYZ Jan 25 Puts @ .45
Sell to open 10 XYZ Jan 25 Calls @ 1.30
Buy to open 10 XYZ Jan 27.50 Calls @ .30

Credit (CR) = 1.35 (–1st leg + 2nd leg + 3rd leg–4th leg)
Lower Breakeven (BE) = 23.65 (middle strike – MG)
Upper Breakeven (BE) = 26.35 (middle strike + MG)
Max Gain (MG) = 1.35 (initial credit amount) (occurs at middle strike)
Max Loss (ML) = –1.15 (1st strike – 2nd strike + MG) (occurs beyond the outside strike prices)

When you set up an order like this, most butterfly order entry systems automatically calculate the market price of this 10/10/10/10 spread. To do so manually, reduce the spread by its greatest common factor of 10 to 1/1/1/1. Then multiply each leg by the market price using the ask price on the legs you are buying and the bid price on the legs you are selling:

1 × –.10 = –.10

1 × +.45 = +.45

1 × +1.30 = +1.30

1 × –.30 = –.30

Net = +1.35 × 10 spreads × 100 shares per contract = $1,350 total initial credit

Figure 7.2 depicts the profit/loss zones of this example, including the breakeven points at the option expiration date.

As you can see, the maximum gain on this strategy, which occurs only at a price of exactly 25 at expiration, is $1,350. There are two breakeven points at 23.65 and 26.35. All prices below 23.65 or

FIGURE 7.2

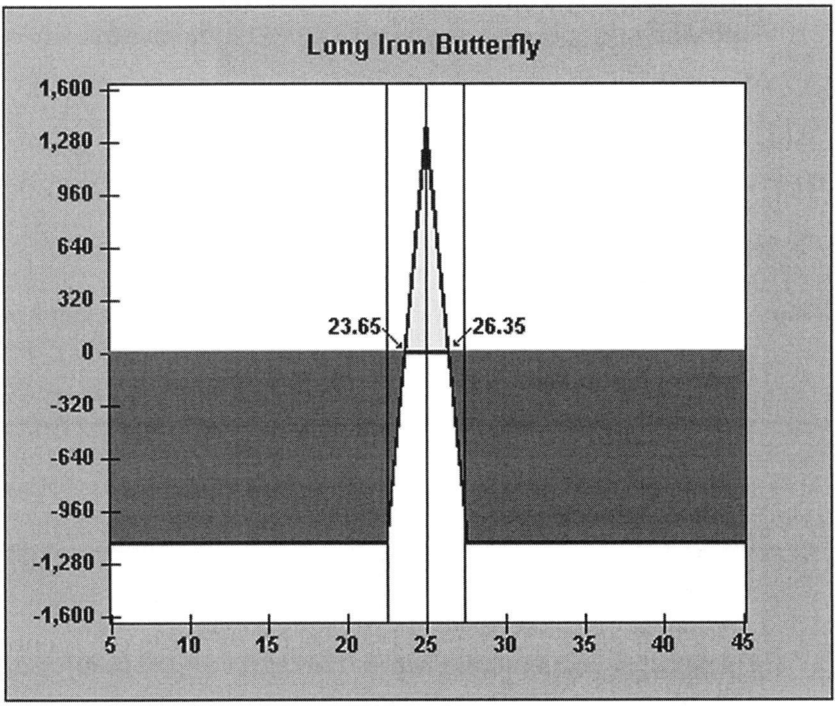

Strategy at Expiration

above 26.35 result in a loss. The maximum loss on the upside or downside is –$1,150. To get a better feel for the profit and loss zones, see the following sample prices at expiration.

XYZ below 22.50 at expiration:	
Initial credit:	$1,350
Exercise long puts:	$22,500
Assigned on short 25 puts to buy 1,000 shares:	($25,000)
All calls expire worthless:	-0-
Net profit/loss:	= **($1,150)**

XYZ at 23.65 at expiration:	
Initial credit:	$1,350
Long puts expire worthless:	-0-
Assigned on 25 puts to buy 1,000 shares:	($25,000)
Sell 1,000 shares @ market:	$23,650
All calls expire worthless:	-0-
Net profit/loss:	= $**0**

XYZ at 25 at expiration:	
Initial credit:	$1,350
All puts expire worthless:	-0-
All calls expire worthless:	-0-
Net profit/loss:	= **$1,350**

XYZ at 26.35 at expiration:	
Initial credit:	$1,350
All puts expire worthless:	-0-
Assigned on 25 calls to sell short 1,000 shares:	$25,000
1,000 short shares bought back @ market:	($26,350)
27.50 calls expire worthless:	-0-
Net profit/loss:	= $**0**

XYZ at 27.50 at expiration:	
Initial credit:	$1,350
All puts expire worthless:	-0-
Assigned on 25 calls to sell short 1,000 shares:	$25,000
1,000 short shares bought back @ market:	($27,500)
27.50 calls expire worthless:	-0-
Net profit/loss:	= **($1,150)**

XYZ above 27.50 at expiration:

Initial credit:	$1,350
All puts expire worthless:	-0-
Assigned on 25 calls to sell short 1,000 shares:	$25,000
Exercise 27.50 calls to cover short stock:	($27,500)
Net profit/loss:	= **($1,150)**

Figure 7.3 is the entry screen within the CyberTrader Pro software that shows the sample trade above. This should help you visualize how this type of order is typically entered.

Short Iron Butterfly—Quick Overview

A short iron butterfly is made up of one short put at the lowest strike, one long put at the middle strike, one long call at the same middle strike, and one short call at the highest strike, with the same strike price interval between all legs. All legs should also have the same expiration month. All sides of this spread are opening transactions,

FIGURE 7.3

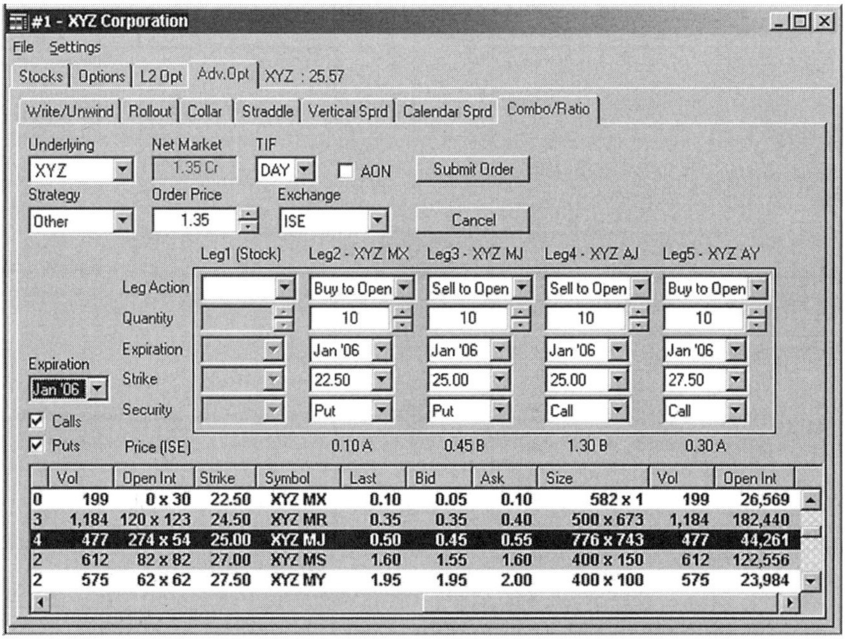

and the ratio of all the legs is always 1/1/1/1. This strategy is actually made up of one debit put spread and one debit call spread combined together as a single strategy (see Figure 7.4).

At Entry The white line in Figure 7.4 represents what the strategy typically looks like at the point of entry. As expiration approaches, the curve moves toward the black lines, which illustrate the final profit and loss boundaries at expiration.

Direction Breakout

When to Use You would typically employ a short iron butterfly in neutral markets and would hope to profit if the underlying stock breaks out in either direction by the expiration date of the options. Generally, the middle strike price should be about the same as the underlying stock price at the time of entry. If you are moderately bullish or bearish, you could use strike prices that are

FIGURE 7.4

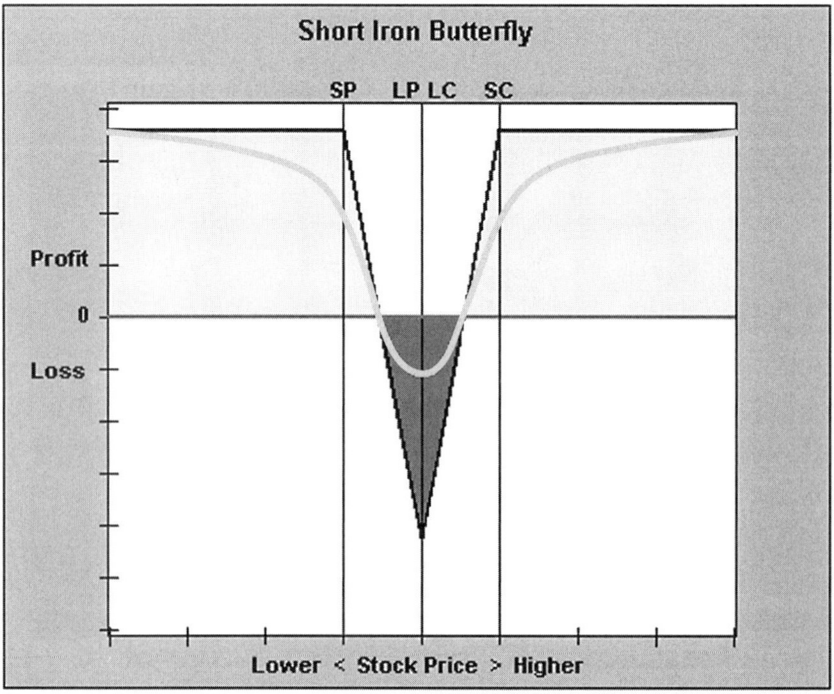

slightly higher or lower, but this strategy generally works best when you stay closest to the middle.

Risk vs. Reward Limited risk with limited profit potential

Volatility The effect of volatility is positive. This strategy benefits from volatility increases.

Time Decay The effect of time decay on this strategy varies with the underlying stock's price level in relation to the strike prices. If the stock price is between the outer strike prices, the effect is negative. If the stock price is above the upper strike price or below the lower strike price, the effect is positive (see Table 7.2).

Prior to Expiration

- Because the highest and lowest strike options have little value to begin with, the middle strike options will lose time value more quickly than either of the long options.
  - As a result, with little or no movement in the underlying stock price, the spread can often be closed out at a loss that is less than the maximum loss possible if held until expiration, because time value will erode the value of the middle strike options more quickly.
- Similarly, if the underlying stock rises or drops sharply enough, the spread can often be closed out at a gain that is less than the maximum gain possible if held until expiration.
  - Comparing the early close gain to the maximum potential gain at expiration can help you decide if holding until expiration makes sense.

TABLE 7.2

Greeks	Below-the-money	At-the-money	Above-the-money
Delta	Negative	Neutral	Positive
Gamma	Positive	Positive	Positive
Theta	Positive	Negative	Positive
Vega	Positive	Positive	Positive

- However, because of the large number of commissions involved, this strategy is typically held until expiration if the stock has begun to move higher or lower.

At Expiration

- Below the lowest strike, the short puts will be assigned, the long puts will be exercised, and max gain will be achieved.
- Between the lowest and middle strikes, short stock will be acquired through exercise of the long puts. The short stock can then be covered in the market. The trade may or may not be profitable.
- Between the middle and highest strikes, long stock will be acquired through exercise of the long calls. The long stock position can then be closed out in the market. The trade may or may not be profitable.
- Above the highest strike, the long calls are exercised, the short calls are assigned, and max gain is achieved.

Short Iron Butterfly—Detail

When you establish a short iron butterfly, the combined debit from the second and third legs will exceed the combined credit of the first and fourth legs. As a result, a short iron butterfly is established at a net debit. This type of strategy is intended to take advantage of a stock that is expected to move sharply in either direction and is therefore considered a breakout strategy.

Example

Sell to open 10 XYZ Dec 40 Puts @ .20
Buy to open 10 XYZ Dec 45 Puts @ 1.05
Buy to open 10 XYZ Dec 45 Calls @ 2.20
Sell to open 10 XYZ Dec 50 Calls @ .30

Debit (DR) = 2.75 (1st leg – 2nd leg – 3rd leg + 4th leg)
Lower Breakeven (BE) = 42.25 (middle strike – ML)
Upper Breakeven (BE) = 47.75 (middle strike + ML)
Max Gain (MG) = 2.25 (2nd strike – 1st strike – ML) (occurs beyond the outside strike prices)
Max Loss (ML) = –2.75 (initial debit amount) (occurs at middle strike)

When you set up an order like this, most butterfly order entry systems automatically calculate the market price of this 10/10/10/10 spread. To do so manually, reduce the spread by its greatest common factor of 10 to 1/1/1/1. Then multiply each leg by the market price, using the ask price on the legs you are buying and the bid price on the legs you are selling:

1 × +.20 = +.20
1 × –1.05 = –1.05
1 × –2.20 = –2.20
1 × +.30 = +.30
Net = –2.75 × 10 spreads = ($2,750) total initial debit

Figure 7.5 depicts the profit/loss zones of this example, including the breakeven points at the option expiration date.

FIGURE 7.5

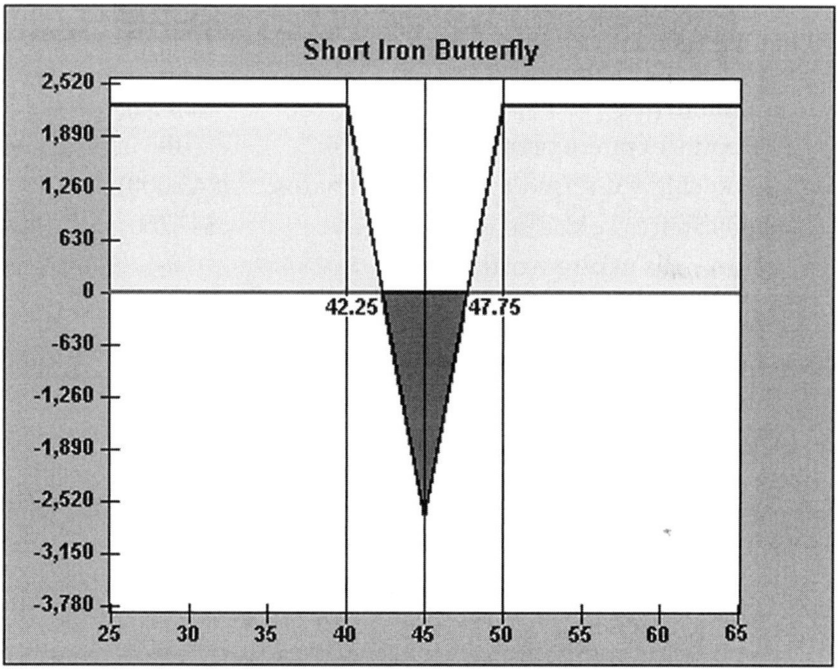

Strategy at Expiration

As you can see, the maximum gain on this strategy, which occurs only above or below the outer strike prices at expiration, is $2,250. There are two breakeven points at 42.25 and 47.75. All prices between 42.25 and 47.75 result in a loss. The maximum loss is –$2,750 and occurs only at the middle strike price of 45. To get a better feel for the profit and loss zones, see the following sample prices at expiration.

XYZ above 50 at expiration:

Initial debit:	($2,750)
All puts expire worthless:	-0-
Long calls exercised to buy 1,000 shares:	($45,000)
Short calls assigned to sell 1,000 shares:	$50,000
Net profit/loss:	= **$2,250**

XYZ at 50 at expiration:

Initial debit:	($2,750)
All puts expire worthless:	-0-
Long calls exercised to buy 1,000 shares:	($45,000)
1,000 shares sold @ market:	$50,000
Short calls expire worthless:	-0-
Net profit/loss:	= **$2,250**

XYZ at 47.75 at expiration:

Initial debit:	($2,750)
All puts expire worthless:	-0-
Long calls exercised to buy 1,000 shares:	($45,000)
1,000 shares sold @ market:	$47,750
Short calls expire worthless:	-0-
Net profit/loss:	= $**0**

XYZ at 45 at expiration:

Initial debit:	($2,750)
All puts expire worthless:	-0-
All calls expire worthless:	-0-
Net profit/loss:	= **($2,750)**

XYZ at 42.25 at expiration:

Initial debit:	($2,750)
Exercise long puts & sell 1,000 shares:	$45,000
Short puts expire worthless:	-0-

Buy back 1,000 shares @ market:	($42,250)
All calls expire worthless	-0-
Net profit/loss:	= $0

XYZ at 40 at expiration:

Initial debit:	($2,750)
Exercise long puts & sell 1,000 shares:	$45,000
Short puts expire worthless:	-0-
Buy back 1,000 shares @ market:	($40,000)
All calls expire worthless	-0-
Net profit/loss:	**= $2,250**

XYZ below 40 at expiration:

Initial debit:	($2,750)
Exercise long puts & sell 1,000 shares:	$45,000
Assigned on short puts to cover 1,000 shares:	($40,000)
All calls expire worthless	-0-
Net profit/loss:	**= $2,250**

FIGURE 7.6

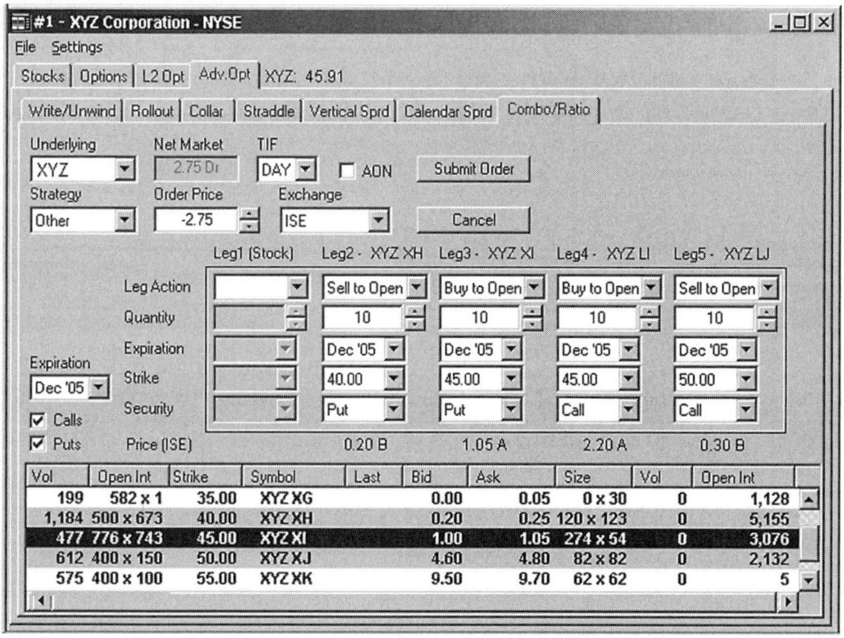

Figure 7.6 is the butterfly order entry screen within the CyberTrader Pro software that shows the sample trade above. This should help you visualize how this type of order is typically entered.

Characteristics

A long iron butterfly is primarily a neutral strategy, and a short iron butterfly is primarily a breakout strategy. Both are typically most effective when the underlying stock is at the middle strike price at the point of entry. If you have a slightly bullish or bearish bias, a standard butterfly is usually a better choice.

As Table 7.3 illustrates, since a long iron butterfly is a credit strategy, it will generally require the underlying stock to remain extremely neutral, due to the typically narrow profit zone. A slightly wider profit zone can sometimes (though not always) be obtained with the same neutral sentiment by using a long standard butterfly spread. However, a long standard butterfly spread will require you to pay a debit up front, rather than receive a credit. A short iron butterfly by contrast is a debit strategy, and will generally require a moderate breakout in order to reach profitability, due to the typically narrow loss zone. This breakout can sometimes (though not always) be slightly less than is required for a short standard butterfly, but it also requires you to pay a debit up front, rather than receive a credit.

Long Iron Butterfly Since your best chance of a profitable trade comes from a stock that stays within a certain range, you

TABLE 7.3

	<< Direction >>				<< Magnitude >>		
Strategy	**Bullish**	**Neutral**	**Breakout**	**Bearish**	**Extreme**	**Moderate**	**Slight**
Long iron butterfly		X			X		
Short iron butterfly			X			X	

need to have a way of identifying which stocks might do this. Common sense would indicate that a stock most likely to stay range-bound in the near future might be one that has been range-bound for an extended period of time in the recent past. Therefore, when you are researching stocks, you can usually find good long iron butterfly candidates by looking for stocks with the following criteria:

- In a 5–15 point channel for about 6–8 weeks or more.
- Currently trading in about the middle of that channel.
- No expected news or events coming up that might cause them to move out of that channel or cause a sharp increase in volatility.
  - Such as earnings or merger and acquisition news.
- Currently trading at a price that is near a standard option strike price, such as 15, 20, 22.50, 25, 27.50, 30, etc.

You will notice that these criteria are identical to those for a long standard butterfly. See the stock chart examples in Chapter 6 on long standard butterflies for illustrations on how to draw the important price levels on a stock chart.

To help you determine which strategy makes the most sense, compare the two side by side for the same underlying stock and then decide based on the advantages or disadvantages. Below is a comparison using the same example used previously in this chapter for the long call butterfly (see Figure 7.7) versus a comparable long iron butterfly (see Figure 7.8).

Example

Long Call Butterfly vs. Long Iron Butterfly

XYZ = 25.57

	Buy 10 XYZ Jan 22.50 Puts @ .10
Buy 10 XYZ Jan 22.50 Calls @ 3.35	Sell 10 XYZ Jan 25 Puts @ .45
Sell 20 XYZ Jan 25 Calls @ 1.30	Sell 10 XYZ Jan 25 Calls @ 1.30
Buy 10 XYZ Jan 27.50 Calls @ .30	Buy 10 XYZ Jan 27.50 Calls @ .30
Debit (DR) = 1.05	Credit (CR) = 1.35
Lower Breakeven (BE) = 23.55	Lower Breakeven (BE) = 23.65
Upper Breakeven (BE) = 26.45	Upper Breakeven (BE) = 26.35
Max Gain (MG) = 1.45	Max Gain (MG) = 1.35
Max Loss (ML) = –1.05	Max Loss (ML) = –1.15

FIGURE 7.7 AND 7.8

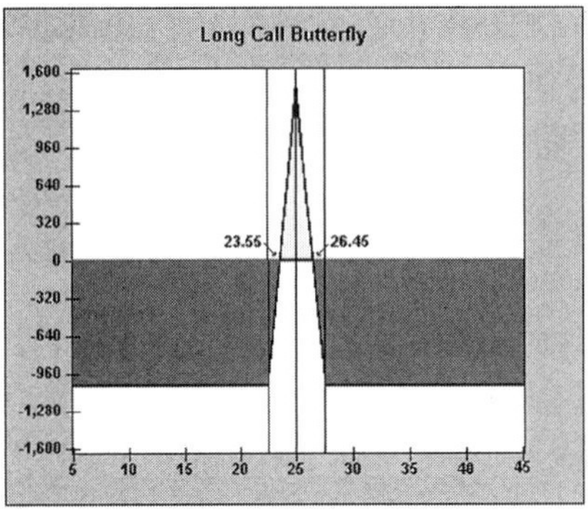

Strategy at Expiration

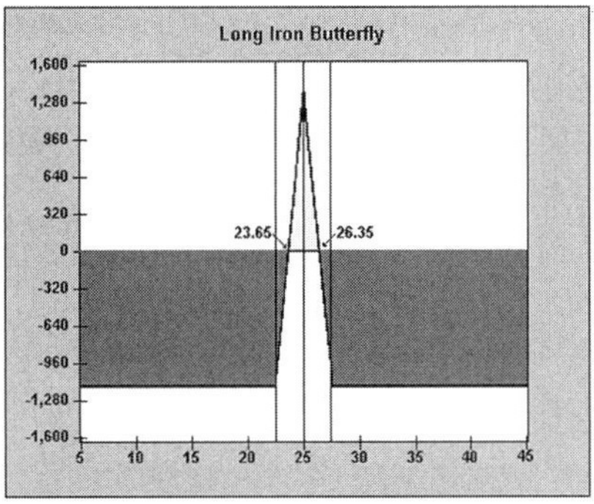

Strategy at Expiration

Advantages of long butterfly vs. long iron butterfly:

- Profit zone is 2.90 points (26.45 – 23.55).
  - Rather than 2.70 points (26.35 – 23.65) for the iron butterfly.
- Maximum loss is $1,050.
  - Rather than $1,150 for the iron butterfly.
- Maximum gain is $1,450.
  - Rather than $1,350 for the iron butterfly.
- Possible commissions savings.
  - Due to three legs instead of four.
- Margin requirements may be lower.
  - Depending upon your broker.

Advantages of long iron butterfly vs. long butterfly:

- A net credit is received at the time the position is established.
  - Rather than paying a net debit for the long butterfly.

Short Iron Butterfly Since a good chance of a profitable trade comes from a stock that breaks out of a certain range, you need to have a way of identifying which stocks might do this. Therefore, when you are researching stocks, you can usually find good short iron butterfly candidates by looking for stocks with the following criteria:

- Expecting a sharp move in either direction due to pending news.
  - Such as an earnings report.
- Typically a volatile stock, but has recently been less volatile than normal.
  - The theory of volatility mean reversion would anticipate a pickup in volatility.
- Recent consolidation around a support or resistance level.
  - After consolidation, stocks typically break out higher or lower.
- Currently trading at a price that is near a standard option strike price, such as 15, 20, 22.50, 25, 27.50, 30, etc.

You will notice that these criteria are identical to those for a short standard butterfly. See the stock chart examples in Chapter 6 on short standard butterflies for illustrations on how to draw the important price levels on a stock chart.

To help you determine which strategy makes the most sense, compare the two side by side for the same underlying stock, and then decide based on the advantages or disadvantages. The following example is a comparison using the same example used previously for the short call butterfly (see Figure 7.9) versus a comparable short iron butterfly (see Figure 7.10).

Example

Short Call Butterfly vs. Short Iron Butterfly

XYZ = 45.91

Sell 10 XYZ Dec 40 Calls @ 6.10
Buy 20 XYZ Dec 45 Calls @ 2.20
Sell 10 XYZ Dec 50 Calls @ .30
  Credit (CR) = 2.00
  Upper Breakeven (BE) = 48
  Lower Breakeven (BE) = 42
  Max Gain (MG) = 2.00
  Max Loss (ML) = –3.00

Sell 10 XYZ Dec 40 Puts @ .20
Buy 10 XYZ Dec 45 Puts @ 1.05
Buy 10 XYZ Dec 45 Calls @ 2.20
Sell 10 XYZ Dec 50 Calls @ .30
  Debit (DR) = 2.75
  Lower Breakeven (BE) = 42.25
  Upper Breakeven (BE) = 47.75
  Max Gain (MG) = 2.25
  Max Loss (ML) = –2.75

FIGURE 7.9 AND 7.10

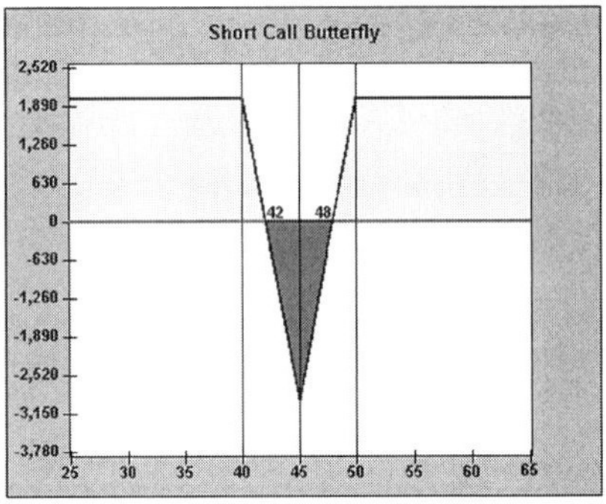

Strategy at Expiration

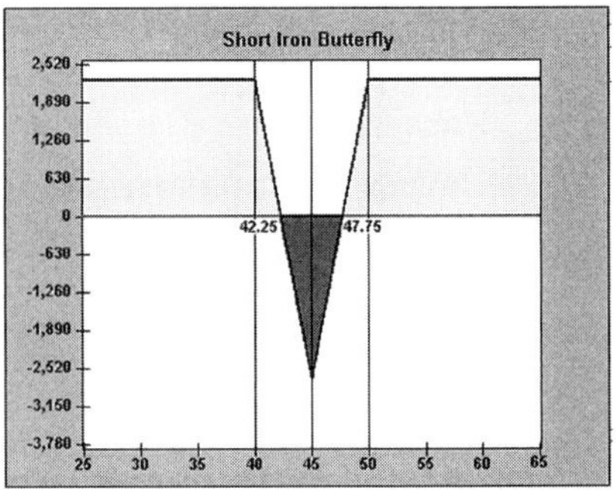

Strategy at Expiration

Advantages of short butterfly vs. short iron butterfly:

- A net credit is received at the time the position is established.
  - Rather than paying a net debit for the iron butterfly.
- Possible commissions savings.
  - Due to three legs instead of four.

Advantages of long iron butterfly vs. long butterfly:

- Loss zone is 5.50 points (47.75 – 42.25).
  - Rather than 6.00 points (48 – 42) for the short butterfly.
- Maximum loss is $2,750.
  - Rather than $3,000 for the short butterfly.
- Maximum gain is $2,250.
  - Rather than $2,000 for the short butterfly.
- There is no margin requirement except for the initial debit amount.
  - Since this strategy is made up of two debit spreads.

While their approach and characteristics are slightly different, both butterflies and iron butterflies are effective in providing ways to help you take advantage of stocks you believe will either remain range-bound or break out one way or the other. The best part is you have a choice, and with both puts and calls at your disposal and a range of strike prices from which to choose, there is a good chance you will be able to construct a spread to suit your sentiment and trading style.

SECTION 5

Condor Spreads

CHAPTER 8

Standard Condor Spreads

Condor spreads offer you the opportunity to limit losses in exchange for a limited gain potential. They involve the simultaneous purchase and sale of options contracts of the same class (puts or calls), in the same expiration month, on the same underlying security, but there are four different strike prices involved.

CONDOR SPREADS EXPLANATION

In many cases, condor spreads may require that you temporarily establish a long or short stock position. That resulting long or short position will need to be closed out in the market to fully realize the profit potential of the strategy. This is explained in more detail later in this chapter.

Two of the key concepts to understand before you begin trading condor spreads are how to determine your sentiment (whether you are breakout or neutral) and how to calculate the maximum loss (ML), maximum gain (MG), and breakeven points (BE). These calculations will vary depending upon whether the spread is initially established as a net debit or net credit and whether or not it is entered using calls or puts. Because of the unique profit and loss characteristics of condor spreads, the amount of the initial margin requirement is likely to be determined more by your broker than by industry regulations. In some cases you may be required to maintain funds in your account that exceed your maximum possible loss.

You can determine your sentiment and calculate the ML, MG, and BE for any condor strategy by applying the following rules:

1. Arrange your condor spread from lowest to highest strike price.
   a. Leg 1 is the contract with the lowest strike price, regardless of whether it is a put or a call.
   b. Leg 2 is the contract with the next highest strike price.
   c. Leg 3 is the contract with the next highest strike price.
   d. Leg 4 is the contract with the highest strike price.
2. Determine whether your sentiment is neutral or breakout on the spread.
   a. If legs 1 and 4 are buys and legs 2 and 3 are sells, you are neutral.
      i. This is considered a long condor.
   b. If legs 1 and 4 are sells and legs 2 and 3 are buys, you are breakout.
      i. This is considered a short condor.
3. Determine whether the spread was entered at a net debit or a net credit.
   a. A long condor is entered at a net debit.
   b. A short condor is entered at a net credit.
4. Calculate the **ML**.
   a. If long condor, the debit is the ML.
      i. The ML will occur at any price above the leg 4 strike price.
      ii. The ML will occur at any price below the leg 1 strike price.
   b. If short condor, the ML is first strike – second strike + the initial credit.
      i. The ML occurs between the second and third strike prices.
5. Calculate the **MG**.
   a. If long condor, the MG is the second strike – first strike – debit.
      i. The MG occurs between the second and third strike prices.
   b. If short condor, the MG is the initial credit received.

i. The MG occurs above the highest strike price or below the lowest strike price.

6. Calculate the **BE**.
   a. If long condor, the upper BE is the third strike price + MG.
   b. If long condor, the lower BE is the second strike price – MG.
   c. If short condor, the upper BE is the third strike price + ML.
   d. If short condor, the lower BE is the second strike price – ML.

LONG CONDOR SPREADS

The two most basic types of long condor spreads are long call condors and long put condors. Both are typically used when you have a neutral sentiment, but they sometimes differ by the amount of the initial debit you must pay to establish them. In both cases, you will buy the lowest strike price, sell the second strike price, sell the third strike price, and buy the highest strike price in an equal quantity on all four legs. Since the outcome at expiration is virtually identical, often the decision whether to establish a long call condor or a long put condor can be made strictly on price alone. The amount of the initial debit may be 10 or 20 cents lower for one versus the other, and you can simply choose the lower one. Because these strategies involve four legs, commissions will be higher than strategies involving fewer legs.

Long Call Condor—Quick Overview

A long call condor is made up of one long call at the lowest strike, one short call at the lower middle strike, one short call at the upper middle strike, and one long call at the highest strike, with the same strike price interval between all legs. All legs should also have the same expiration month. All sides of this spread are opening transactions, and the quantity of all four legs is always the same. This strategy is actually made up of one debit call spread and one credit call spread combined together as a single strategy (see Figure 8.1). Your broker will require you to deposit a margin requirement for the credit spread part of this strategy.

FIGURE 8.1

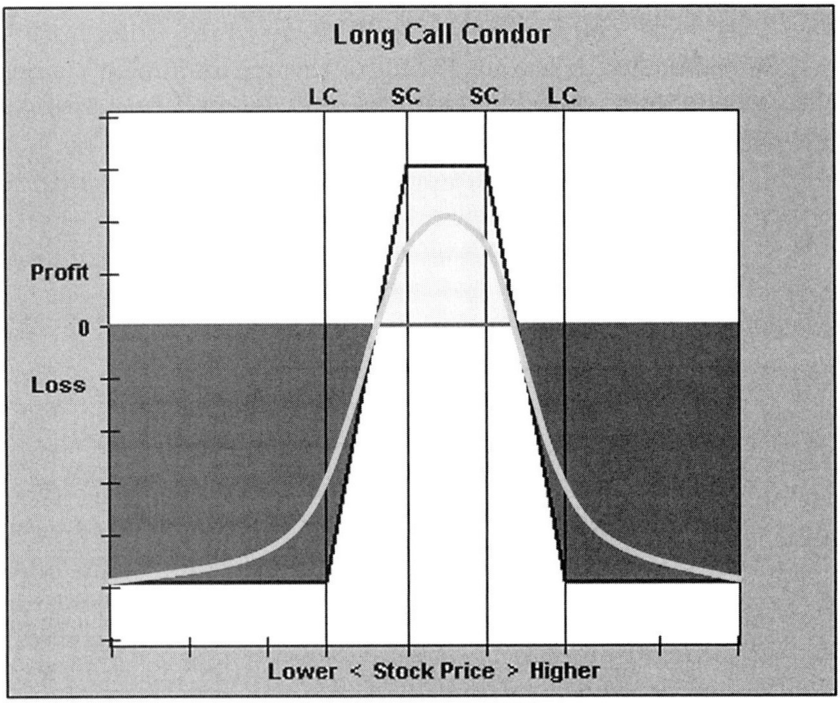

At Entry The white line in Figure 8.1 represents what the strategy typically looks like at the point of entry. As expiration approaches, the curve moves toward the black lines, which illustrate the final profit and loss boundaries at expiration.

Direction Neutral with a bullish or bearish bias, depending upon the strike prices selected

When to Use You would typically employ a long call condor in neutral markets and would hope to profit if the underlying stock remains relatively flat until the expiration date of the options. Generally, the underlying stock price should be between the two middle strike prices at the time of entry. If you are moderately bullish, higher strike prices should be used, and if you are moderately bearish, lower strike prices should be used.

Risk vs. Reward Limited risk with limited profit potential

Volatility The effect of volatility varies depending upon the strike prices chosen. The strategy generally benefits moderately from volatility decreases. Volatility increases will cause the strategy to lose value.

Time Decay The effect of time decay on this strategy varies with the underlying stock's price level in relation to the strike prices. If the stock price is between the outer strike prices, the effect is positive. If the stock price is above the highest strike price or below the lowest strike price, the effect is negative (see Table 8.1).

Prior to Expiration

- Because the highest strike options have little value to begin with and the lowest strike options are usually in-the-money and have a relatively small time value component, the two middle strike options may lose time value more quickly than either of the long options.
  - As a result, with little or no movement in the underlying stock price, the spread can often be closed out at a profit prior to expiration, once time value has eroded sufficiently.
  - However, because of the large number of commissions involved, this strategy is typically held until expiration if the stock has remained relatively stable.
- Similarly, if the underlying stock rises or drops sharply enough, the spread can often be closed out at a loss that is less than the maximum loss possible if held until expiration, because time value will erode the value of the middle strike options more quickly.

TABLE 8.1

Greeks	Below-the-money	At-the-money	Above-the-money
Delta	Positive	Neutral	Negative
Gamma	Negative	Negative	Negative
Theta	Negative	Positive	Negative
Vega	Positive	Negative	Positive

- Comparing the early close loss to the maximum potential loss at expiration can help you decide if holding until expiration makes sense.

At Expiration

- Below the lowest strike, all options expire worthless and the max loss is sustained.
- Between the lowest and lower middle strike, long stock will be acquired through exercise of the lowest strike. The long stock can then be sold in the market. The trade may or may not be profitable.
- Between the two middle strikes, the lowest strike is exercised, the lower middle strike is assigned, and max gain is achieved.
- Between the upper middle and highest strike, short stock will be obtained through the exercise of the lowest strike and the assignment on the lower and upper middle strikes. The short stock position can then be closed out. The trade may or may not be profitable.
- Above the highest strike, all options are exercised and/or assigned and the max loss is sustained.

Long Call Condor—Detail

When you establish a long call condor, the combined cost of the first and fourth legs will exceed the amount you receive in on the second and third legs. As a result, a long call condor is established at a net debit. This type of strategy is intended to take advantage of a stock that is moving sideways and is therefore considered a neutral strategy.

Example

Buy to open 10 XYZ Dec 110 Calls @ 7.70
Sell to open 10 XYZ Dec 115 Calls @ 3.70
Sell to open 10 XYZ Dec 120 Calls @ 1.30
Buy to open 10 XYZ Dec 125 Calls @ .40

Debit (DR) = –3.10 (–1st leg + 2nd leg + 3rd leg – 4th leg)
Lower Breakeven (BE) = 113.10 (2nd strike – MG)
Upper Breakeven (BE) = 121.90 (3rd strike + MG)
Max Gain (MG) = 1.90 (2nd strike – 1st strike – debit) (occurs between 2nd & 3rd strikes)
Max Loss (ML) = –3.10 (debit paid) (occurs beyond the outside strike prices)

When you set up an order like this, most condor order entry systems automatically calculate the market price of this 10/10/10/10 spread. To do so manually, reduce the spread by its greatest common factor of 10 to 1/1/1/1. Then multiply each leg by the market price, using the ask price on the legs you are buying and the bid price on the legs you are selling.

1 × –6 = –7.70

1 × +1.50 = +3.70

1 × +1.50 = +1.30

1 × –.50 = –.40

Net = –3.10 × 10 spreads × 100 shares per contract = ($3,100) total up-front cost

Figure 8.2 depicts the profit/loss zones of this example, including the breakeven points at the option expiration date.

FIGURE 8.2

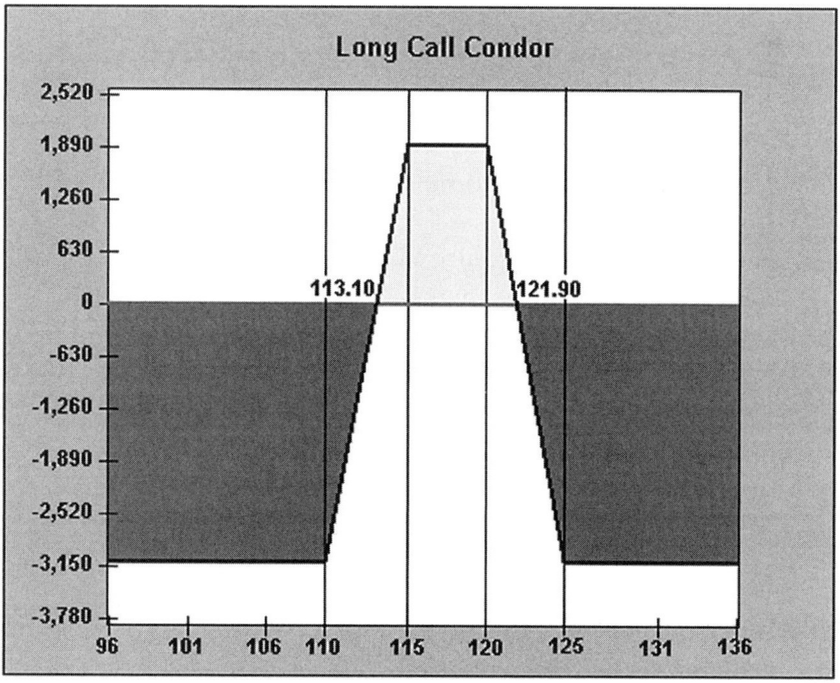

Strategy at Expiration

As you can see, the maximum gain on this strategy, which occurs between the two middle strike prices of 115 and 120, is $1,900. There are two breakeven points at 113.10 and 121.90. All prices below 113.10 or above 121.90 result in a loss. The maximum loss on the upside or downside is –$3,100. To get a better feel for the profit and loss zones, see the following sample prices at expiration.

XYZ at 110 or below at expiration:	
Initial cost:	($3,100)
All options expire worthless:	-0-
Net loss of 3.10 × 10 spreads:	= **($3,100)**
XYZ at 113.10 at expiration:	
Initial cost:	($3,100)
Exercise 110 calls & acquire 1,000 shares:	($110,000)
1,000 shares sold @ market:	$113,100
115, 120, and 125 calls expire worthless:	-0-
Net profit/loss:	= **$0**
XYZ at 115 at expiration:	
Initial cost:	($3,100)
Exercise 110 calls & acquire 1,000 shares:	($110,000)
1,000 shares sold @ market:	$115,000
115, 120, and 125 calls expire worthless:	-0-
Net profit/loss:	= **$1,900**
XYZ at 121.90 at expiration:	
Initial cost:	($3,100)
Exercise 110 calls & acquire 1,000 shares:	($110,000)
Called away on 1,000 shares @ 115:	$115,000
Called away on 1,000 shares @ 120:	$120,000
Buy back 1,000 short shares @ market:	($121,900)
125 calls expire worthless:	-0-
Net profit/loss:	= **$0**
XYZ at 125 at expiration:	
Initial cost:	($3,100)
Exercise 110 calls & acquire 1,000 shares:	($110,000)
Called away on 1,000 shares @ 115:	$115,000
Called away on 1,000 shares @ 120:	$120,000
Buy back 1,000 short shares @ market:	($125,000)

125 calls expire worthless:	-0-
Net profit/loss:	**= ($3,100)**

XYZ above 125 at expiration:

Initial cost:	($3,100)
Exercise 110 calls & acquire 1,000 shares:	($110,000)
Called away on 1,000 shares @ 115:	$115,000
Called away on 1,000 shares @ 120:	$120,000
Exercise 125 calls to close short shares:	($125,000)
Net profit/loss:	**= ($3,100)**

Figure 8.3 is the condor order entry screen within the CyberTrader Pro software that shows the sample trade above. This should help you visualize how this type of order is typically entered.

Long Put Condor—Quick Overview

A long put condor is made up of one long put at the lowest strike, one short put at the lower middle strike, one short put at the upper

FIGURE 8.3

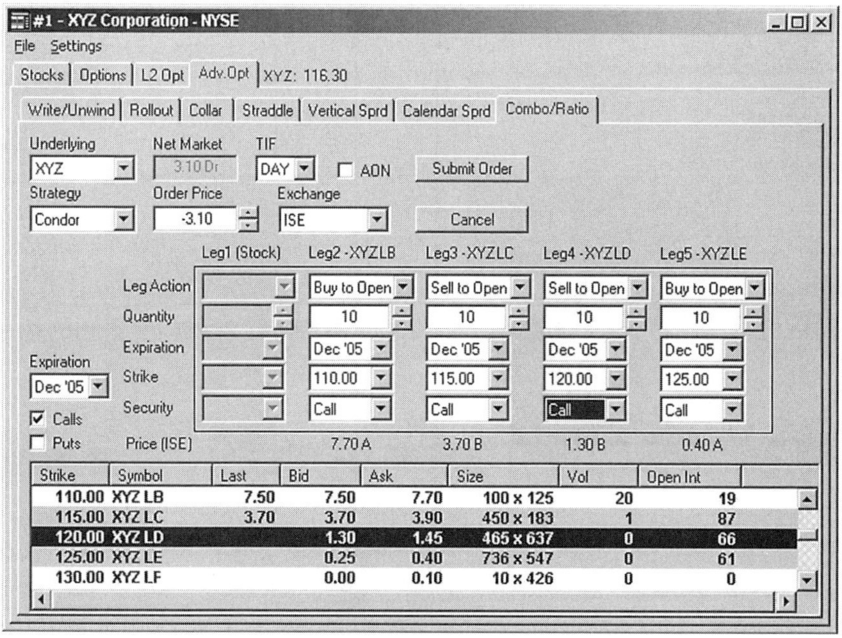

middle strike, and one long put at the highest strike, with the same strike price interval between all legs. All legs should also have the same expiration month. All sides of this spread are opening transactions, and the quantity of all four legs is always the same. This strategy is actually made up of one debit put spread and one credit put spread combined together as a single strategy (see Figure 8.4). Your broker will require you to deposit a margin requirement for the credit spread part of this strategy.

At Entry The white line in Figure 8.4 represents what the strategy typically looks like at the point of entry. As expiration approaches, the curve moves toward the black lines, which illustrate the final profit and loss boundaries at expiration.

Direction Neutral with a bullish or bearish bias, depending upon the strike prices selected

FIGURE 8.4

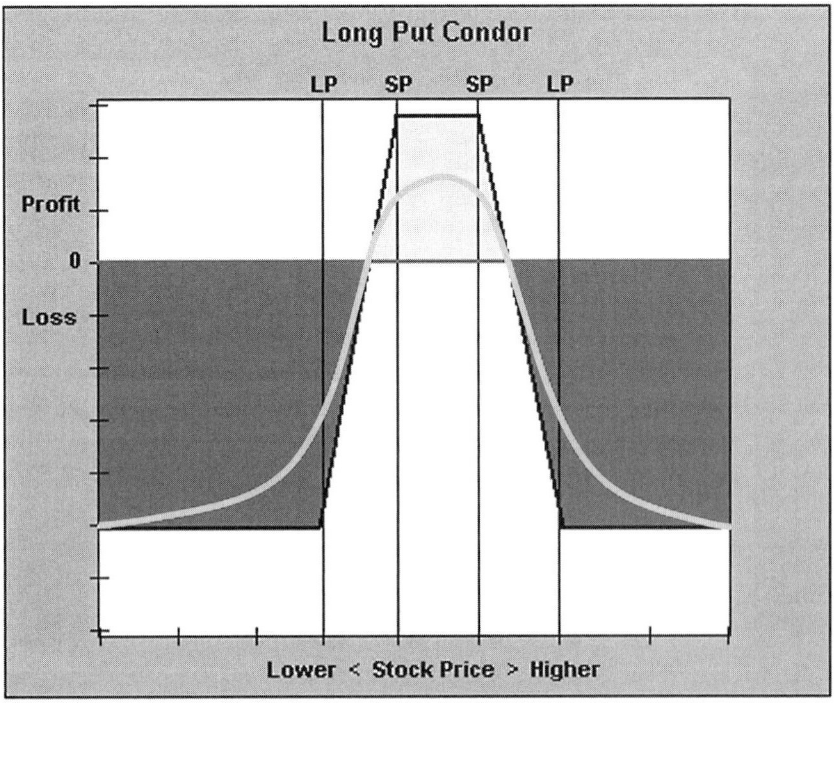

When to Use You would typically employ a long put condor in neutral markets and would hope to profit if the underlying stock remains relatively flat until the expiration date of the options. Generally, the underlying stock price should be between the two middle strike prices at the time of entry. If you are moderately bullish, lower strike prices should be used, and if you are moderately bearish, higher strike prices should be used.

Risk vs. Reward Limited risk with limited profit potential

Volatility The effect of volatility varies depending upon the strike prices chosen. The strategy generally benefits moderately from volatility decreases.

Time Decay The effect of time decay on this strategy varies with the underlying stock's price level in relation to the strike prices. If the stock price is between the outer strike prices, the effect is positive. If the stock price is above the upper strike price or below the lower strike price, the effect is negative (see Table 8.2).

Prior to Expiration

- Because the lowest strike options have little value to begin with and the highest strike options are usually in-the-money and have a relatively small time value component, the two middle strike options may lose time value more quickly than either of the long options.
  - As a result, with little or no movement in the underlying stock price, the spread can often be closed out at a profit prior to expiration once time value has eroded sufficiently.
  - However, because of the large number of commissions involved, this strategy is typically held until expiration if the stock has remained relatively stable.

TABLE 8.2

Greeks	Below-the-money	At-the-money	Above-the-money
Delta	Positive	Neutral	Negative
Gamma	Negative	Negative	Negative
Theta	Negative	Positive	Negative
Vega	Positive	Negative	Positive

- Similarly, if the underlying stock rises or drops sharply enough, the spread can often be closed out at a loss that is less than the maximum loss possible if held until expiration, because time value will erode the value of the middle strike options more quickly.
    - Comparing the early close loss to the maximum potential loss at expiration can help you decide if holding until expiration makes sense.

At Expiration

- Above the highest strike, all options expire worthless and max loss is sustained.
- Between the highest and upper middle strike, short stock will be acquired through exercise of the highest strike. The short stock position can then be closed out in the market. The trade may or may not be profitable.
- Between the two middle strikes, the highest strike is exercised, the upper middle strike is assigned, and max gain is achieved.
- Between the lower middle and lowest strike, long stock will be obtained through the exercise of the highest strike and the assignment on the upper and lower middle strikes. The long stock can then be sold in the market. The trade may or may not be profitable.
- Below the lowest strike, all options are exercised and/or assigned and max loss is sustained.

Long Put Condor—Detail

When you establish a long put condor, the combined cost of the first and fourth legs will exceed the amount you receive in on the second and third legs. As a result, a long put condor is established at a net debit. This type of strategy is intended to take advantage of a stock that is moving sideways and is therefore considered a neutral strategy.

Example

Buy to open 5 XYZ Dec 50 Puts @ .50
Sell to open 5 XYZ Dec 55 Puts @ 1.55
Sell to open 5 XYZ Dec 60 Puts @ 4.20
Buy to open 5 XYZ Dec 65 Puts @ 8.50

Debit (DR) = –3.25 (–1st leg + 2nd leg + 3rd leg – 4th leg)
Lower Breakeven (BE) = 53.25 (2nd strike – MG)
Upper Breakeven (BE) = 61.75 (3rd strike + MG)
Max Gain (MG) = 1.75 (2nd strike – 1st strike – debit) (occurs between 2nd & 3rd strikes)
Max Loss (ML) = –3.25 (debit paid) (occurs beyond the outside strike prices)

When you set up an order like this most condor order entry systems automatically calculate the market price of this 5/5/5/5 spread. To do so manually, reduce the spread by its greatest common factor of 5 to 1/1/1/1. Then multiply each leg by the market price using the ask price on the legs you are buying and the bid price on the leg you are selling:

1 × –1 = –.50
1 × +2.80 = +1.55
1 × +2.80 = +4.20
1 × –6.00 = –8.50
Net = –3.25 × 5 spreads × 100 shares per contract = ($1,625) total up-front cost

Figure 8.5 depicts the profit/loss zones of this example, including the breakeven points, at the option expiration date.

As you can see, the maximum gain on this strategy, which occurs between the two middle strike prices of 55 and 60, is $875. There are two breakeven points at 53.25 and 61.75. All prices below 53.25 or above 61.75 result in a loss. The maximum loss on the upside or downside is –$1,625. To get a better feel for the profit and loss zones, see the following sample prices at expiration.

XYZ at 65 or above at expiration:

Initial cost:	($1,625)
All options expire worthless:	-0-
Net loss of 1.40 × 5 spreads:	= **($1,625)**

XYZ at 61.75 at expiration:

Initial cost:	($1,625)
Exercise (5) 65 puts to sell short 500 shares:	$32,500
Buy back 500 shares @ market:	($30,875)
60, 55, and 50 puts expire worthless:	-0-
Net profit/loss:	= **$0**

FIGURE 8.5

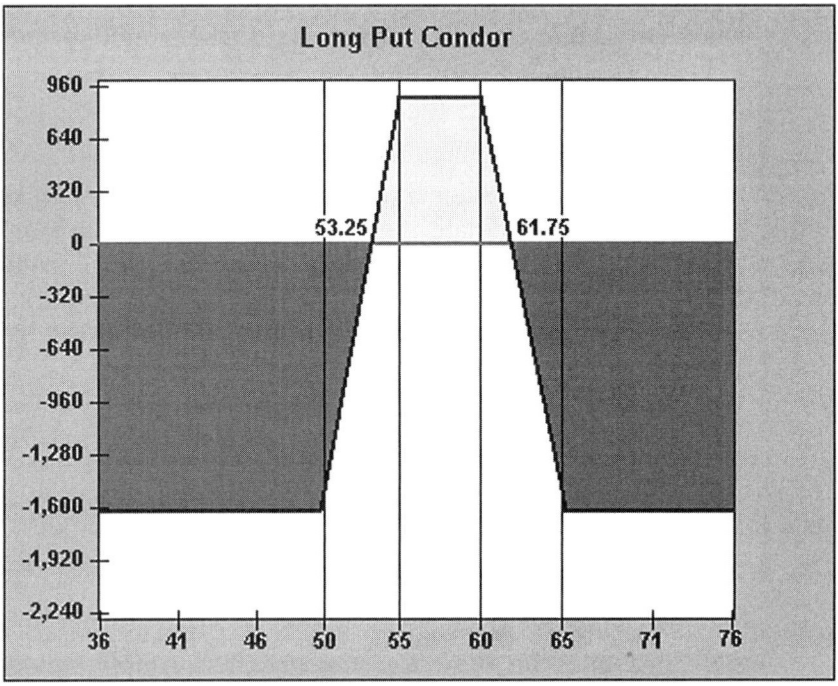

Strategy at Expiration

XYZ at 60 at expiration:	
Initial cost:	($1,625)
Exercise (5) 65 puts to sell short 500 shares:	$32,500
Buy back 500 shares @ market:	($30,000)
60, 55, and 50 puts expire worthless:	-0-
Net profit/loss:	= **$875**
XYZ at 55 at expiration:	
Initial cost:	($1,625)
Exercise (5) 65 puts to sell short 500 shares:	$32,500
Assigned on (5) 60 puts to buy 500 shares:	($30,000)
55 and 50 puts expire worthless:	-0-
Net profit/loss:	= **$875**
XYZ at 53.25 at expiration:	
Initial cost:	($1,625)

Exercise (5) 65 puts to sell short 500 shares:	$32,500
Assigned on (5) 60 puts to buy 500 shares:	($30,000)
Assigned on (5) 55 puts to buy 500 shares:	($27,500)
Sell 500 shares @ market:	$26,625
50 puts expire worthless:	-0-
Net profit/loss:	= $**0**

XYZ below 50 at expiration:

Initial cost:	($1,625)
Exercise (5) 65 puts to sell short 500 shares:	$32,500
Assigned on (5) 60 puts to buy 500 shares:	($30,000)
Assigned on (5) 55 puts to buy 500 shares:	($27,500)
Exercise (5) 50 puts to sell 500 shares:	$25,000
Net profit/loss:	= **($1,625)**

Figure 8.6 is the condor order entry screen within the Cyber-Trader Pro software that shows the sample trade above. This should help you visualize how this type of order is typically entered.

FIGURE 8.6

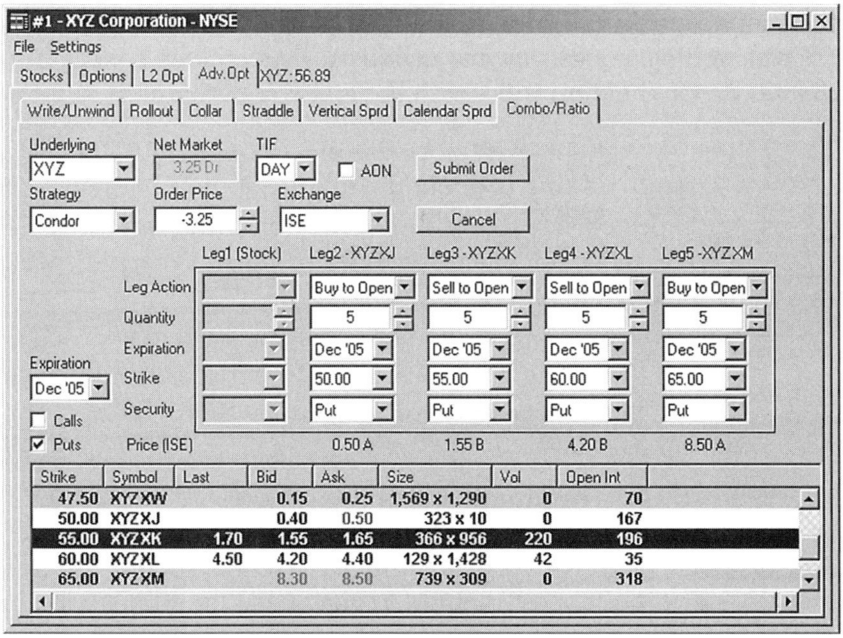

Characteristics

While a long condor is primarily a neutral strategy, it is possible to put a slightly bullish or bearish bias on it depending upon which strike prices you use. If you are completely neutral, you would want the stock to be halfway between the two middle strike prices at the time the condor is established. This would be an around-the-money (RTM) condor.

Table 8.3 illustrates how to properly structure a long condor spread to match your level of bullishness or bearishness. For example, if you are slightly bullish, you may want to consider a long call condor that is above-the-money (ABTM) or a long put condor that is below-the-money (BTM). By contrast, if you are slightly bearish, you may want to consider a long call condor that is below-the-money (BTM) or a long put condor that is above-the-money (ABTM). Remember, while large up or down moves in the stock could result in losses, to maximize your potential profit, you want the stock to be between the two middle strike prices on option expiration day.

While the two strategies are very similar, one benefit of a condor over a butterfly is that the profit zone is wider and it therefore requires less outcome precision at expiration in order to end up in the profitable zone. While good butterfly candidates can often be found in any price range, because of their wider price zone, it is more likely that you will find condor candidates if you limit your selection to stocks trading over $50 per share. Therefore, when you are researching stocks, you can usually find good long condor candidates by looking for stocks with the following criteria:

- In a 10–20 point channel for about 6–8 weeks or more
- Currently trading in about the middle of that channel
- No expected news or events coming up that might cause them to move out of that channel, or cause a sharp increase in volatility.
  - Such as earnings or merger and acquisition news.
- Currently trading at a price over $50 per share and is near the midpoint between two standard option strike prices, such as 55, 60, 65, 75, 80, 90, etc.

While these criteria might sound overly restrictive, you may be surprised how many good candidates you will find with only a little research. Once you have identified a potential condor through this process, it is often very helpful to view what the strategy might

TABLE 8.3

Strategy	<< Direction >>				<< Magnitude >>		
	Bullish	Neutral	Breakout	Bearish	Extreme	Moderate	Slight
Long call condor ABTM	X						X
Long call condor RTM		X			X		
Long call condor BTM				X			X
Long put condor ABTM				X			X
Long put condor RTM		X			X		
Long put condor BTM	X						X

look like by drawing the important price levels on a chart. This will help you visualize where you will be profitable and how much the stock must break out in order for your strategy to be unprofitable. First, calculate the key price levels on a sample 10 point condor, so we will know where to draw the lines.

Example 1A

Buy 10 XYZ Feb 180 Calls @ 19.40
Sell 10 XYZ Feb 190 Calls @ 12.20
Sell 10 XYZ Feb 200 Calls @ 7.10
Buy 10 XYZ Feb 210 Calls @ 3.90

DR (Debit) = 4.00 (–19.40 + 12.20 + 7.10 – 3.90)

MG (Maximum Gain) = 6.00 (2nd strike – 1st strike – debit) (occurs between 2nd & 3rd strikes)

ML (Maximum Loss) = 4.00 (debit paid) (occurs at outside strike prices)

Upper BE (Breakeven) = 206 (3rd strike + MG)

Lower BE (Breakeven) = 184 (2nd strike – MG)

Total cost of this trade = $4,000 (DR × # of spreads × option multiplier) or (4.00 × 10 × 100)

Once you have calculated the key price levels, you can draw them on a chart. The lines you will want to show on the chart are the outside strike prices of 180 and 210 (max loss levels) and the upper and lower breakeven levels of 206 and 184. On CyberTrader Pro or Schwab's StreetSmart Pro software, you can do this using the support line tool (red line) for the outer maximum loss lines and the resistance line tool (green line) for the breakeven thresholds as illustrated below in Figure 8.7.

The upper and lower red lines represent the outer strike (max loss) levels. The inner green lines represent the breakeven levels.

To ensure that the risk/reward characteristics of the condor you are considering are favorable, it is advisable to also calculate the MG/ML ratio and look for a value of at least 50%. In the example above, the MG/ML would be 6.00/4.00 = 150%; this means the maximum potential profit is 150% of the maximum potential loss. Since Figure 8.7 presents data as of around January 19, the February condor being considered has about 29 days until expiration. As you can see, if XYZ is between 184 and 206 at the February option expiration, this trade will be profitable. The maximum profit will

FIGURE 8.7

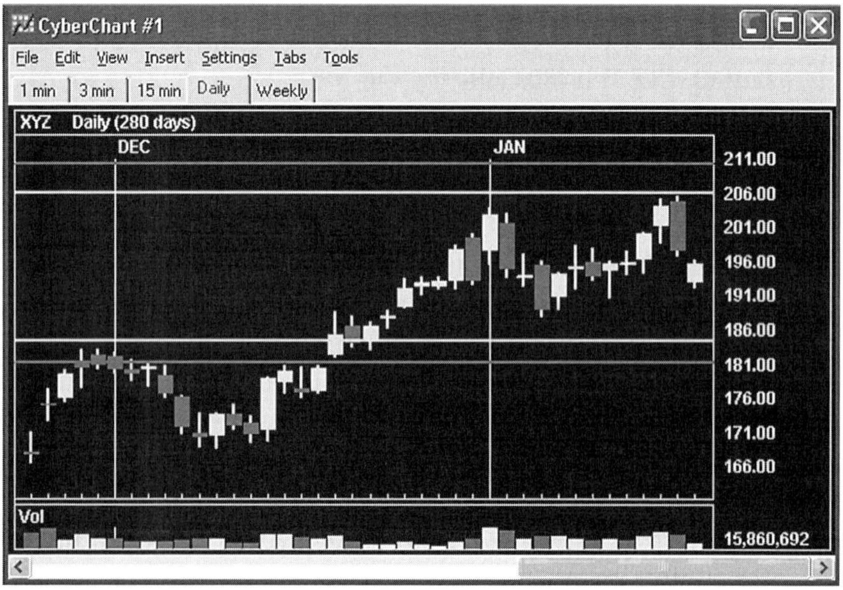

be reached if XYZ is anywhere between 190 and 200 (the inner strike prices) at expiration. Losses will be incurred if XYZ closes above 206 at expiration, with the maximum loss of $4,000 occurring at any price above 210. Likewise, losses will be incurred if XYZ closes below 184 at expiration, with the maximum loss of $4,000 also occurring at any price below 180.

Unlike butterfly spreads, with which it is very difficult to hit maximum profit, condor spreads more frequently hit maximum profit because it occurs over a range of prices rather than just at a single price. In this example, the profit zone is 22 points (206 – 184) and the maximum profit zone is 10 points (200 – 190), allowing plenty of room for normal market fluctuation and a good chance of ending up profitable if the stock remains relatively stable. If the trade ends up profitable, the rate of return can be calculated by dividing the amount of the eventual gain ($0 up to $6,000) by the amount invested ($4,000). Thus, your rate of return will be somewhere between 0% and 150%.

Example 1B illustrates a good 5 point condor candidate with different profit and loss characteristics.

ZYX has the following characteristics:

- In a 10 point channel between about 75 and 90 for about six weeks
- Currently trading in about the middle of that channel (81.90)
- No expected news or events (such as an earnings report) coming up that might cause it to move out of that channel or cause a sharp increase in volatility
- Currently trading at a price of 81.90, which is near the midpoint between two standard option strike prices of 80 and 85

Example 1B

Buy 5 ZYX Apr 75 Calls @ 7.60
Sell 5 ZYX Apr 80 Calls @ 3.70
Sell 5 ZYX Apr 85 Calls @ 1.35
Buy 5 ZYX Apr 90 Calls @ .40

DR (Debit) = 2.95 (–7.60 + 3.70 + 1.35 – .40)

MG (Maximum Gain) = 2.05 (2nd strike –1st strike – debit) (occurs between 2nd & 3rd strikes)

ML (Maximum Loss) = 2.95 (debit paid) (occurs at outside strike prices)

Upper BE (Breakeven) = 87.05 (3rd strike + MG)

Lower BE (Breakeven) = 77.95 (2nd strike – MG)

Total cost of this trade = $1,475 (DR × # of spreads × option multiplier) or (2.95 × 5 × 100)

To ensure that the risk/reward characteristics of this condor are favorable, you calculate the MG/ML ratio and look for a value of at least 50%. In this example the MG/ML would be 2.05/2.95 = 69%; this means the maximum potential profit is 69% of the maximum potential loss.

The lines you will want to show on the chart are the outside strike prices of 75 and 90 (represented by the red lines) and the upper and lower breakeven levels of 87.05 and 77.95 (represented by the green lines). Using the support and resistance line tools creates a chart as illustrated below in Figure 8.8.

The upper and lower red lines represent the outer strike (max loss) levels. The inner green lines represent the breakeven levels.

FIGURE 8.8

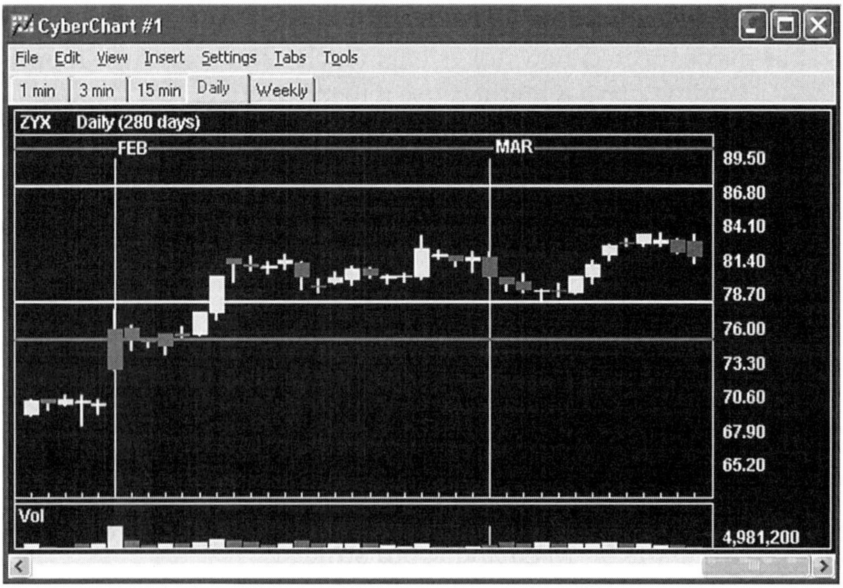

Since Figure 8.8 presents data as of around March 17, the April condor being considered has about 28 days until expiration. As you can see, if ZYX is between 77.95 and 87.05 at the April option expiration, this trade will be profitable. The maximum profit will be reached if ZYX is anywhere between 80 and 85 (the inner strike prices) at expiration. Losses will be incurred if ZYX closes above 87.05 at expiration, with the maximum loss of $1,475 occurring at any price above 90. Likewise, losses will be incurred if XYZ closes below 77.95 at expiration, with the maximum loss of $1,475 also occurring at any price below 75.

Since the profit zone on condor spreads occurs over a much wider range of prices than on a butterfly spread, this strategy has a higher probability of being profitable. In this example, the profit zone is 9.10 points (87.05 – 77.95) and the maximum profit zone is 5 points (85 – 80) allowing plenty of room for normal market fluctuation and a good chance of ending up profitable if the stock remains relatively stable. If the trade ends up profitable, the rate of return can be calculated by dividing the amount of the eventual gain ($0 up to $1,025) by the amount invested ($1,475). Thus, your rate of return will be somewhere between 0% and 69%.

While entering a four-legged order may seem complicated, there are a number of reasons why it makes sense to enter a condor as a single order rather than two separate spreads.

Advantages

- Since you can specify a single price for the whole strategy, the market can fluctuate while your order is open, and there are a number of different prices among the four options that will work out to your specified net debit.
- Since all four legs are part of the same order they must execute in an equal 1×1×1×1 ratio or not at all.

Disadvantages

- Most of the option exchanges handle these orders manually, which could result is slower fill reports than you are used to on simpler orders.
- As of year-end 2005, only the International Securities Exchange (ISE) and the Chicago Board Options Exchange (CBOE) had the ability to execute condors in a fully electronic manner.

SHORT CONDOR SPREADS

The two most basic types of short condor spreads are short call condors and short put condors. Both are typically used when you have a breakout sentiment, but they sometimes differ by the amount of the initial credit you can receive to establish them. In both cases, you will sell the lowest strike price, buy the second strike price, buy the third strike price, and sell the highest strike price, all in equal quantity. Because these strategies involve four legs, commissions will be higher than strategies involving fewer legs.

Any stock that you might consider a good candidate for a long strangle is probably a good candidate for a short condor. While a long strangle will generally only be profitable with a significant move in either direction, a short condor, by contrast, requires less movement, since a potential profit beyond a certain level in both directions is sold for a small premium. This premium lowers the maximum loss, since it moves the breakeven points closer to the starting point, requiring less movement to reach the profit zone.

Since the outcome at expiration is virtually identical, often the decision whether to establish a short call condor or a short put condor can be made strictly on price alone. The amount of the initial credit may be 10 or 20 cents higher for one versus the other, and you can simply choose the higher one.

Short Call Condor—Quick Overview

A short call condor is made up of one short call at the lowest strike, one long call at the lower middle strike, one long call at the upper middle strike, and one short call at the highest strike, with the same strike price interval between all legs. All legs should also have the same expiration month. All sides of this spread are opening transactions, and the quantity of all four legs is always the same. This strategy is actually made up of one debit call spread and one credit call spread combined together as a single strategy (see Figure 8.9). Your broker will require you to deposit a margin requirement for the credit spread part of this strategy.

At Entry The white line in Figure 8.9 represents what the strategy typically looks like at the point of entry. As expiration approaches, the curve moves toward the black lines, which illustrate the final profit and loss boundaries at expiration.

FIGURE 8.9

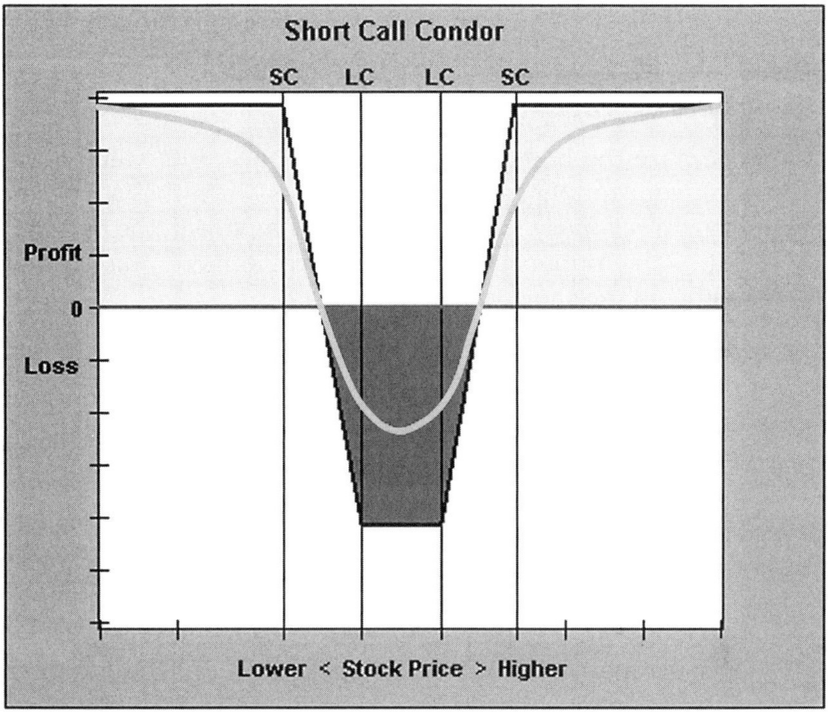

Direction Breakout with a bullish or bearish bias, depending upon the strike prices selected

When to Use You would typically employ a short call condor in uncertain markets and would hope to profit if the underlying stock breaks out either higher or lower than the current price by the expiration date of the options. Generally, the underlying stock price should be between the two middle strike prices at the time of entry. If you are moderately bullish, lower strike prices should be used, and if you are moderately bearish, higher strike prices should be used.

Risk vs. Reward Limited risk with limited profit potential

Volatility The effect of volatility varies depending upon the strike prices chosen. The strategy generally benefits moderately from volatility increases.

Time Decay The effect of time decay on this strategy varies with the underlying stock's price level in relation to the strike prices. If the stock price is between the outer strike prices, the effect is negative. If the stock price is above the upper strike price or below the lower strike price, the effect is positive (see Table 8.4).

Prior to Expiration

- Because the highest strike options have little value to begin with and the lowest strike options are in-the-money and have a relatively small time value component, the two middle strike options will lose time value more quickly than either of the short options.
  - As a result, with little or no movement in the underlying stock price, the spread can often be closed out at a loss that is less than the maximum loss possible if held until expiration, because time value will erode the value of the middle strike options more quickly.
- Similarly, if the underlying stock rises or drops sharply enough, the spread can often be closed out at a gain that is less than the maximum gain possible if held until expiration.
  - Comparing the early close gain to the maximum potential gain at expiration can help you decide if holding until expiration makes sense.
  - However, because of the large number of commissions involved, this strategy is typically held until expiration if the stock has begun to move higher or lower.

At Expiration

- Below the lowest strike, all options expire worthless and max gain is achieved.

TABLE 8.4

Greeks	Below-the-money	At-the-money	Above-the-money
Delta	Negative	Neutral	Positive
Gamma	Positive	Positive	Positive
Theta	Positive	Negative	Positive
Vega	Positive	Positive	Positive

- Between the lowest and lower middle strike, short stock will be acquired through assignment of the lowest strike. The short stock position can then be closed out in the market. The trade may or may not be profitable.
- Between the two middle strikes, the lowest strike is assigned, the lower middle strike is exercised, and max loss is sustained.
- Between the upper middle and highest strike, long stock will be obtained through the assignment of the lowest strike and the exercise of the lower and upper middle strikes. The long stock position can then be closed out in the market. The trade may or may not be profitable.
- Above the highest strike, all options are exercised and/or assigned and max gain is achieved.

Short Call Condor—Detail

When you establish a short call condor, the combined credit from the first and fourth legs will be greater than the amount you spend on the second and third legs. As a result, a short call condor is established at a net credit. This type of strategy is intended to take advantage of a stock that is expected to rise or drop sharply and is therefore considered a breakout strategy.

Example

Sell to open 10 XYZ Dec 65 Calls @ 9.40

Buy to open 10 XYZ Dec 70 Calls @ 5.40

Buy to open 10 XYZ Dec 75 Calls @ 2.35

Sell to open 10 XYZ Dec 80 Calls @ .75

Credit (CR) = 2.40 (1st leg – 2nd leg – 3rd leg + 4th leg)

Upper Breakeven (BE) = 77.60 (3rd strike + ML)

Lower Breakeven (BE) = 67.40 (2nd strike – ML)

Max Gain (MG) = 2.40 (credit received) (occurs beyond the outside strike prices)

Max Loss (ML) = 2.60 (1st strike – 2nd strike + credit) (occurs between the 2nd & 3rd strikes)

When you set up an order like this, most condor order entry systems automatically calculate the market price of this 10/10/10/10 spread. To do so manually, reduce the spread by its greatest common factor of 10 to 1/1/1/1. Then multiply each leg by the market price using the ask price on the leg you are buying and the bid price on the legs you are selling:

$1 \times +9.40 = +9.40$

$1 \times -5.40 = -5.40$

$1 \times -2.35 = -2.35$

$1 \times +.75 = +.75$

Net = $+2.40 \times 10$ spreads $\times$ 100 shares per contract = \$2,400 total credit received

Figure 8.10 depicts the profit/loss zones of this example, including the breakeven points at the option expiration date.

As you can see, the maximum gain on this strategy, which occurs only above or below the outer strike prices at expiration, is

FIGURE 8.10

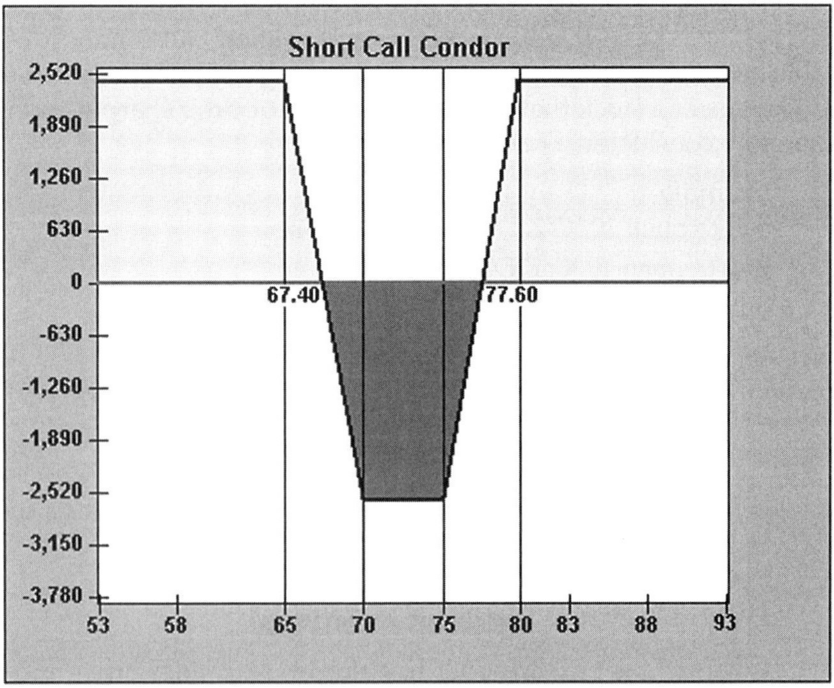

Strategy at Expiration

$2,400. There are two breakeven points, at 67.40 and 77.60. All prices between 67.40 and 77.60 result in a loss. The maximum loss is –$2,600 and occurs only between the two middle strike prices of 70 and 75. To get a better feel for the profit and loss zones, see the following sample prices at expiration.

XYZ at 65 or below at expiration:

Initial credit:	$2,400
All options expire worthless:	-0-
Net gain of 2.40 × 10 spreads:	= **$2,400**

XYZ at 67.40 at expiration:

Initial credit:	$2,400
Called away on 1,000 shares @ 65:	$65,000
Buy back 1,000 shares @ market:	($67,400)
70, 75, and 80 calls expire worthless:	-0-
Net profit/loss:	= $**0**

XYZ at 70 at expiration:

Initial credit:	$2,400
Called away on 1,000 shares @ 65:	$65,000
Buy back 1,000 shares @ market:	($70,000)
70, 75, and 80 calls expire worthless:	-0-
Net profit:	= **($2,600)**

XYZ at 77.60 at expiration:

Initial credit:	$2,400
Called away on 1,000 shares @ 65:	$65,000
Exercise 70 calls to buy 1,000 shares:	($70,000)
Exercise 75 calls to buy 1,000 shares:	($75,000)
Sell 1,000 shares at market:	$77,600
80 calls expire worthless:	-0-
Net profit/loss:	= $**0**

XYZ at 80 at expiration:

Initial credit:	$2,400
Called away on 1,000 shares @ 65:	$65,000
Exercise 70 calls to buy 1,000 shares:	($70,000)
Exercise 75 calls to buy 1,000 shares:	($75,000)

Sell 1,000 shares at market:	$80,000
80 calls expire worthless:	-0-
Net profit/loss:	= **$2,400**

XYZ above 80 at expiration:

Initial credit:	$2,400
Called away on 1,000 shares @ 65:	$65,000
Exercise 70 calls to buy 1,000 shares:	($70,000)
Exercise 75 calls to buy 1,000 shares:	($75,000)
Called away on 1,000 shares @ 80:	$80,000
Net profit/loss:	= **$2,400**

Figure 8.11 is the condor order entry screen within the Cyber-Trader Pro software that shows the sample trade above. This should help you visualize how this type of order is typically entered.

FIGURE 8.11

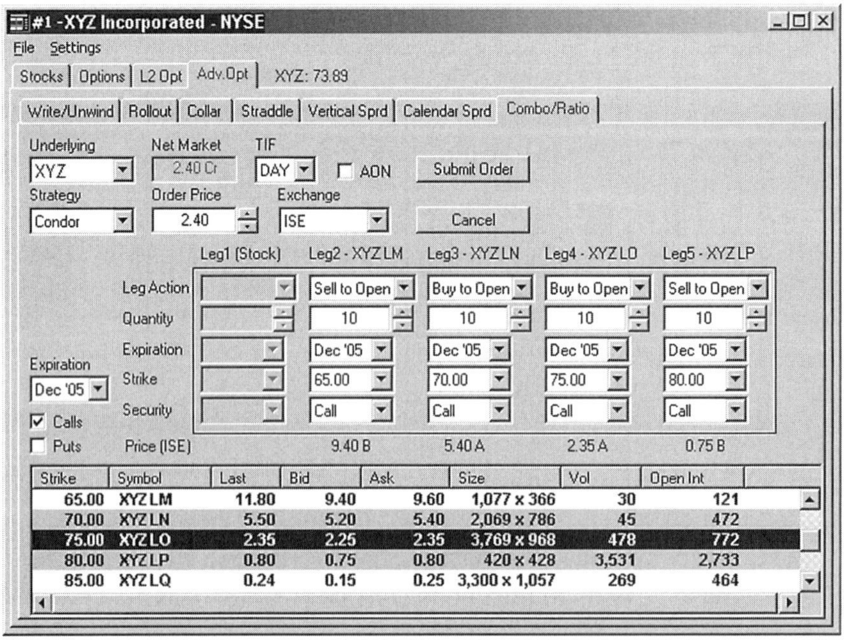

Short Put Condor—Quick Overview

A short put condor is made up of one short put at the lowest strike, one long put at the lower middle strike, one long put at the upper middle strike, and one short put at the highest strike, with the same strike price interval between all legs. All legs should also have the same expiration month. All sides of this spread are opening transactions, and the quantity of all four legs is always the same. This strategy is actually made up of one debit put spread and one credit put spread combined together as a single strategy (see Figure 8.12). Your broker will require you to deposit a margin requirement for the credit spread part of this strategy.

At Entry The white line in Figure 8.12 represents what the strategy typically looks like at the point of entry. As expiration

FIGURE 8.12

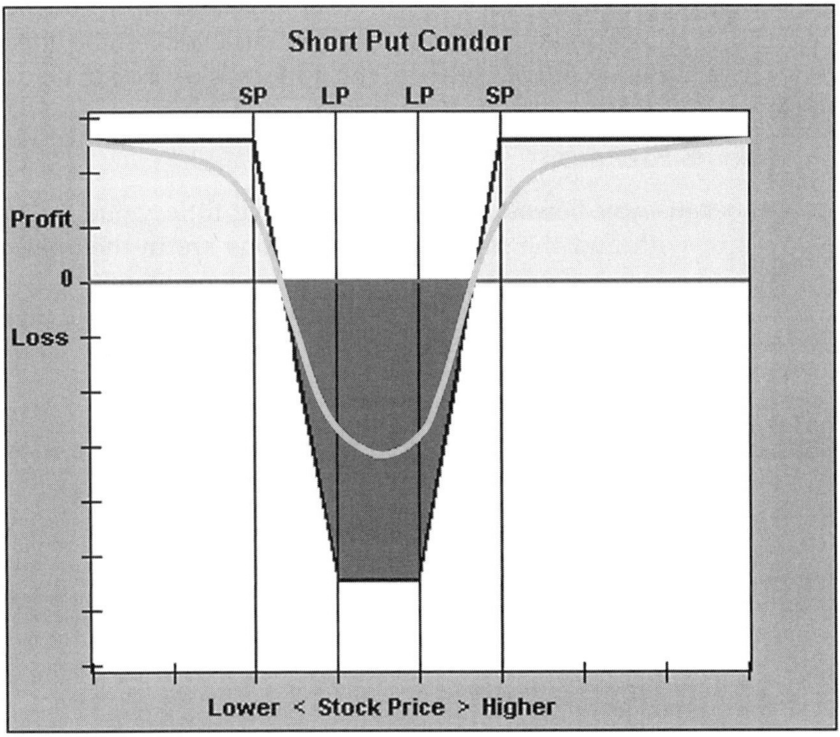

approaches, the curve moves toward the black lines, which illustrate the final profit and loss boundaries at expiration.

Direction Breakout with a bullish or bearish bias, depending upon the strike prices selected

When to Use You would typically employ a short put condor in uncertain markets and would hope to profit if the underlying stock breaks out either higher or lower than the current price by the expiration date of the options. Generally, the underlying stock price should be between the two middle strike prices at the time of entry. If you are moderately bullish, higher strike prices should be used, and if you are moderately bearish, lower strike prices should be used.

Risk vs. Reward Limited risk with limited profit potential

Volatility he effect of volatility varies depending upon the strike prices chosen. This strategy generally benefits moderately from volatility increases.

Time Decay The effect of time decay on this strategy varies with the underlying stock's price level in relation to the strike prices. If the stock price is between the outer strike prices, the effect is negative. If the stock price is above the upper strike price or below the lower strike price, the effect is positive (see Table 8.5).

Prior to Expiration

- Because the lowest strike options have little value to begin with and the highest strike options are in-the-money and have a relatively small time value component, the two middle strike options will lose time value more quickly than either of the short options.

TABLE 8.5

Greeks	Below-the-money	At-the-money	Above-the-money
Delta	Negative	Neutral	Positive
Gamma	Positive	Positive	Positive
Theta	Positive	Negative	Positive
Vega	Positive	Positive	Positive

- As a result, with little or no movement in the underlying stock price the spread can often be closed out at a loss that is less than the maximum loss possible if held until expiration, because time value will erode the value of the middle strike options more quickly.

- Similarly, if the underlying stock rises or drops sharply enough, the spread can often be closed out at a gain that is less than the maximum gain possible if held until expiration.
  - Comparing the early close gain to the maximum potential gain at expiration can help you decide if holding until expiration makes sense.
  - However, because of the large number of commissions involved, this strategy is typically held until expiration if the stock has begun to move higher or lower.

At Expiration

- Below the lowest strike, all options are exercised and/or assigned and max gain is achieved.
- Between the lowest and lower middle strike, short stock will be obtained through the assignment of the highest strike and the exercise of the upper and lower middle strikes. The short stock position can then be closed out in the market. The trade may or may not be profitable.
- Between the two middle strikes, the highest strike is assigned, the upper middle strike is exercised, and max loss is sustained.
- Between the upper middle and highest strike, long stock will be acquired through assignment of the highest strike. The long stock position can then be closed out in the market. The trade may or may not be profitable.
- Above the highest strike, all options expire worthless and max gain is achieved.

Short Put Condor—Detail

When you establish a short put condor, the combined credit from the first and fourth legs will be greater than the amount you spend on the second and third legs. As a result, a short put condor is established at a net credit. This type of strategy is intended to take advantage of a stock that is expected to rise or drop sharply and is therefore considered a breakout strategy.

Example

Sell to open 4 XYZ Jan 75 Puts @ .55
Buy to open 4 XYZ Jan 80 Puts @ 1.55
Buy to open 4 XYZ Jan 85 Puts @ 3.40
Sell to open 4 XYZ Jan 90 Puts @ 6.00

Credit (CR) = 1.60 (1st leg – 2nd leg – 3rd leg + 4th leg)
Upper Breakeven (BE) = 88.40 (3rd strike + ML)
Lower Breakeven (BE) = 76.60 (2nd strike –ML)
Max Gain (MG) = 1.60 (credit received) (occurs beyond the outside strike prices)
Max Loss (ML) = 3.40 (1st strike – 2nd strike + credit) (occurs between 2nd & 3rd strikes)

When you set up an order like this, most condor order entry systems automatically calculate the market price of this 4/4/4/4 spread. To do so manually, reduce the spread by its greatest common factor of 4 to 1/1/1/1. Then multiply each leg by the market price using the ask price on the leg you are buying and the bid price on the legs you are selling:

1 × +.55 = +.55
1 × –1.55 = –1.55
1 × –3.40 = –3.40
1 × +6.00 = +6.00
Net = +1.60 × 4 spreads × 100 shares per contract = $640 total credit received

Figure 8.13 depicts the profit/loss zones of this example, including the breakeven points at the option expiration date.

As you can see, the maximum gain on this strategy, which occurs only above or below the outer strike prices at expiration, is $640. There are two breakeven points at 76.60 and 88.40. All prices between 76.60 and 88.40 result in a loss. The maximum loss is –$1,360 and occurs only between the two middle strike prices of 80 and 85. To get a better feel for the profit and loss zones, see the following sample prices at expiration.

FIGURE 8.13

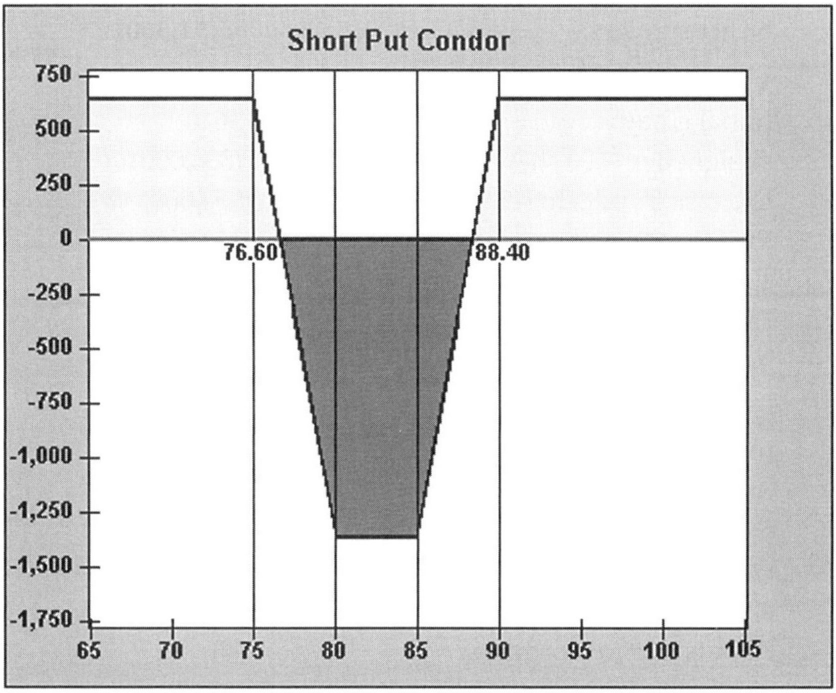

Strategy at Expiration

XYZ above 90 at expiration:	
Initial credit:	$640
All options expire worthless:	-0-
Net gain of 1.60 × 4 spreads:	= **$640**
XYZ at 88.40 at expiration:	
Initial credit:	$640
Assigned on 400 shares @ 90:	($36,000)
400 shares sold @ market:	$35,360
75, 80, and 85 puts expire worthless:	-0-
Net profit/loss:	= **$0**
XYZ at 85 at expiration:	
Initial credit:	$640

Assigned on 400 shares @ 90:	($36,000)
400 shares sold @ market:	$34,000
75, 80, and 85 puts expire worthless:	-0-
Net profit/loss:	= **($1,360)**
XYZ at 76.60 at expiration:	
Initial credit:	$640
Assigned on 400 shares @ 90:	($36,000)
Exercise 85 puts to sell 400 shares:	$34,000
Exercise 80 puts to sell 400 shares:	$32,000
400 shares bought back @ market:	($30,640)
75 puts expire worthless:	-0-
Net profit/loss:	= **$0**
XYZ at 75 at expiration:	
Initial credit:	$640
Assigned on 400 shares @ 90:	($36,000)
Exercise 85 puts to sell 400 shares:	$34,000
Exercise 80 puts to sell 400 shares:	$32,000
400 shares bought back @ market:	($30,000)
75 puts expire worthless:	-0-
Net profit/loss:	= **$640**
XYZ below 75 at expiration:	
Initial credit:	$640
Assigned on 400 shares @ 90:	($36,000)
Exercise 85 puts to sell 400 shares:	$34,000
Exercise 80 puts to sell 400 shares:	$32,000
Assigned on 400 shares @ 75:	($30,000)
Net profit/loss:	= **$640**

Figure 8.14 is the condor order entry screen within the CyberTrader Pro software that shows the sample trade above. This should help you visualize how this type of order is typically entered.

Characteristics

While a short condor is primarily a breakout strategy, it is possible to put a slightly bullish or bearish bias on it, depending upon which strike prices you use. If you are completely neutral, you would want

FIGURE 8.14

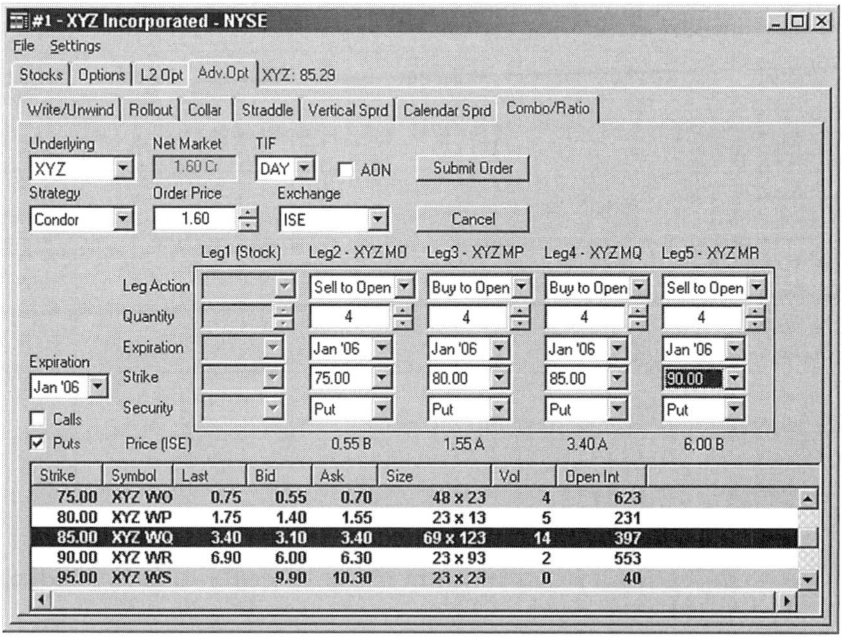

the stock to be halfway between the two middle strike prices at the time the condor is established. This would be an around-the-money (RTM) condor.

Table 8.6 illustrates how to properly structure a short condor spread to match your level of bullishness or bearishness. For example, if you are slightly bullish you may want to consider a short call condor that is below-the-money (BTM) or a short put condor that is above-the-money (ABTM). By contrast, if you are slightly bearish you may want to consider a short call condor that is above-the-money (ABTM) or a short put condor that is below-the-money (BTM). Remember, while little or no up or down moves in the stock could result in losses, to maximize your profit you want the stock above the highest strike price or below the lowest strike price on option expiration day.

Since your best chance of a profitable trade comes from a stock that breaks out of a certain range, you need to have a way of identifying which stocks might do this. Therefore, when you are researching stocks you can usually find good short condor candidates by looking for stocks with the following criteria:

TABLE 8.6

	<< Direction >>				<< Magnitude >>		
Strategy	**Bullish**	**Neutral**	**Breakout**	**Bearish**	**Extreme**	**Moderate**	**Slight**
Short call condor ABTM				X		X	
Short call condor RTM			X			X	
Short call condor BTM	X					X	
Short put condor ABTM	X					X	
Short put condor RTM			X			X	
Short put condor BTM				X		X	

- Expecting a sharp move in either direction due to pending news
  - Such as an earnings report.
- Typically a volatile stock but has recently been less volatile than normal.
  - The theory of volatility mean reversion would anticipate a pickup in volatility.
- Recent consolidation around a support or resistance level.
  - After consolidation stocks typically break out higher or lower.
- Currently trading at a price over $50 per share and is near the midpoint between two standard option strike prices, such as 55, 60, 65, 75, 80, 90, etc.

While these criteria might sound overly restrictive, you may be surprised how many good candidates you will find with only a little research. Once you have identified a potential short condor through this process, it is often very helpful to view what the strategy might look like by drawing the important price levels on a chart. This will help you visualize where you will be unprofitable and how much the stock must break out in order for your strategy to be profitable.

Using the sample 5 point short call condor discussed previously in this chapter, review the key price levels so you will know where to draw the lines on the chart.

Example 2A

Sell to open 10 XYZ Dec 65 Calls @ 9.40
Buy to open 10 XYZ Dec 70 Calls @ 5.40
Buy to open 10 XYZ Dec 75 Calls @ 2.35
Sell to open 10 XYZ Dec 80 Calls @ .75

Credit (CR) = 2.40 (1st leg - 2nd leg - 3rd leg + 4th leg)
Upper Breakeven (BE) = 77.60 (3rd strike + ML)
Lower Breakeven (BE) = 67.40 (2nd strike - ML)
Max Gain (MG) = 2.40 (credit received) (occurs beyond the outside strike prices)
Max Loss (ML) = 2.60 (1st strike - 2nd strike + credit) (occurs between the 2nd & 3rd strikes)
Total credit from this trade = $2,400 (CR × # of spreads × option multiplier) or (2.40 × 10 × 100)

Once you have calculated the key price levels, you can draw them on a chart. The lines you will want to show on the chart are the outside strike prices of 65 and 80 (max gain levels) and the upper and lower breakeven levels of 77.60 and 67.40. On CyberTrader Pro or Schwab's StreetSmart Pro software, you can do this using the support line tool (red line) for the outer BE lines and the resistance line tool (green line) for the MG thresholds as illustrated in Figure 8.15.

The upper and lower green lines represent the outer strike (max gain) levels. The inner red lines represent the breakeven levels. To be profitable XYZ must be outside the red lines by December option expiration.

Since Figure 8.15 presents data as of around November 2, the December short call condor has about 44 days until expiration. If XYZ is below 67.40 or above 77.60 at the December option expiration, this trade will be profitable. The maximum profit will be reached if XYZ is below 65 or above 80 at expiration. Losses will be incurred if XYZ closes between 67.40 and 77.60 at expiration with the maximum loss of $2,600 occurring at all prices between 70 and 75.

As with most short condor spreads, the maximum loss price range is much wider than that of a short butterfly. Therefore, this

FIGURE 8.15

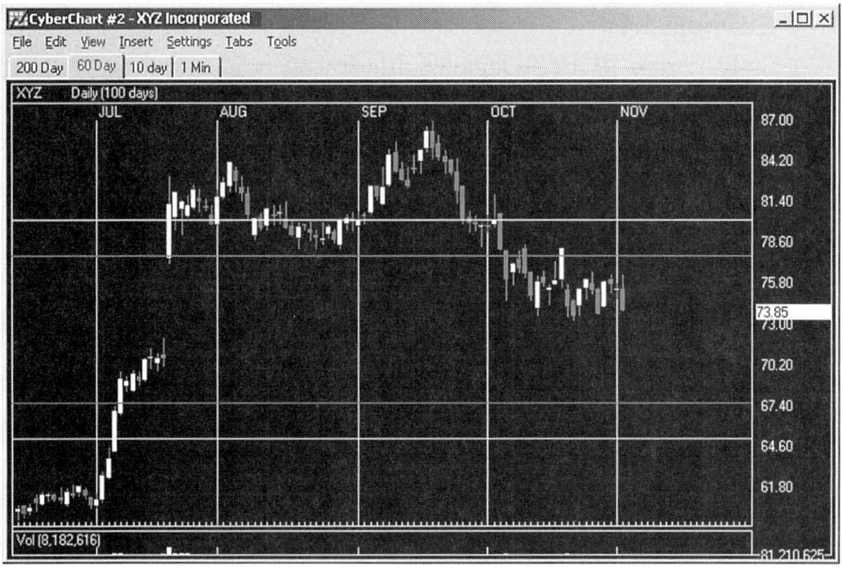

stock must move up or down sharply to be profitable. Though Figure 8.15 shows a stock that has been very volatile with a loss zone of 10.20 points (67.40–77.60) this stock needs to move up at least 3.75 points or down at least 6.45 points to be profitable. Your broker will also require you to hold a margin deposit equal to the maximum loss amount of $2,600 in your account to cover any possible losses.

Using the sample 5 point short put condor discussed previously in this chapter, review the key price levels so you will know where to draw the lines on the chart.

Example 2B

Sell to open 4 XYZ Jan 75 Puts @ .55
Buy to open 4 XYZ Jan 80 Puts @ 1.55
Buy to open 4 XYZ Jan 85 Puts @ 3.40
Sell to open 4 XYZ Jan 90 Puts @ 6.00

Credit (CR) = 1.60 (1st leg – 2nd leg – 3rd leg + 4th leg)
Upper Breakeven (BE) = 76.60 (3rd strike + ML)
Lower Breakeven (BE) = 88.40 (2nd strike – ML)

Max Gain (MG) = 1.60 (credit received) (occurs beyond the outside strike prices)

Max Loss (ML) = 3.40 (1st strike – 2nd strike + credit) (occurs between 2nd & 3rd strikes)

Total credit from this trade = $640 (CR × # of spreads × option multiplier) or (1.60 × 4 × 100)

Once you have calculated the key price levels, you can draw them on a chart. The lines you will want to show on the chart are the outside strike prices of 75 and 90 (max gain levels) and the upper and lower breakeven levels of 88.40 and 76.60. On CyberTrader Pro or Schwab's StreetSmart Pro software, you can do this using the support line tool (red line) for the outer BE lines and the resistance line tool (green line) for the MG thresholds as illustrated in Figure 8.16.

The upper and lower green lines represent the outer strike (max gain) levels. The inner red lines represent the breakeven levels. To be profitable, XYZ must be outside the red lines by December option expiration.

FIGURE 8.16

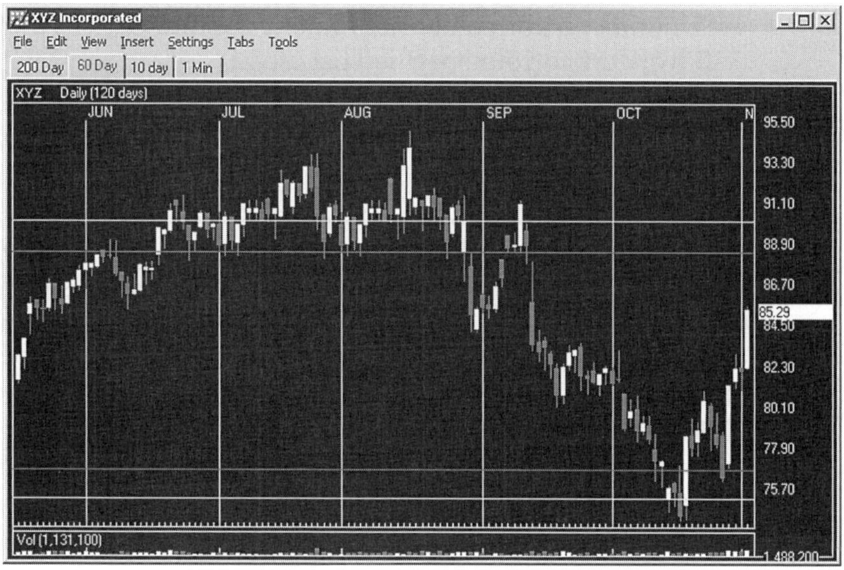

Since Figure 8.16 presents data as of around November 2, the January short put condor has about 78 days until expiration. If XYZ is below 76.60 or above 88.40 at the January option expiration, this trade will be profitable. The maximum profit will be reached if XYZ is below 75 or above 90 at expiration. Losses will be incurred if XYZ closes between 76.60 and 88.40 at expiration, with the maximum loss of $1,360 occurring at all prices between 80 and 85.

As with most short condor spreads, the maximum loss price range is much wider than that of a short butterfly. Therefore, this stock must move up or down sharply to be profitable. Though this chart shows a stock that has been very volatile, with a loss zone of 11.80 points (76.60–88.40), this stock needs to move up at least 3.11 points or down at least 8.69 points to be profitable. Your broker will also require you to hold a margin deposit equal to the maximum loss amount of $1,300 in your account to cover any possible losses.

While entering a four-legged order may seem complicated, there are a number of reasons why it makes sense to enter a condor as a single order rather than two separate spreads.

Advantages

- Since you can specify a single price for the whole strategy, the market can fluctuate while your order is open and there are a number of different prices among the four options that will work out to your specified net credit.
- Since all four legs are part of the same order, they must execute in an equal 1×1×1×1 ratio or not at all.

Disadvantages

- Most of the option exchanges handle these orders manually, which could result is slower fill reports than you are used to on simpler orders.
- As of year-end 2005, only the International Securities Exchange (ISE) and the Chicago Board Options Exchange (CBOE) had the ability to execute condors in a fully electronic manner.

CHAPTER 9

Iron Condor Spreads

Standard condor spreads offer you the opportunity to limit losses in exchange for a limited gain potential. They involve the simultaneous purchase and sale of options contracts of the same class (puts or calls), in the same expiration month, on the same underlying security, at four different strike prices. By contrast, iron condors involve buying and selling of both puts *and* calls at four different strike prices.

IRON CONDOR SPREADS EXPLANATION

In many cases, condor spreads may require that you temporarily establish a long or short stock position. The resulting long or short position will need to be closed out in the market to fully realize the profit potential of the strategy. This is explained in more detail later in this chapter.

Author's Note: While their approach and characteristics are slightly different, both condors and iron condors are equally effective in providing ways for you to take advantage of higher priced stocks you believe will either remain range-bound or will break out one way or the other. The best part is you have a choice, and with both puts and calls at your disposal and a range of strike prices from which to choose, there is a good chance you will be able to construct one to suit your sentiment and trading style.

Two of the key concepts to understand before you begin trading condor spreads are how to determine your sentiment (whether you are breakout or neutral) and how to calculate the maximum loss (ML), maximum gain (MG), and breakeven points (BE). With iron condors, these calculations will vary depending upon whether the spread is initially established as a net debit or net credit. Because of the unique profit and loss characteristics of iron condor spreads, the amount of the initial margin requirement and the maintenance margin requirement is likely to be determined more by your broker than by industry regulations. In some cases, you may be required to maintain funds in your account that exceed your maximum possible loss. You can determine your sentiment and calculate the ML, MG, and BE for any iron condor strategy by applying the following rules:

1. Arrange your iron condor spread from lowest to highest strike price.
   a. Leg 1 is the put contract with the lowest strike price.
   b. Leg 2 is the put contract with the next highest strike price.
   c. Leg 3 is the call contract with the next highest strike price.
   d. Leg 4 is the call contract with the highest strike price.
2. Determine whether your sentiment is neutral or breakout on the spread.
   a. If legs 1 and 4 are buys, you are neutral.
      i. This is considered a long iron condor.
   b. If legs 1 and 4 are sells, you are breakout.
      i. This is considered a short iron condor.
3. Determine whether the spread was entered at a net debit or a net credit.
   a. A long iron condor is entered at a net credit.
   b. A short iron condor is entered at a net debit.
4. Calculate the **ML**.
   a. If long iron condor, the ML is lower strike – second strike + the initial credit.
      i. The ML will occur at any price above the leg 4 strike price.
      ii. The ML will occur at any price below the leg 1 strike price.
   b. If short iron condor, the debit is the ML.
      i. The ML occurs between the two middle strike prices.

5. Calculate the **MG**.
   a. If long iron condor, then the MG is the initial credit received.
      i. The MG occurs only between the two middle strike prices.
   b. If short iron condor, the MG is the second strike – lowest strike – debit.
      i. The MG occurs above the highest strike price or below the lowest strike price.
6. Calculate the **BE**.
   a. If long iron condor, the upper BE is the third strike price + MG.
   b. If long iron condor, the lower BE is the second strike price – MG.
   c. If short iron condor, the upper BE is the third strike price + ML.
   d. If short iron condor, the lower BE is the second strike price – ML.

TYPES OF IRON CONDOR SPREADS

The are only two types of iron condor spreads, long iron condors and short iron condors. Long iron condors are used when you have a neutral sentiment, and short iron condors are used when you have a breakout sentiment. They also differ by whether you pay an initial debit or receive an initial credit when you establish them. Unlike standard long and short condors, iron condors involve buying and selling of both puts and calls. Since a long iron condor has profit and loss characteristics that are very similar to a long condor, which one you choose may be based primarily on whether you would rather receive a credit initially or pay a debit up front. If you are considering a long iron condor, it is a good idea to calculate the breakeven points for both the long iron condor and the long condor to ensure that you trade the one that is most beneficial. This comparison will be made in more detail later in this chapter.

Long Iron Condor—Quick Overview

A long iron condor is made up of one long put at the lowest strike, one short put at the lower middle strike, one short call at the upper middle strike, and one long call at the highest strike, with the same strike price interval between all legs. All legs should also have the same expiration month. All sides of this spread are opening transactions, and the quantity of all four legs is always the same. This strategy is actually made up of one credit put spread and one credit call spread. If you are familiar with strangles, this can also be viewed as being made up of one short strangle and one long strangle combined together as a single strategy (see Figure 9.1).

At Entry The white line in Figure 9.1 represents what the strategy typically looks like at the point of entry. As expiration approaches, the curve moves toward the black lines, which illustrate the final profit and loss boundaries at expiration.

Direction Neutral

When to Use You would typically employ a long iron condor in neutral markets and would hope to profit if the underlying stock

FIGURE 9.1

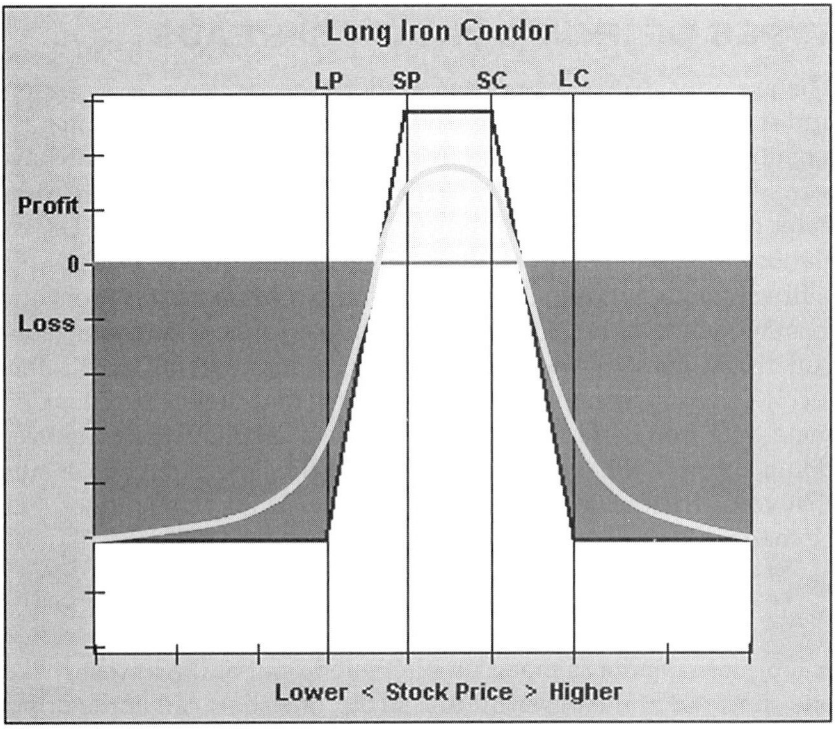

remains relatively flat until the expiration date of the options. Generally, the underlying stock price should be between the two middle strike prices at the time of entry. If you are moderately bullish or bearish, you could use strike prices that are slightly higher or lower, but this strategy generally works best when you stay closest to the middle.

Risk vs. Reward Limited risk with limited profit potential

Volatility The effect of volatility varies depending upon the strike prices chosen. The strategy generally benefits moderately from volatility decreases.

Time Decay The effect of time decay on this strategy varies with the underlying stock's price level in relation to the strike prices. If the stock price is between the outer strike prices, the effect is positive. If the stock price is above the upper strike price or below the lower strike price, the effect is negative (see Table 9.1).

Prior to Expiration

- Because the highest and lowest strike options have little value to begin with, the two middle strike options will lose time value more quickly than either of the long options.
  - As a result, with little or no movement in the underlying stock price, the spread can often be closed out at a profit prior to expiration once time value has eroded sufficiently.
  - However, because of the large number of commissions involved, this strategy is typically held until expiration if the stock has remained relatively stable.
- Similarly, if the underlying stock rises or drops sharply enough, the spread can often be closed out at a loss that is

TABLE 9.1

Greeks	Below-the-money	At-the-money	Above-the-money
Delta	Positive	Neutral	Negative
Gamma	Negative	Negative	Negative
Theta	Negative	Positive	Negative
Vega	Positive	Negative	Positive

less than the maximum loss possible if held until expiration, because time value will erode the value of the middle strike options more quickly.

- Comparing the early close loss to the maximum potential loss at expiration can help you decide if holding until expiration makes sense.

At Expiration

- Below the lowest strike, all call options expire worthless, but all put options are exercised and/or assigned and max loss is sustained.
- Between the lowest and lower middle strikes, all call options expire worthless and the long put expires worthless. Long stock will be acquired through assignment of the short put. The long stock can then be sold in the market. The trade may or may not be profitable.
- Between the two middle strikes, all options expire worthless and max gain is achieved.
- Between the upper middle and highest strikes, all put options expire worthless and the long call expires worthless. Short stock will be obtained through the assignment of the short call. The short stock position can then be closed out in the market. The trade may or may not be profitable.
- Above the highest strike, all put options expire worthless but all call options are exercised and/or assigned and max loss is sustained.

Long Iron Condor—Detail

When you establish a long iron condor, the combined credit from the second and third legs will exceed the combined cost of the first and fourth legs. As a result, a long iron condor is established at a net credit. This type of strategy is intended to take advantage of a stock that is moving sideways and is therefore considered a neutral strategy.

Example

Buy to open 5 XYZ Dec 50 Puts @ .50
Sell to open 5 XYZ Dec 55 Puts @ 1.55
Sell to open 5 XYZ Dec 60 Calls @ 1.10
Buy to open 5 XYZ Dec 65 Calls @ .40

Credit (CR) = 1.75 (–1st leg + 2nd leg + 3rd leg – 4th leg)
Lower Breakeven (BE) = 53.25 (2nd strike – MG)
Upper Breakeven (BE) = 61.75 (3rd strike + MG)
Max Gain (MG) = 1.75 (credit received) (occurs between 2nd & 3rd strikes)
Max Loss (ML) = –3.25 (1st strike – 2nd strike + credit) (occurs beyond the outside strike prices)

When you set up an order like this, most condor order entry systems automatically calculate the market price of this 5/5/5/5 spread. To do so manually, reduce the spread by its greatest common factor of 5 to 1/1/1/1. Then multiply each leg by the market price using the ask price on the legs you are buying and the bid price on the legs you are selling:

1 × –.50A = –.50
1 × +1.55B = +1.55
1 × +1.10B = +1.10
1 × –.40A = –.40
Net = +1.75 × 5 spreads × 100 shares per contract = $875 total initial credit

Figure 9.2 depicts the profit/loss zones of this example, including the breakeven points at the option expiration date.

As you can see, the maximum gain on this strategy, which occurs between the prices of 55 and 60 at expiration, is $875. There are two breakeven points at 53.25 and 61.75. All prices below 53.25 or above 61.75 result in a loss. The maximum loss on the upside or downside is –$1,625. To get a better feel for the profit and loss zones, see the following sample prices at expiration.

XYZ at 50 at expiration:

Initial credit:	$875
Assigned on 55 puts to buy 500 shares:	($27,500)
500 shares sold @ market:	$25,000
All other options expire worthless:	-0-
Net profit/loss:	= **($1,625)**

XYZ at 53.25 at expiration:

Initial credit:	$875
Assigned on 55 puts to buy 500 shares:	($27,500)

FIGURE 9.2

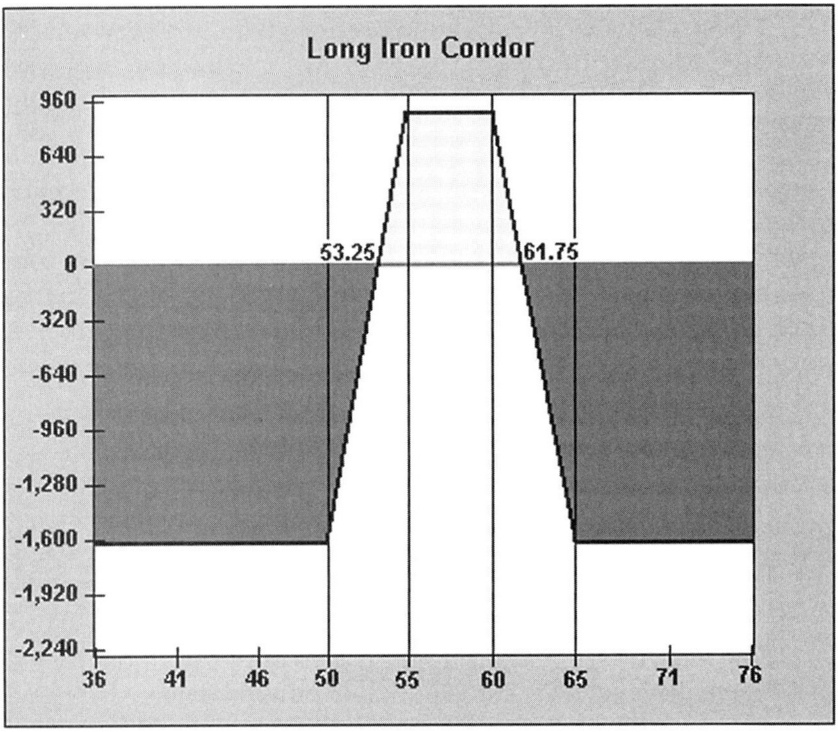

Strategy at Expiration

500 shares sold @ market:	$26,625
All other options expire worthless:	-0-
Net profit/loss:	= **$0**

XYZ at 55 at expiration:

Initial credit:	$875
All options expire worthless:	-0-
Net profit/loss:	= **$875**

XYZ at 60 at expiration:

Initial credit:	$875
All options expire worthless:	-0-
Net profit/loss:	= **$875**

XYZ at 61.75 at expiration:

Initial credit:	$875
Assigned on 60 calls to short 500 shares:	$30,000
500 shares bought back @ market:	($30,875)
All puts expire worthless:	-0-
Net profit/loss:	= **$0**

XYZ above 65 at expiration:

Initial credit:	$875
Assigned on 60 calls to short 500 shares:	$30,000
Exercise 65 calls:	($32,500)
All puts expire worthless:	-0-
Net profit/loss:	= **($1,625)**

Figure 9.3 is the order entry screen within the CyberTrader Pro software that shows the sample trade above. This should help you visualize how this type of order is typically entered.

FIGURE 9.3

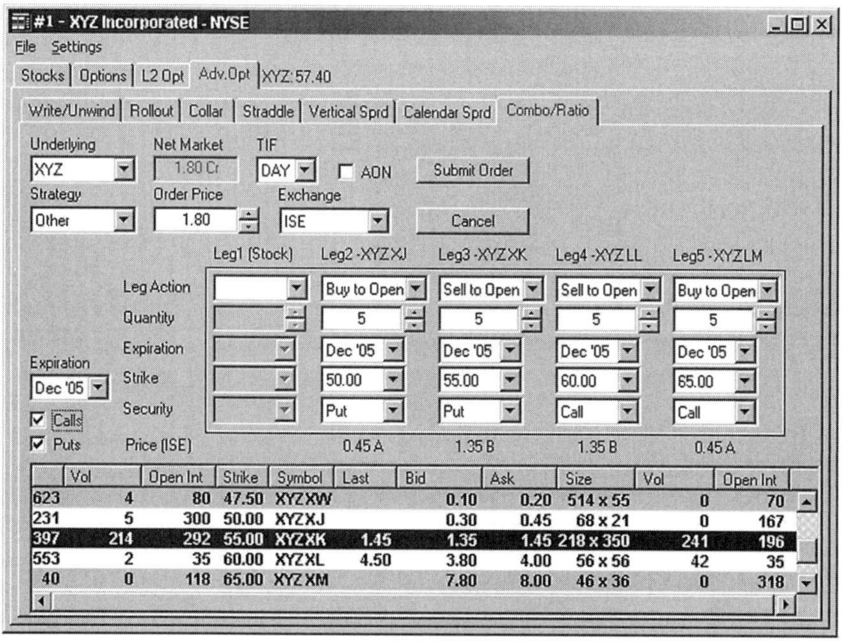

Short Iron Condor—Quick Overview

A short iron condor is made up of one short put at the lowest strike, one long put at the lower middle strike, one long call at the upper middle strike, and one short call at the highest strike, with the same strike price interval between all legs. All legs should also have the same expiration month. All sides of this spread are opening transactions, and the quantity of all four legs is always the same. This strategy is actually made up of one long strangle and one short strangle combined together as a single strategy. This can also be viewed as being made up of one put debit spread and one call debit spread (see Figure 9.4).

At Entry The white line in Figure 9.4 represents what the strategy typically looks like at the point of entry. As expiration

FIGURE 9.4

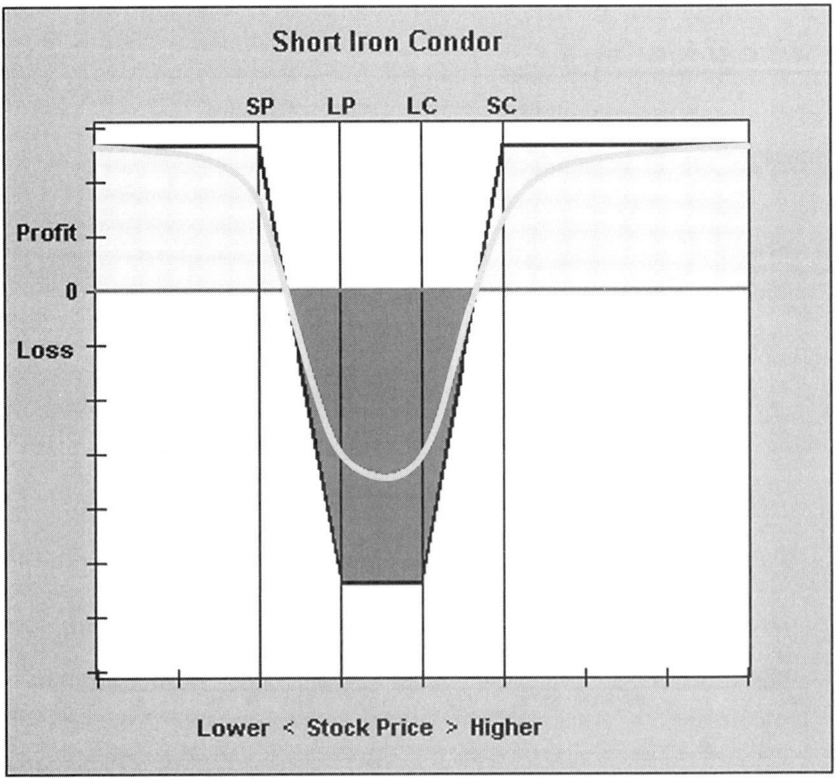

approaches, the curve moves toward the black lines, which illustrate the final profit and loss boundaries at expiration.

Direction Breakout

When to Use You would typically employ a short iron condor in uncertain markets and would hope to profit if the underlying stock breaks out either higher or lower than the current price by the expiration date of the options. Generally, the underlying stock price should be between the two middle strike prices at the time of entry. If you are moderately bullish or bearish, you could use strike prices that are slightly higher or lower, but this strategy generally works best when you stay closest to the middle.

Risk vs. Reward Limited risk with limited profit potential

Volatility The effect of volatility varies depending upon the strike prices chosen. This strategy generally benefits moderately from volatility increases.

Time Decay The effect of time decay on this strategy varies with the underlying stock's price level in relation to the strike prices. If the stock price is between the outer strike prices, the effect is negative. If the stock price is above the upper strike price or below the lower strike price, the effect is positive (see Table 9.2).

Prior to Expiration

- Because the highest and lowest strike options have little value to begin with, the two middle strike options will lose time value more quickly than either of the long options.
  - As a result, with little or no movement in the underlying stock price, the spread can often be closed out at a loss that is less than the maximum loss possible if held until

TABLE 9.2

Greeks	Below-the-money	At-the-money	Above-the-money
Delta	Negative	Neutral	Positive
Gamma	Positive	Positive	Positive
Theta	Positive	Negative	Positive
Vega	Positive	Positive	Positive

  expiration, because time value will erode the value of the middle strike options more quickly.
- Similarly, if the underlying stock rises or drops sharply enough, the spread can often be closed out at a gain that is less than the maximum gain possible if held until expiration.
  - Comparing the early close gain to the maximum potential gain at expiration can help you decide if holding until expiration makes sense.
  - However, because of the large number of commissions involved, this strategy is typically held until expiration if the stock has begun to move higher or lower.

At Expiration

- Below the lowest strike, all call options expire worthless and all put options are exercised and/or assigned and max gain is achieved.
- Between the lowest and lower middle strikes, all call options expire worthless and the short put expires worthless. Short stock will be acquired through exercise of the long put. The short stock position can then be closed out in the market. The trade may or may not be profitable.
- Between the two middle strikes, all options expire worthless and the max loss is sustained.
- Between the upper middle and highest strikes, all put options expire worthless and the short call expires worthless. Long stock will be obtained through the exercise of the long call. The long stock position can then be sold in the market. The trade may or may not be profitable.
- Above the highest strike, all put options expire worthless and all call options are exercised and/or assigned and the max gain is achieved.

Short Iron Condor—Detail

When you establish a short iron condor, the combined debit from the second and third legs will exceed the combined credit of the first and fourth legs. As a result, a short iron condor is always established at a net debit. This type of strategy is intended to take advantage of a stock that is expected to move sharply in either direction and is therefore considered a breakout strategy.

Example

Sell to open 4 XYZ Jan 75 Puts @ .55
Buy to open 4 XYZ Jan 80 Puts @ 1.55
Buy to open 4 XYZ Jan 85 Calls @ 4.10
Sell to open 4 XYZ Jan 90 Calls @ 1.75

Debit (DR) = 3.35 (1st leg – 2nd leg – 3rd leg + 4th leg)
Lower Breakeven (BE) = 76.65 (2nd strike – ML)
Upper Breakeven (BE) = 88.35 (3rd strike + ML)
Max Gain (MG) = 1.65 (2nd strike – 1st strike – debit) (occurs beyond the outside strike prices)
Max Loss (ML) = –3.35 (debit paid) (occurs between 2nd & 3rd strikes)

When you set up an order like this most condor order entry systems automatically calculate the market price of this 4/4/4/4 spread. To do so manually, reduce the spread by its greatest common factor of 4 to 1/1/1/1. Then multiply each leg by the market price using the ask price on the legs you are buying and the bid price on the legs you are selling:

1 × +.20 = +.55
1 × –1.05 = –1.55
1 × –2.20 = –4.10
1 × +.30 = +1.75
Net = –3.35 × 4 spreads × 100 shares per contract = ($1,340) total initial debit

Figure 9.5 depicts the profit/loss zones of this example, including the breakeven points at the option expiration date.

As you can see, the maximum gain on this strategy, which occurs only above or below the outer strike prices at expiration, is $660. There are two breakeven points at 76.65 and 88.35. All prices between 76.65 and 88.35 result in a loss. The maximum loss is –$1,340 and occurs only between the two middle strike prices of 80 and 85. To get a better feel for the profit and loss zones, see the following sample prices at expiration.

XYZ above 90 at expiration:

Initial debit:	($1,340)
Long 85 calls exercised to buy 400 shares:	($34,000)
Short 90 calls assigned to sell 400 shares:	$36,000

FIGURE 9.5

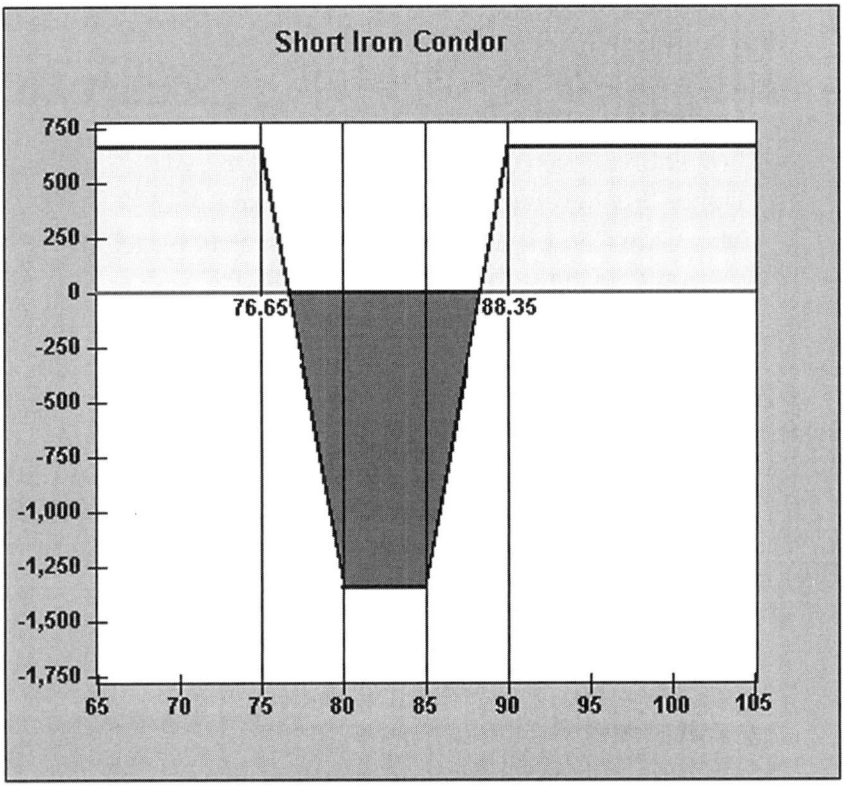

Strategy at Expiration

All puts expire worthless:	-0-
Net profit/loss:	= **$660**

XYZ at 90 at expiration:

Initial debit:	($1,340)
Long 85 calls exercised to buy 400 shares:	($34,000)
400 shares sold @ market:	$36,000
All puts expire worthless:	-0-
Net profit/loss:	= **$660**

XYZ at 88.35 at expiration:

Initial debit:	($1,340)
Long 85 calls exercised to buy 400 shares:	($34,000)

400 shares sold @ market:	$35,340
All puts expire worthless:	-0-
Net profit/loss:	= **$0**
XYZ at 85 at expiration:	
Initial debit:	($1,340)
All options expire worthless:	-0-
Net profit/loss:	= **($1,340)**
XYZ at 76.65 at expiration:	
Initial debit:	($1,340)
Exercise long puts & sell 400 shares:	$32,000
Buy back 400 shares @ market:	($30,660)
All calls expire worthless	-0-
Net profit/loss:	= **$0**
XYZ below 75 at expiration:	
Initial debit:	($1,340)
Exercise long puts & sell 400 shares:	$32,000
Assigned on short 75 puts:	($30,000)
All calls expire worthless	-0-
Net profit/loss:	**= $660**

Figure 9.6 is the condor order entry screen within the Cyber-Trader Pro software that shows the sample trade above. This should help you visualize how this type of order is typically entered.

Characteristics

A long iron condor is primarily a neutral strategy, and a short iron condor is primarily a breakout strategy. Both are typically most effective when the underlying stock is at the middle strike price at the point of entry. If you have a slightly bullish or bearish bias, a standard condor is usually a better choice.

As Table 9.3 illustrates, since a long iron condor is a credit strategy, it will generally require the underlying stock to remain fairly neutral, due to the typically narrow profit zone. A slightly wider profit zone can sometimes (though not always) be obtained with the same neutral sentiment by using a long standard condor spread. However, a long standard condor spread will require you to pay a debit up front rather than receive a credit. A short iron condor, by contrast, is a debit strategy and will generally require a moderate

FIGURE 9.6

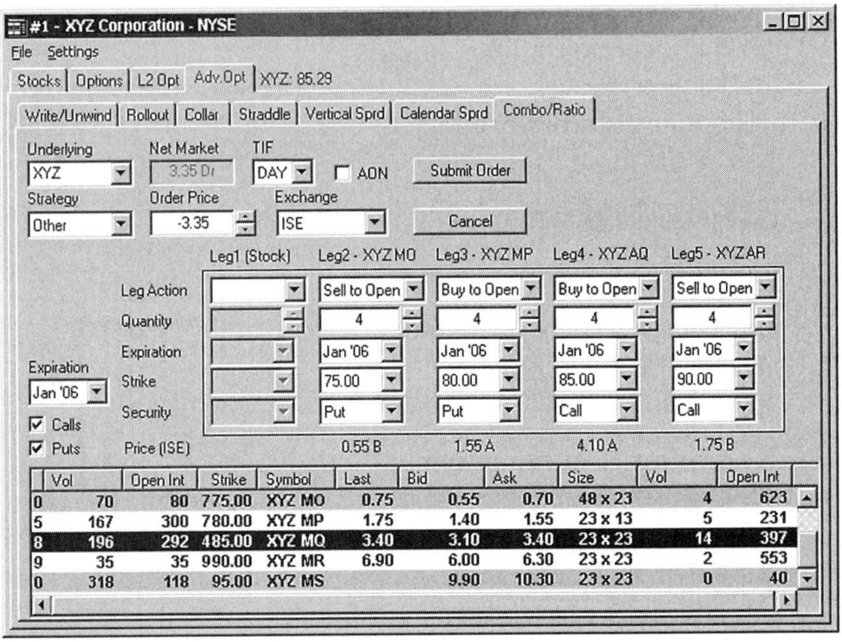

breakout in order to reach profitability due to the fairly narrow loss zone. This breakout can sometimes (though not always) be slightly less than is required for a short standard condor, but it also requires you to pay a debit up front rather than receive a credit.

Long Iron Condor While the two strategies are very similar, one benefit of an iron condor over an iron butterfly is that the profit

TABLE 9.3

	<< Direction >>				<< Magnitude >>		
Strategy	**Bullish**	**Neutral**	**Breakout**	**Bearish**	**Extreme**	**Moderate**	**Slight**
Long iron condor		X			X		
Short iron condor			X			X	

zone is wider and it therefore requires less outcome precision at expiration in order to end up in the profitable zone. While good iron butterfly candidates can often be found in any price range because of their wider price zone, it is more likely that you will find iron condor candidates if you limit your selection to stocks trading over $50 per share. Therefore, when you are researching stocks you can usually find good long iron condor candidates by looking for stocks with the following criteria:

- In a 10–20 point channel for about 6–8 weeks or more
- Currently trading in about the middle of that channel
- No expected news or events coming up that might cause them to move out of that channel or cause a sharp increase in volatility.
  - Such as earnings or merger and acquisition news.
- Currently trading at a price over $50 per share and is near the midpoint between two standard option strike prices, such as 55, 60, 65, 75, 80, 90, etc.

You will notice that these criteria are identical to those for a long standard condor. Therefore, take a look at the stock chart examples used in the section on long standard condors (Chapter 8) for illustrations on how to draw the important price levels on a stock chart.

To help you determine which strategy makes the most sense, compare the two side by side for the same underlying stock and then decide based on the advantages or disadvantages. The following example is a comparison using the same example used previously in this chapter for the long put condor (see Figure 9.7) versus a comparable long iron condor (see Figure 9.8).

Example

Long Put Condor vs. Long Iron Condor

XYZ = 56.89

Buy 5 XYZ Dec 50 Puts @ .50A	Buy 5 XYZ Dec 50 Puts @ .50A
Sell 5 XYZ Dec 55 Puts @ 1.55B	Sell 5 XYZ Dec 55 Puts @ 1.55B
Sell 5 XYZ Dec 60 Puts @ 4.20B	Sell 5 XYZ Dec 60 Calls @ 1.10B
Buy 5 XYZ Dec 65 Puts @ 8.50A	Buy 5 XYZ Dec 65 Calls @ .40A
Debit (DR) = –3.25	Credit (CR) = 1.75
Lower Breakeven (BE) = 53.25	Lower Breakeven (BE) = 53.25
Upper Breakeven (BE) = 61.75	Upper Breakeven (BE) = 61.75
Max Gain (MG) = 1.75	Max Gain (MG) = 1.75
Max Loss (ML) = –3.25	Max Loss (ML) = –3.25

FIGURE 9.7 AND 9.8

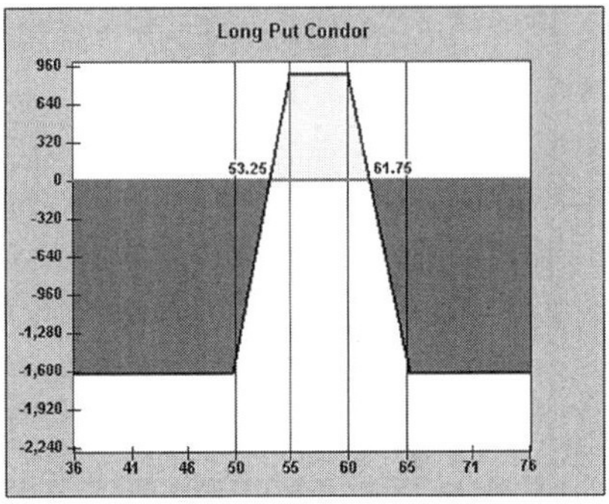

Strategy at Expiration

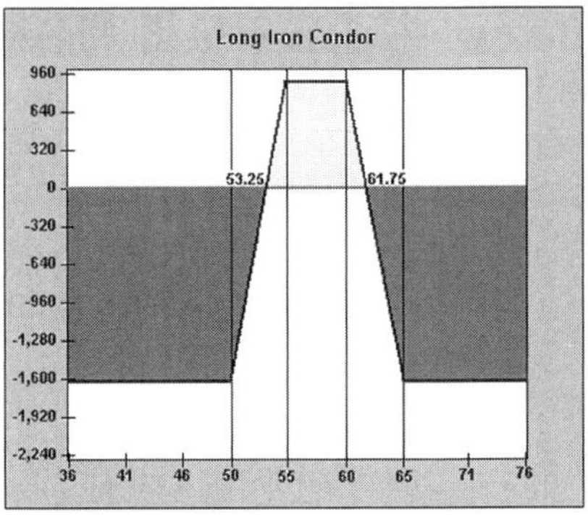

Strategy at Expiration

Advantages of long condor vs. long iron condor:

- Margin requirements may be lower.
  - Depending upon your broker.

Advantages of long iron condor vs. long condor:

- A net credit is received at the time the position is established.
  - Rather than paying a net debit for the long condor.

Short Iron Condor Since your best chance of a profitable trade comes from a stock that breaks out of a certain range, you need to have a way of identifying which stocks might do this. Therefore, when you are researching stocks you can usually find good short iron condor candidates by looking for stocks with the following criteria:

- Expecting a sharp move in either direction due to pending news
  - Such as an earnings report.
- Typically a volatile stock but has recently been less volatile than normal.
  - The theory of volatility mean reversion would anticipate a pickup in volatility.
- Recent consolidation around a support or resistance level.
  - After consolidation stocks typically break out higher or lower.

- Currently trading at a price over $50 per share and is near the midpoint between two standard option strike prices, such as 55, 60, 65, 75, 80, 90, etc.

You will notice that these criteria are identical to those for a short standard condor. Therefore, take a look at the stock chart examples used in the section on short standard condors (Chapter 8) for illustrations on how to draw the important price levels on a stock chart.

To help you determine which strategy makes the most sense, compare the two side by side for the same underlying stock and then decide based on the advantages or disadvantages. The following example is a comparison using the same example used previously is this chapter for the short put condor (see Figure 9.9) versus a comparable short iron condor (see Figure 9.10).

Example

Short Put Condor vs. Short Iron Condor

XYZ = 85.29

Sell 4 XYZ Jan 75 Puts @ .55B
Buy 4 XYZ Jan 80 Puts @ 1.55A
Buy 4 XYZ Jan 85 Puts @ 3.40A
Sell 4 XYZ Jan 90 Puts @ 6.00B
Credit (CR) = 1.60
Upper Breakeven (BE) = 88.40
Lower Breakeven (BE) = 76.60
Max Gain (MG) = 1.60
Max Loss (ML) = –3.40

Sell 4 XYZ Jan 75 Puts @ .55B
Buy 4 XYZ Jan 80 Puts @ 1.55A
Buy 4 XYZ Jan 85 Calls @ 4.10A
Sell 4 XYZ Jan 90 Calls @ 1.75B
Debit (DR) = 3.35
Lower Breakeven (BE) = 76.65
Upper Breakeven (BE) = 88.35
Max Gain (MG) = 1.65
Max Loss (ML) = –3.35

FIGURE 9.9 AND 9.10

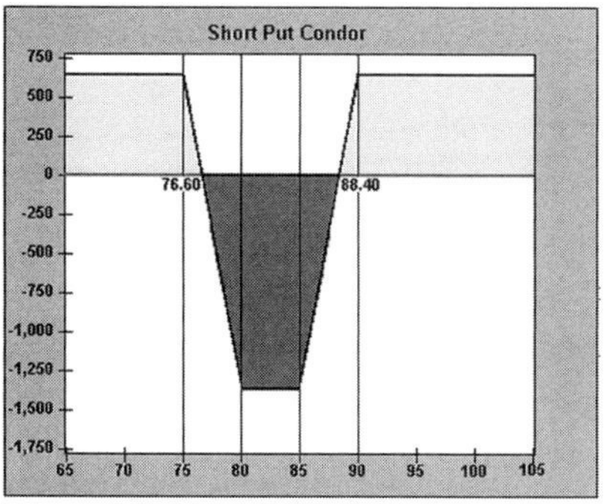

Strategy at Expiration

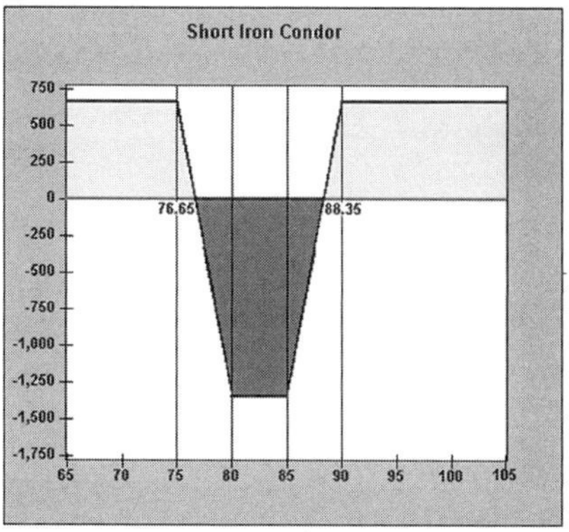

Strategy at Expiration

Advantages of short condor vs. short iron condor:

- A net credit is received at the time the position is established.
  - Rather than paying a net debit for the iron condor.

Advantages of short iron condor vs. short condor:

- Loss zone is 11.70 points (88.35 – 76.65).
  - Rather than 11.80 points (88.40 –76.60) for the short condor.
- Maximum loss is $1,340.
  - Rather than $1,360 for the short condor.
- Maximum gain is $660.
  - Rather than $640 for the short condor.
- There is no margin requirement.
  - Since this strategy is made up of two debit spreads.

SECTION 6

Arbitrage Spreads

CHAPTER 10

Box Spreads

A box spread is a trade designed to lock in a near riskless profit, when the combination of a long call / short put (or short call / long put) at a single strike price and a long put / short call (or short put / long call) of a different strike price can be established for less than the difference between the two strike prices. When this can be done, an arbitrage situation has been created that is completely independent of any movement in the underlying stock. All four legs of a box spread are of the same quantity, the same expiration month, and the same underlying security, but at only two different strike prices.

BOX SPREADS EXPLANATION

Since a properly executed box spread locks in a near riskless profit, it seems that this would be the perfect strategy. However, since a box spread is solely dependent upon a favorable pricing discrepancy

---

Author's Note: Opportunities to trade either short or long box spreads are very difficult to find without the use of options with many months until expiration. However, since many brokers now offer streaming quote data and order entry screens that can accommodate four-legged option orders, you may occasionally find them. I cannot stress enough how important it is to calculate the commissions before entering a box spread to ensure that it will still be profitable after all transaction costs of both establishing and closing the position have been taken into account.

between four different option contracts, instances where this discrepancy exists are very difficult to find. When opportunities do exist, the amount of profit available is generally very small and often will not be sufficient to cover commission costs.

Since box spreads are an option strategy most often utilized by option market makers, as a retail option trader you may find it necessary to employ sophisticated quote monitoring systems or computerized algorithms to find such opportunities. As automated trading becomes more and more common even among retail traders, box spreads are a strategy you should be aware of despite the fact that very few opportunities for establishing them will exist. Even if you never have the opportunity to trade a box spread, understanding the structure and profit and loss characteristics is valuable in building your overall knowledge of option strategies.

Commissions are an important consideration with box spreads. Since a box spread typically requires six commission charges, it is important to net the commission costs against the locked-in profit. If the commissions exceed the profit, the trade should be avoided. It is also critically important that a box spread be executed as a single trade. If you attempt to create a box spread by pairing two simple spreads together, it is very likely that the pricing will not be favorable enough to ensure a profit, unless the first simple spread has moved in your favor before the second simple spread is established.

Depending upon the price at expiration, box spreads may require that you temporarily establish a long or short stock position. The long or short positions that result from exercise or assignment will need to be closed out in the market to fully realize the profit opportunity. In some cases an assignment or exercise will be offset by an assignment or exercise of another leg in the strategy. The end result will always be a net cash amount equal to the difference between the initial credit or debit and the strike price difference. This is explained in more detail later in this chapter.

Two of the key concepts to understand before you begin trading box spreads are how to determine your sentiment and how to calculate the maximum loss (ML), maximum gain (MG), and breakeven points (BE). With box spreads these calculations are quite simple, because they are fixed throughout the life of the strategy. You can determine your sentiment and calculate the ML, MG, and BE for a box spread by applying the following rules:

1. Arrange your box spread from lowest to highest strike price.
   a. Leg 1 is the call contract with the lower strike price.
   b. Leg 2 is the put contract with the lower strike price.
   c. Leg 3 is the put contract with the higher strike price.
   d. Leg 4 is the call contract with the higher strike price.
2. Determine your sentiment.
   a. A box spread is always neutral.
3. Determine whether the spread was entered at a net debit or a net credit.
   a. A short box spread is entered at a net credit.
      i. Calculated as (1st leg –2nd leg + 3rd leg –4th leg)
   b. A long box spread is entered at a net debit.
      i. Calculated as (–1st leg + 2nd leg –3rd leg + 4th leg)
4. Calculate the **ML**.
   a. If the initial debit is greater than the difference between the two strike prices, there will be a guaranteed loss.
5. Calculate the **MG**.
   a. If the initial debit is less than the difference between the two strike prices, there will be a guaranteed gain.
6. Calculate the **BE**.
   a. If the initial debit is equal to the difference between the two strike prices, the trade will break even.

TYPES OF BOX SPREADS

There are only two types of box spreads, long box spreads and short box spreads. Both can be used regardless of your sentiment. They differ mainly by whether you pay an initial debit or receive an initial credit when you establish them. Since both are static strategies, which one you choose may be based primarily on whether you would rather receive a credit initially or pay a debit up front. Keep in mind, however, that a long box spread is made up of two debit spreads and, therefore, has no margin requirement. A short box spread is made up of two credit spreads, and despite the fact that it is a near riskless trade, your broker may not be able to pair all four legs up as a single strategy and may require margin maintenance equal to the difference between the low strike price and the high strike price times the number of spreads in the strategy.

Long Box Spread—Quick Overview

A long box spread is made up of one long call at the lower strike, one short put at the same lower strike, one long put at a higher strike, and one short call at the same higher strike. All legs should also have the same expiration month. All sides of this spread are opening transactions, and the quantity of all four legs is always the same (see Figure 10.1).

The greatest likelihood of finding a favorable long box spread opportunity exists the longer the time you have until options expiration, such as with LEAPs. This is primarily because of the cost of carry. However, when you can lock in a specific profit over the long term, it is likely to be no higher than the interest you would have been able to earn if the funds used to establish the long box spread were simply deposited into a money market account or invested in a Treasury bill for the same period of time.

FIGURE 10.1

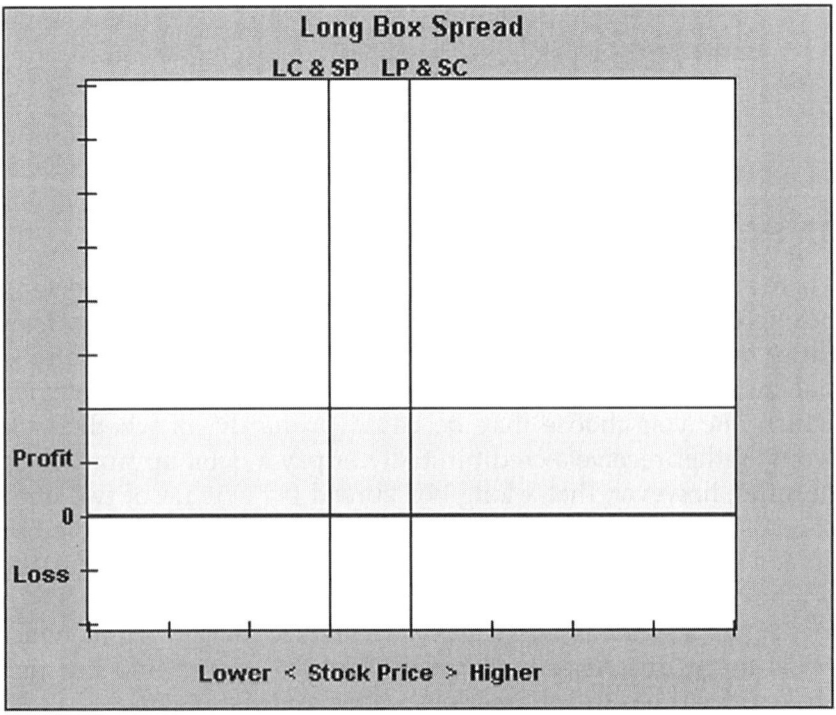

At Entry Since a long box spread is neutral to the market, the profit and loss chart looks the same throughout the life of the strategy.

Direction Static

When to Use You would typically employ a long box spread in an attempt to take advantage of option pricing inefficiencies. Since a long box spread is an arbitrage trade, if the spread can be established at a net debit price that is less than the difference between the two strikes, it locks in a profit. If the spread is established at a net debit price that is greater than the difference between the two strikes, it locks in a loss.

Risk vs. Reward Certain gain, certain breakeven, or certain loss

Volatility Neutral

Time Decay Neutral (see Table 10.1)

Prior to Expiration

- Because a short-term long box spread is established when there is a temporary price disparity, it may also be possible to close it out early if an opposite price disparity occurs such that the net credit that can be obtained is greater than the difference between the two strike prices. If this occurs, it may be possible to close the spread with a profit that is slightly higher than the profit that will occur at expiration, unless the commissions from doing so would exceed the commissions charged at expiration.
  - This is extremely unlikely to occur, and as a result, most box spreads are held until expiration.

TABLE 10.1

Greeks	Below-the-money	At-the-money	Above-the-money
Delta	Neutral	Neutral	Neutral
Gamma	Neutral	Neutral	Neutral
Theta	Neutral	Neutral	Neutral
Vega	Neutral	Neutral	Neutral

- If you have established a long box spread with several months until expiration, the value of the spread will increase as expiration approaches, and closing the spread early at a net profit is likely. However, since the strategy is neutral to the market, this should only be done if the net credit received from closing the spread early is equal to or greater than the difference between the two strike prices.
  - Again, it is important to evaluate the commission costs involved in closing the spread early. If the commissions are greater than they would be at expiration, they may negate any advantage of closing the spread early.

At Expiration

- Below the lower strike, the call options expire worthless but the put options are exercised and assigned, and the gain or loss will be equal to the difference between the initial debit and the strike difference.
- Between the two strikes, the short call and short put options expire worthless but the long call and long put options are exercised, and the gain or loss will be equal to the difference between the initial debit and the strike difference.
- Above the higher strike, the put options expire worthless but the call options are exercised and assigned, and the gain or loss will be equal to the difference between the initial debit and the strike difference.

Long Box Spread—Detail

When you establish a long box spread, the combined cost of the two long legs (first and third legs) will exceed the combined proceeds from the two short legs (second and fourth legs). If the cost of the long legs exceeds the proceeds from the short legs by less than the difference between the two strike prices, a locked-in profit will result at expiration. If the cost of the long legs exceeds the proceeds from the short legs by more than the difference between the two strike prices, a locked-in loss will result at expiration. This type of strategy is intended to take advantage of pricing inefficiencies that may exist in the marketplace and is therefore considered a static or neutral strategy.

Example

Buy to open 10 XYZ Jan 50 Calls @ 10.50
Sell to open 10 XYZ Jan 50 Puts @ .20
Buy to open 10 XYZ Jan 60 Puts @ 2.75
Sell to open 10 XYZ Jan 60 Calls @ 3.10

Debit (DR) = 9.95 (–1st leg + 2nd leg – 3rd leg + 4th leg)
Breakeven (BE) = n/a (when initial debit equals difference between strikes)
Max Gain (MG) = .05 (amount of difference) (when initial debit is less than difference between strikes)
Max Loss (ML) = n/a (amount of difference) (when initial debit is greater than difference between strikes)

When you set up an order like this, most order entry systems automatically calculate the market price of this 10/10/10/10 spread. To do so manually, reduce the spread by its greatest common factor of 10 to 1/1/1/1. Then multiply each leg by the market price using the ask price on the legs you are buying and the bid price on the legs you are selling:

1 × –10.50 = –10.50
1 × +.20 = +.20
1 × –2.75 = –2.75
1 × +3.10 = +3.10
Net = –9.95 × 10 spreads × 100 shares per contract = ($9,950) total initial debit

Figure 10.2 depicts the profit/loss zones of this example, including the breakeven points at the option expiration date.

As you can see, the maximum gain on this strategy, which occurs regardless of the underlying stock price at expiration, is $50. There are no breakeven points. There are no prices that result in a loss. To get a better feel for how this strategy works, see for the following sample prices at expiration.

XYZ at 45 at expiration:

Initial debit:	($9,950)
Assigned on 50 puts to buy 1,000 shares:	($50,000)
Exercise 60 puts to sell 1,000 shares:	$60,000

FIGURE 10.2

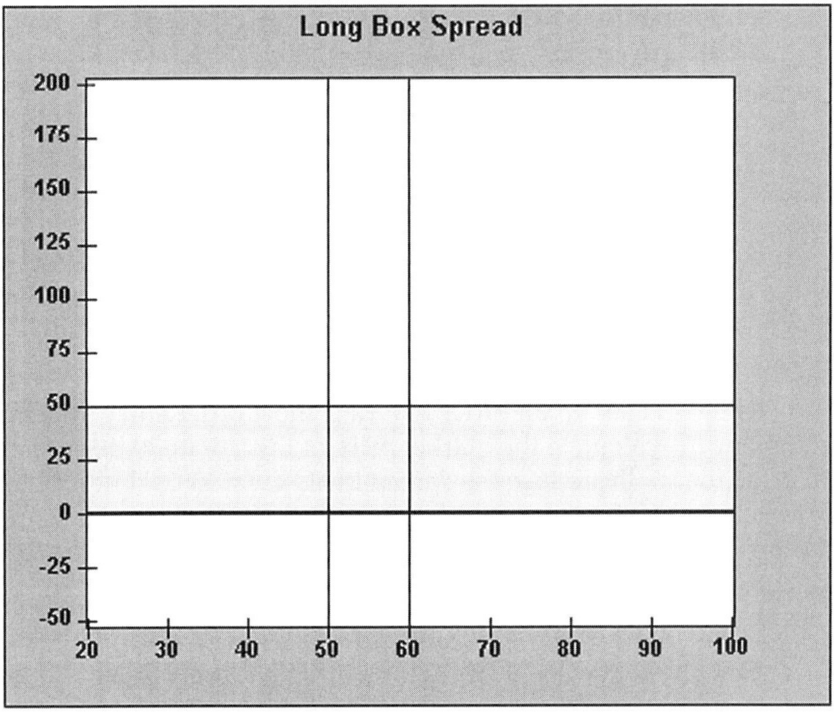

Strategy at Expiration

All call options expire worthless:	-0-
Net profit/loss:	= **$50**

XYZ at 50 at expiration:

Initial debit:	($9,950)
Exercise 60 puts to sell 1,000 shares:	$60,000
Buy 1,000 shares back @ market:	($50,000)
All other options expire worthless:	-0-
Net profit/loss:	= **$50**

XYZ at 55 at expiration:

Initial debit:	($9,950)
Exercise 50 calls to buy 1,000 shares:	($50,000)
Exercise 60 puts to sell 1,000 shares:	$60,000
Short 50 puts and 60 calls expire worthless:	-0-

Net profit/loss:	= **$50**
XYZ at 60 at expiration:	
Initial debit:	($9,950)
Exercise 50 calls to buy 1,000 shares:	($50,000)
Sell 1,000 shares @ market:	$60,000
All other options expire worthless:	-0-
Net profit/loss:	= **$50**
XYZ at 65 at expiration:	
Initial debit:	($9,950)
Exercise 50 calls to buy 1,000 shares:	($50,000)
Assigned on 60 calls to sell 1,000 shares:	$60,000
All put options expire worthless:	-0-
Net profit/loss:	= **$50**

Figure 10.3 is the order entry screen within the CyberTrader Pro software that shows the sample trade above. This should help you visualize how this type of order is typically entered.

FIGURE 10.3

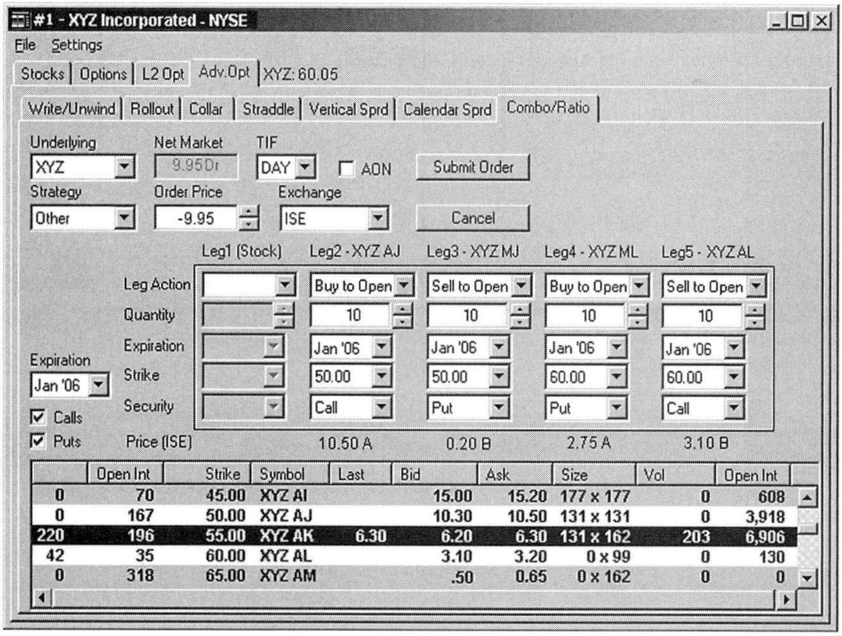

Short Box Spread–Quick Overview

A short box spread is made up of one short call at the lower strike, one long put at the same lower strike, one short put at a higher strike, and one long call at the same higher strike. All legs should also have the same expiration month. All sides of this spread are opening transactions, and the quantity of all four legs is always the same (see Figure 10.4).

The greatest likelihood of finding a favorable short box spread opportunity exists the shorter the time you have until options expiration. This is primarily because of the cost of carry. Once the cost of carry becomes negligible, pricing inefficiencies can sometimes be exploited. However, when you can lock in a specific profit over the short term, it is unlikely to be high enough to cover commission costs. It is very important to calculate commission costs before you establish a short box spread to ensure the trade will be profitable afterward.

FIGURE 10.4

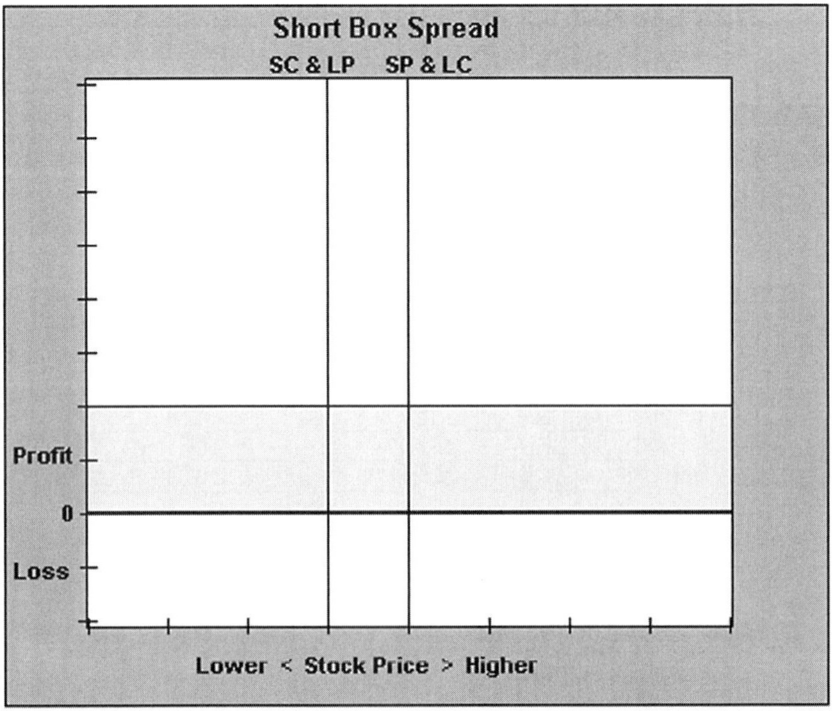

At Entry Since a short box spread is neutral to the market, the profit and loss chart looks the same throughout the life of the strategy.

Direction Static

When to Use You would typically employ a short box spread in an attempt to take advantage of option pricing inefficiencies. Since a short box spread is an arbitrage trade, if the spread can be established at a net credit that is greater than the difference between the two strikes, it locks in a profit. If the spread is established at a net credit that is less than the difference between the two strikes, it locks in a loss.

Risk vs. Reward Certain gain, certain breakeven, or certain loss

Volatility Neutral

Time Decay Neutral (see Table 10.2)

Prior to Expiration

- Because a short-term short box spread is established when there is a temporary price disparity, it may also be possible to close it out early if an opposite price disparity occurs such that the net debit that you would incur is less than the difference between the two strike prices. If this occurs, it may be possible to close the spread with a profit that is slightly higher than the profit that will occur at expiration, unless the commissions from doing so would exceed the commissions charged at expiration.
  - This is extremely unlikely to occur, and as a result, most box spreads are held until expiration.

TABLE 10.2

Greeks	Below-the-money	At-the-money	Above-the-money
Delta	Neutral	Neutral	Neutral
Gamma	Neutral	Neutral	Neutral
Theta	Neutral	Neutral	Neutral
Vega	Neutral	Neutral	Neutral

- If you have established a short box spread with several months until expiration, the value of the spread will increase as expiration approaches, so closing the spread early at a net profit becomes less and less likely over time. However, since it is very rare to find a short box spread opportunity with several months until expiration, it is likely that an opportunity to close the spread early will occur soon after the spread is established once the disparity is discovered.
    - Again, it is important to evaluate the commission costs involved in closing the spread early. If the commissions are greater than they would be at expiration, they may negate any advantage of closing the spread early.

At Expiration

- Below the lower strike, the call options expire worthless but the put options are exercised and assigned, and the gain or loss will be equal to difference between the initial credit and the strike difference.
- Between the two strikes, the long call and long put options expire worthless but the short call and short put options are assigned, and the gain or loss will be equal to difference between the initial credit and the strike difference.
- Above the higher strike, the put options expire worthless but the call options are exercised and assigned, and the gain or loss will be equal to difference between the initial credit and the strike difference.

Short Box Spread–Detail

When you establish a short box spread, the combined credit from the two short legs (first and third legs) will exceed the combined cost of the two long legs (second and fourth legs). If the credit from the short legs exceeds the cost of the long legs by more than the difference between the two strike prices, a locked-in profit will result at expiration. If the credit from the short legs exceeds the cost of the long legs by less than the difference between the two strike prices, a locked-in loss will result at expiration. This type of strategy is intended to take advantage of pricing inefficiencies that may exist in the marketplace and is therefore considered a static or neutral strategy.

Example

Sell to open 10 XYZ Nov 25 Calls @ 3.00
Buy to open 10 XYZ Nov 25 Puts @ .10
Sell to open 10 XYZ Nov 30 Puts @ 2.30
Buy to open 10 XYZ Nov 30 Calls @ .15

Credit (CR) = 5.05 (1st leg – 2nd leg + 3rd leg – 4th leg)
Breakeven (BE) = n/a (when initial credit equals difference between strikes)
Max Gain (MG) = .05 (amount of difference) (when initial credit is greater than difference between strikes)
Max Loss (ML) = n/a (amount of difference) (when initial credit is less than difference between strikes)

When you set up an order like this, most order entry systems automatically calculate the market price of this 10/10/10/10 spread. To do so manually, reduce the spread by its greatest common factor of 10 to 1/1/1/1. Then multiply each leg by the market price using the ask price on the legs you are buying and the bid price on the legs you are selling:

1 × +3.00 = +3.00
1 × –.10 = –.10
1 × +2.30 = +2.30
1 × –.15 = –.15
Net = +5.05 × 10 spreads × 100 shares per contract = $5,050 total initial credit

Figure 10.5 depicts the profit/loss zones of this example, including the breakeven points at the option expiration date.

As you can see, the maximum gain on this strategy, which occurs regardless of the underlying stock price at expiration, is $50. There are no breakeven points. There are no prices that result in a loss. To get a better feel for how this strategy works, see the following sample prices at expiration.

XYZ at 35 at expiration:

Initial credit:	$5,050
Assigned on 25 calls to sell 1,000 shares:	$25,000
Exercise 30 calls to buy 1,000 shares:	($30,000)
All put options expire worthless:	-0-
Net profit/loss:	= **$50**

FIGURE 10.5

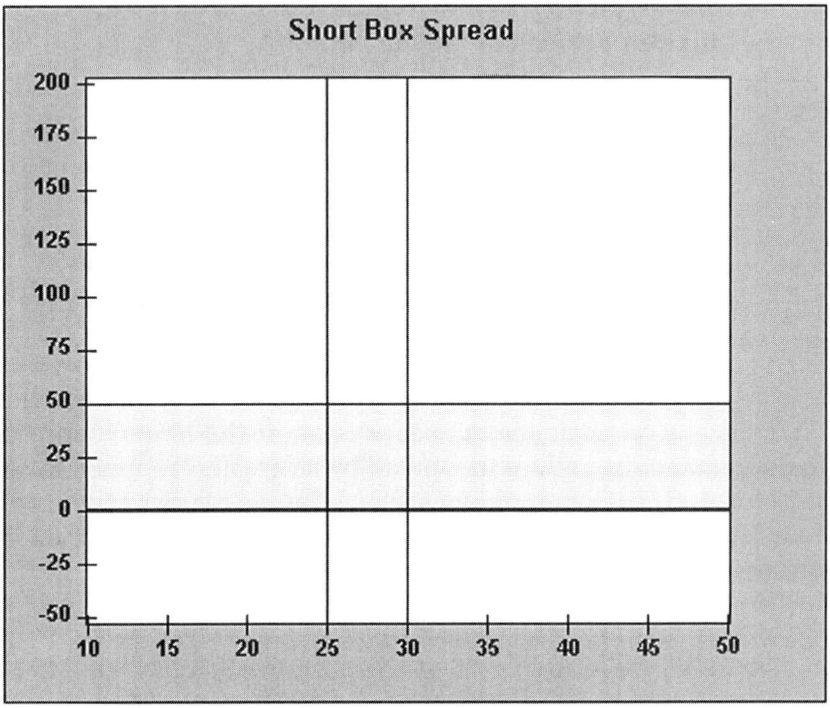

Strategy at Expiration

XYZ at 30 at expiration:	
Initial credit:	$5,050
Assigned on 25 calls to sell 1,000 shares:	$25,000
Buy 1,000 shares back @ market:	($30,000)
All other options expire worthless:	-0-
Net profit/loss:	= **$50**
XYZ at 27.50 at expiration:	
Initial credit:	$5,050
Assigned on 25 calls to sell 1,000 shares:	$25,000
Assigned on 30 puts to buy 1,000 shares:	($30,000)
30 calls and 25 puts expire worthless:	-0-
Net profit/loss:	= **$50**

XYZ at 25 at expiration:	
Initial credit:	$5,050
Assigned on 30 puts to buy 1,000 shares:	($30,000)
Sell 1,000 shares @ market:	$25,000
All other options expire worthless:	-0-
Net profit/loss:	= **$50**
XYZ at 20 at expiration:	
Initial credit:	$5,050
Assigned on 30 puts to buy 1,000 shares:	($30,000)
Exercise 25 puts to sell 1,000 shares:	$25,000
All call options expire worthless:	-0-
Net profit/loss:	= **$50**

Figure 10.6 is the order entry screen within the CyberTrader Pro software that shows the sample trade above. This should help you visualize how this type of order is typically entered.

FIGURE 10.6

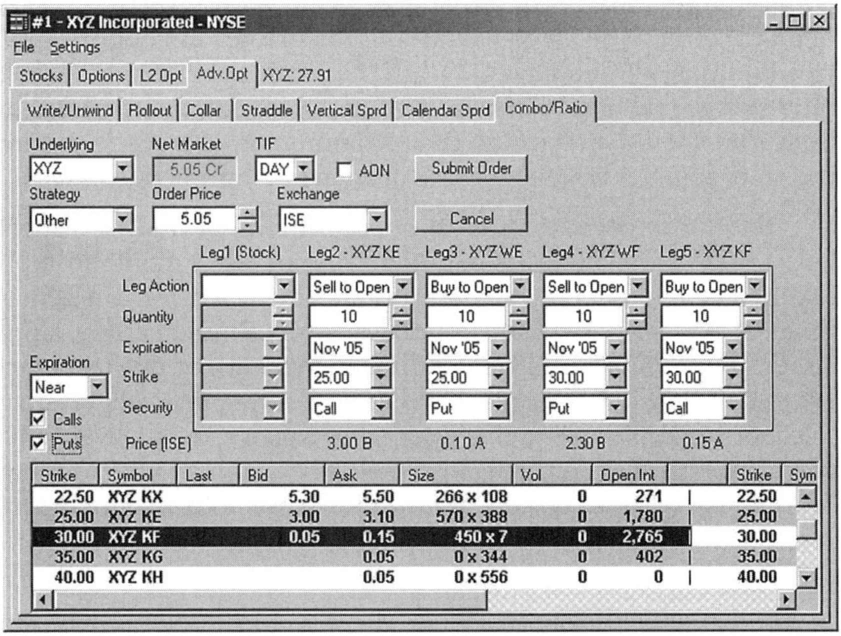

TABLE 10.3

	<< Direction >>				<< Magnitude >>		
Strategy	Bullish	Neutral	Breakout	Bearish	Extreme	Moderate	Slight
Long box spread		X			X		
Short box spread		X			X		

Characteristics

As Table 10.3 illustrates, box spreads are considered extremely neutral. Unlike other spread strategies, you do not have to hope the stock remains neutral. In this sense, neutral does not mean the stock must remain neutral, it simply means you are indifferent to movement in the underlying stock because it has no effect on the strategy. Once a box spread is established, you immediately know whether the outcome will be profitable or not.

Long Box Spread Your best opportunity of finding a long box spread candidate is by looking for stocks with available LEAPS. The farther out you go to expiration, the greater the opportunity. However, you should always weigh the profit opportunity against the risk-free rate of return on those funds over that same period of time. You should also factor in six commission charges to ensure the profit will not be completely consumed by transaction costs.

Short Box Spread Your best opportunity of finding a short box spread candidate exists in options of the closest month to expiration. Though difficult to find, pricing inefficiencies can sometimes be exploited. This can occur because of rounding errors, since options only trade in nickel and dime increments, or due to a market maker's option pricing tools that do not automatically update the quotes. Keep in mind that even when you can lock in a specific profit over the short term, it is unlikely to be high enough to cover commission costs, so be sure to take those costs into account before you establish a short box spread.

SECTION 7

Ratio Spreads

CHAPTER 11

Ratio Spreads and Ratio Backspreads

Unlike standard spreads, which offer you the opportunity to limit losses in exchange for a limited gain potential, ratio spreads sometimes involve significant risk or significant gain potential. They involve the simultaneous purchase and sale of two different series of options contracts of the same type (puts or calls) on the same underlying security. The main difference is that, while they are called spreads, the options are only partially spread. Because the quantity of options bought and sold is different, the remaining part is either left long or uncovered (naked).

RATIO SPREADS EXPLANATION

With standard ratio spreads (which includes both ratio spreads and ratio backspreads), the expiration month is the same, but the strike price will be different. In many cases ratio spreads may require that you temporarily establish a long or short stock position. That resulting long or short position will need to be closed out in the market to fully realize the profit potential of the strategy. This is explained in more detail later in this chapter.

Two of the key concepts to understand before you begin trading ratio spreads are how to determine your sentiment (whether

---

Author's Note: Since ratio spreads and ratio backspreads always result in some contracts not being spread, it is especially important to consider your risk tolerance before you establish your positions.

you are bullish or bearish) and how to calculate the maximum gain (MG), maximum loss (ML), and breakeven points (BE). These calculations will vary depending upon whether the spread is initially established with a net debit or net credit and whether or not it is entered using calls or puts. Ratio spreads are typically established at a small debit, and ratio backspreads are established at a small credit. You can determine your sentiment and calculate the MG, ML, and BE for any 1×2 ratio spread or 1×2 ratio backspread by applying the following rules:

1. Determine the main leg of the spread.
   a. For all ratio spreads, the main leg is simply the long option leg.
2. Determine whether you are bullish or bearish on the main leg.
   a. Long one call is moderately bullish.
   b. Long two calls is very bullish.
   c. Long one put is moderately bearish.
   d. Long two puts is very bearish.
3. Determine whether you are bullish or bearish on the spread.
   a. Your answer to step 2 holds true for the entire spread strategy.
4. Calculate the **MG**.
   a. MG is the net of the two strike prices + the initial credit.
   b. MG is the net of the two strike prices – the initial debit.
5. Calculate the **ML**.
   a. If call spread
      i. ML is unlimited to the upside.
      ii. ML is the initial debit to the downside.
         1. Or zero if entered at even or a net credit.
   b. If put spread
      i. ML to the downside is the short strike price – maximum gain.
      ii. ML to the upside is the initial debit.
         1. Or zero if entered at even or a net credit.
6. Calculate the **BE**.
   a. If call spread

            i. The lower BE is the long strike price + initial debit.
                1. Or zero if entered at even or a net credit.
            ii. The upper BE is the short strike price + MG.
        b. If put spread
            i. The upper BE is the long strike price – initial debit.
                1. Or zero if entered at even or a net credit.
            ii. The lower BE is the short strike price – MG.

RATIO BACKSPREADS EXPLANATION

1. Determine the main leg of the spread.
    - For all ratio spreads, the main leg is simply the long option leg.
2. Determine whether you are bullish or bearish on the main leg.
    - Long one call is moderately bullish.
    - Long two calls is very bullish.
    - Long one put is moderately bearish.
    - Long two puts is very bearish.
3. Determine whether you are bullish or bearish on the spread.
    - Your answer to step 2 holds true for the entire spread strategy.
4. Calculate the **ML**.
    - If entered at a net credit, ML is the net of the two strike prices – the initial credit.
    - If entered at a net debit, ML is the net of the two strike prices + the initial debit.
5. Calculate the **BE**.
    - If call backspread
        i. The lower BE is the short strike price + initial credit.
            1. Or zero if entered at even or a net debit.
        ii. The upper BE is the long strike price + ML.
    - If put backspread
        i. The upper BE is the short strike price – initial credit.
            1. Or zero if entered at even or a net debit.
        ii. The lower BE is the long strike price – ML.

6. Calculate the **MG**.
    - If call backspread
        i. MG is unlimited to the upside.
        ii. MG is the initial credit to the downside.
            1. Or zero if entered at even or a net debit.
    - If put backspread
        i. MG to the downside is the long strike – ML.
        ii. MG to the upside is the initial credit.
            1. Or zero if entered at even or a net debit.

TYPES OF RATIO SPREADS

The two main types of ratio spreads are 1×2 ratio spreads and 1×2 ratio backspreads. Both types of spreads involving call options are typically used when you are bullish, but they differ by your degree of bullishness. Call ratio backspreads are more bullish than call ratio spreads. Similarly, both types of spreads involving put options are typically used when you are bearish, but they too differ by your degree of bearishness. Put ratio backspreads are more bearish than put ratio spreads.

Since ratio backspreads are made up of a credit spread and an additional long option, your broker will require you to meet an initial margin requirement and maintain funds in your account equal to the maximum loss amount for the spread. Since ratio spreads are made up of a debit spread and an additional uncovered (naked) option, your broker will require a substantial margin deposit to cover the naked options, which cannot be spread against the long options. Although you may establish these types of spreads by entering them as a single order, most brokers will not display them as ratio spreads or ratio backspreads in your account. They will most likely be paired up as simple two-legged spreads and unrelated long or naked options. The basic structure of ratio spreads and ratio backspreads is as follows:

- **Call Ratio Spread**—Long one call at a low strike, short two calls at a higher strike.
    - Comprised of one debit call spread and one naked call option.
- **Put Ratio Spread**—Long one put at a high strike, short two puts at a lower strike.

   - Comprised of one debit put spread and one naked put option.
- **CallRatio Backspread**—Short one call at a low strike, long two calls at a higher strike.
   - Comprised of one credit call spread and one long call option.
- **Put Ratio Backspread**—Short one put at a high strike, long two puts at a lower strike.
   - Comprised of one credit put spread and one long put option.

Calculate Your Limit Price

An important thing to learn about ratio spreads is how to specify a net debit or credit when entering an order. With a normal spread, you simply net the two prices together. With a ratio spread, that will not work. In the example below, the first step is to reduce the ratio spread to the smallest common fraction. You do this by dividing by the greatest common factor. Then you would figure out the market price (also called the natural) by multiplying the number of contracts by the price and then netting the two legs together.

Example

Buy 15 XYZ May 60 Calls @ 3
Sell 18 XYZ May 65 Calls @ .75

15×18 reduces to 5×6
Then:
$5 \times -3 = -15$
$6 \times +.75 = +4.5$

The natural or market price is 10.50 debit for each 5 × 6 spread. Since you divided by 3 to reduce the ratio, you know that there are 3 (5×6) spreads.

To calculate the total cost of this trade, you would multiply the net price by the number of spreads times the options multiplier: $-10.50 \times 3 \times 100 = -\$3{,}150$.

Another way to approach this is to start with the amount you want to spend (or receive if entered for a credit) and work backward to determine your entry price.

Example If you want to enter the following trade:

ZYX = 33
and you only have $ 3,315 available to spend

Buy 10 ZYXAG quoting 4.70–5
Sell 5 ZYXAH quoting 3–3.20

Step 1 Reduce the 10 × 5 fraction to 2 × 1

Step 2 Multiply the buy side by the ask and net it against the sell side times the bid:

2 × –5 = –10
1 × 3 = 3

Net debit at the market price would be –7. You know there are 5 spreads (since you divided by 5 to reduce the ratio), so the cost of the trade at the market would be $3,500. Since you only have $3,315 to spend, you must find a net debit (less than 7) that will cost no more than $3,315.

Figure this out with the following steps:

1. Divide 3,315 by 100 (the options multiplier) = 33.15.
2. Divide 33.15 by the number of spreads (5) = 6.63.
3. Convert 6.63 to the next lower nickel or dime increment.
   a. Dime if both options are priced > 3 or nickel if at least one is < 3.
4. This spread could be entered at 6.60.
5. Calculate the total cost as 6.60 × 5 spreads × 100 = $3,300

Call Ratio Spreads—Quick Overview

A call ratio spread is made up of one long call at a lower strike and two short calls at a higher strike. Both legs should have the same expiration month. Both sides of this spread are opening transactions, and the number of contracts of the short leg should always be the twice the number of the long leg (see Figure 11.1).

At Entry The white line in Figure 11.1 represents what the strategy typically looks like at the point of entry. As expiration

FIGURE 11.1

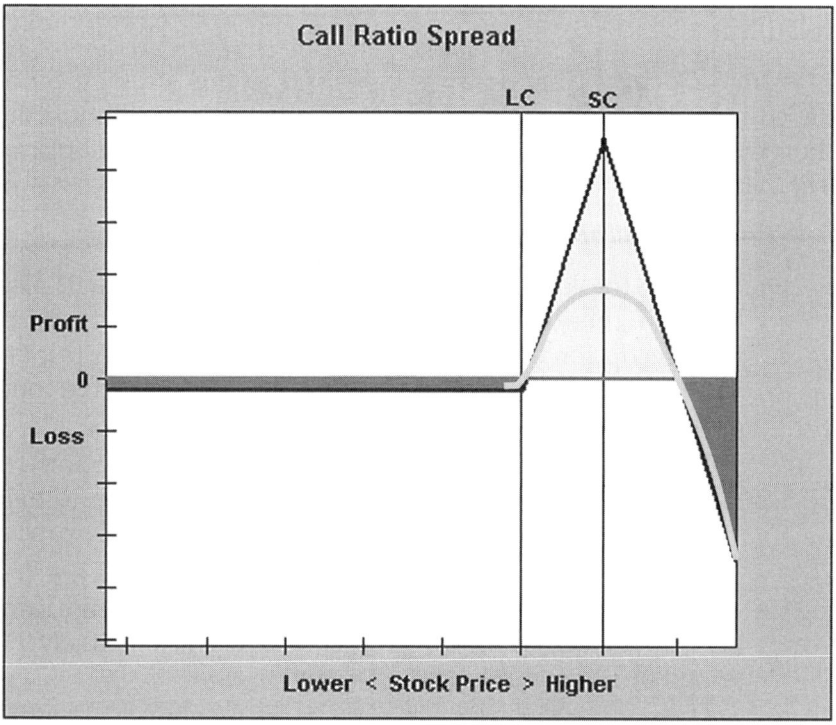

approaches, the curve moves toward the black lines, which illustrate the final profit and loss boundaries at expiration.

Direction Neutral to moderately bullish

When to Use You would typically employ a call ratio spread in a neutral to moderately bullish market or when you think the underlying stock will rise moderately, but not beyond a certain point by the expiration date of the options. Generally, you would select a long strike price that is close to the underlying stock price and a short strike price that is out-of-the-money. If the stock is between the two strike prices on option expiration or slightly above the short strike price, your spread will be profitable. Maximum profit will occur if the stock is at the short leg strike price on option expiration.

Risk vs. Reward Unlimited risk to the upside, with limited profit potential

Volatility This strategy generally benefits from a decrease in volatility.

Time Decay Time decay is beneficial to this strategy. Since the strategy has twice as many short options as long options, the short options lose more aggregate time value than the long options (see Table 11.1).

Prior to Expiration

- Because the long call has a lower strike price, it will also have a higher delta. As the underlying stock rises in price, the long option will gain value faster than the short options. Likewise, as the underlying stock drops in price, the long option will lose value faster than the short options.
  - However, since there are twice as many short options, if the delta on the short options is anywhere close to half the delta on the long options, the two will nearly cancel each other out.
- If the underlying stock rises or drops sharply enough, any loss savings from closing the spread early will likely be wiped out by commissions in many cases.
  - Comparing the early close loss to the maximum potential loss at expiration can help you decide if holding until expiration makes sense.
- Since this strategy benefits from time decay, it may be possible to close the spread out at a profit prior to expiration. That profit will be less than the maximum profit at expiration but

TABLE 11.1

Greeks	In-the-money	At-the-money	Out-of-the-money
Delta	Negative	Positive	Negative
Gamma	Negative	Positive	Negative
Theta	Positive	Positive	Positive
Vega	Negative	Negative	Negative

will approach the maximum profit as expiration approaches if the underlying stock is near the short strike price.

- Comparing the early close profit to the maximum potential profit at expiration can help you decide if holding until expiration makes sense.

At Expiration

- Below the lower strike, all options expire worthless and the initial debit is lost.
- Between the lower and upper strike, long stock will be acquired through exercise of the lower strike. The long stock can then be sold in the market. The trade will probably be profitable.
- Slightly above the higher strike, both options are exercised and/or assigned and the remaining short stock is covered in the market. The trade will probably be profitable.
- Significantly above the higher strike, both options are exercised and/or assigned and the remaining short stock is covered in the market. The trade will probably be unprofitable.

Call Ratio Spreads—Detail

When you establish a position using a call ratio spread, you will usually pay a slightly higher premium for the options you purchase than the amount you will receive on the premiums from the options sold. As a result, a call ratio spread is usually established at a small net debit. This type of spread is best used when you are neutral to only slightly bullish.

Example

Buy 5 XYZ Dec 65 Calls @ 1.90

Sell 10 XYZ Dec 70 Calls @ .85

Debit (DR) = .20

Lower BE = 65.20 (long strike price + the debit)

Upper BE = 74.80 (short strike price + MG)

MG = 4.80 (net of strikes – the debit) (occurs at the short strike price)

Upper ML = Unlimited

Lower ML = .20 (initial debit) (occurs below the long strike price)

When you set up an order like this, most order entry systems automatically calculate the market price of this 5/10 spread. To do so manually, reduce the spread by its greatest common factor of 5 to 1/2. Then multiply each leg by the market price using the ask price on the legs you are buying and the bid price on the legs you are selling:

1 × –1.90 = –1.90

2 × +.85 = +1.70

Net = –.20 × 5 spreads × 100 shares per contract = ($100) total up-front cost

Figure 11.2 depicts the profit/loss zones of this example, including the breakeven points at the option expiration date.

FIGURE 11.2

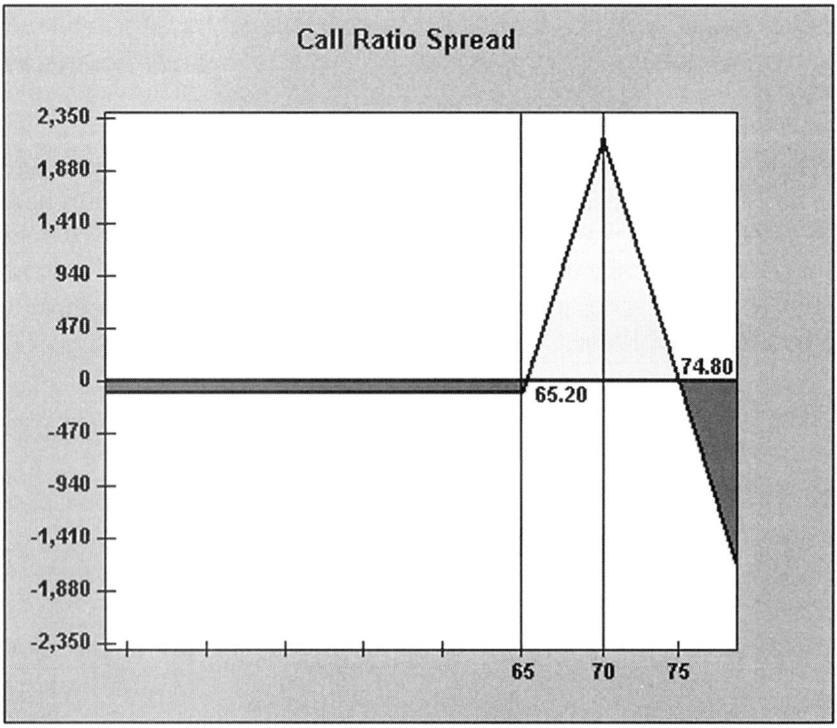

Strategy at Expiration

As you can see, the maximum gain on this strategy, which occurs only at the short strike price of 70, is $2,400. There are two breakeven points at 65.20 and 74.80. All prices below 65.20 or above 74.80 result in a loss. The maximum loss on the upside is unlimited, and the maximum loss on the downside is –$100. To get a better feel for the profit and loss zones, see for the following sample prices at expiration.

XYZ below 65 at expiration:	
Initial cost:	($100)
All options expire worthless:	-0-
Net loss of .20 × 5 spreads:	= **($100)**

XYZ at 65.20 at expiration:	
Initial cost:	($100)
Exercise 65 calls & acquire 500 shares:	($32,500)
500 shares sold @ market:	$32,600
70 calls expire worthless:	-0-
Net profit/loss:	= **$0**

XYZ at 70 at expiration:	
Initial cost:	($100)
Exercise 65 calls & acquire 500 shares:	($32,500)
500 shares sold @ market:	$35,000
70 calls expire worthless:	-0-
Net profit/loss:	= **$2,400**

XYZ at 72 at expiration:	
Initial cost:	($100)
Exercise 65 calls & acquire 500 shares:	($32,500)
Assigned on 70 calls to sell 1,000 shares:	$70,000
500 short shares bought back @ market:	($36,000)
Net profit/loss:	= **$1,400**

XYZ at 74.80 at expiration:	
Initial cost:	($100)
Exercise 65 calls & acquire 500 shares:	($32,500)
Assigned on 70 calls to sell 1,000 shares:	$70,000
500 short shares bought back @ market:	($37,400)
Net profit/loss:	= **$0**

XYZ at 76 at expiration:

Initial cost:	($100)
Exercise 65 calls & acquire 500 shares:	($32,500)
Assigned on 70 calls to sell 1,000 shares:	$70,000
500 short shares bought back @ market:	($38,000)
Net profit/loss:	= **($600)**

Figure 11.3 is the order entry screen within the CyberTrader Pro software that shows the sample trade above. This should help you visualize how this type of order is typically entered.

In this example, you would be bullish and would believe that XYZ will rally up past 65 but will probably not exceed 70. If XYZ is slightly above or below 70 at the December option expiration, this trade will be profitable. If XYZ exceeds 74.80, losses will begin to grow and can become substantial.

FIGURE 11.3

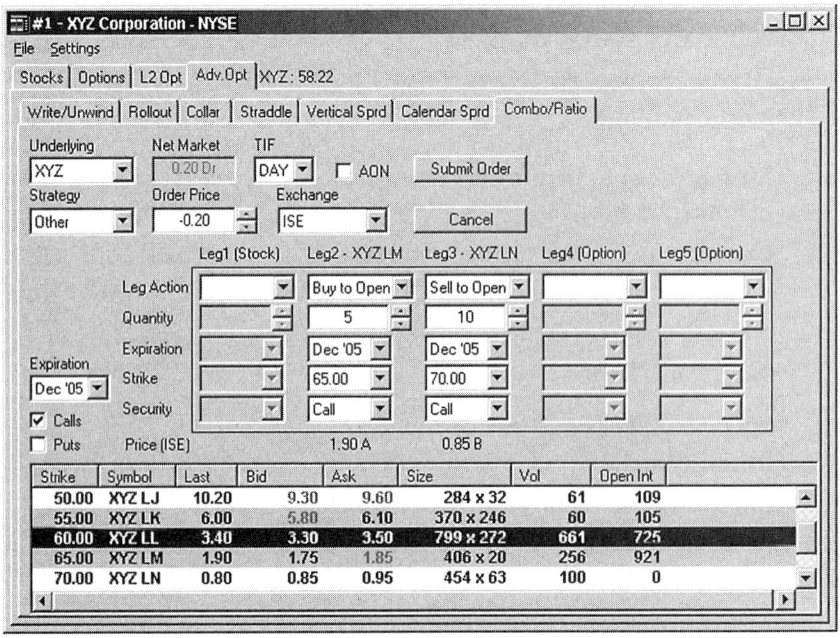

Put Ratio Spreads—Quick Overview

A put ratio spread is made up of one long put at a higher strike and two short puts at a lower strike. Both legs should have the same expiration month. Both sides of this spread are opening transactions, and the number of contracts of the short leg should always be the twice the number of the long leg (see Figure 11.4).

At Entry The white line in Figure 11.4 represents what the strategy typically looks like at the point of entry. As expiration approaches, the curve moves toward the black lines, which illustrate the final profit and loss boundaries at expiration.

Direction Neutral to moderately bearish

When to Use You would typically employ a put ratio spread in a neutral to moderately bearish market or when you think the underlying stock will drop moderately, but not beyond a certain

FIGURE 11.4

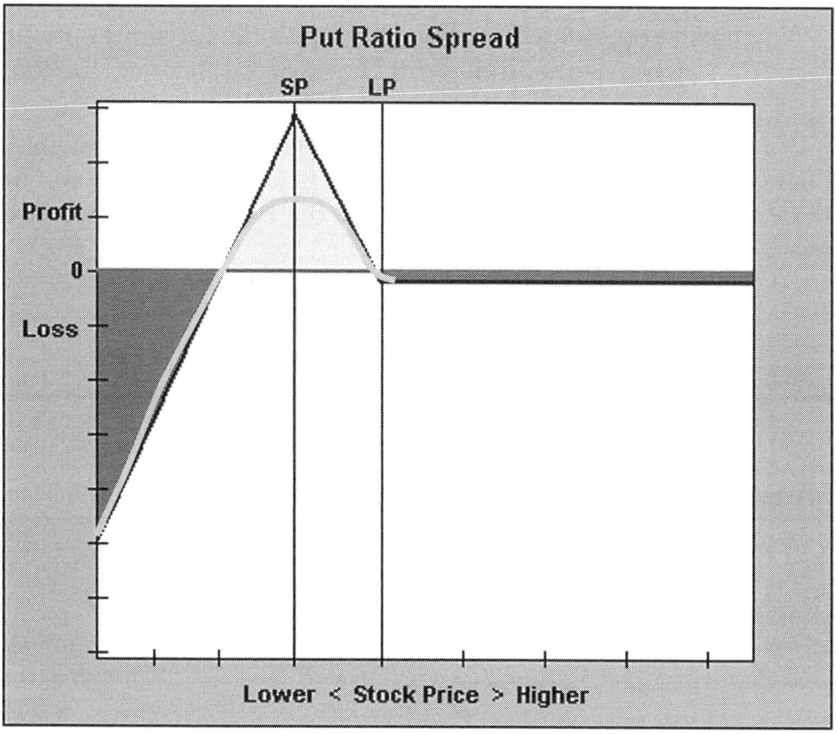

point by the expiration date of the options. Generally, you would select a long strike price that is close to the underlying stock price and a short strike price that is out-of-the-money. Typically, if the stock is between the two strike prices on option expiration or slightly below the short strike price, your spread will be profitable. Maximum profit will occur if the stock is at the short leg strike price on option expiration.

Risk vs. Reward Significant risk to the downside, with limited profit potential

Volatility This strategy generally benefits from a decrease in volatility.

Time Decay Time decay is beneficial to this strategy. Since the strategy has twice as many short options as long options, the short options lose more aggregate time value than the long options (see Table 11.2).

Prior to Expiration

- Because the long put has a higher strike price, it will also have a higher delta. As the underlying stock rises in price, the long option will lose value faster than the short options. Likewise, as the underlying stock drops in price, the long option will gain value faster than the short options.
  - However, since there are twice as many short options, if the delta on the short options is anywhere close to half the delta on the long options, the two will nearly cancel each other out.

TABLE 11.2

Greeks	In-the-money	At-the-money	Out-of-the-money
Delta	Positive	Negative	Positive
Gamma	Negative	Positive	Negative
Theta	Positive	Positive	Positive
Vega	Negative	Negative	Negative

- If the underlying stock rises or drops sharply enough, any loss savings from closing the spread early will likely be wiped out by commissions in many cases.
  - Comparing the early close loss to the maximum potential loss at expiration can help you decide if holding until expiration makes sense.
- Since this strategy benefits from time decay, it may be possible to close the spread out at a profit prior to expiration. That profit will be less than the maximum profit at expiration but will approach the maximum profit as expiration approaches if the underlying stock is near the short strike price.
  - Comparing the early close profit to the maximum potential profit at expiration can help you decide if holding until expiration makes sense.

At Expiration

- Above the higher strike, all options expire worthless and the initial debit is lost.
- Between the upper and lower strike, short stock will be acquired through exercise of the higher strike. The short stock can then be closed out in the market. The trade will probably be profitable.
- Slightly below the lower strike, both options are exercised and/or assigned and the remaining long stock is sold in the market. The trade will probably be profitable.
- Significantly below the lower strike, both options are exercised and/or assigned and the remaining long stock is sold in the market. The trade will probably be unprofitable.

Put Ratio Spreads—Detail

When you establish a position using a put ratio spread, you will usually pay a slightly higher premium for the options you purchase than the amount you will receive on the premiums from the options sold. As a result, a put ratio spread is usually established at a small net debit. This type of spread is best used when you are neutral to only slightly bearish.

Example

Buy 10 XYZ Jan 47.50 Puts @ 1.15
Sell 20 XYZ Jan 45 Puts @ .50

Debit (DR) = .15
Upper BE = 47.35 (long strike price – the debit)
Lower BE = 42.65 (short strike price – MG)
MG = 2.35 (net of strikes – the debit) (occurs at the short strike price)
Lower ML = 42.65 (short strike price – MG)
Upper ML = .15 (initial debit) (occurs above the long strike price)

When you set up an order like this, most order entry systems automatically calculate the market price of this 10/20 spread. To do so manually, reduce the spread by its greatest common factor of 10 to 1/2. Then multiply each leg by the market price using the ask price on the legs you are buying and the bid price on the legs you are selling:

$1 \times -1.15 = -1.15$
$2 \times +.50 = +1.00$
Net = $-.15 \times 10$ spreads $\times$ 100 shares per contract = ($150) total up-front cost

Figure 11.5 depicts the profit/loss zones of this example, including the breakeven points at the option expiration date.

As you can see, the maximum gain on this strategy, which occurs only at the short strike price of 45, is $2,350. There are two breakeven points at 42.65 and 47.35. All prices below 42.65 or above 47.35 result in a loss. The maximum loss on the downside is $42,650, and the maximum loss to the upside is –$150. To get a better feel for the profit and loss zones, see the following sample prices at expiration.

XYZ above 47.50 at expiration:

Initial cost:	($150)
All options expire worthless:	-0-
Net loss of .15 × 10 spreads:	**= ($150)**

XYZ at 47.35 at expiration:

Initial cost:	($150)
Exercise 47.50 puts & short 1,000 shares:	$47,500

FIGURE 11.5

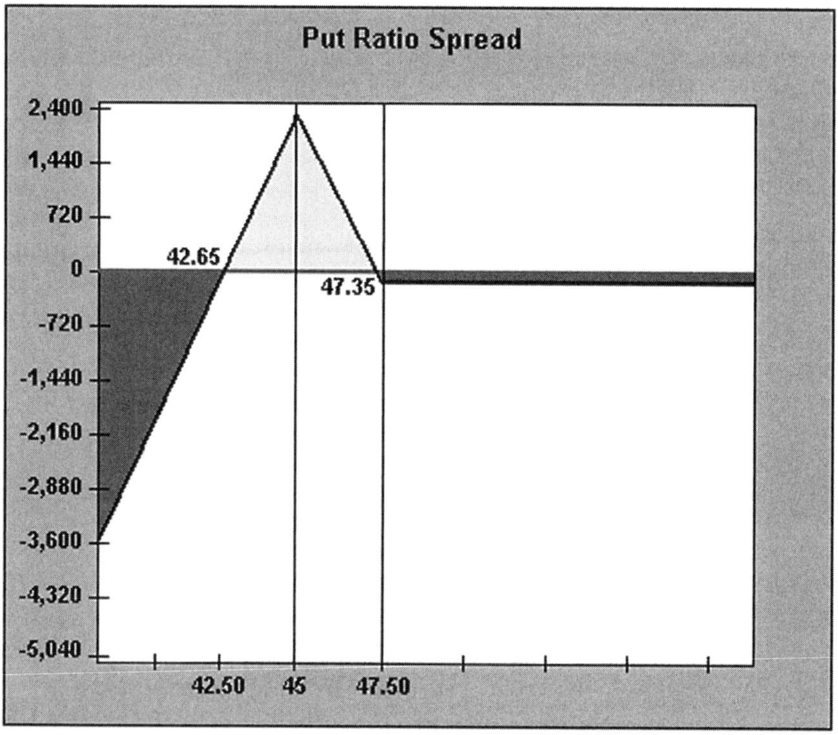

Strategy at Expiration

1,000 shares bought back @ market:	($47,350)
45 puts expire worthless:	-0-
Net profit/loss:	= **$0**

XYZ at 45 at expiration:

Initial cost:	($150)
Exercise 47.50 puts & short 1,000 shares:	$47,500
1,000 shares bought back @ market:	($45,000)
45 puts expire worthless:	-0-
Net profit/loss:	= **$2,350**

XYZ at 43 at expiration:

Initial cost:	($150)
Exercise 47.50 puts & short 1,000 shares:	$47,500

Assigned on 45 puts; buy 2,000 shares:	($90,000)
1,000 shares sold @ market:	$43,000
Net profit/loss:	= **$350**

XYZ at 42.65 at expiration:

Initial cost:	($150)
Exercise 47.50 puts & short 1,000 shares:	$47,500
Assigned on 45 puts; buy 2,000 shares:	($90,000)
1,000 shares sold @ market:	$42,650
Net profit/loss:	= **$0**

XYZ at 40 at expiration:

Initial cost:	($150)
Exercise 47.50 puts & short 1,000 shares:	$47,500
Assigned on 45 puts; buy 2,000 shares:	($90,000)
1,000 shares sold @ market:	$40,000
Net profit/loss:	= **($2,650)**

Figure 11.6 is the order entry screen within the CyberTrader Pro software that shows the sample trade above. This should help you visualize how this type of order is typically entered.

In this example, you would be bearish and would believe that XYZ will fall below 47.50, but probably not past 45. If XYZ is slightly above or below 45 at the January option expiration, this trade will be profitable. If XYZ drops below 42.65, losses will begin to grow and can become substantial. Always consider the impact of commissions on any profit or loss calculations you may make.

Call Ratio Backspreads—Quick Overview

A call ratio backspread is made up of one short call at a low strike and two long calls at a higher strike. Both legs should have the same expiration month. Both sides of this spread are opening transactions, and the number of contracts of the long leg should always be the twice the number of the short leg (see Figure 11.7).

At Entry The white line in Figure 11.7 represents what the strategy typically looks like at the point of entry. As expiration

FIGURE 11.6

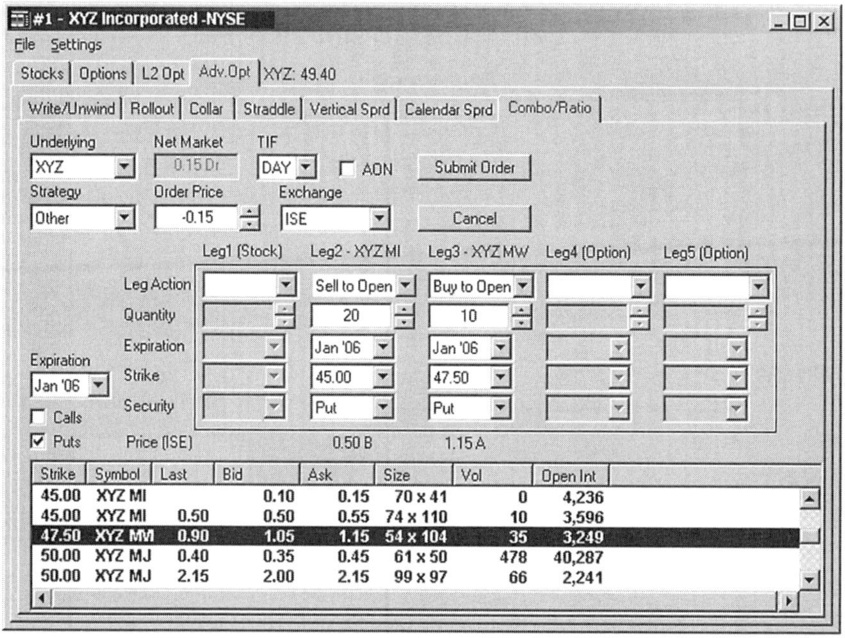

approaches, the curve moves toward the black lines, which illustrate the final profit and loss boundaries at expiration.

Direction Very bullish

When to Use You would typically employ a call ratio backspread in a very bullish market or when you think the underlying stock will rise substantially by the expiration date of the options. Generally, you would select a short strike price that is close to the underlying stock price and a long strike price that is out-of-the-money. If the stock is between the two strike prices or only slightly above the long strike price on option expiration, your spread will be unprofitable. Maximum loss will occur if the stock is at the long leg strike price on option expiration. Maximum profit will occur if the stock is significantly above the long leg strike price on option expiration.

Risk vs. Reward Unlimited profit potential to the upside, limited profit potential to the downside, with limited risk

FIGURE 11.7

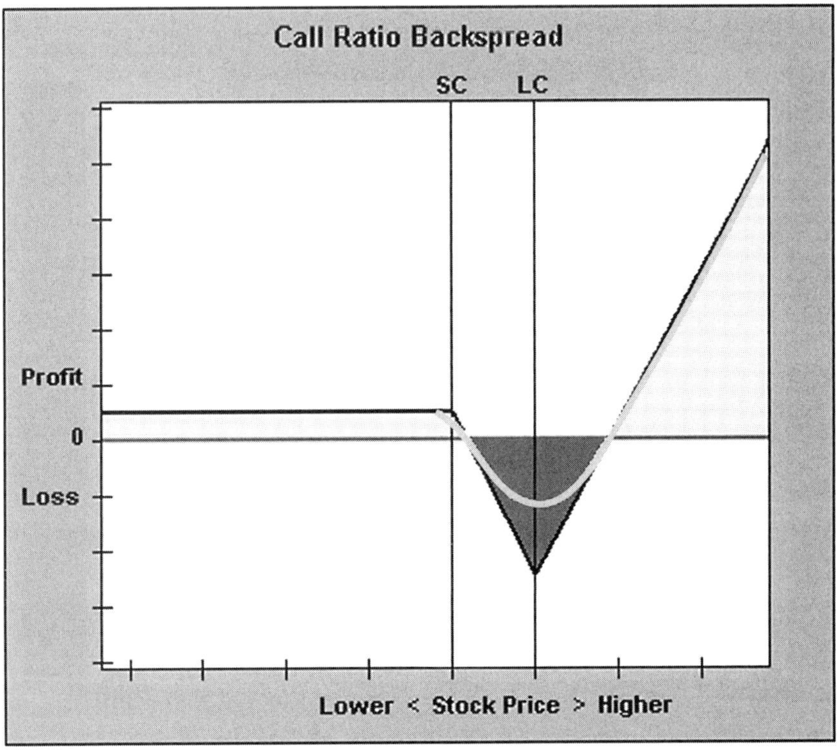

Volatility This strategy generally benefits from an increase in volatility.

Time Decay Time decay has a generally adverse effect on this strategy. Since the strategy has twice as many long options as short options, the long options lose more aggregate time value than the short options (see Table 11.3).

Prior to Expiration

- Because the short call has a lower strike price, it will also have a higher delta. As the underlying stock rises in price, the short option will gain value faster than the long options. Likewise, as the underlying stock drops in price, the short option will lose value faster than the long options.

TABLE 11.3

Greeks	In-the-money	At-the-money	Out-of-the-money
Delta	Positive	Negative	Positive
Gamma	Negative	Positive	Negative
Theta	Negative	Negative	Negative
Vega	Positive	Positive	Positive

- However, since there are twice as many long options, if the delta on the long options is anywhere close to half the delta on the short options, the two will nearly cancel each other out.
- If the underlying stock rises or drops sharply enough, it may be possible to close the spread out at a profit prior to expiration. That profit will be less than the maximum profit at expiration but will approach the maximum profit as expiration approaches.
  - Comparing the early close profit to the maximum potential profit at expiration can help you decide if holding until expiration makes sense.
- Since time decay works against you in this strategy, it may be possible to close the spread out at a loss prior to expiration. That loss will be less than the maximum loss at expiration but will approach the maximum loss as expiration approaches if the underlying stock is near the long strike price.
  - Comparing the early close loss to the maximum potential loss at expiration can help you decide if holding until expiration makes sense.

At Expiration

- Below the lower strike, all options expire worthless and the initial credit is retained.
- Between the lower and upper strike, short stock will be acquired through assignment of the lower strike. The short stock position can then be closed in the market. The trade will probably be unprofitable.

- Slightly above the higher strike, both options are exercised and/or assigned and the remaining long stock is sold in the market. The trade will probably be unprofitable.
- Significantly above the higher strike, both options are exercised and/or assigned and the remaining long stock is sold in the market. The trade will probably be profitable.

Call Ratio Backspreads—Detail

When you establish a position using a call ratio backspread, you will usually pay a slightly lower premium for the options you purchase than the amount you will receive on the premiums from the options sold. As a result, a call ratio backspread is usually established at a small net credit. This type of spread is best used when you are very bullish.

Example

Sell 4 XYZ Dec 25 Calls @ 1.30
Buy 8 XYZ Dec 30 Calls @ .25
Credit (CR) = .80
Lower BE = 25.80 (short strike price + the credit)
Upper BE = 34.20 (long strike price + ML)
Upper MG = unlimited
Lower MG = .80 (initial credit) (occurs below the short strike price)
ML = –4.20 (net of strikes – the credit) (occurs at long strike price)

When you set up an order like this, most order entry systems automatically calculate the market price of this 4/8 spread. To do so manually, reduce the spread by its greatest common factor of 4 to 1/2. Then multiply each leg by the market price using the ask price on the legs you are buying and the bid price on the legs you are selling:

$1 \times +1.30 = +1.30$
$2 \times -.25 = -.50$
Net = +.80 × 4 spreads = $320 total up-front credit

Figure 11.8 depicts the profit/loss zones of this example, including the breakeven points at the option expiration date.

FIGURE 11.8

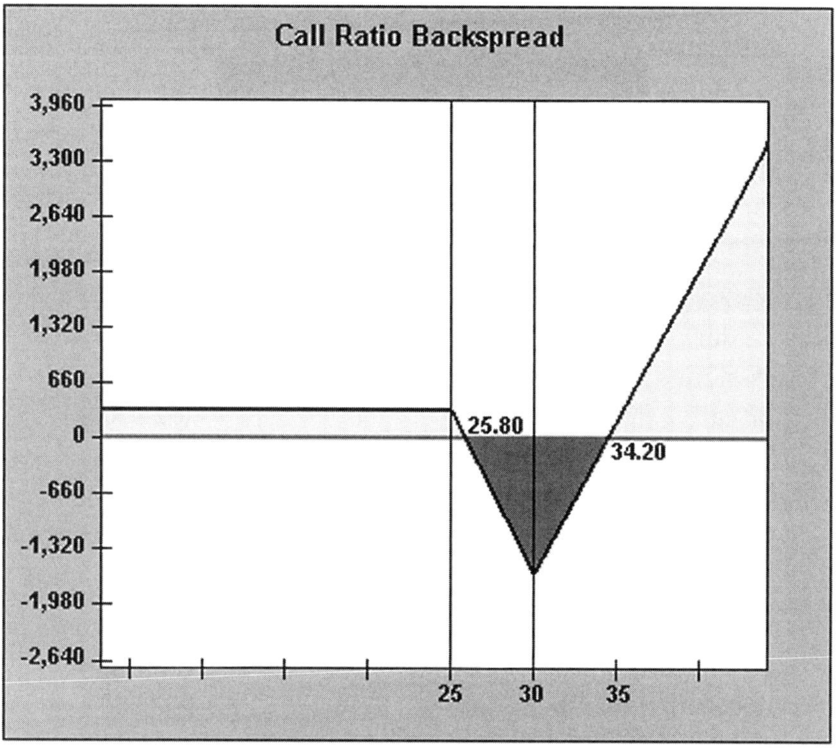

Strategy at Expiration

As you can see, the maximum loss on this strategy, which occurs at a price of 30, is $1,680. There are two breakeven points at 25.80 and 34.20. All prices above 25.80 or below 34.20 result in a loss. The maximum gain on the upside is unlimited, and the maximum gain on the downside is $320. To get a better feel for the profit and loss zones, see the following sample prices at expiration.

XYZ below 25 at expiration:

Initial credit:	$320
All options expire worthless:	-0-
Net gain of .80 × 4 spreads:	= **$320**

XYZ at 25.80 at expiration:

Initial credit:	$320
Assigned on 25 calls to sell 400 shares:	$10,000

400 shares bought back @ market:	($10,320)
30 calls expire worthless:	-0-
Net profit/loss:	= **$0**
XYZ at 30 at expiration:	
Initial credit:	$320
Assigned on 25 calls to sell 400 shares:	$10,000
400 shares bought back @ market:	($12,000)
30 calls expire worthless:	-0-
Net profit/loss:	= **($1,680)**
XYZ at 32 at expiration:	
Initial credit:	$320
Assigned on 25 calls to sell 400 shares:	$10,000
30 calls exercised:	($24,000)
400 shares sold @ market:	$12,800
Net profit/loss:	= **($880)**
XYZ at 34.20 at expiration:	
Initial credit:	$320
Assigned on 25 calls to sell 400 shares:	$10,000
30 calls exercised:	($24,000)
400 shares sold @ market:	$13,680
Net profit/loss:	= **$0**
XYZ at 36 at expiration:	
Initial credit:	$320
Assigned on 25 calls to sell 400 shares:	$10,000
30 calls exercised:	($24,000)
400 shares sold @ market:	$14,400
Net profit/loss:	= **$720**

Figure 11.9 is the order entry screen within the CyberTrader Pro software that shows the sample trade above. This should help you visualize how this type of order is typically entered.

In this example, you would be very bullish and would believe that XYZ will rally up past 34.20 by the option expiration date. If XYZ is slightly above or below 30 at the December option expiration, this trade will be unprofitable. If XYZ exceeds 34.20, profits will begin to grow and can become substantial. If you are completely wrong,

FIGURE 11.9

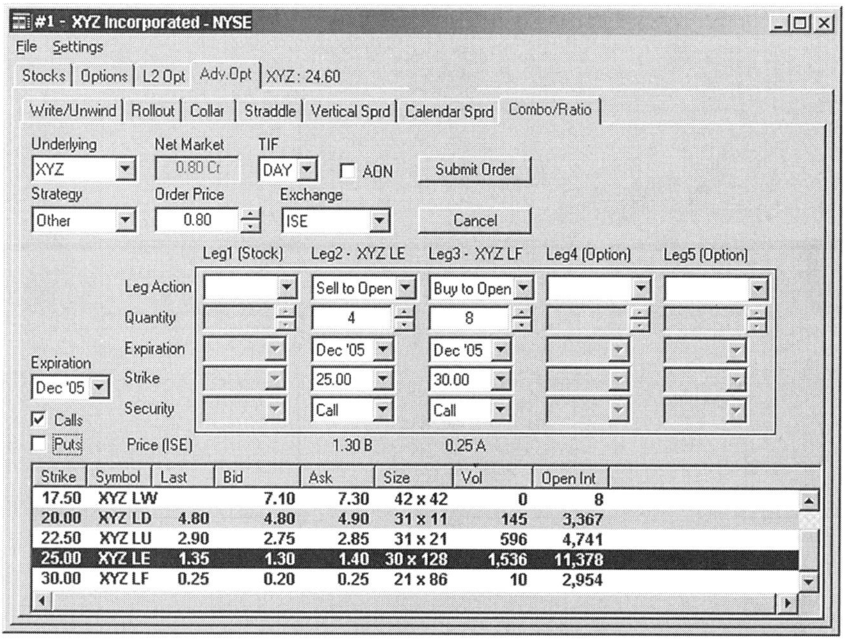

and XYZ remains below 25.80, you will keep your initial credit for a small gain.

Put Ratio Backspreads—Quick Overview

A put ratio backspread is made up of one long put at a high strike and two short puts at a lower strike. Both legs should have the same expiration month. Both sides of this spread are opening transactions, and the number of contracts of the long leg should always be twice the number of the short leg (see Figure 11.10).

At Entry The white line in Figure 11.10 represents what the strategy typically looks like at the point of entry. As expiration approaches, the curve moves toward the black lines, which illustrate the final profit and loss boundaries at expiration.

Direction Very bearish

When to Use You would typically employ a put ratio backspread in a very bearish market or when you think the underlying stock will drop dramatically by the expiration date of the options. Generally,

FIGURE 11.10

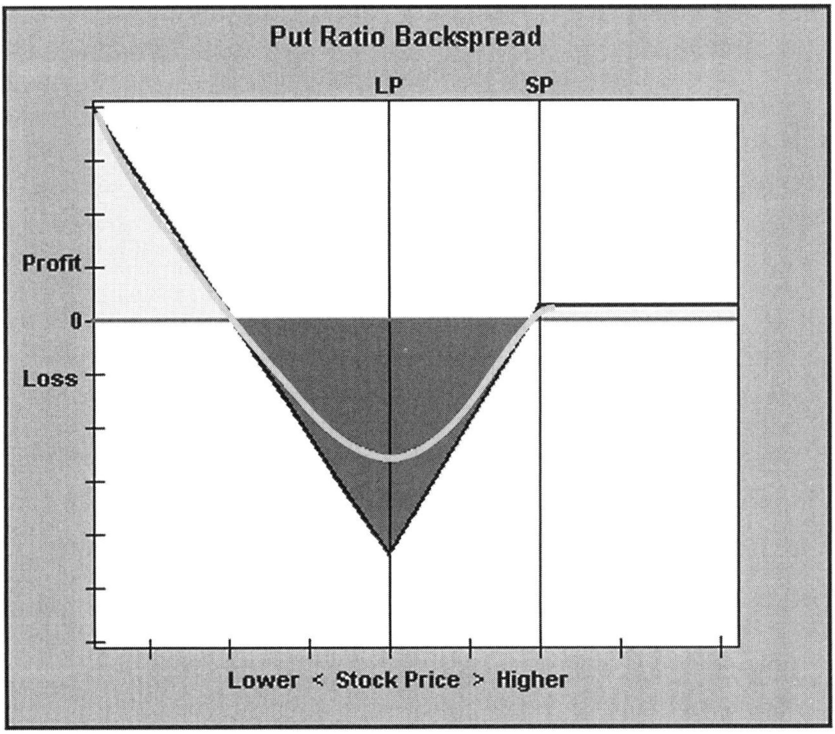

you would select a short strike price that is close to the underlying stock price and a long strike price that is out-of-the-money. Typically, if the stock is between the two strike prices on option expiration or slightly below the long strike price, your spread will be unprofitable. Maximum loss will occur if the stock is at the long leg strike price on option expiration. Maximum profit will occur if the stock is significantly below the long leg strike price on option expiration.

Risk vs. Reward Significant profit potential to the downside, limited profit potential to the upside, and limited risk

Volatility This strategy generally benefits from an increase in volatility.

Time Decay Time decay has a generally adverse effect on this strategy. Since the strategy has twice as many long options as short options, the long options lose more aggregate time value than the short options (see Table 11.4).

Prior to Expiration

- Because the short put has a higher strike price, it will also have a higher delta. As the underlying stock rises in price, the short option will lose value faster than the long options. Likewise, as the underlying stock drops in price, the short option will gain value faster than the long options.
    - However, since there are twice as many long options, if the delta on the long options is anywhere close to half the delta on the short options, the two will nearly cancel each other out.
- If the underlying stock rises or drops sharply enough, it may be possible to close the spread out at a profit prior to expiration. That profit will be less than the maximum profit at expiration but will approach the maximum profit as expiration approaches.
    - Comparing the early close profit to the maximum potential profit at expiration can help you decide if holding until expiration makes sense.
- Since time decay works against you in this strategy, it may be possible to close the spread out at a loss prior to expiration. That loss will be less than the maximum loss at expiration but will approach the maximum loss as expiration approaches, if the underlying stock is near the long strike price.

TABLE 11.4

Greeks	In-the-money	At-the-money	Out-of-the-money
Delta	Negative	Positive	Negative
Gamma	Negative	Positive	Negative
Theta	Negative	Negative	Negative
Vega	Positive	Positive	Positive

- Comparing the early close loss to the maximum potential loss at expiration can help you decide if holding until expiration makes sense.

At Expiration

- Above the higher strike, all options expire worthless and the initial credit is retained.
- Between the lower and upper strike, long stock will be acquired through assignment of the higher strike. The long stock position can then be sold in the market. The trade will probably be unprofitable.
- Slightly below the lower strike, both options are exercised and/or assigned and the remaining short stock is covered in the market. The trade will probably be unprofitable.
- Significantly below the lower strike, both options are exercised and/or assigned and the remaining short stock is covered in the market. The trade will probably be profitable.

Put Ratio Backspreads—Detail

When you establish a position using a put ratio backspread, you will usually pay a slightly lower premium for the options you purchase than the amount you will receive on the premiums from the options sold. As a result, a put ratio backspread is usually established at a small net credit. This type of spread is best used when you are very bearish.

Example

Sell 7 XYZ Jan 30 Puts @ 4.60

Buy 14 XYZ Jan 25 Puts @ 2.15

Credit (CR) = .30

Upper BE = 29.70 (short strike price – the credit)

Lower BE = 20.30 (long strike price – ML)

ML = 4.70 (net of the two strike prices – the credit)

Upper MG = .30 points (initial credit) (occurs beyond the short strike price)

Lower MG = 20.30 points (long strike – ML)

When you set up an order like this, most order entry systems automatically calculate the market price of this 7/14 spread. To do so manually, reduce the spread by its greatest common factor of 7 to 1/2. Then multiply each leg by the market price using the ask price on the legs you are buying and the bid price on the legs you are selling:

1 × +4.60 = +4.60

2 × −2.15 = −4.30

Net = +.30 × 7 spreads × 100 shares per contract = $210 total up-front credit

Figure 11.11 depicts the profit/loss zones of this example, including the breakeven points at the option expiration date.

FIGURE 11.11

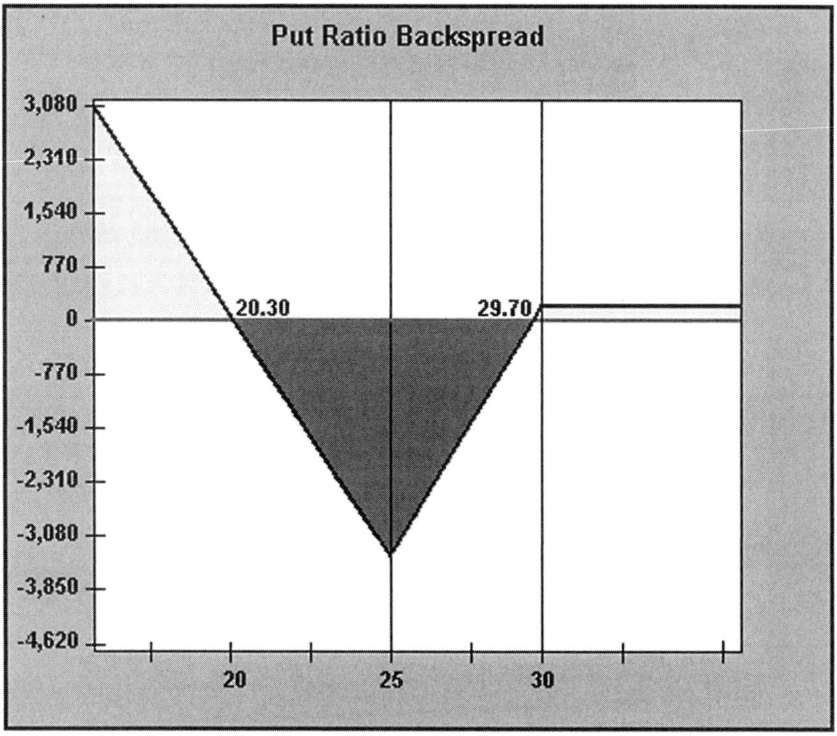

Strategy at Expiration

As you can see, the maximum loss on this strategy, which occurs at a price of 25, is $3,290. There are two breakeven points at 20.30 and 29.70. All prices between 20.30 and 29.70 result in a loss. The maximum gain to the downside is $14,210, and the maximum gain to the upside is $210. To get a better feel for the profit and loss zones, see the following sample prices at expiration.

XYZ above 30 at expiration:

Initial credit:	$210
All options expire worthless:	-0-
Net gain of .30 × 7 spreads:	= **$210**

XYZ at 29.70 at expiration:

Initial credit:	$210
Assigned on 30 puts to buy 700 shares:	($21,000)
700 shares sold @ market:	$20,790
25 puts expire worthless:	-0-
Net profit/loss:	= **$0**

XYZ at 25 at expiration:

Initial credit:	$210
Assigned on 30 puts to buy 700 shares:	($21,000)
700 shares sold @ market:	$17,500
25 puts expire worthless:	-0-
Net profit/loss:	= **($3,290)**

XYZ at 23 at expiration:

Initial credit:	$210
Assigned on 30 puts to buy 700 shares:	($21,000)
25 puts exercised:	$35,000
700 short shares bought back @ market:	($16,100)
Net profit/loss:	= **($1,890)**

XYZ at 20.30 at expiration:

Initial credit:	$210
Assigned on 30 puts to buy 700 shares:	($21,000)
25 puts exercised:	$35,000
700 short shares bought back @ market:	($14,210)
Net profit/loss:	= **$0**

XYZ at 19 at expiration:

Initial credit:	$210
Assigned on 30 puts to buy 700 shares:	($21,000)
25 puts exercised:	$35,000
700 short shares bought back @ market:	($13,300)
Net profit/loss:	= **$910**

Figure 11.12 is the order entry screen within the CyberTrader Pro software that shows the sample trade above. This should help you visualize how this type of order is typically entered.

In this example, you would be very bearish and would believe that XYZ will drop below 20.30 by the option expiration date. If XYZ is slightly above or below 25 at the January option expiration, this trade will be unprofitable. If XYZ drops below 20.30, profits will begin to grow and can become substantial. If you are completely wrong, and XYZ rallies up beyond 29.70, you will keep your initial credit for a small gain.

FIGURE 11.12

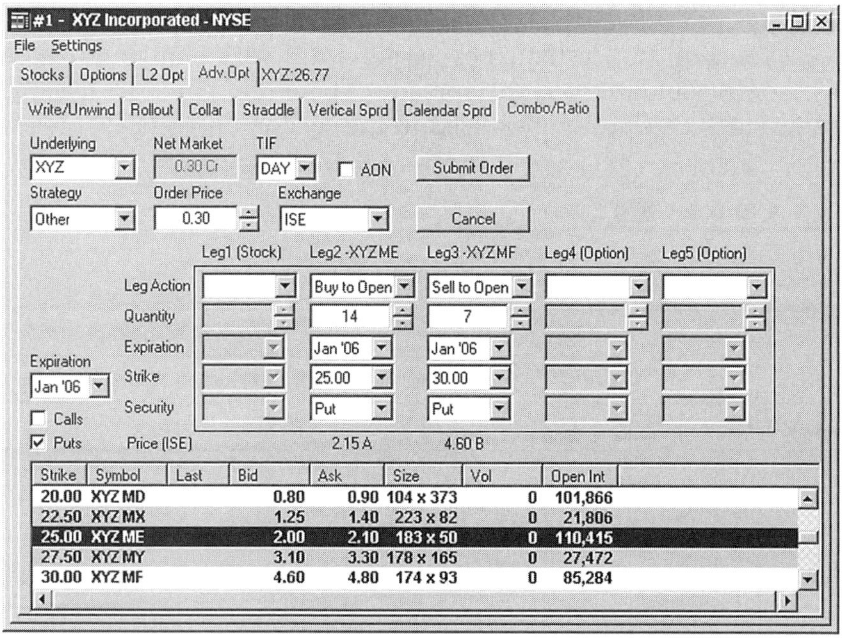

Characteristics

Ratio spreads, like other spreads, require you to decide which strike prices to use and how wide to make the spreads. Which strike prices you use and whether or not those strike prices are in, at, or out-of-the-money will affect the magnitude of the underlying move needed to reach profitability and will also determine whether or not the spread can be profitable if the underlying remains unchanged.

Table 11.5 illustrates how to properly structure a ratio spread or ratio backspread to match your level of bullishness or bearishness. For example, if you are extremely bullish, you would want to use a call ratio backspread, while a call ratio spread would be more appropriate if you are neutral to moderately bullish. Generally the more bullish you are, the higher the strike prices you will use. If you want a call ratio spread to be profitable with no movement in the underlying stock, be sure the long leg of the spread is in-the-money when the strategy is initiated.

Similarly, if you are extremely bearish, you would want to use a put ratio backspread, while a put ratio spread would be more appropriate if you are neutral to moderately bearish. Generally, the more bearish you are, the lower the strike prices you will use.

You will notice that these criteria are very similar to those for some standard vertical spreads. Therefore, you can use the same stock chart examples used in the section on vertical spreads

TABLE 11.5

	<< Direction >>				<< Magnitude >>		
Strategy	**Bullish**	**Neutral**	**Breakout**	**Bearish**	**Extreme**	**Moderate**	**Slight**
Ratio Spread							
Call ratio spread	X						X
Put ratio spread				X			X
Ratio Back Spread							
Call ratio backspread	X				X		
Put ratio backspread				X	X		

(Chapters 2 and 3) for examples on how to find good ratio spread and ratio backspread candidates.

Since they can often be entered at a much lower debit, ratio spreads may be an appealing alternative to traditional spreads. Though the risks are often higher, you may want to consider the following substitutions:

- A call ratio spread can be a lower cost substitute for an in-the-money or at-the-money debit call spread.
  - Keep in mind that this strategy will have a naked margin requirement on half the short options.
- A put ratio spread can be a lower cost substitute for an in-the-money or at-the-money debit put spread.
  - Keep in mind that this strategy will have a naked margin requirement on half the short options.

Since they can often be entered at a net credit, ratio backspreads may be an appealing alternative to traditional spreads. Though the risks are often higher, you may want to consider the following substitutions:

- A call ratio backspread can be a lower cost substitute for an out-of-the-money debit call spread.
- A put ratio backspread can be a lower cost substitute for an out-of-the-money debit put spread.

To help you determine which strategy makes the most sense, compare the two side by side for the same underlying stock and then decide based on the advantages or disadvantages. Below are some comparisons using the examples above.

Example 1

Debit Call Spread (see Figure 11.13) vs. Call Ratio Spread (see Figure 11.14)

XYZ = 58.22

Buy 10 XYZ Dec 65 Calls @ 1.90	Buy 5 XYZ Dec 65 Calls @ 1.90
Sell 10 XYZ Dec 70 Calls @ .85	Sell 10 XYZ Dec 70 Calls @ .85
Debit (DR) = –1.05	Debit (DR) = –.20
	Lower BE = 65.20
Breakeven (BE) = 66.05	Upper BE = 74.80
Max Gain (MG) = 3.95	MG = 4.80
Max Loss (ML) = –1.05	Upper ML = Unlimited
	Lower ML = –.20

FIGURE 11.13 AND 11.14

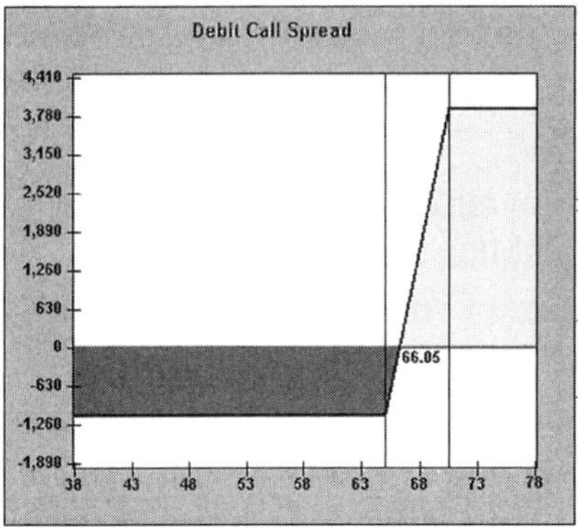

Strategy at Expiration

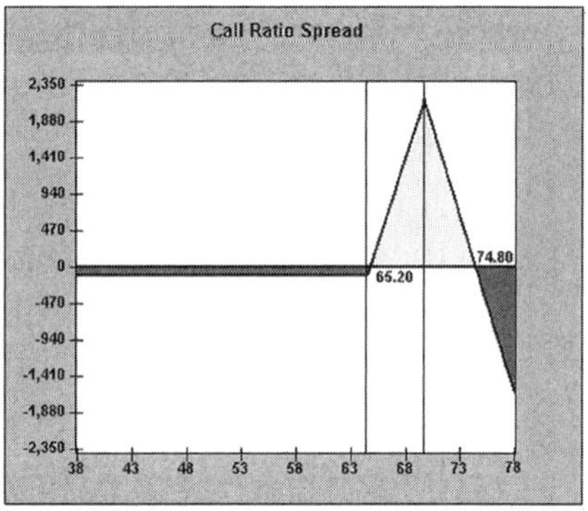

Strategy at Expiration

Advantages of debit call spread vs. call ratio spread:

- No upside risk
  - Versus unlimited upside risk for the call ratio spread
- Maximum gain of $3,950
  - Versus $2,400 for the call ratio spread
- Lower margin requirements due to no naked option

Advantages of call ratio spread vs. debit call spread:

- Lower initial debit of $100
  - Versus $1,050 for the debit call spread
- Downside risk is $100
  - Versus $1,050 for the debit call spread
- Lower breakeven price of 65.20
  - Versus 66.05 for the debit call spread

Example 2:

Debit Put Spread (see Figure 11.15) vs. Put Ratio Spread (see Figure 11.16)

XYZ = 49.40

Buy 20 XYZ Jan 47.50 Puts @ 1.15
Sell 20 XYZ Jan 45 Puts @ .50
Debit (DR) = –.65

Breakeven (BE) = 46.85

Buy 10 XYZ Jan 47.50 Puts @ 1.15
Sell 20 XYZ Jan 45 Puts @ .50
Debit (DR) = –.15
Lower BE = 42.65
Upper BE = 47.35

FIGURE 11.15 AND 11.16

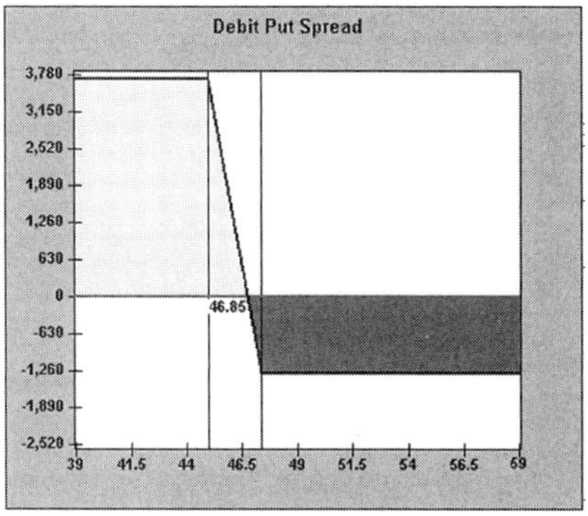

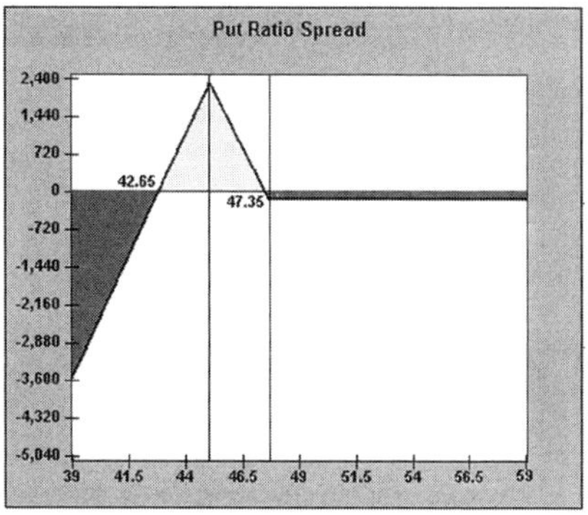

Strategy at Expiration	**Strategy at Expiration**
Max Gain (MG) = 1.85	MG = 2.35
Max Loss (ML) = –.65	Lower ML = –42.65
	Upper ML = –.15

Advantages of debit put spread vs. put ratio spread:

- No downside risk
  - Versus $42,650 downside risk for the put ratio spread
- Maximum gain of $3,700
  - Versus $2,350 for the put ratio spread
- Lower margin requirements due to no naked option

Advantages of put ratio spread vs. debit put spread:

- Lower initial debit of $150
  - Versus $1,300 for the debit put spread
- Upside risk is $150
  - Versus $1,300 for the debit put spread
- Lower breakeven price of 42.65
  - Versus 46.85 for the debit put spread

Example 3:

Debit Call Spread (see Figure 11.17) vs. Call Ratio Backspread (see Figure 11.18)

XYZ = 58.22

Buy 10 XYZ Dec 65 Calls @ 1.90	Sell 5 XYZ Dec 65 Calls @ 1.85
Sell 10 XYZ Dec 70 Calls @ .85	Buy 10 XYZ Dec 70 Calls @ .90

FIGURE 11.17 AND 11.18

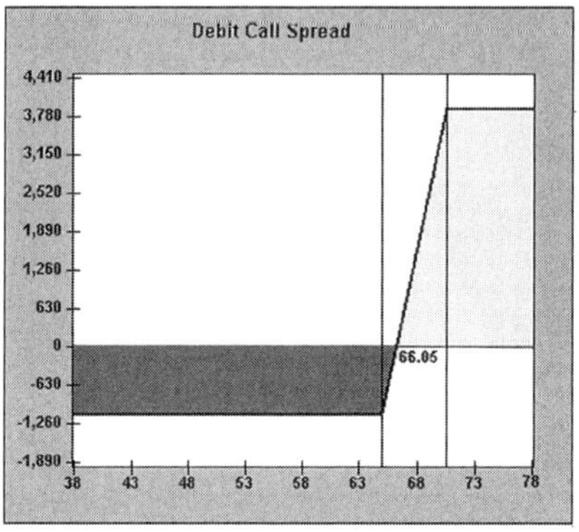

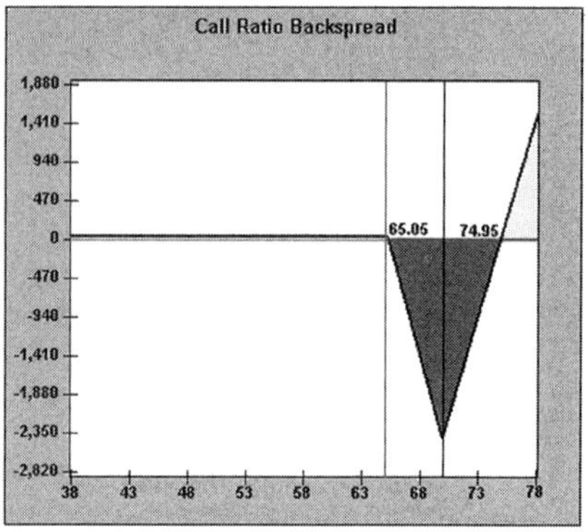

Strategy at Expiration

Debit (DR) = –1.05
Breakeven (BE) = 66.05
Max Gain (MG) = 3.95
Max Loss (ML) = –1.05

Strategy at Expiration

Credit (CR) = .05 Lower BE = 65.05
Upper BE = 74.95
Upper MG = Unlimited
Lower MG = .05 ML = –4.95

Advantages of debit call spread vs. call ratio backspread:

- Lower upside breakeven of 66.05
  - Versus 74.95 for the call ratio backspread
- Lower maximum loss of $1,050
  - Versus $2,475 for the call ratio backspread

Advantages of call ratio backspread vs. debit call spread:

- Unlimited maximum gain
  - Versus $3,950 for the debit call spread
- Initial credit of $25
  - Versus $1,050 debit for the debit call spread
- Downside maximum gain of $25
  - Versus losses for the debit call spread

Example 4:

Debit Put Spread (see Figure 11.19) vs. Put Ratio Backspread (see Figure 11.20)

XYZ = 49.40

Buy 20 XYZ Jan 47.50 Puts @ 1.15
Sell 20 XYZ Jan 45 Puts @ .50

Sell 10 XYZ Jan 47.50 Puts @ 1.10
Buy 20 XYZ Jan 45 Puts @ .55

FIGURE 11.19 AND 11.20

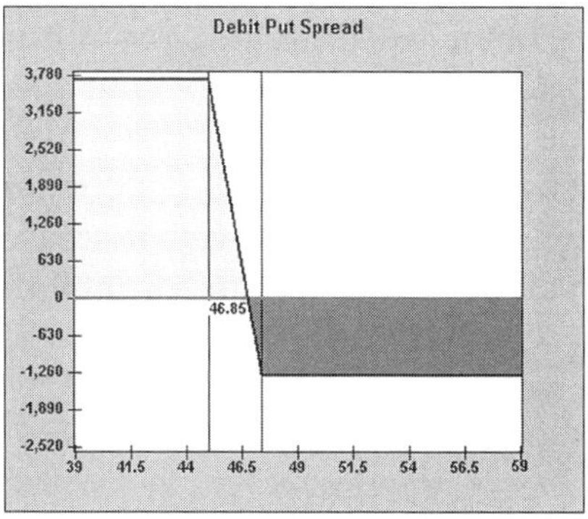

Strategy at Expiration

Debit (DR) = –.65

Breakeven (BE) = 46.85
Max Gain (MG) = 1.85
Max Loss (ML) = –.65

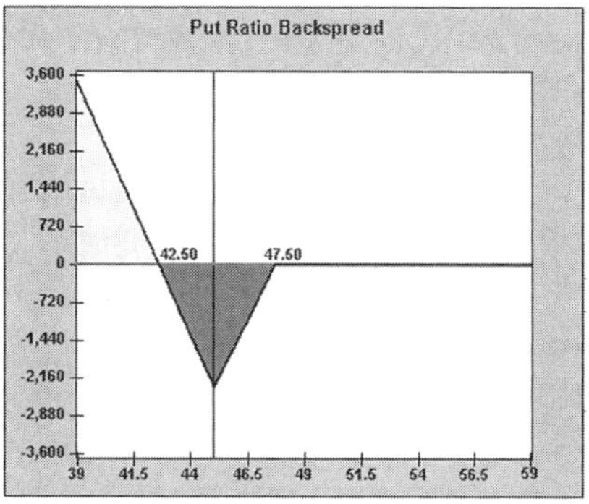

Strategy at Expiration

Credit (CR) = Even
Upper BE = 47.50
Lower BE = 42.50
Upper MG = 0.00
Lower MG = 42.50
ML = –2.50

Advantages of debit put spread vs. put ratio backspread:

- Higher downside breakeven of 46.85
  - Versus 42.50 for the put ratio backspread
- Lower maximum loss of $1,300
  - Versus $2,500 for the put ratio backspread

Advantages of put ratio backspread vs. debit put spread:

- Higher maximum gain of $42,500
  - Versus $3,700 for the debit put spread
- Initial debit/credit of $0 (even)
  - Versus $1,300 debit for the debit put spread
- Upside maximum loss of $0
  - Versus losses for the debit put spread

The examples in this chapter focused exclusively on ratio spreads and ratio backspreads with a 1 to 2 ratio between the legs. It is possible to structure a ratio spread with a 1 to 3 ratio, a 2 to 3 ratio, or any other possible ratio you can come up with. While the profit and loss charts will look similar to these, the important thing to realize is that your risk will go up substantially on a ratio spread with greater than a 1 to 2 ratio because you will be naked a higher number of contracts. This increase in risk could result in higher profitability if the trade is profitable, but a much greater loss if it is not. Similarly, if you lower the ratio such as a 2 to 3 ratio, your risk will go down accordingly, as will your potential profit.

With ratio backspreads, a higher ratio would result in a greater number of additional long options, which would effectively increase your costs. This additional cost can create either greater profitability or greater loss, depending upon whether your sentiment in the underlying security is ultimately correct or not.

SECTION 8

Advanced Spreads

CHAPTER 12

Combination Spreads

Most standard spreads offer you the opportunity to limit losses in exchange for a limited gain potential. There are a number of lesser known spreads with similar characteristics, as well as many that sometimes involve significant risk and/or significant gain potential. These spreads may involve the purchase and sale of two, three, or four different options and may involve either puts, calls, or both. Some might even involve long or short stock positions as well. Some of them may not be spreads at all and should probably just be called combinations to be completely accurate. You can use the term *spread* rather loosely from here on. With dozens of different strike prices, numerous expiration dates, puts and calls, the number of different combinations you can come up with is virtually unlimited.

The spreads covered here may require that you temporarily establish a long or short stock position. That resulting long or short position will need to be closed out in the market to fully realize the profit potential of the strategy. This is explained in more detail later in this chapter.

Most of the previous chapters were intended to cover the most common types of spreads, but this chapter will cover a number of the less common ones. Some of them have a number of different names, and what they are called can sometimes depend upon who you talk to. Whatever you call them, their profit and loss characteristics and the sentiment held by those who use them deserve at least a brief overview in this book.

Since most of the previous chapters dealt with a common spread strategy, it was fairly easy to establish specific rules for determining your sentiment (whether you are bullish or bearish) and how to calculate the maximum gain (MG), maximum loss (ML), and breakeven points (BE). Since the spreads covered in this chapter are all very different, it is not possible to have any standardized formulas for these values. Probably the best way to determine the values is to plot these strategies on a graphical analysis tool, which is pretty easy to come by these days, or simply work through the scenarios at expiration the way it was done in the previous chapters.

Always remember that industry regulations require most spreads be done in a margin account. Always be sure to take commissions into account when calculating potential profits, especially on three- and four-legged strategies where commissions can be significant.

TYPES OF COMBINATION SPREADS

The two main types of combination (combo) spreads are long combo spreads and short combo spreads. Neither is technically a spread, but because they both involve buying and selling of puts and calls, they are often referred to as such. Combo spreads are often used as substitutes for outright stock positions.

Long Combo Spreads—Quick Overview

A long combo spread is made up of one long call at a high strike and one short put at a lower strike. Both legs should have the same expiration month. Both sides of this spread are opening transactions, and the number of contracts of the short leg should always be the same as the number of the long leg. This type of combo can substitute for a long stock position because the profit and loss characteristics are very similar. To make it a true synthetic long stock position, the trade can be modified so the call and put have the exact same strike price (see Figure 12.1).

Since this strategy is made up of a long call and an uncovered (naked) put, your broker will require a significant margin deposit to offset some of the risk associated with the uncovered put.

At Entry The white line in Figure 12.1 represents what the strategy typically looks like at the point of entry. As expiration approaches, the curve moves toward the black lines, which illustrate the final profit and loss boundaries at expiration.

FIGURE 12.1

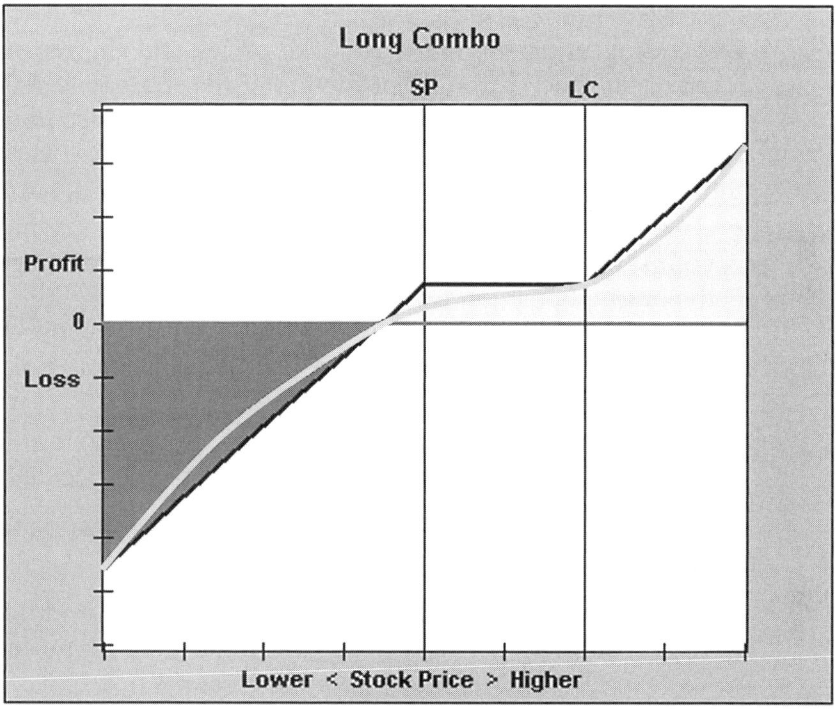

Direction Bullish

When to Use You would typically employ a long combo spread in a bullish market or when you think the underlying stock will rise sharply by the expiration date of the options. Figure 12.1 illustrates a long combo entered at a net credit. If the stock is below the breakeven point on option expiration, the strategy will be unprofitable. If the stock is between the two strike prices, the strategy will be moderately profitable. If the stock is above the call strike price, the strategy will be profitable. Maximum potential profit is unlimited, and above the call strike price, profit is positively correlated with the stock price increases.

Risk vs. Reward Significant risk to the downside, unlimited profit potential to the upside

Volatility This strategy is generally fairly neutral to volatility.

Time Decay The effect of time decay varies depending upon the strike prices selected and the price of the underlying stock.

Prior to Expiration

- Depending upon the original strike prices and the movement of the stock throughout the life of the strategy, it will often be possible to close out this spread at a loss less than the maximum loss at expiration or a gain less than the maximum gain at expiration.
  - Often the decision to do so depends upon whether or not your sentiment of the underlying stock has changed since the original position was established.
  - Regardless of whether the stock has risen or dropped, if you are still bullish you may want to continue to hold your positions.
  - Comparing the early close gain or loss to the maximum potential gain or loss at expiration can help you decide if holding until expiration makes sense.

At Expiration

- Above the call strike, the long call will be exercised and the short put will expire worthless. The trade may be profitable.
- Between the two strikes, both options will be expire worthless and any initial credit is retained for a profit. If the trade was entered at a net debit, the trade will result in a loss.
- Below the put strike, the short put will be assigned and the call will expire worthless. The trade will probably be unprofitable.

Long Combo Spreads—Detail

Depending upon which strike prices you choose, this strategy might be entered at a net debit, a net credit, or even. If entered at a net debit, the breakeven price will be above the call strike price. If entered at even, the breakeven price will equal the call strike price, the put strike price, and all points between. If entered at a net credit, the breakeven price will be below the put strike price. This type of spread is best used as a substitute for a long stock strategy when you are bullish.

Example

Sell 10 XYZ Dec 40 Puts @ 1.75
Buy 10 XYZ Dec 45 Calls @ .40
Credit (CR) = 1.35
BE = 38.65 (put strike price – the credit) (or call strike price + the debit)
MG = Unlimited
ML = 38.65 points (occurs at zero)

When you set up an order like this, most order entry systems automatically calculate the market price of this 10/10 spread. To do so manually, reduce the spread by its greatest common factor of 10 to 1/1. Then multiply each leg by the market price using the ask price on the legs you are buying and the bid price on the legs you are selling:

1 × +1.75 = +1.75
1 × –.40 = –.40
Net = +1.35 × 10 spreads × 100 shares per contract = $1,350 total up-front credit

Figure 12.2 depicts the profit/loss zones of this example, including the breakeven point, at the option expiration date.

As you can see, the maximum gain on this strategy is unlimited to the upside. There is only one breakeven point at 38.65. All prices below 38.65 result in a loss. The maximum loss to the downside is $38,650. To get a better feel for the profit and loss zones, see the following sample prices at expiration.

XYZ at 37 at expiration:

Initial credit:	$1,350
Assigned on short puts to buy 1,000 shares:	($40,000)
Long shares sold at market:	$37,000
Long 45 calls expire worthless:	-0-
Net profit/loss:	= **($1,650)**

XYZ at 38.65 at expiration:

Initial credit:	$1,350
Assigned on short puts to buy 1,000 shares:	($40,000)
Long shares sold at market:	$38,650

FIGURE 12.2

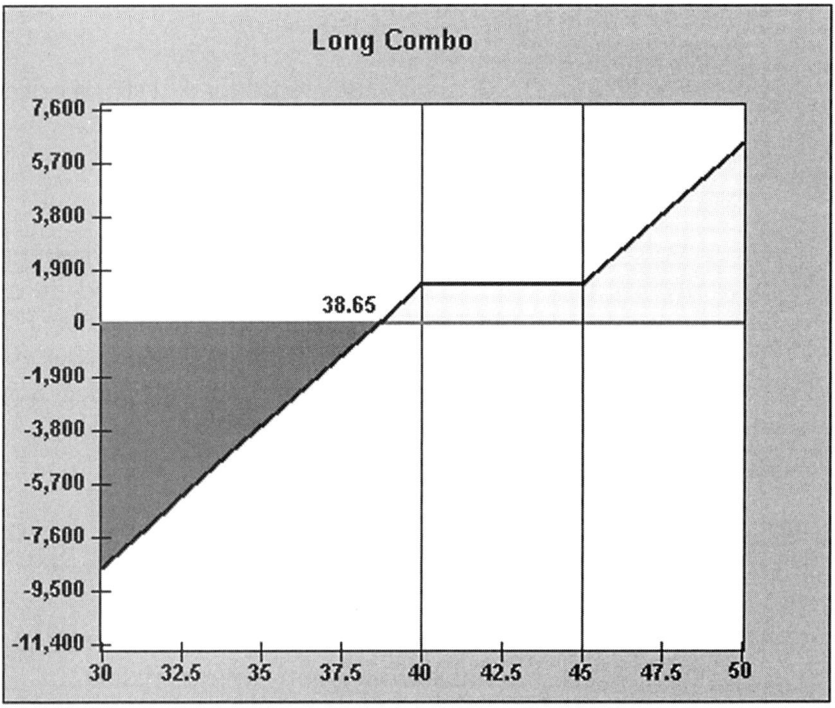

Strategy at Expiration

Long 45 calls expire worthless:	-0-
Net profit/loss:	= **$0**
XYZ at 40 at expiration:	
Initial credit:	$1,350
Short 40 puts expire worthless:	-0-
Long 45 calls expire worthless:	-0-
Net profit/loss:	= **$1,350**
XYZ at 42 at expiration:	
Initial credit:	$1,350
Short 40 puts expire worthless:	-0-
Long 45 calls expire worthless:	-0-
Net profit/loss:	= **$1,350**
XYZ at 45 at expiration:	
Initial credit:	$1,350

Short 40 puts expire worthless:	-0-
Long 45 calls expire worthless:	-0-
Net profit/loss:	= **$1,350**
XYZ at 47 at expiration:	
Initial credit:	$1,350
Short 40 puts expire worthless:	-0-
Exercise 45 calls to buy 1,000 shares:	($45,000)
1,000 shares sold @ market:	$47,000
Net profit/loss:	= **$3,350**

You may notice this order has very similar profit and loss characteristics to a long stock position, but the key benefit is that you get to bring in a credit up front, rather than investing a significant amount of capital.

Short Combo Spreads—Quick Overview

A short combo spread is made up of one long put at a low strike and one short call at a higher strike. Both legs should have the same expiration month. Both sides of this spread are opening transactions, and the number of contracts of the short leg should always be the same as the number of the long leg. This type of combo can substitute for a short stock position because the profit and loss characteristics are very similar. To make it a true synthetic short stock position, the trade can be modified so the call and put have the exact same strike price (see Figure 12.3).

Since this strategy is made up of a long put and an uncovered (naked) call, your broker will require a significant margin deposit to offset some of the risk associated with the uncovered call.

At Entry The white line in Figure 12.3 represents what the strategy typically looks like at the point of entry. As expiration approaches, the curve moves toward the black lines, which illustrate the final profit and loss boundaries at expiration.

Direction Bearish

When to Use You would typically employ a short combo spread in a bearish market or when you think the underlying stock will drop sharply by the expiration date of the options. The example above illustrates a short combo entered at a net debit. If the stock is below the breakeven point on option expiration, the strategy will be profitable. If the stock is between the two strike prices, the strategy

FIGURE 12.3

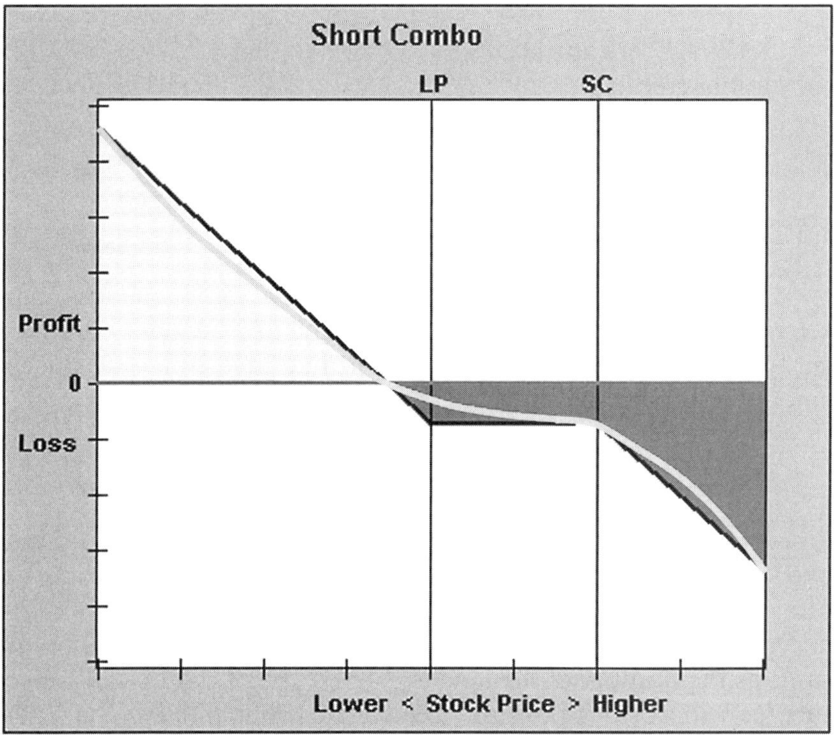

will be unprofitable. If the stock is above the call strike price, the strategy will be unprofitable. Maximum profit will occur if the stock drops all the way to zero by option expiration.

Risk vs. Reward Unlimited risk to the upside, significant profit potential to the downside

Volatility This strategy is generally fairly neutral to volatility.

Time Decay The effect of time decay varies depending upon the strike prices selected and the price of the underlying stock.

Prior to Expiration

- Depending upon the original strike prices and the movement of the stock throughout the life of the strategy, it will often be possible to close out this spread at a loss less than the maximum loss at expiration or a gain less than the maximum gain at expiration.

- Often the decision to do so depends upon whether or not your sentiment of the underlying stock has changed since the original position was established.
- Regardless of whether the stock has risen or dropped, if you are still bearish you may want to continue to hold your positions.
- Comparing the early close gain or loss to the maximum potential gain or loss at expiration can help you decide if holding until expiration makes sense.

At Expiration

- Below the put strike, the long put will be exercised and the short call will expire worthless. The trade may or may not be profitable.
- Between the two strikes, both options will expire worthless and the initial debit is forfeited for a small loss.
- Above the call strike, the short call will be assigned and the put will expire worthless. The trade will be unprofitable.

Short Combo Spreads—Detail

Depending upon which strike prices you choose, this strategy might be entered at a net debit, a net credit, or even. If entered at a net debit, the breakeven price will be below the put strike price. If entered at even, the breakeven price will equal the put strike price, the call strike price, and all points in between. If entered at a net credit, the breakeven price will be above the put strike price. This type of spread is best used as a substitute for a short stock strategy when you are bearish.

Example

Buy 10 XYZ Dec 40 Puts @ 1.75

Sell 10 XYZ Dec 45 Calls @ .40

Debit (DR) = 1.35

BE = 38.65 (put strike price – the debit) (or call strike price + the credit)

MG = 38.65 points (put strike price – the debit) (occurs at zero)

ML = Unlimited

When you set up an order like this, most order entry systems automatically calculate the market price of this 10/10 spread. To do so manually, reduce the spread by its greatest common factor of 10 to 1/1. Then multiply each leg by the market price using the ask price on the legs you are buying and the bid price on the legs you are selling:

1 × –1.75 = –1.75

1 × +.40 = .40

Net = –1.35 × 10 spreads × 100 shares per contract = ($1,350) total up-front cost

Figure 12.4 depicts the profit/loss zones of this example, including the breakeven point at the option expiration date.

As you can see, the maximum gain on this strategy, which occurs at a stock price of zero, is $38,650. There is only one

FIGURE 12.4

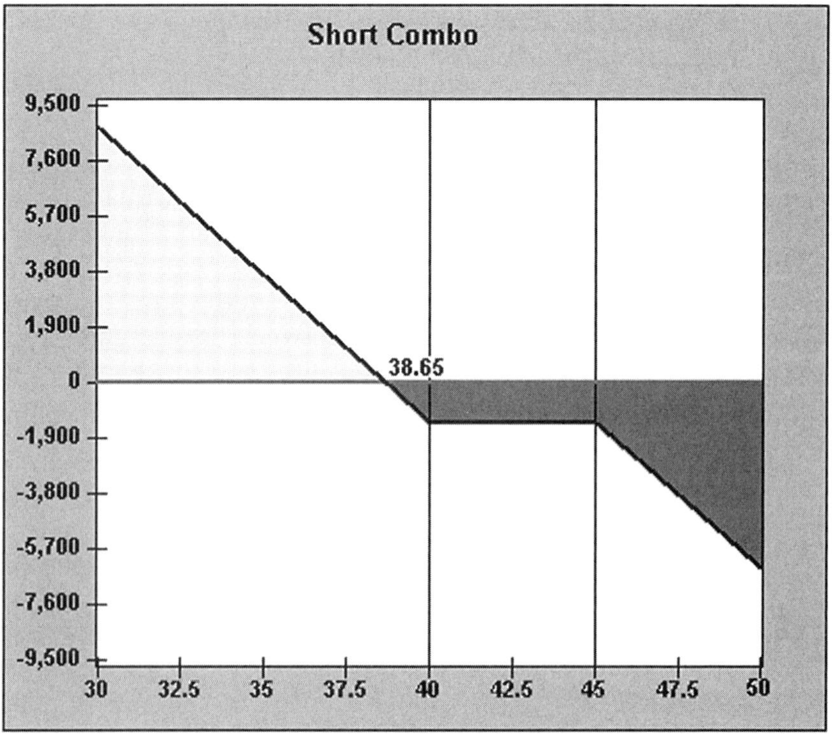

Strategy at Expiration

breakeven point at 38.65. All prices above 38.65 result in a loss. The maximum loss on the upside is unlimited. To get a better feel for the profit and loss zones, see the following sample prices at expiration.

XYZ at 37 at expiration:

Initial cost:	($1,350)
Exercise long puts to sell 1,000 shares:	$40,000
Short shares bought back @ market:	($37,000)
Short 45 calls expire worthless:	-0-
Net profit/loss:	= **$1,650**

XYZ at 38.65 at expiration:

Initial cost:	($1,350)
Exercise long puts to sell 1,000 shares:	$40,000
Short shares bought back @ market:	($38,650)
Short 45 calls expire worthless:	-0-
Net profit/loss:	= **$0**

XYZ at 40 at expiration:

Initial cost:	($1,350)
Long 40 puts expire worthless:	-0-
Short 45 calls expire worthless:	-0-
Net profit/loss:	= **($1,350)**

XYZ at 42 at expiration:

Initial cost:	($1,350)
Long 40 puts expire worthless:	-0-
Short 45 calls expire worthless:	-0-
Net profit/loss:	= **($1,350)**

XYZ at 45 at expiration:

Initial cost:	($1,350)
Long 40 puts expire worthless:	-0-
Short 45 calls expire worthless:	-0-
Net profit/loss:	= **($1,350)**

XYZ at 47 at expiration:

Initial cost:	($1,350)
Long 40 puts expire worthless:	-0-
Assigned on 45 calls to sell 1,000 shares:	$45,000

1,000 shares bought back @ market:	($47,000)
Net profit/loss:	= **($3,350)**

As you can see, this order has very similar profit and loss characteristics to a short stock position, but the key benefit is that the initial cost is significantly lower.

CHAPTER 13

Albatross Spreads

An albatross spread is very similar to a condor spread. The only real distinction is that while a condor spread requires the exact same difference between the strike prices of all the legs, an albatross actually has a wider gap between the two middle strike prices than between the two upper or the two lower legs. Like condors, albatrosses can be established as either long or short.

Always remember that industry regulations require most spreads be done in a margin account. Be sure to take commissions into account when calculating potential profit or loss, especially on three- and four-legged strategies where commissions can be significant.

TYPES OF LONG ALBATROSS SPREADS

The two most basic types of long albatross spreads are long call albatrosses and long put albatrosses. Both are typically used when you have a neutral sentiment, but they sometimes differ by the amount of the initial debit you must pay to establish them. In both cases, you will buy the lowest strike price, sell the second strike price, sell the third strike price, and buy the highest strike price in an equal quantity on all four legs. Since the outcome at expiration is virtually identical, often the decision whether to establish a long call albatross or a long put albatross can be made strictly on price alone. The amount of the initial debit may be 10 or 20 cents lower for one versus the other, and you can simply choose the lower one. Because of the wide range of strikes used in establishing an albatross, it is most appropriate for stock priced over 100.

Long Call Albatross—Quick Overview

A long call albatross is made up of one long call at the lowest strike, one short call at the lower middle strike, one short call at the upper middle strike, and one long call at the highest strike, with the same strike price interval between the first two and the last two legs. The strike price interval between the second and third legs is larger than the interval between the first and second legs or between the third and fourth legs. All legs should also have the same expiration month. All sides of this spread are opening transactions, and the quantity of all four legs is always the same. Like a long condor, this strategy is actually made up of one debit call spread and one credit call spread combined together as a single strategy (see Figure 13.1).

FIGURE 13.1

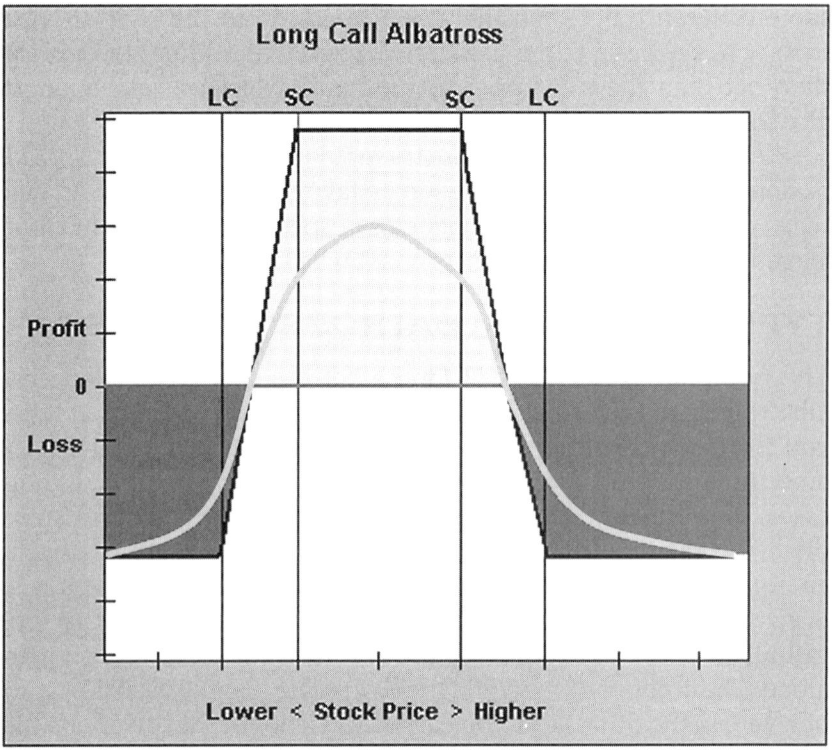

Since this strategy includes a credit call spread, your broker will require a margin deposit to offset the risk associated with the credit spread.

At Entry The white line in Figure 13.1 represents what the strategy typically looks like at the point of entry. As expiration approaches, the curve moves toward the black lines, which illustrate the final profit and loss boundaries at expiration.

Direction Neutral with a bullish or bearish bias, depending upon the strike prices selected

When to Use You would typically employ a long call albatross in neutral markets and would hope to profit if the underlying stock remains relatively flat until the expiration date of the options. Generally, the underlying stock price should be between the two middle strike prices at the time of entry. If you are moderately bullish, higher strike prices should be used, and if you are moderately bearish, lower strike prices should be used. Because of the large strike range between legs 2 and 3, a long albatross has a relatively wide profit range.

Risk vs. Reward Limited risk with limited profit potential

Volatility The effect of volatility varies depending upon the strike prices chosen. Generally the strategy benefits moderately from volatility decreases.

Time Decay The effect of time decay on this strategy varies with the underlying stock's price level in relation to the strike prices. If the stock price is between the outer strike prices, the effect is positive. If the stock price is above the highest strike price or below the lowest strike price, the effect is negative.

Prior to Expiration

- Because the highest strike options have little value to begin with and the lowest strike options are in-the-money and have a relatively small time value component, the two middle strike options will lose time value more quickly than either of the long options.
    - As a result, with little or no movement in the underlying stock price, the spread can often be closed out at a profit prior to expiration, once time value has eroded sufficiently.

- However, because of the large number of commissions involved, this strategy is typically held until expiration if the stock has remained relatively stable.
- Similarly, if the underlying stock rises or drops sharply enough, the spread can often be closed out at a loss that is less than the maximum loss possible if held until expiration, because time decay will erode the value of the middle strike options more quickly.
  - Comparing the early close loss to the maximum potential loss at expiration can help you decide if holding until expiration makes sense.

At Expiration

- Below the lowest strike, all options expire worthless and max loss is sustained.
- Between the lowest and lower middle strike, long stock will be acquired through exercise of the lowest strike. The long stock can then be sold in the market. The trade may or may not be profitable.
- Between the two middle strikes, the lowest strike is exercised, the lower middle strike is assigned, and max gain is achieved.
- Between the upper middle and highest strike, a net short stock position will be obtained through the exercise of the lowest strike and the assignment on the lower and upper middle strikes. The short stock position can then be closed out in the market. The trade may or may not be profitable.
- Above the highest strike, all options are exercised and/or assigned and max loss is sustained.

Long Call Albatross—Detail

When you establish a long call albatross, the combined cost of the first and fourth legs will exceed the amount you receive in on the second and third legs. As a result, a long call albatross is established at a net debit. This type of strategy is intended to take advantage of a stock that is moving sideways and is therefore considered a neutral strategy.

Example

Buy to open 10 XYZ Dec 105 Calls @ 14.40
Sell to open 10 XYZ Dec 110 Calls @ 10.50
Sell to open 10 XYZ Dec 120 Calls @ 4.70
Buy to open 10 XYZ Dec 125 Calls @ 2.80

Debit (DR) = –2.00 (–1st leg + 2nd leg + 3rd leg – 4th leg)
Lower Breakeven (BE) = 107 (2nd strike – MG)
Upper Breakeven (BE) = 123 (3rd strike + MG)
Max Gain (MG) = 3.00 (2nd strike – 1st strike – debit) (occurs between 2nd & 3rd strikes)
Max Loss (ML) = –2.00 points (debit paid) (occurs beyond the outside strike prices)

When you set up an order like this, most albatross order entry systems automatically calculate the market price of this 10/10/10/10 spread. To do so manually, reduce the spread by its greatest common factor of 10 to 1/1/1/1. Then multiply each leg by the market price using the ask price on the legs you are buying and the bid price on the legs you are selling:

1 × –14.40 = –14.40
1 × +10.50 = +10.50
1 × +4.70 = +4.70
1 × –2.80 = –2.80
Net = –2.00 × 10 spreads × 100 shares per contract = ($2,000) total up-front cost

Figure 13.2 depicts the profit/loss zones of this example, including the breakeven points at the option expiration date.

As you can see, the maximum gain on this strategy, which occurs between the two middle strike prices of 110 and 120, is $3,000. There are two breakeven points at 107 and 123. All prices below 107 or above 123 result in a loss. The maximum loss on the upside or downside is -$2,000. To get a better feel for the profit and loss zones, see the following sample prices at expiration.

XYZ at 105 or below at expiration:

Initial cost:	($2,000)
All options expire worthless:	-0-
Net loss of 2.00 × 10 spreads:	**= ($2,000)**

FIGURE 13.2

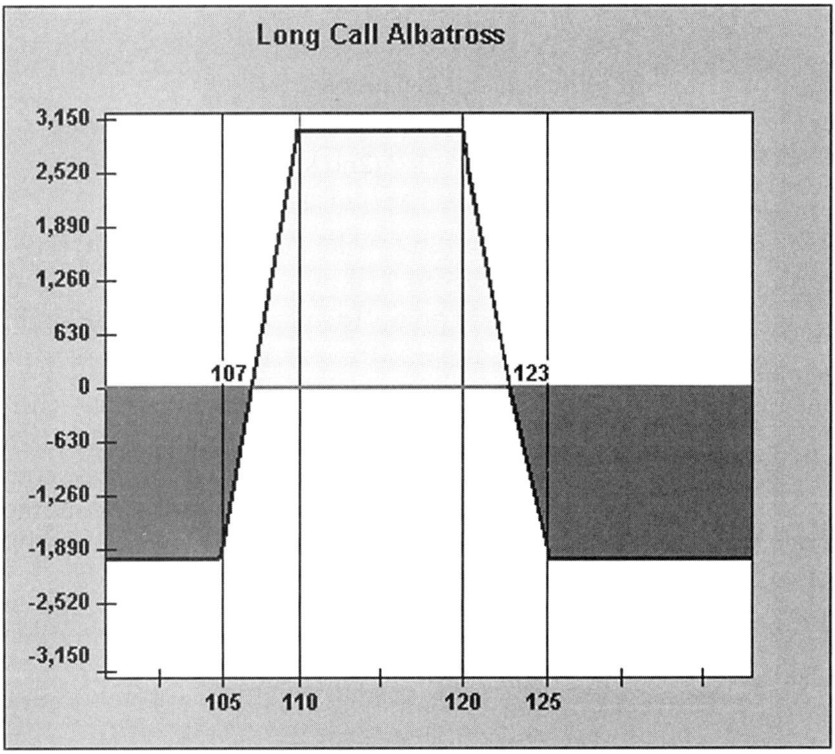

Strategy at Expiration

XYZ at 107 at expiration:

Initial cost:	($2,000)
Exercise 105 calls & acquire 1,000 shares:	($105,000)
1,000 shares sold @ market:	$107,000
110, 120, and 125 calls expire worthless:	-0-
Net profit/loss:	= **$0**

XYZ at 110 at expiration:

Initial cost:	($2,000)
Exercise 105 calls & acquire 1,000 shares:	($105,000)
1,000 shares sold @ market:	$110,000
110, 120, and 125 calls expire worthless:	-0-
Net profit/loss:	= **$3,000**

XYZ at 123 at expiration:

Initial cost:	($2,000)
Exercise 105 calls & acquire 1,000 shares:	($105,000)
Called away on 1,000 shares @ 110:	$110,000
Called away on 1,000 shares @ 120:	$120,000
Buy back 1,000 short shares @ market:	($123,000)
125 calls expire worthless:	-0-
Net profit/loss:	= **$0**

XYZ at 125 at expiration:

Initial cost:	($2,000)
Exercise 105 calls & acquire 1,000 shares:	($105,000)
Called away on 1,000 shares @ 110:	$110,000
Called away on 1,000 shares @ 120:	$120,000
Buy back 1,000 short shares @ market:	($125,000)
125 calls expire worthless:	-0-
Net profit/loss:	= **($2,000)**

XYZ above 125 at expiration:

Initial cost:	($2,000)
Exercise 105 calls & acquire 1,000 shares:	($105,000)
Called away on 1,000 shares @ 110:	$110,000
Called away on 1,000 shares @ 120:	$120,000
Exercise 125 calls to buy short shares:	($125,000)
Net profit/loss:	= **($2,000)**

As you can see, this strategy has very similar profit and loss characteristics to a long call condor. Since it has a wider profit zone in the middle, it will not require as much stability in the underlying stock to remain in the profit zone. However, it will probably generate smaller profits than a comparable long call condor.

TYPES OF SHORT ALBATROSS SPREADS

The two most basic types of short albatross spreads are short call albatrosses and short put albatrosses. Both are typically used when you have a breakout sentiment, but they sometimes differ by the amount of the initial credit you bring in when you establish them. In both cases, you will sell the lowest strike price, buy the second strike price, buy the third strike price, and sell the highest strike price in an equal quantity on all four legs. Since the outcome at expiration is virtually identical, often the decision whether to establish a short call albatross or a short put albatross can be made strictly on the credit alone. The amount of the initial credit may be 10 or 20 cents higher for one versus the other and you can simply choose the higher one. Because of the wide range of strikes used in establishing an albatross, it is most appropriate for stock priced over 100.

Short Put Albatross—Quick Overview

A short put albatross is made up of one short put at the lowest strike, one long put at the lower middle strike, one long put at the upper middle strike, and one short put at the highest strike, with the same strike price interval between the first two and the last two legs. The strike price interval between the second and third legs is larger than the interval between the first and second legs or between the third and fourth legs. All legs should also have the same expiration month. All sides of this spread are opening transactions, and the quantity of all four legs is always the same. Like a short condor, this strategy is actually made up of one debit put spread and one credit put spread combined together as a single strategy (see Figure 13.3).

Since this strategy includes a credit put spread, your broker will require a margin deposit to offset the risk associated with the credit spread.

At Entry The white line in Figure 13.3 represents what the strategy typically looks like at the point of entry. As expiration approaches, the curve moves toward the black lines, which illustrate the final profit and loss boundaries at expiration.

Direction Breakout with a bullish or bearish bias, depending upon the strike prices selected

When to Use You would typically employ a short put albatross in uncertain markets and would hope to profit if the underlying stock breaks out either higher or lower than the current price by the expiration date of the options. Generally, the underlying stock price should be between the two middle strike prices at the time of entry. If you are moderately bullish, higher strike prices should be used, and if you are moderately bearish, lower strike prices should be used.

FIGURE 13.3

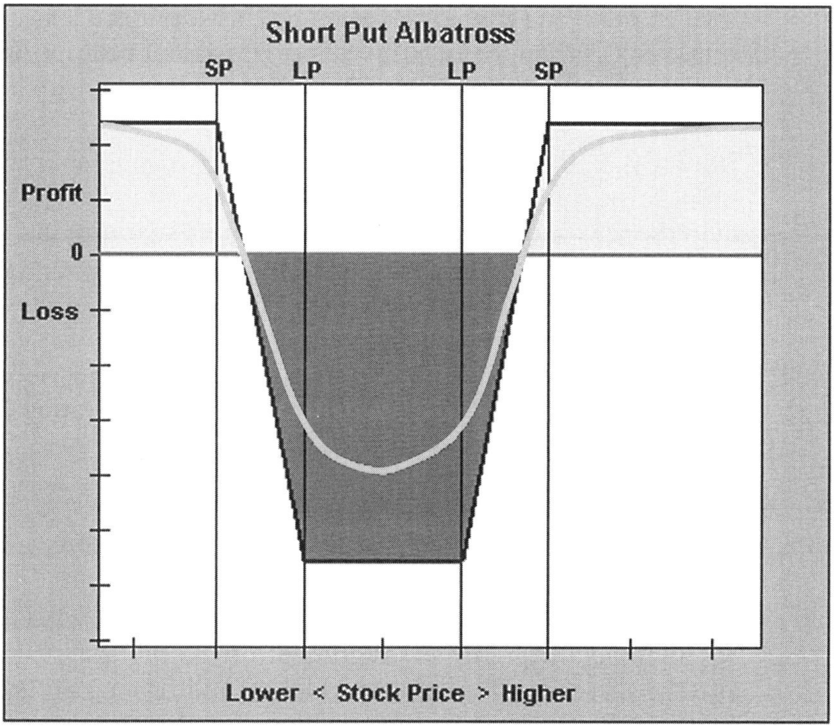

Risk vs. Reward Limited risk with limited profit potential

Volatility The effect of volatility varies depending upon the strike prices chosen. Generally the strategy benefits moderately from volatility increases.

Time Decay The effect of time decay on this strategy varies with the underlying stock's price level in relation to the strike prices. If the stock price is between the outer strike prices, the effect is negative. If the stock price is above the upper strike price or below the lower strike price, the effect is positive.

Prior to Expiration

- Because the lowest strike options have little value to begin with and the highest strike options are in-the-money and have a relatively small time value component, the two middle strike options will lose time value more quickly than either of the short options.

  - As a result, with little or no movement in the underlying stock price, the spread can often be closed out at a loss that is less than the maximum loss possible if held until expiration, because time decay will erode the value of the middle strike options more quickly.

- Similarly, if the underlying stock rises or drops sharply enough, the spread can often be closed out at a gain that is less than the maximum gain possible if held until expiration.
  - Comparing the early close gain to the maximum potential gain at expiration can help you decide if holding until expiration makes sense.
  - However, because of the large number of commissions involved, this strategy is typically held until expiration if the stock has begun to move higher or lower.

At Expiration

- Below the lowest strike, all options are exercised and/or assigned and max gain is achieved.
- Between the lowest and lower middle strike, short stock will be obtained through the assignment of the highest strike and the exercise of the upper and lower middle strikes. The short stock position can then be closed out in the market. The trade may or may not be profitable.
- Between the two middle strikes, the highest strike is assigned, the upper middle strike is exercised, and max loss is sustained.
- Between the upper middle and highest strike, long stock will be acquired through assignment of the highest strike. The long stock position can then be closed out in the market. The trade may or may not be profitable.
- Above the highest strike, all options expire worthless and max gain is achieved.

Short Put Albatross—Detail

When you establish a short put albatross, the combined credit from the first and fourth legs will be greater than the amount you spend on the second and third legs. As a result, a short put albatross is established at a net credit. This type of strategy is intended to take advantage of a stock that is expected to rise or drop sharply and is therefore considered a breakout strategy.

Example

Sell to open 10 XYZ Jan 105 Puts @ .80
Buy to open 10 XYZ Jan 110 Puts @ 2.10
Buy to open 10 XYZ Jan 120 Puts @ 6.40
Sell to open 10 XYZ Jan 125 Puts @ 9.20

Credit (CR) = 1.50 (1st leg – 2nd leg – 3rd leg + 4th leg)
Upper Breakeven (BE) = 123.50 (3rd strike + ML)
Lower Breakeven (BE) = 106.50 (2nd strike – ML)
Max Gain (MG) = 1.50 (credit received) (occurs beyond the outside strike prices)
Max Loss (ML) = 3.50 points (1st strike – 2nd strike + credit) (occurs between 2nd & 3rd strikes)

When you set up an order like this, most albatross order entry systems automatically calculate the market price of this 10/10/10/10 spread. To do so manually, reduce the spread by its greatest common factor of 10 to 1/1/1/1. Then multiply each leg by the market price using the ask price on the leg you are buying and the bid price on the legs you are selling:

1 × +.80 = +.80
1 × –2.10 = –2.10
1 × –6.40 = –6.40
1 × +9.20 = +9.20
Net = +1.50 × 10 spreads × 100 shares per contract = $1,500 total credit received

Figure 13.4 depicts the profit/loss zones of this example, including the breakeven points at the option expiration date.

As you can see, the maximum gain on this strategy, which occurs only above or below the outer strike prices at expiration, is $1,500. There are two breakeven points at 106.50 and 123.50. All prices between 106.50 and 123.50 result in a loss. The maximum loss is –$3,500 and occurs only between the two middle strike prices of 110 and 120. To get a better feel for the profit and loss zones, see the following sample prices at expiration.

FIGURE 13.4

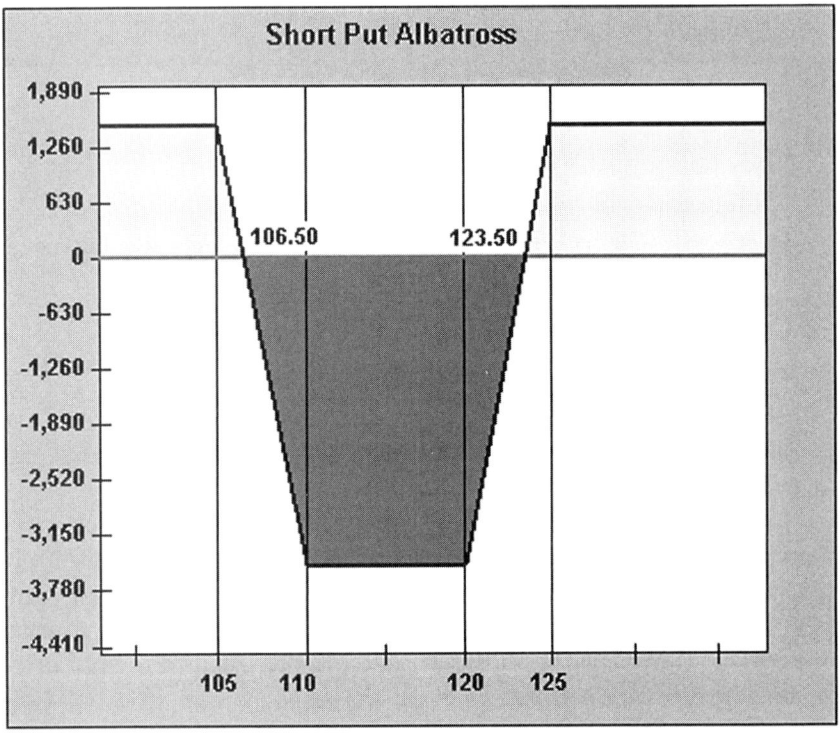

Strategy at Expiration

XYZ above 125 at expiration:	
Initial credit:	$1,500
All options expire worthless:	-0-
Net gain of 1.50 × 10 spreads:	= **$1,500**

XYZ at 123.50 at expiration:	
Initial credit:	$1,500
Assigned on 1,000 shares @ 125:	($125,000)
1,000 shares sold @ market:	$123,500
105, 110, and 120 puts expire worthless:	-0-
Net profit/loss:	= **$0**

XYZ at 120 at expiration:

Initial credit:	$1,500
Assigned on 1,000 shares @ 125:	($125,000)
1,000 shares sold @ market:	$120,000
105, 110, and 120 puts expire worthless:	-0-
Net profit/loss:	= **($3,500)**

XYZ at 106.50 at expiration:

Initial credit:	$1,500
Assigned on 1,000 shares @ 125:	($125,000)
Exercise 120 puts to sell 1,000 shares:	$120,000
Exercise 110 puts to sell 1,000 shares:	$110,000
1,000 shares bought back @ market:	($106,500)
105 puts expire worthless:	-0-
Net profit/loss:	= **$0**

XYZ at 105 at expiration:

Initial credit:	$1,500
Assigned on 1,000 shares @ 125:	($125,000)
Exercise 120 puts to sell 1,000 shares:	$120,000
Exercise 110 puts to sell 1,000 shares:	$110,000
1,000 shares bought back @ market:	($105,000)
105 puts expire worthless:	-0-
Net profit/loss:	= **$1,500**

XYZ below 105 at expiration:

Initial credit:	$1,500
Assigned on 1,000 shares @ 125:	($125,000)
Exercise 120 puts to sell 1,000 shares:	$120,000
Exercise 110 puts to sell 1,000 shares:	$110,000
Assigned on 1,000 shares @ 105:	($105,000)
Net profit/loss:	= **$1,500**

As you can see, this strategy has very similar profit and loss characteristics to a short put condor. Since it has a wider loss zone in the middle, it will require a greater move in either direction to be profitable than a short put condor requires.

IRON ALBATROSS SPREADS

An iron albatross spread is very similar to an iron condor spread. The only real distinction is that while an iron condor spread requires the exact same difference between the strike prices of all the legs, an iron albatross actually has a wider gap between the two middle strike prices than between the two upper or the two lower legs. Like iron condors, iron albatrosses involve buying and selling of both puts *and* calls at four different strike prices.

There are only two types of iron albatross spreads, long iron albatrosses and short iron albatrosses. Long iron albatrosses are used when you have a neutral sentiment, and short iron albatrosses are used when you have a breakout sentiment. They also differ by whether you pay an initial debit or receive an initial credit when you establish them. Because of the wide range of strikes used in establishing an iron albatross, it is most appropriate for stock priced over 100.

Long Iron Albatross—Quick Overview

A long iron albatross is made up of one long put at the lowest strike, one short put at the lower middle strike, one short call at the upper middle strike, and one long call at the highest strike, with the same strike price interval between the first two and the last two legs. The strike price interval between the second and third legs is larger than the interval between the first and second legs or between the third and fourth legs. All legs should also have the same expiration month. All sides of this spread are opening transactions, and the quantity of all four legs is always the same. This strategy is actually made up of one short strangle and one long strangle combined together as a single strategy. This can also be viewed as being made up of one credit put spread and one credit call spread (see Figure 13.5).

Since this strategy includes two credit spreads, your broker will require a margin deposit to offset the risk associated with at least one of the credit spreads.

At Entry The white line in Figure 13.5 represents what the strategy typically looks like at the point of entry. As expiration approaches, the curve moves toward the black lines, which illustrate the final profit and loss boundaries at expiration.

Direction Neutral

FIGURE 13.5

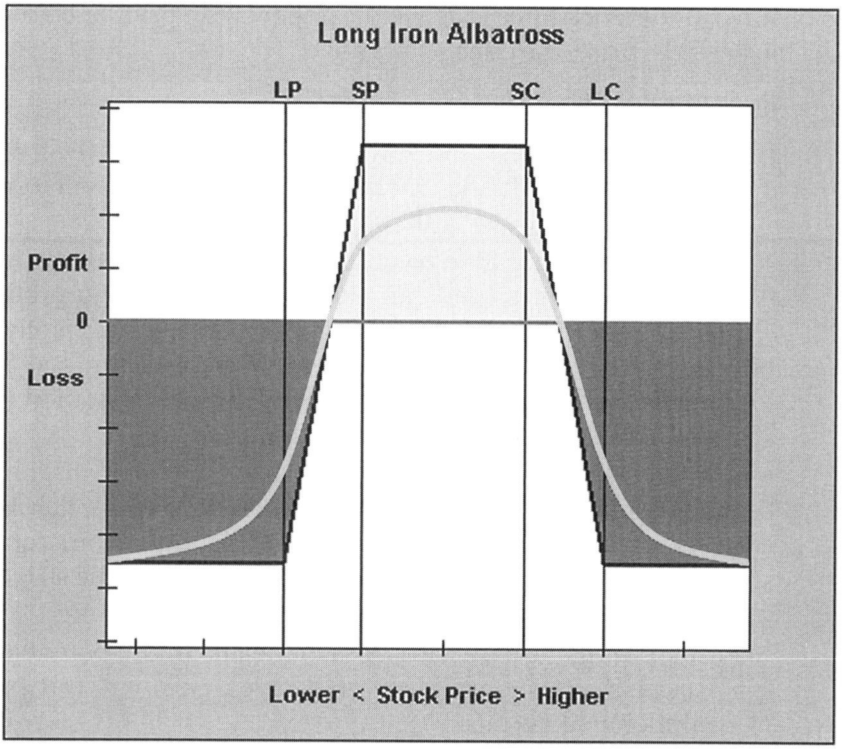

When to Use You would typically employ a long iron albatross in neutral markets and would hope to profit if the underlying stock remains relatively flat until the expiration date of the options. Generally, the underlying stock price should be between the two middle strike prices at the time of entry. If you are moderately bullish or bearish you could use strike prices that are slightly higher or lower, respectively, but this strategy generally works best when you stay closest to the middle.

Risk vs. Reward Limited risk with limited profit potential

Volatility The effect of volatility varies depending upon the strike prices chosen. Generally the strategy benefits moderately from volatility decreases.

Time Decay The effect of time decay on this strategy varies with the underlying stock's price level in relation to the strike prices. If the stock price is between the outer strike prices, the effect is positive. If the stock price is above the upper strike price or below the lower strike price, the effect is negative.

Prior to Expiration

- Because the highest and lowest strike options have little value to begin with, the two middle strike options will lose time value more quickly than either of the long options.
  - As a result, with little or no movement in the underlying stock price, the spread can often be closed out at a profit prior to expiration, once time value has eroded sufficiently.
  - However, because of the large number of commissions involved, this strategy is typically held until expiration if the stock has remained relatively stable.
- Similarly, if the underlying stock rises or drops sharply enough, the spread can often be closed out at a loss that is less than the maximum loss possible if held until expiration, because time decay will erode the value of the middle strike options more quickly.
  - Comparing the early close loss to the maximum potential loss at expiration can help you decide if holding until expiration makes sense.

At Expiration

- Below the lowest strike, all call options expire worthless but all put options are exercised and/or assigned and max loss is sustained.
- Between the lowest and lower middle strikes, all call options expire worthless and the long put expires worthless. Long stock will be acquired through assignment of the short put. The long stock can then be sold in the market. The trade may or may not be profitable.
- Between the two middle strikes, all options expire worthless and max gain is achieved.
- Between the upper middle and highest strikes, all put options expire worthless and the long call expires worthless. Short stock will be obtained through the assignment of the

short call. The short stock position can then be closed out in the market. The trade may or may not be profitable.

- Above the highest strike, all put options expire worthless but all call options are exercised and/or assigned and max loss is sustained.

Long Iron Albatross—Detail

When you establish a long iron albatross, the combined credit from the second and third legs will exceed the combined cost of the first and fourth legs. As a result, a long iron albatross is established at a net credit. This type of strategy is intended to take advantage of a stock that is moving sideways and is therefore considered a neutral strategy.

Example

Buy to open 5 XYZ Dec 115 Puts @ .75
Sell to open 5 XYZ Dec 120 Puts @ 1.90
Sell to open 5 XYZ Dec 130 Calls @ 1.75
Buy to open 5 XYZ Dec 135 Calls @ .80

Credit (CR) = 2.10 (–1st leg + 2nd leg + 3rd leg – 4th leg)
Lower Breakeven (BE) = 117.90 (2nd strike – MG)
Upper Breakeven (BE) = 132.10 (3rd strike + MG)
Max Gain (MG) = 2.10 (credit received) (occurs between 2nd & 3rd strikes)
Max Loss (ML) = –2.90 points (1st strike – 2nd strike + credit) (occurs beyond the outside strike prices)

When you set up an order like this, most condor order entry systems automatically calculate the market price of this 5/5/5/5 spread. To do so manually, reduce the spread by its greatest common factor of 5 to 1/1/1/1. Then multiply each leg by the market price using the ask price on the legs you are buying and the bid price on the legs you are selling:

$1 \times -.75 = -.75$
$1 \times +1.90 = +1.90$
$1 \times +1.75 = +1.75$
$1 \times -.80 = -.80$

Net = +2.10 × 5 spreads × 100 shares per contract = $1,050 total initial credit

Figure 13.6 depicts the profit/loss zones of this example, including the breakeven points, at the option expiration date.

As you can see, the maximum gain on this strategy, which occurs between the prices of 120 and 135 at expiration, is $1,050. There are two breakeven points at 117.90 and 132.10. All prices below 117.90 or above 132.10 result in a loss. The maximum loss on the upside or downside is –$1,450. To get a better feel for the profit and loss zones, see the following sample prices at expiration.

XYZ at 115 at expiration:

Initial credit:	$1,050
Assigned on 120 puts to buy 500 shares:	($60,000)

FIGURE 13.6

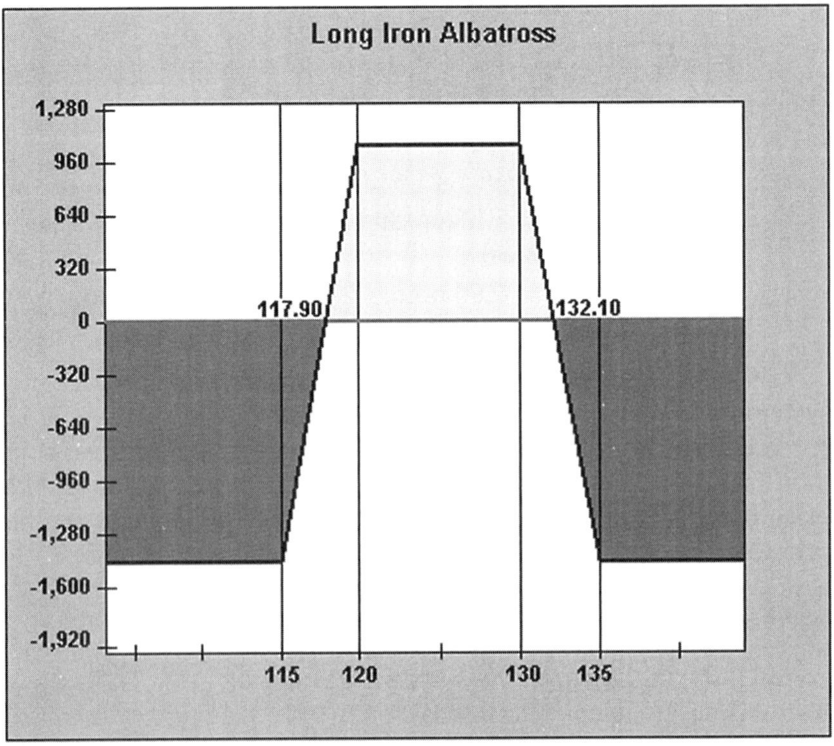

Strategy at Expiration

500 shares sold @ market:	$57,500
All other options expire worthless:	-0-
Net profit/loss:	= **($1,450)**

XYZ at 117.90 at expiration:

Initial credit:	$1,050
Assigned on 120 puts to buy 500 shares:	($60,000)
500 shares sold @ market:	$58,950
All other options expire worthless:	-0-
Net profit/loss:	= **$0**

XYZ at 120 at expiration:

Initial credit:	$1,050
All options expire worthless:	-0-
Net profit/loss:	= **$1,050**

XYZ at 130 at expiration:

Initial credit:	$1,050
All options expire worthless:	-0-
Net profit/loss:	= **$1,050**

XYZ at 132.10 at expiration:

Initial credit:	$1,050
Assigned on (5) 130 calls to short 500 shares:	$65,000
500 shares bought back @ market:	($66,050)
All puts expire worthless:	-0-
Net profit/loss:	= **$0**

XYZ above 135 at expiration:

Initial credit:	$1,050
Assigned on (5) 130 calls to short 500 shares:	$65,000
Exercise (5) 135 calls to cover 500 shares:	($67,500)
All puts expire worthless:	-0-
Net profit/loss:	= **($1,450)**

As you can see, this strategy has very similar profit and loss characteristics to a long iron condor. Since it has a wider profit zone in the middle, it will not require as much stability in the underlying stock to remain in the profit zone. However, it will probably generate smaller profits than a comparable long iron condor.

Short Iron Albatross—Quick Overview

A short iron albatross is made up of one short put at the lowest strike, one long put at the lower middle strike, one long call at the upper middle strike, and one short call at the highest strike, with the same strike price interval between the first two and the last two legs. The strike price interval between the second and third legs is larger than the interval between the first and second legs or between the third and fourth legs. All legs should also have the same expiration month. All sides of this spread are opening transactions, and the quantity of all four legs is always the same. This strategy is actually made up of one long strangle and one short strangle combined together as a single strategy. This can also be viewed as being made up of one put debit spread and one call debit spread (see Figure 13.7).

At Entry The white line in Figure 13.7 represents what the strategy typically looks like at the point of entry. As expiration approaches, the curve moves toward the black lines, which illustrate the final profit and loss boundaries at expiration

Direction Breakout

When to Use You would typically employ a short iron albatross in uncertain markets and would hope to profit if the underlying stock breaks out either higher or lower than the current price by the expiration date of the options. Generally, the underlying stock price should be between the two middle strike prices at the time of entry. If you are moderately bullish or bearish you could use strike prices that are slightly higher or lower, respectively, but this strategy generally works best when you stay closest to the middle.

Risk vs. Reward Limited risk with limited profit potential

Volatility The effect of volatility varies depending upon the strike prices chosen. Generally the strategy benefits moderately from volatility increases.

Time Decay The effect of time decay on this strategy varies with the underlying stock's price level in relation to the strike prices. If the stock price is between the outer strike prices, the effect is negative. If the stock price is above the upper strike price or below the lower strike price, the effect is positive.

FIGURE 13.7

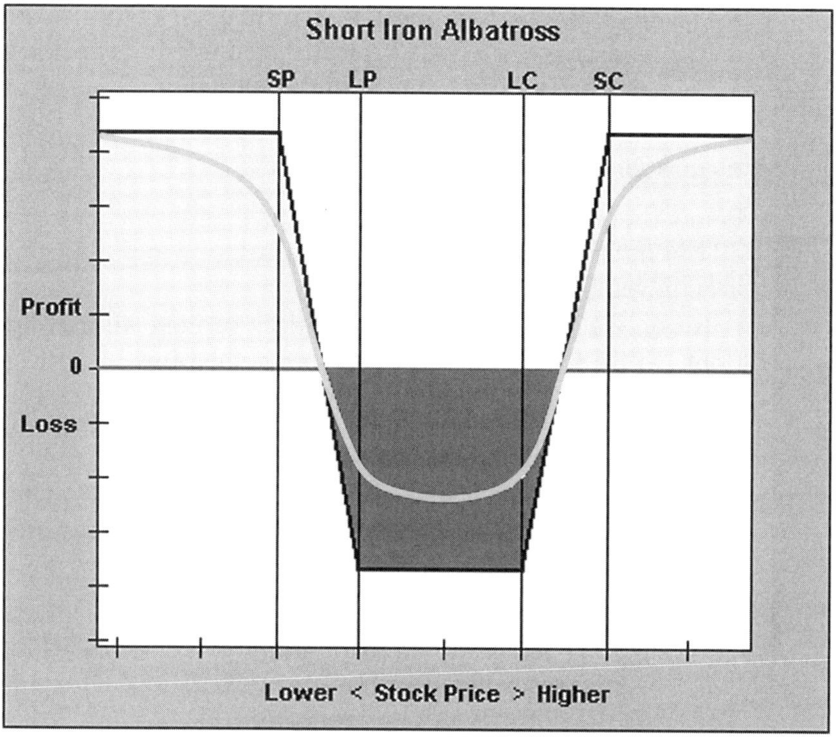

Prior to Expiration

- Because the highest and lowest strike options have little value to begin with, the two middle strike options will lose time value more quickly than either of the long options.
  - As a result, with little or no movement in the underlying stock price, the spread can often be closed out at a loss that is less than the maximum loss possible if held until expiration, because time decay will erode the value of the middle strike options more quickly.
- Similarly, if the underlying stock rises or drops sharply enough, the spread can often be closed out at a gain that is less than the maximum gain possible if held until expiration.

- Comparing the early close gain to the maximum potential gain at expiration can help you decide if holding until expiration makes sense.
- However, because of the large number of commissions involved, this strategy is typically held until expiration if the stock has begun to move higher or lower.

At Expiration

- Below the lowest strike, all call options expire worthless but all put options are exercised and/or assigned and max gain is achieved.
- Between the lowest and lower middle strikes, all call options expire worthless and the short put expires worthless. Short stock will be acquired through exercise of the long put. The short stock position can then be closed out in the market. The trade may or may not be profitable.
- Between the two middle strikes, all options expire worthless and max loss is sustained.
- Between the upper middle and highest strikes, all put options expire worthless and the short call expires worthless. Long stock will be obtained through the exercise of the long call. The long stock position can then be sold in the market. The trade may or may not be profitable.
- Above the highest strike, all put options expire worthless but all call options are exercised and/or assigned and max gain is achieved.

Short Iron Albatross—Detail

When you establish a short iron albatross, the combined debit from the second and third legs will exceed the combined credit of the first and fourth legs. As a result, a short iron albatross is established at a net debit. This type of strategy is intended to take advantage of a stock that is expected to move sharply in either direction and is therefore considered a breakout strategy.

Example

Sell to open 4 XYZ Jan 115 Puts @ .70

Buy to open 4 XYZ Jan 120 Puts @ 1.95

Buy to open 4 XYZ Jan 130 Calls @ 1.80
Sell to open 4 XYZ Jan 135 Calls @ .75
Debit (DR) = 2.30 (1st leg – 2nd leg – 3rd leg + 4th leg)
Lower Breakeven (BE) = 117.70 (2nd strike – ML)
Upper Breakeven (BE) = 132.30 (3rd strike + ML)
Max Gain (MG) = 2.70 (2nd strike – 1st strike – debit) (occurs beyond the outside strike prices)
Max Loss (ML) = –2.30 points (debit paid) (occurs between 2nd & 3rd strikes)

When you set up an order like this, most condor order entry systems automatically calculate the market price of this 4/4/4/4 spread. To do so manually, reduce the spread by its greatest common factor of 4 to 1/1/1/1. Then multiply each leg by the market price, using the ask price on the legs you are buying and the bid price on the legs you are selling:

1 × +.70 = +.70
1 × –1.95 = –1.95
1 × –1.80 = –1.80
1 × +.75 = +.75
Net = –2.30 × 4 spreads × 100 shares per contract = ($920) total initial debit

Figure 13.8 depicts the profit/loss zones of this example, including the breakeven points at the option expiration date.

As you can see, the maximum gain on this strategy, which occurs only above or below the outer strike prices at expiration, is $1,080. There are two breakeven points at 117.70 and 132.30. All prices between 117.70 and 132.30 result in a loss. The maximum loss is –$920 and occurs only between the two middle strike prices of 120 and 130. To get a better feel for the profit and loss zones, see the following sample prices at expiration.

XYZ above 135 at expiration:

Initial debit:	($920)
Long 130 calls exercised to buy 400 shares:	($52,000)
Short 135 calls assigned to sell 400 shares:	$54,000
All puts expire worthless:	-0-
Net profit/loss:	= **$1,080**

FIGURE 13.8

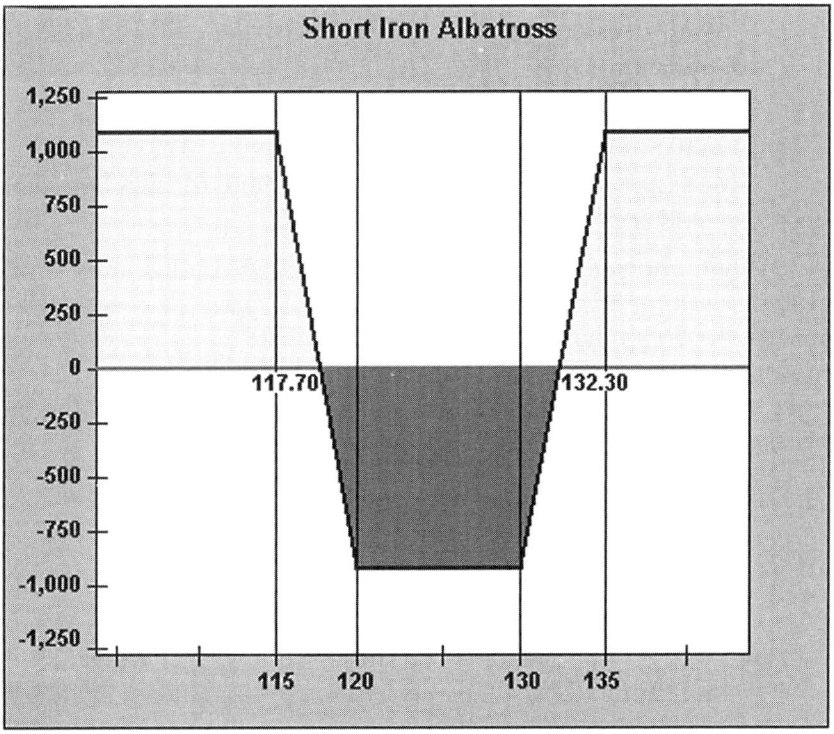

Strategy at Expiration

XYZ at 135 at expiration:

Initial debit:	($920)
Long 130 calls exercised to buy 400 shares:	($52,000)
400 shares sold @ market:	$54,000
All puts expire worthless:	-0-
Net profit/loss:	= **$1,080**

XYZ at 132.30 at expiration:

Initial debit:	($920)
Long 130 calls exercised to buy 400 shares:	($52,000)
400 shares sold @ market:	$52,920
All puts expire worthless:	-0-
Net profit/loss:	= $**0**

XYZ at 130 at expiration:	
Initial debit:	($920)
All options expire worthless:	-0-
Net profit/loss:	= **($920)**
XYZ at 117.70 at expiration:	
Initial debit:	($920)
Long 120 puts exercised to sell 400 shares:	$48,000
Buy back 400 shares @ market:	($47,080)
All calls expire worthless	-0-
Net profit/loss:	= $**0**
XYZ below 115 at expiration:	
Initial debit:	($920)
Long 120 puts exercised to sell 400 shares:	$48,000
Assigned on short puts to buy 400 shares:	($46,000)
Net profit/loss:	**= $1,080**

As you can see, this strategy has very similar profit and loss characteristics to a short iron condor. Since it has a wider loss zone in the middle, it will require a much greater move in the underlying stock to reach the profit zones.

CHAPTER 14

Ladder Spreads

A ladder spread (also known as a Christmas tree spread) is a three-legged strategy made up of either calls or puts at three different strike prices. Because the number of long options is never equal to the number of short options, a ladder spread is a type of ratio spread. Like many other spreads, a ladder spread can be established as either long or short using either calls or puts.

Since short ladder spreads are made up of a credit spread and an additional long option, your broker will require you to meet an initial margin requirement and maintain funds in your account equal to the maximum loss amount for the spread. Since long ladder spreads are made up of a debit spread and an additional uncovered (naked) option, your broker will require a substantial margin deposit to cover any naked options that cannot be spread against long options. Although you may establish these types of spreads by entering them as a single order, most brokers will not display them as ladder spreads in your account. They will most likely be paired up as simple two-legged spreads and unrelated long or naked options. The basic structure of ladder spreads is as follows:

- **Long Call Ladder Spread**—Long one call at a low strike, short one call at a higher strike, short one call at an even higher strike.
  - Comprised of one debit call spread and one naked call option.

- **Long Put Ladder Spread**—Long one put at a high strike, short one put at a lower strike, short one put at an even lower strike.
    - Comprised of one debit put spread and one naked put option.
- **Short Call Ladder Spread**—Short one call at a low strike, long one call at a higher strike, long one call at an even higher strike.
    - Comprised of one credit call spread and one long call option.
- **Short Put Ladder Spread**—Short one put at a high strike, long one put at a lower strike, long one put at an even lower strike.
    - Comprised of one credit put spread and one long put option.

TYPES OF LONG LADDER SPREADS

The two basic types of long ladder spreads are long call ladders and long put ladders. Long call ladders are typically used when you are neutral to moderately bearish, while long put ladders are typically used when you are neutral to moderately bullish. It is possible to make long call ladders completely neutral or even slightly bullish, depending upon the underlying price at the time of entry. Similarly, it is possible to make a long put ladder completely neutral or even slightly bearish, depending upon the underlying price of the time of entry.

Long Call Ladder—Quick Overview

A long call ladder is made up of one long call at a low strike, one short call at a higher strike, and one short call at an even higher strike. All three legs should have the same expiration month. All sides of this spread are opening transactions, and the number of contracts should be equal on all three legs (see Figure 14.1).

At Entry The white line in Figure 14.1 represents what the strategy typically looks like at the point of entry. As expiration approaches, the curve moves toward the black lines, which illustrate the final profit and loss boundaries at expiration.

FIGURE 14.1

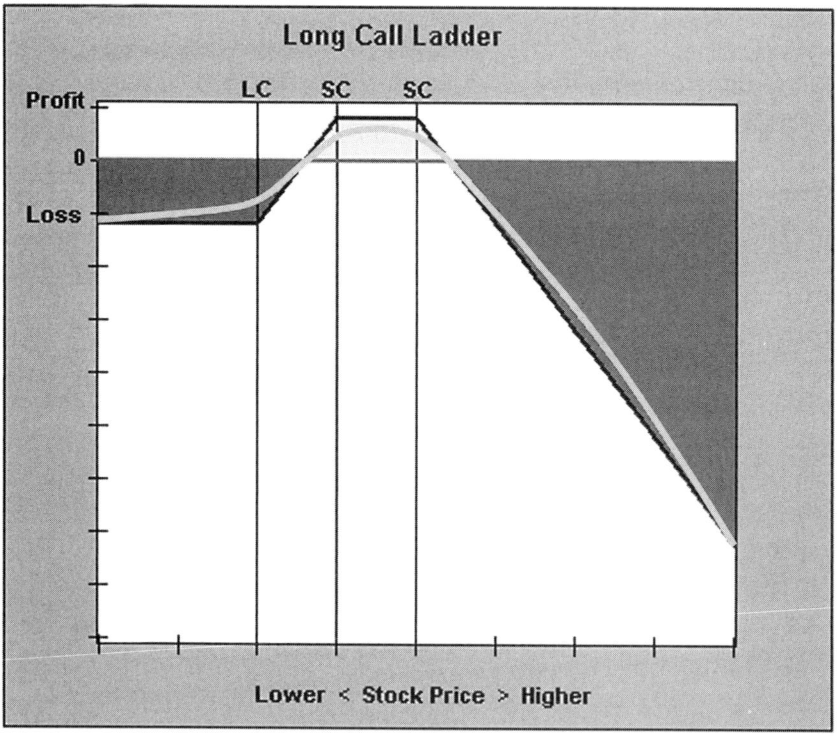

Direction Neutral to moderately bullish or moderately bearish, depending upon the strike prices used

When to Use You would typically employ a long call ladder in a neutral market or when you think the underlying stock will stay within a certain price range until the expiration date of the options. If you were moderately bullish, you would select a second leg strike price that is close to the underlying stock price. If you were moderately bearish, you would select a third leg strike price that is close to the underlying stock price. Maximum profit will occur if the stock is between the two short legs' strike prices on option expiration.

Risk vs. Reward Limited risk to the downside, unlimited risk to the upside, with limited profit potential

Volatility This strategy generally benefits from a decrease in volatility.

Time Decay Time decay is beneficial to this strategy. Since the strategy has twice as many short options as long options, the short options lose more aggregate time value than the long options.

Prior to Expiration

- Because the long call has the lowest strike price, it will also have the highest delta. As the underlying stock rises in price, the long option will gain value faster than the short options. Likewise, as the underlying stock drops in price, the long option will lose value faster than the short options.
  - However, since there are twice as many short options, often the combined deltas on the short options will offset much of the higher delta of the long option.
- If the underlying stock rises or drops sharply enough, any loss mitigation from closing the spread early will likely be wiped out by commissions in many cases.
  - Comparing the early close loss to the maximum potential loss at expiration can help you decide if holding until expiration makes sense.
- Since this strategy benefits from time decay, it may be possible to close the spread out at a profit prior to expiration. That profit will be less than the maximum profit at expiration but will approach the maximum profit as expiration approaches if the underlying stock is between the two short strike prices.
  - Comparing the early close profit to the maximum potential profit at expiration can help you decide if holding until expiration makes sense.

At Expiration

- Below the lower strike, all options expire worthless and the initial debit is lost.
- Between the lower and middle strike, long stock will be acquired through exercise of the lower strike. The long stock can then be sold in the market. The trade may or may not be profitable.

- Between the middle and higher strikes, the lower strike is exercised and the middle strike is assigned. The trade will probably be profitable.
- Significantly above the higher strike, the lower strike is exercised, the middle and highest strikes are assigned, and the remaining short stock is covered in the market. The trade will probably be unprofitable.

Long Call Ladder—Detail

When you establish a long call ladder, the debit you pay on the first leg will typically exceed the combined credit of the second and third legs. As a result, a long call ladder is typically established at a net debit. This type of strategy is intended to take advantage of a stock that is expected to stay relatively unchanged and is therefore considered a neutral strategy.

Example

Buy 10 XYZ Dec 55 Calls @ 10.50

Sell 10 XYZ Dec 60 Calls @ 5.50

Sell 10 XYZ Dec 65 Calls @ 2.00

Debit (DR) = 3.00 (–1st leg + 2nd leg + 3rd leg)

Lower Breakeven (BE) = 58 (1st strike + DR)

Upper Breakeven (BE) = 67 (3rd strike + MG)

Max Gain (MG) = 2.00 (2nd strike – 1st strike – debit) (occurs between 2nd & 3rd strikes)

Upper Max Loss (ML) = Unlimited (occurs above upper BE)

Lower Max Loss (ML) = –3.00 points (debit paid) (occurs below 1st strike)

When you set up an order like this, most order entry systems automatically calculate the market price of this 10/10/10 spread. To do so manually, reduce the spread by its greatest common factor of 10 to 1/1/1. Then multiply each leg by the market price using the ask price on the legs you are buying and the bid price on the legs you are selling:

1 × –10.50 = –10.50

1 × +5.50 = +5.50

1 × +2.00 = +2.00

Net = –3.00 × 10 spreads × 100 shares per contract = ($3,000) total initial debit

Figure 14.2 depicts the profit/loss zones of this example, including the breakeven points at the option expiration date.

As you can see, the maximum gain on this strategy, which occurs between the middle and upper strike prices of 60 and 65 is $2,000. There are two breakeven points at 58 and 67. All prices below 58 or above 67 result in a loss. The maximum loss on the upside is unlimited, and the maximum loss on the downside is –$3,000. To get a better feel for the profit and loss zones, see the following sample prices at expiration.

XYZ below 55 at expiration:

Initial cost: ($3,000)

FIGURE 14.2

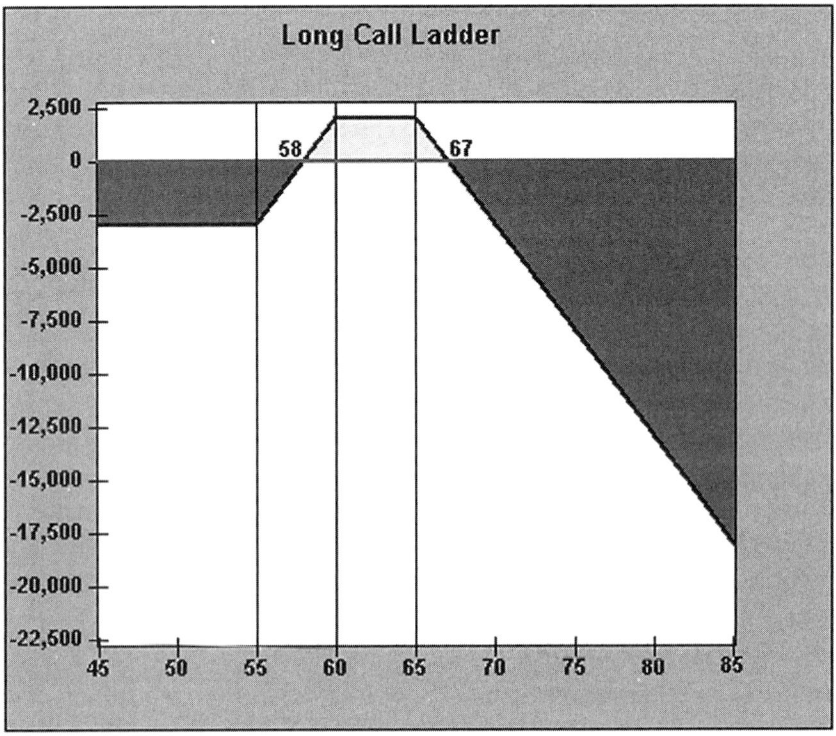

Strategy at Expiration

All options expire worthless:	-0-
Net loss of 3.00 × 10 spreads:	= **($3,000)**

XYZ at 58 at expiration:

Initial cost:	($3,000)
55 calls exercised to buy 1,000 shares:	($55,000)
1,000 shares sold @ market:	$58,000
60 and 65 calls expire worthless:	-0-
Net profit/loss:	= **$0**

XYZ at 60 at expiration:

Initial cost:	($3,000)
55 calls exercised to buy 1,000 shares:	($55,000)
1,000 shares sold @ market:	$60,000
60 and 65 calls expire worthless:	-0-
Net profit/loss:	= **$2,000**

XYZ at 65 at expiration:

Initial cost:	($3,000)
55 calls exercised to buy 1,000 shares:	($55,000)
Assigned on 60 calls to sell 1,000 shares:	$60,000
65 calls expire worthless:	-0-
Net profit/loss:	= **$2,000**

XYZ at 67 at expiration:

Initial cost:	($3,000)
55 calls exercised to buy 1,000 shares:	($55,000)
Assigned on 60 calls to sell 1,000 shares:	$60,000
Assigned on 65 calls to sell 1,000 shares:	$65,000
1,000 shares bought back @ market:	($67,000)
Net profit/loss:	= **$0**

XYZ above 70 at expiration:

Initial cost:	($3,000)
55 calls exercised to buy 1,000 shares:	($55,000)
Assigned on 60 calls to sell 1,000 shares:	$60,000
Assigned on 65 calls to sell 1,000 shares:	$65,000
1,000 shares bought back @ market:	($70,000)
Net profit/loss:	= **($3,000)**

Long Put Ladder—Quick Overview

A long put ladder is made up of one long put at a high strike, one short put at a lower strike, and one short put at an even lower strike. All legs should have the same expiration month, and the number of contracts should be equal on all three legs (see Figure 14.3).

At Entry The white line in Figure 14.3 represents what the strategy typically looks like at the point of entry. As expiration approaches, the curve moves toward the black lines, which illustrate the final profit and loss boundaries at expiration.

Direction Neutral to moderately bullish or moderately bearish, depending upon the strike prices used

When to Use You would typically employ a long put ladder in a neutral market or when you think the underlying stock will

FIGURE 14.3

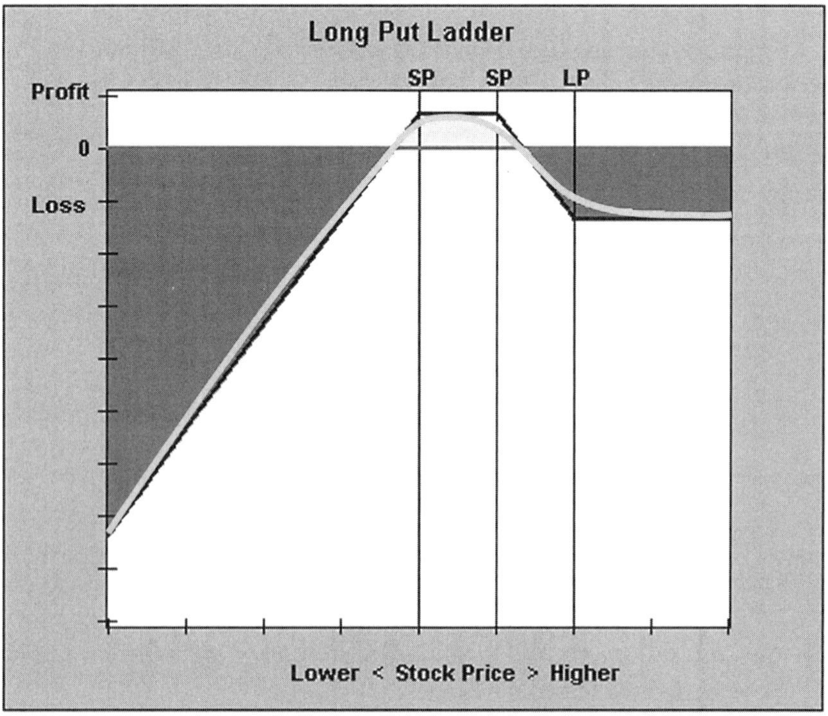

stay within a certain price range until the expiration date of the options. If you were moderately bullish, you would select a first leg strike price that is close to the underlying stock price. If you were moderately bearish, you would select a second leg strike price that is close to the underlying stock price. Maximum profit will occur if the stock is between the two short legs' strike prices on option expiration.

Risk vs. Reward Significant risk to the downside, limited risk to the upside, with limited profit potential

Volatility This strategy generally benefits from a decrease in volatility.

Time Decay Time decay is beneficial to this strategy. Since the strategy has twice as many short options as long options, the short options lose more aggregate time value than the long options.

Prior to Expiration

- Because the long put has the highest strike price, it will also have the highest delta. As the underlying stock rises in price, the long option will lose value faster than the short options. Likewise, as the underlying stock drops in price, the long option will gain value faster than the short options.
  - However, since there are twice as many short options, often the combined deltas on the short options will offset much of the higher delta of the long option.
- If the underlying stock rises or drops sharply enough, any loss mitigation from closing the spread early will likely be wiped out by commissions in many cases.
  - Comparing the early close loss to the maximum potential loss at expiration can help you decide if holding until expiration makes sense.
- Since this strategy benefits from time decay, it may be possible to close the spread out at a profit prior to expiration. That profit will be less than the maximum profit at expiration but will approach the maximum profit as expiration approaches if the underlying stock is between the two short strike prices.
  - Comparing the early close profit to the maximum potential profit at expiration can help you decide if holding until expiration makes sense.

At Expiration

- Above the highest strike, all options expire worthless and the initial debit is lost.
- Between the upper and middle strike, a short stock position will be created through exercise of the higher strike. The short stock can then be closed out in the market. The trade may or may not be profitable.
- Between the middle and lower strike, the upper strike is exercised, the middle strike is assigned, and maximum gain is achieved.
- Significantly below the lower strike, the upper strike is exercised, the middle and lower strikes are both assigned, and the remaining long stock is sold in the market. The trade will probably be unprofitable.

Long Put Ladder—Detail

When you establish a long put ladder, the debit you pay on the third leg will typically exceed the combined credit of the second and first legs. As a result, a long put ladder is typically established at a net debit. This type of strategy is intended to take advantage of a stock that is expected to stay relatively unchanged and is therefore considered a neutral strategy.

Example

Sell 10 XYZ Jan 55 Puts @ 1.50

Sell 10 XYZ Jan 60 Puts @ 5.10

Buy 10 XYZ Jan 65 Puts @ 10.00

Debit (DR) = 3.40 (1st leg + 2nd leg – 3rd leg)

Lower Breakeven (BE) = 53.40 (1st strike – MG)

Upper Breakeven (BE) = 61.60 (2nd strike + MG)

Max Gain (MG) = 1.60 (3rd strike – 2nd strike – debit) (occurs between 2nd & 3rd strikes)

Upper Max Loss (ML) = –3.40 points (occurs above the 3rd strike)

Lower Max Loss (ML) = –53.40 points (debit paid) (occurs below the lower BE)

When you set up an order like this, most order entry systems automatically calculate the market price of this 10/10/10 spread. To do so manually, reduce the spread by its greatest common factor of 10 to 1/1/1. Then multiply each leg by the market price, using the ask price on the legs you are buying and the bid price on the legs you are selling:

1 × +1.50 = +1.50
1 × +5.10 = +5.10
1 × –10.00 = –10.00
Net = –3.40 × 10 spreads × 100 shares per contract = ($3,400) total up-front cost

Figure 14.4 depicts the profit/loss zones of this example, including the breakeven points at the option expiration date.

As you can see, the maximum gain on this strategy, which occurs between the first and second strike prices of 55 and 60, is $1,600. There are two breakeven points at 53.40 and 61.60. All prices

FIGURE 14.4

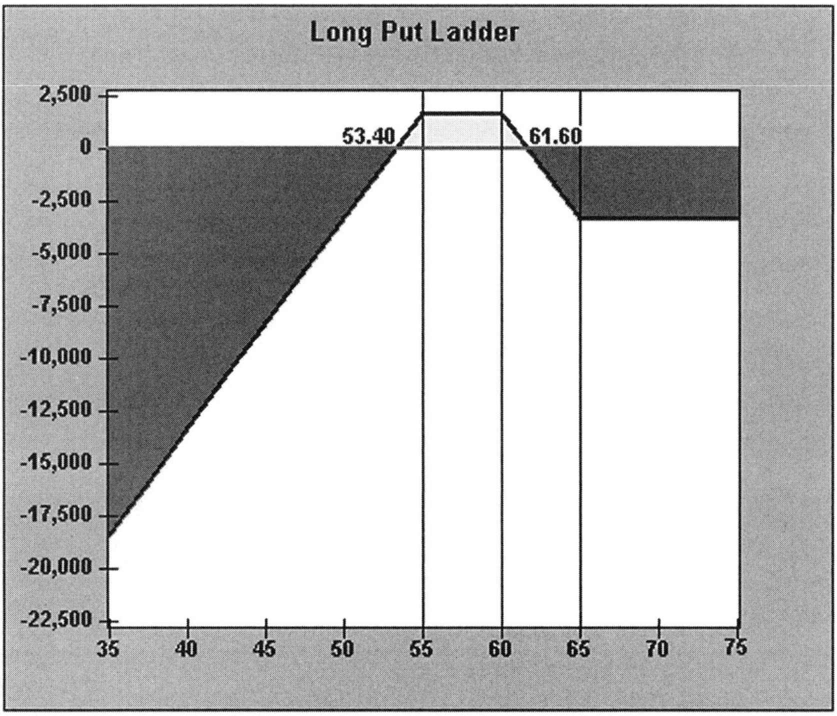

Strategy at Expiration

below 53.40 or above 61.60 result in a loss. The maximum loss on the downside is $53,400, and the maximum loss to the upside is –$3,400. To get a better feel for the profit and loss zones, see the following sample prices at expiration.

XYZ above 65 at expiration:	
Initial cost:	($3,400)
All options expire worthless:	-0-
Net loss of 3.40 × 10 spreads:	**= ($3,400)**

XYZ at 61.60 at expiration:	
Initial cost:	($3,400)
Exercise 65 puts & short 1,000 shares:	$65,000
1,000 shares bought back @ market:	($61,600)
55 and 60 puts expire worthless:	-0-
Net profit/loss:	**= $0**

XYZ at 60 at expiration:	
Initial cost:	($3,400)
Exercise 65 puts & short 1,000 shares:	$65,000
1,000 shares bought back @ market:	($60,000)
55 and 60 puts expire worthless:	-0-
Net profit/loss:	**= $1,600**

XYZ at 55 at expiration:	
Initial cost:	($3,400)
Exercise 65 puts & short 1,000 shares:	$65,000
Assigned on 60 puts to buy 1,000 shares:	($60,000)
55 puts expire worthless:	-0-
Net profit/loss:	**= $1,600**

XYZ at 53.40 at expiration:	
Initial cost:	($3,400)
Exercise 65 puts & short 1,000 shares:	$65,000
Assigned on 60 puts to buy 1,000 shares:	($60,000)
Assigned on 55 puts to buy 1,000 shares:	($55,000)
1,000 shares sold @ market:	$53,400
Net profit/loss:	**= $0**

XYZ at 52 at expiration:	
Initial cost:	($3,400)
Exercise 65 puts & short 1,000 shares:	$65,000
Assigned on 60 puts to buy 1,000 shares:	($60,000)
Assigned on 55 puts to buy 1,000 shares:	($55,000)
1,000 shares sold @ market:	$52,000
Net profit/loss:	= **($1,400)**

As you can see, long ladder spreads are very similar to long ratio spreads. The main differences are that while long ladder spreads allow for a wider maximum profit zone, that maximum profit when earned will be lower than it would be on a comparable ratio spread. Additionally, the debit to establish a long ladder spread will usually be higher than for a comparable ratio spread.

TYPES OF SHORT LADDER SPREADS

The two basic types of short ladder spreads are short call ladders and short put ladders. Short call ladders are typically used when you are neutral to moderately bullish, while short put ladders are typically used when you are neutral to moderately bearish. It is possible to make short call ladders completely neutral or even slightly bearish, depending upon the underlying price at the time of entry. Similarly, it is possible to make a short put ladder completely neutral or even slightly bullish, depending upon the underlying price of the time of entry.

Short Call Ladder—Quick Overview

A short call ladder is made up of one short call at a low strike, one long call at a higher strike, and one long call at an even higher strike. All legs should have the same expiration month. All sides of this spread are opening transactions, and the number of contracts should be equal on all three legs (see Figure 14.5).

At Entry The white line in Figure 14.5 represents what the strategy typically looks like at the point of entry. As expiration approaches, the curve moves toward the black lines, which illustrate the final profit and loss boundaries at expiration.

FIGURE 14.5

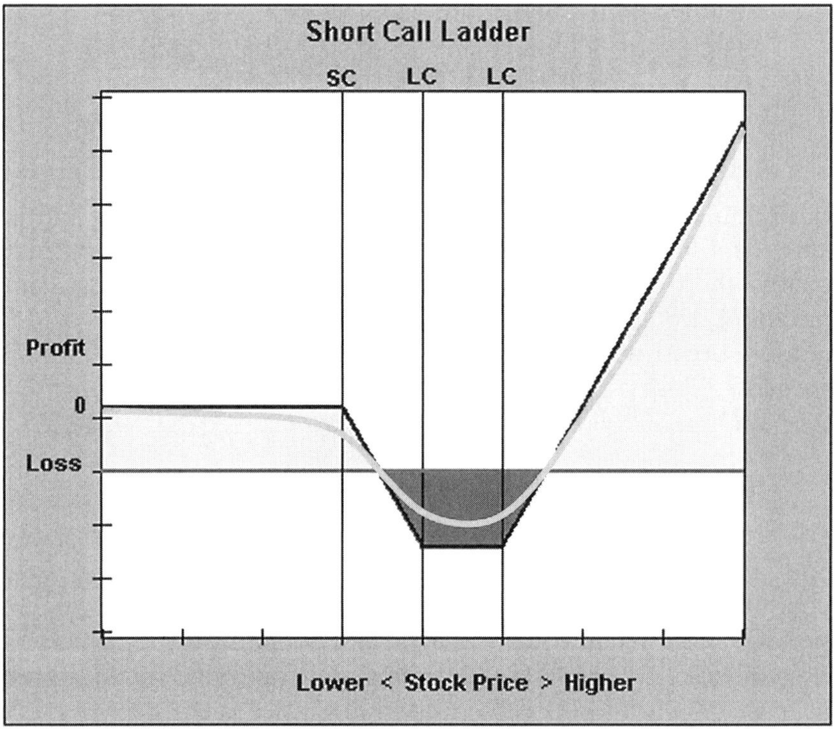

Direction Breakout with a bullish preference

When to Use You would typically employ a short call ladder when you think the underlying stock will break out higher or lower by the expiration date of the options and you believe a breakout higher is more likely.

Risk vs. Reward Unlimited profit potential to the upside, limited profit potential to the downside, with limited risk

Volatility This strategy generally benefits from an increase in volatility.

Time Decay Time decay has a generally adverse effect on this strategy. Since the strategy has twice as many long options as short options, the long options lose more aggregate time value than the short options.

Prior to Expiration

- Because the short call has the lowest strike price, it will also have the highest delta. As the underlying stock rises in price, the short option will gain value faster than the long options. Likewise, as the underlying stock drops in price, the short option will lose value faster than the long options.
  - However, since there are twice as many long options, often the combined deltas on the long options will offset much of the higher delta of the short option.
- If the underlying stock rises or drops sharply enough, it may be possible to close the spread out at a profit prior to expiration. That profit will be less than the maximum profit at expiration but will approach the maximum profit as expiration approaches.
  - Comparing the early close profit to the maximum potential profit at expiration can help you decide if holding until expiration makes sense.
- Since time decay works against you in this strategy, it may be possible to close the spread out at a loss prior to expiration. That loss will be less than the maximum loss at expiration but will approach the maximum loss as expiration approaches if the underlying stock is near the long strike price.
  - Comparing the early close loss to the maximum potential loss at expiration can help you decide if holding until expiration makes sense.

At Expiration

- Below the lower strike, all options expire worthless and the initial credit is retained.
- Between the lower and middle strike, a short stock position will be created through assignment of the lower strike options. The short stock position can then be closed in the market. The trade may or may not be profitable.
- Between the middle and higher strike, the lower strike options will be assigned and the middle strike options will be exercised. The trade will be unprofitable.
- Significantly above the higher strike, the lower strike options are assigned, the middle and upper strike options are

exercised, and long stock is acquired. The long stock positions can then be sold in the market. The trade will probably be profitable.

Short Call Ladder—Detail

When you establish a position using a short call ladder, you will usually pay a slightly lower premium for the options you purchase than the amount you will receive on the premiums from the options sold, even though you are buying more options than you are selling. As a result, a short call ladder is usually established at a net credit.

Example

Sell 10 XYZ Dec 55 Calls @ 5.80
Buy 10 XYZ Dec 60 Calls @ 2.60
Buy 10 XYZ Dec 65 Calls @ .90

Credit (CR) = 2.30
Lower BE = 57.30 (short strike price + the credit)
Upper BE = 67.70 (highest strike price + ML)
Upper MG = Unlimited
Lower MG = 2.30 points (initial credit) (occurs below the short strike price)
ML = 2.70 points (1st strike – 2nd strike – the credit) (occurs between the middle and higher strikes)

When you set up an order like this, most order entry systems automatically calculate the market price of this 10/10/10 spread. To do so manually, reduce the spread by its greatest common factor of 10 to 1/1/1. Then multiply each leg by the market price, using the ask price on the legs you are buying and the bid price on the legs you are selling:

1 × +5.80 = +5.80
1 × –2.60 = –2.60
1 × –.90 = –.90
Net = +2.30 × 10 spreads × 100 shares per contract = $2,300 total up-front credit

Figure 14.6 depicts the profit/loss zones of this example, including the breakeven points at the option expiration date.

As you can see, the maximum loss on this strategy, which occurs between the two long strike prices of 60 and 65, is $2,700.

There are two breakeven points at 57.30 and 67.70. All prices above 57.30 or below 67.70 result in a loss. The maximum gain on the upside is unlimited, and the maximum gain on the downside is $2,300. To get a better feel for the profit and loss zones, see the following sample prices at expiration.

XYZ below 55 at expiration:

Initial credit:	$2,300
All options expire worthless:	-0-
Net gain of 2.30 × 10 spreads:	= **$2,300**

XYZ at 57.30 at expiration:

Initial credit:	$2,300
Assigned on 55 calls to sell 1,000 shares:	$55,000
1,000 shares bought back @ market:	($57,300)

FIGURE 14.6

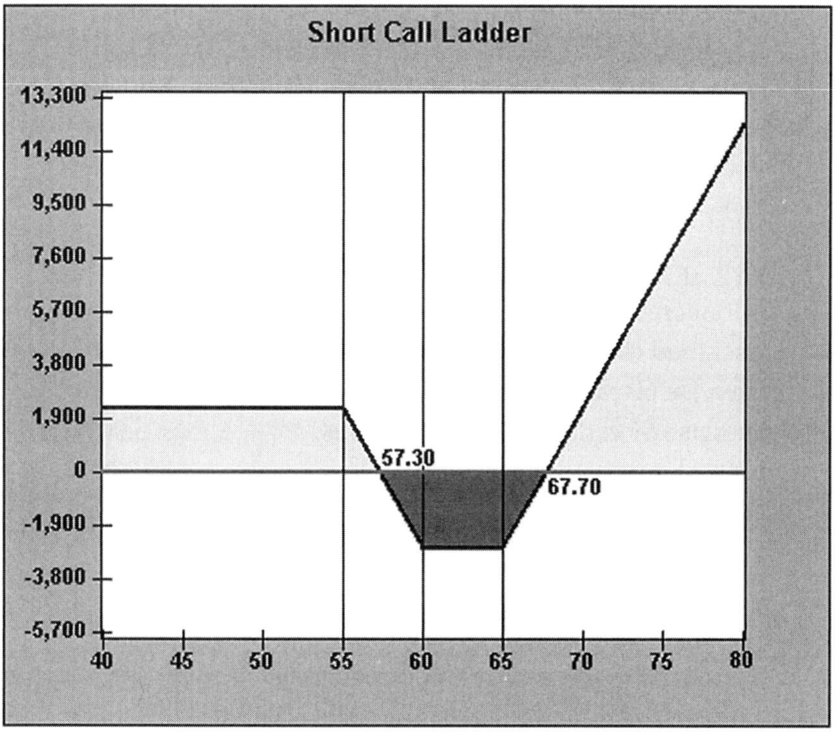

Strategy at Expiration

60 and 65 calls expire worthless:	-0-
Net profit/loss:	= **$0**

XYZ at 60 at expiration:	
Initial credit:	$2,300
Assigned on 55 calls to sell 1,000 shares:	$55,000
1,000 shares bought back @ market:	($60,000)
60 and 65 calls expire worthless:	-0-
Net profit/loss:	= **($2,700)**

XYZ at 65 at expiration:	
Initial credit:	$2,300
Assigned on 55 calls to sell 1,000 shares:	$55,000
Exercise 60 calls to buy 1,000 shares:	($60,000)
65 calls expire worthless:	-0-
Net profit/loss:	= **($2,700)**

XYZ at 67.70 at expiration:	
Initial credit:	$2,300
Assigned on 55 calls to sell 1,000 shares:	$55,000
Exercise 60 calls to buy 1,000 shares:	($60,000)
Exercise 65 calls to buy 1,000 shares:	($65,000)
1,000 shares sold @ market:	$67,700
Net profit/loss:	= **$0**

XYZ at 70 at expiration:	
Initial credit:	$2,300
Assigned on 55 calls to sell 1,000 shares:	$55,000
Exercise 60 calls to buy 1,000 shares:	($60,000)
Exercise 65 calls to buy 1,000 shares:	($65,000)
1,000 shares sold @ market:	$70,000
Net profit/loss:	= **$2,300**

Short Put Ladder—Quick Overview

A short put ladder is made up of one long put at a low strike, one long put at a higher strike, and one short put at an even higher strike. All legs should have the same expiration month. All sides of this spread are opening transactions, and the number of contracts should be equal on all three legs (see Figure 14.7).

At Entry The white line in Figure 14.7 represents what the strategy typically looks like at the point of entry. As expiration approaches, the curve moves toward the black lines, which illustrate the final profit and loss boundaries at expiration.

Direction Breakout with a bearish preference

When to Use You would typically employ a short put ladder when you think the underlying stock will break out higher or lower by the expiration date of the options and you believe a breakout lower is more likely.

Risk vs. Reward Significant profit potential to the downside, limited profit potential to the upside, and limited risk

FIGURE 14.7

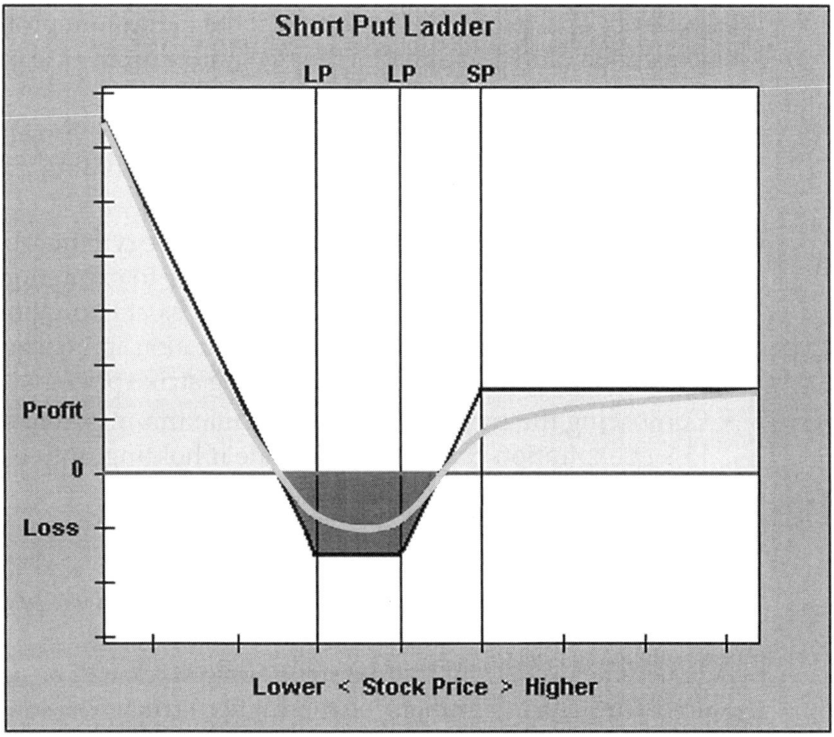

Volatility This strategy generally benefits from an increase in volatility.

Time Decay Time decay has a generally adverse effect on this strategy. Since the strategy has twice as many long options as short options, the long options lose more aggregate time value than the short options.

Prior to Expiration

- Because the short put has the highest strike price, it will also have the highest delta. As the underlying stock rises in price, the short option will lose value faster than the long options. Likewise, as the underlying stock drops in price, the short option will gain value faster than the long options.
  - However, since there are twice as many long options, often the combined deltas on the long options will offset much of the higher delta of the short option.
- If the underlying stock rises or drops sharply enough, it may be possible to close the spread out at a profit prior to expiration. That profit will be less than the maximum profit at expiration but will approach the maximum profit as expiration approaches.
  - Comparing the early close profit to the maximum potential profit at expiration can help you decide if holding until expiration makes sense.
- Since time decay works against you in this strategy, it may be possible to close the spread out at a loss prior to expiration. That loss will be less than the maximum loss at expiration but will approach the maximum loss as expiration approaches if the underlying stock is between the long strike prices.
  - Comparing the early close loss to the maximum potential loss at expiration can help you decide if holding until expiration makes sense.

At Expiration

- Above the higher strike, all options expire worthless and the initial credit is retained.
- Between the upper and middle strike, long stock will be acquired through assignment of the higher strike. The long

stock position can then be sold in the market. The trade may or may not be profitable.

- Between the middle and lower strike, the highest strike options are assigned and the middle strike options are exercised. The trade will probably be unprofitable.
- Significantly below the lower strike, the highest strike options are assigned, the middle and lower strike options are exercised and a short stock position results. The short stock can then be covered in the market. The trade will probably be profitable.

Short Put Ladder—Detail

When you establish a position using a short put ladder, you will usually pay a slightly lower premium for the options you purchase than the amount you will receive on the premiums from the options sold, even though you are buying more options than you are selling. As a result, a short put ladder is usually established at a net credit.

Example

Buy 5 XYZ Jan 65 Puts @ .10
Buy 5 XYZ Jan 70 Puts @ .85
Sell 5 XYZ Jan 75 Puts @ 3.50

Credit (CR) = 2.55
Upper BE = 72.45 (highest strike price – the credit)
Lower BE = 62.55 (lowest strike price – ML)
Upper MG = 2.55 points (initial credit) (occurs beyond the highest strike price)
Lower MG = 62.55 points (lowest strike – ML)
ML = 2.45 points (3rd strike – 2nd strike – the credit) (occurs between the lower and middle strike prices)

When you set up an order like this, most order entry systems automatically calculate the market price of this 5/5/5 spread. To do so manually, reduce the spread by its greatest common factor of 5 to 1/1/1. Then multiply each leg by the market price using the ask price on the legs you are buying and the bid price on the legs you are selling:

1 × –.10 = –.10
1 × –.85 = –.85
1 × +3.50 = +3.50

Net = +2.55 × 5 spreads × 100 shares per contract = $1,275 total up-front credit

Figure 14.8 depicts the profit/loss zones of this example, including the breakeven points at the option expiration date.

As you can see, the maximum loss on this strategy, which occurs between the two long strike prices of 65 and 70, is $1,225. There are two breakeven points at 62.55 and 72.45. All prices above 62.55 or below 72.45 result in a loss. The maximum gain to the downside is $31,275, and the maximum gain to the upside is $1,275. To get a better feel for the profit and loss zones, see the following sample prices at expiration.

XYZ above 75 at expiration:

Initial credit:	$1,275
All options expire worthless:	-0-
Net gain of 2.55 × 5 spreads:	= **$1,275**

FIGURE 14.8

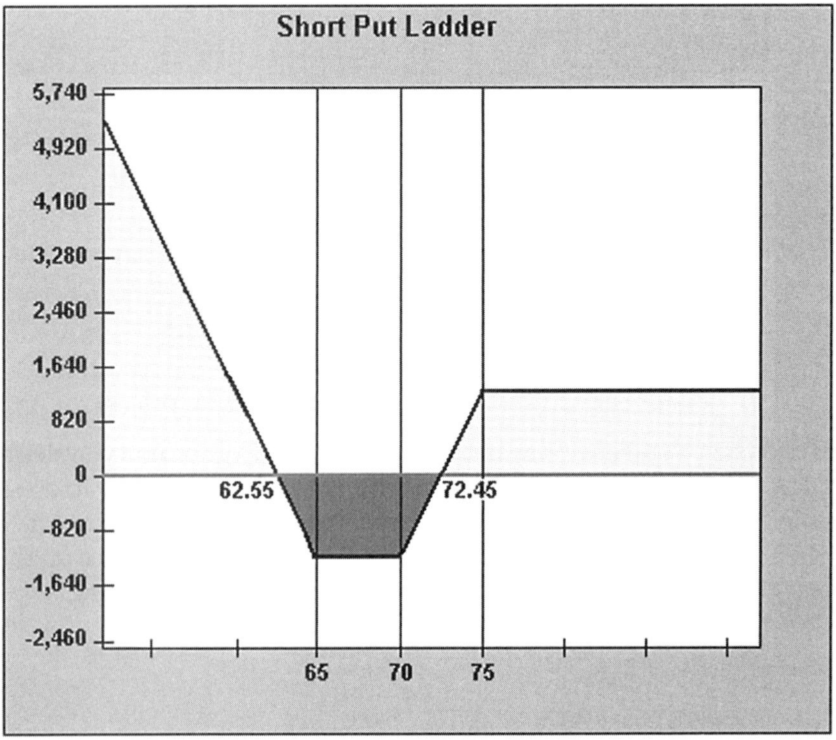

Strategy at Expiration

XYZ at 72.45 at expiration:	
Initial credit:	$1,275
Assigned on 75 puts to buy 500 shares:	($37,500)
500 shares sold @ market:	$36,225
65 and 70 puts expire worthless:	-0-
Net profit/loss:	= **$0**

XYZ at 70 at expiration:	
Initial credit:	$1,275
Assigned on 75 puts to buy 500 shares:	($37,500)
500 shares sold @ market:	$35,000
65 and 70 puts expire worthless:	-0-
Net profit/loss:	= **($1,225)**

XYZ at 65 at expiration:	
Initial credit:	$1,275
Assigned on 75 puts to buy 500 shares:	($37,500)
70 puts exercised to sell 500 shares:	$35,000
65 puts expire worthless:	-0-
Net profit/loss:	= **($1,225)**

XYZ at 62.55 at expiration:	
Initial credit:	$1,275
Assigned on 75 puts to buy 500 shares:	($37,500)
70 puts exercised to sell 500 shares:	$35,000
65 puts exercised to sell 500 shares:	$32,500
500 shares bought back @ market:	($31,275)
Net profit/loss:	= **$0**

XYZ at 60 at expiration:	
Initial credit:	$1,275
Assigned on 75 puts to buy 500 shares:	($37,500)
70 puts exercised to sell 500 shares:	$35,000
65 puts exercised to sell 500 shares:	$32,500
500 shares bought back @ market:	($30,000)
Net profit/loss:	= **$1,275**

As you can see, short ladder spreads are very similar to ratio backspreads. The main differences are that while short ladder spreads have a wider maximum loss zone when the maximum loss is reached, it will be lower than on a comparable ratio backspread. In addition, the credit received upon establishing a short ladder spread will be higher than the credit received on a comparable ratio backspread.

Combo spreads can be used to set up profit and loss characteristics similar to long or short stock, but at a greatly reduced price. Albatross spreads are simply condors for very high priced stocks, and ladder spreads are nothing more than modified ratio spreads. The important thing to gather from this section is that your imagination is the only limitation in the different types of spreads and combinations you can come up with. The important thing is to have an understanding of how the profit and loss characteristics work and a grasp of the risks you take for the rewards you are trying to obtain.

SECTION 9

Gut Spreads

CHAPTER 15

Standard Gut Spreads

Most standard two-legged spreads typically involve being both long and short either puts or calls. By contrast, because of how they are structured, gut spreads involve being either long calls and puts or short calls and puts. As a result, it would probably be more accurate to think of a gut spread as a type of strangle. The difference, however, is that with strangles, the put strike is always lower than the call strike; gut spreads are exactly the opposite. In other words, the call strike is always lower than the put strike for both long and short gut spreads. Despite this key difference, the profit and loss chart of a gut spread looks very similar to that of a strangle.

TYPES OF GUT SPREADS

The two main types of gut spreads are long gut spreads and short gut spreads. A long gut spread involves buying a call and buying a put, and a short gut spread involves selling a call and selling a put. The concept of a gut spread, where the call strike price is lower than the put strike price, can also be incorporated with a number of other more common spreads such as butterflies, condors, and albatrosses. These will be explained in the next 3 chapters.

Long Gut Spreads—Quick Overview

A long gut spread is made up of one long call at a low strike and one long put at a higher strike. Both legs should have the same expiration month. Both sides of this spread are opening transactions, and the number of contracts of the call leg can be the same or different from the number of the put leg. This strategy has similar profit and loss characteristics to a long strangle (see Figure 15.1).

At Entry The white line in Figure 15.1 represents what the strategy typically looks like at the point of entry. As expiration approaches, the curve moves toward the black lines, which illustrate the final profit and loss boundaries at expiration.

Direction Breakout

When to Use You would typically employ a long gut spread in a volatile market, or when you think the underlying stock will become more volatile soon. Breakout strategies are often used before earnings or other significant news announcements. If the stock is significantly below the call strike price on option expiration, the strategy will likely be profitable. Likewise, if the stock is significantly

FIGURE 15.1

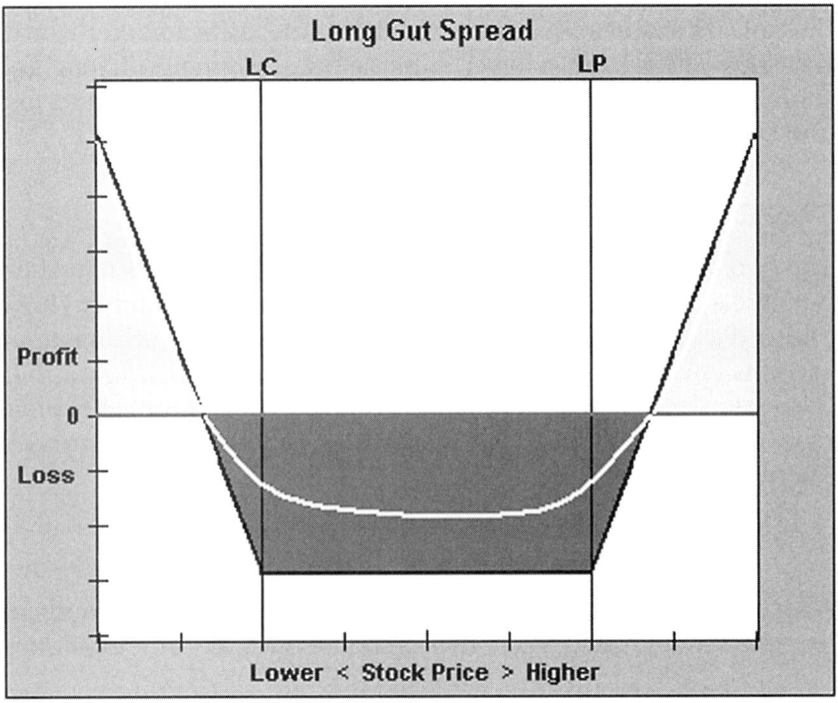

above the put strike price, it will likely be profitable. If the stock is near the two strike prices, it will be unprofitable. Maximum loss occurs anywhere between the two strike prices.

Risk vs. Reward Unlimited profit potential to the upside, substantial profit potential to the downside, with limited risk

Volatility This strategy benefits greatly from an increase in volatility.

Time Decay This strategy loses significant value with time decay, especially in the month of expiration.

Prior to Expiration

- Depending upon the original strike prices and the movement of the stock throughout the life of the strategy, it will often be possible to close out this spread at a loss that is less than the maximum loss at expiration or a gain that is less than the maximum gain at expiration.
  - Often the decision to do so depends upon whether or not your sentiment of the underlying stock has changed since the original position was established.
  - If the underlying stock has remained relatively unchanged but you are still expecting a breakout, you may want to continue to hold your positions.
  - If the underlying stock has already broken out and you believe a pullback closer to where it started is unlikely, you may want to continue to hold your positions
  - If the underlying stock has remained relatively unchanged and you now believe it will remain relatively unchanged, you may want to close your positions to cut your losses.
  - If the underlying stock has already broken out and you now believe it may pull back closer to where it started, you may want to close your positions to preserve your profits.
  - Comparing the early close gain or loss to the maximum potential gain or loss at expiration can help you decide if holding until expiration makes sense.

At Expiration

- Below the call strike, the long put will be exercised and the short call will expire worthless. If the stock is slightly below the call strike, the strategy will be unprofitable. If it is significantly below the call strike, it will be profitable.

- Between the two strikes, both options are exercised and the max loss is sustained.
- Above the put strike, the long call will be exercised and the put will expire worthless. If the stock is slightly above the put strike, the strategy will be unprofitable. If it is significantly above the put strike, it will be profitable.

Long Gut Spreads–Detail

Since both options are long, this strategy is entered at a net debit. This strategy typically requires a significant move in either direction to be profitable.

Example

Buy 10 XYZ Dec 55 Calls @ 6.00

Buy 10 XYZ Dec 65 Puts @ 5.80 for a net debit of 11.80

Upper BE = 66.80 (call strike price + the debit)

Lower BE = 53.20 (put strike price – the debit)

Upper MG = Unlimited

Lower MG = 53.20 (put strike price – the debit)

ML = 1.80 points or $1,800 (difference in strike prices – debit) (occurs between the strike prices)

When you set up an order like this, most order entry systems automatically calculate the market price of this 10/10 spread. To do so manually, reduce the spread by its greatest common factor of 10 to 1/1. Then multiply each leg by the market price using the ask price on the legs you are buying and the bid price on the legs you are selling:

1 × –6.00 = –6.00

1 × –5.80 = –5.80

Net = –11.80 × 10 spreads × 100 shares per contract = $11,800 total up-front debit

Figure 15.2 depicts the profit/loss zones of this example, including the breakeven points, at the option expiration date.

As you can see, the maximum gain on this strategy is unlimited to the upside and substantial to the downside. There are two breakeven points at 53.20 and 66.80. All prices between 53.20 and 66.80 result in a loss. The maximum loss is $1,800. To get a better

FIGURE 15.2

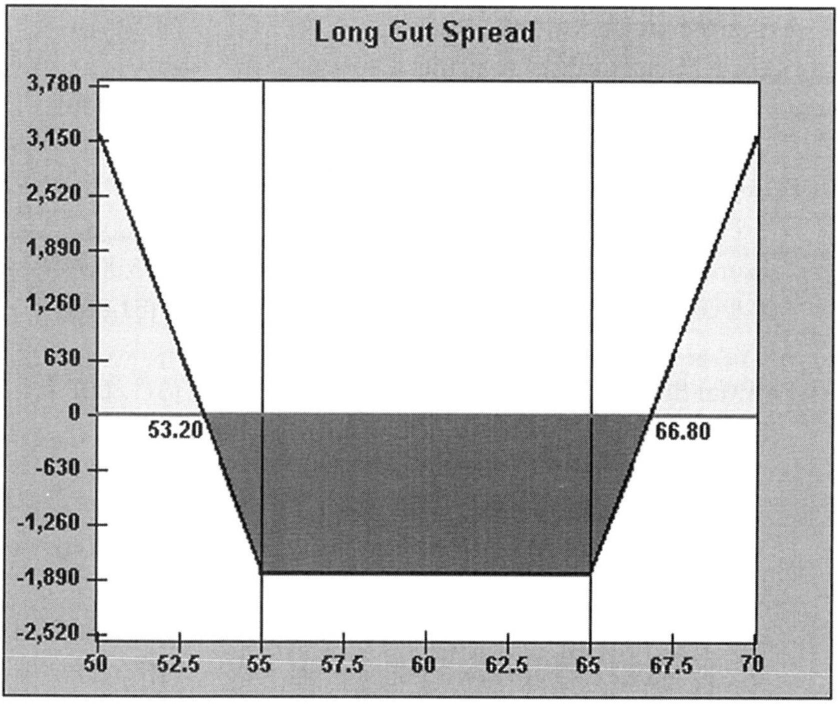

Strategy at Expiration

feel for the profit and loss zones, see the following sample prices at expiration.

XYZ at 52 at expiration:	
Initial debit:	($11,800)
Exercise long puts to sell 1,000 shares:	$65,000
Short shares covered @ market:	($52,000)
Long 55 calls expire worthless:	-0-
Net profit/loss:	= **$1,200**
XYZ at 53.20 at expiration:	
Initial debit:	($11,800)
Exercise long puts to sell 1,000 shares:	$65,000
Short shares covered @ market:	($53,200)
Long 55 calls expire worthless:	-0-
Net profit/loss:	= **$0**

XYZ at 55 at expiration:	
Initial debit:	($11,800)
Exercise long puts to sell 1,000 shares:	$65,000
Short shares covered @ market:	($55,000)
Long 55 calls expire worthless:	-0-
Net profit/loss:	= **($1,800)**
XYZ at 60 at expiration:	
Initial debit:	($11,800)
Exercise long puts to sell 1,000 shares:	$65,000
Exercise long calls to buy 1,000 shares:	($55,000)
Net profit/loss:	= **($1,800)**
XYZ at 65 at expiration:	
Initial debit:	($11,800)
Exercise long calls to buy 1,000 shares:	($55,000)
1,000 shares sold @ market:	$65,000
Long 65 puts expire worthless:	-0-
Net profit/loss:	= **($1,800)**
XYZ at 66.80 at expiration:	
Initial debit:	($11,800)
Exercise long calls to buy 1,000 shares:	($55,000)
1,000 shares sold @ market:	$66,800
Long 65 puts expire worthless:	-0-
Net profit/loss:	= **$0**
XYZ at 70 at expiration:	
Initial debit:	($11,800)
Exercise long calls to buy 1,000 shares:	($55,000)
1,000 shares sold @ market:	$70,000
Long 65 puts expire worthless:	-0-
Net profit/loss:	= **$3,200**

As you can see, this strategy has very similar profit and loss characteristics to a long strangle, but unless you can enter it with a much lower maximum loss, the additional initial debit probably makes this strategy less favorable than a long strangle.

Short Gut Spreads—Quick Overview

A short gut spread is made up of one short call at a low strike and one short put at a higher strike. Both legs should have the same expiration month. Both sides of this spread are opening transactions, and the number of contracts of the call leg can be the same or different from the number of the put leg. This strategy has similar profit and loss characteristics to a short strangle (see Figure 15.3).

At Entry The white line in Figure 15.3 represents what the strategy typically looks like at the point of entry. As expiration approaches, the curve moves toward the black lines, which illustrate the final profit and loss boundaries at expiration.

Direction Neutral

When to Use You would typically employ a short gut spread in a stable market, or when you think the underlying stock will remain relatively flat until the option expiration date. Neutral strategies are often used shortly after earnings reports have come out, when volatility has dropped and the stock has settled back down into a sideways channel. At that point you would have two and a half months or so until the next earnings report. If the stock

FIGURE 15.3

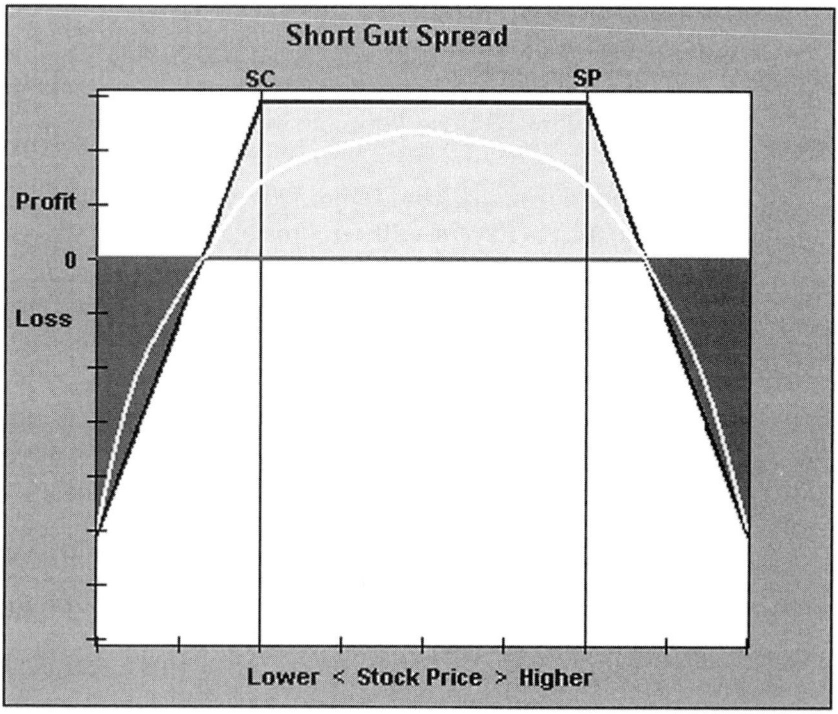

is significantly below the call strike price on option expiration, the strategy will likely be unprofitable. Likewise, if the stock is significantly above the put strike price, it will likely be unprofitable. If the stock is near the two strike prices, it will be profitable. Maximum profit occurs anywhere between the two strike prices.

Risk vs. Reward Unlimited risk to the upside, substantial risk to the downside, with limited profit potential in the middle.

Volatility This strategy benefits greatly from a decrease in volatility.

Time Decay This strategy gains significant value with time decay, especially in the month of expiration.

Prior to Expiration

- Depending upon the original strike prices and the movement of the stock throughout the life of the strategy, it will often be possible to close out this spread at a loss that is less than the maximum loss at expiration or a gain that is less than the maximum gain at expiration.
  - Often the decision to do so depends upon whether or not your sentiment of the underlying stock has changed since the original position was established.
  - If the underlying stock has remained relatively unchanged but you are now expecting a possible breakout, you may want to close your positions to preserve your profits.
  - If the underlying stock has remained relatively unchanged and you still believe it will remain relatively unchanged, you may want to continue to hold your positions.
  - If the underlying stock has already broken out and you now believe it may pull back closer to where it started, you may want to continue to hold your positions.
  - If the underlying stock has already broken out and you believe it is unlikely to pull back closer to where it started, you may want to close your positions to cut your losses.
  - Comparing the early close gain or loss to the maximum potential gain or loss at expiration can help you decide if holding until expiration makes sense.

At Expiration

- Below the call strike, the short put will be assigned and the short call will expire worthless. If the stock is slightly below the call strike, the strategy will be profitable. If it is significantly below the call strike, it will be unprofitable.
- Between the two strikes, both options are assigned and the max gain is achieved.
- Above the put strike, the short call will be assigned and the put will expire worthless. If the stock is slightly above the put strike, the strategy will be profitable. If it is significantly above the put strike, it will be unprofitable.

Short Gut Spreads—Detail

Since both options are short, this strategy is entered at a net credit. This strategy typically requires the underlying stock to remain relatively stable to be profitable.

Example

Short 10 XYZ Dec 55 Calls @ 6.00

Short 10 XYZ Dec 65 Puts @ 5.80 for a net credit of 11.80

Upper BE = 66.80 (call strike price + the credit)

Lower BE = 53.20 (put strike price – the credit)

Upper ML = Unlimited

Lower ML = 53.20 (put strike price – the credit)

MG = 1.80 points or $1,800 (difference in strike prices – credit) (occurs between the strike prices)

When you set up an order like this, most order entry systems automatically calculate the market price of this 10/10 spread. To do so manually, reduce the spread by its greatest common factor of 10 to 1/1. Then multiply each leg by the market price, using the ask price on the legs you are buying and the bid price on the legs you are selling:

$1 \times +6.00 = +6.00$

$1 \times +5.80 = +5.80$

Net = +11.80 × 10 spreads × 100 shares per contract = $11,800 total up-front credit

Figure 15.4 depicts the profit/loss zones of this example, including the breakeven points at the option expiration date.

As you can see, the maximum loss on this strategy is unlimited to the upside and significant to the downside. There are two breakeven points at 53.20 and 66.80. All prices between 53.20 and 66.80 result in a gain. The maximum gain is $1,800. To get a better feel for the profit and loss zones, see the following sample prices at expiration.

XYZ at 52 at expiration:

Initial credit:	$11,800
Assigned on short puts to buy 1,000 shares:	($65,000)
Long shares sold @ market:	$52,000
Short 55 calls expire worthless:	-0-
Net profit/loss:	= **($1,200)**

FIGURE 15.4

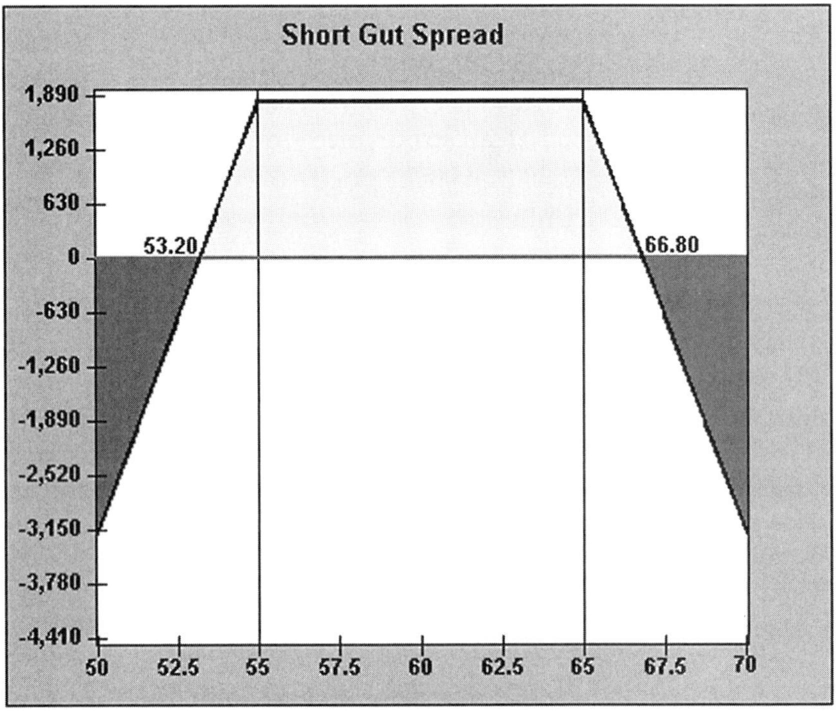

Strategy at Expiration

XYZ at 53.20 at expiration:	
Initial credit:	$11,800
Assigned on short puts to buy 1,000 shares:	($65,000)
Long shares sold @ market:	$53,200
Short 55 calls expire worthless:	-0-
Net profit/loss:	= **$0**
XYZ at 55 at expiration:	
Initial credit:	$11,800
Assigned on short puts to buy 1,000 shares:	($65,000)
Long shares sold @ market:	$55,000
Short 55 calls expire worthless:	-0-
Net profit/loss:	= **$1,800**
XYZ at 60 at expiration:	
Initial credit:	$11,800
Assigned on short puts to buy 1,000 shares:	($65,000)
Assigned on short calls to sell 1,000 shares:	$55,000
Net profit/loss:	= **$1,800**
XYZ at 65 at expiration:	
Initial credit:	$11,800
Assigned on short calls to sell 1,000 shares:	$55,000
Short shares covered @ market:	($65,000)
Short 65 puts expire worthless:	-0-
Net profit/loss:	= **$1,800**
XYZ at 66.80 at expiration:	
Initial credit:	$11,800
Assigned on short calls to sell 1,000 shares:	$55,000
Short shares covered @ market:	($66,800)
Short 65 puts expire worthless:	-0-
Net profit/loss:	= **$0**
XYZ at 70 at expiration:	
Initial credit:	$11,800
Assigned on short calls to sell 1,000 shares:	$55,000
Short shares covered @ market:	($70,000)
Short 65 puts expire worthless:	-0-
Net profit/loss:	= **($3,200)**

As you can see, this strategy has very similar profit and loss characteristics to a short strangle. Since it can be entered with a much larger initial credit, it may be considered more favorable than a long strangle if your broker pays you interest on your full credit balances.

CHAPTER 16

Gut Iron Butterfly Spreads

A gut iron butterfly spread is very similar to an iron butterfly spread. The only real difference is that with an iron butterfly spread, the put strike prices are lower than the call strike prices. As with other gut spreads, gut iron butterflies are exactly the opposite. In other words, the call strikes are lower than the put strikes for both long and short iron butterfly spreads. Despite this key difference, the profit and loss chart of a gut iron butterfly spread looks very similar to that of an iron butterfly spread. Like iron butterflies, gut iron butterflies involve buying and selling of both puts and calls at 3 different strike prices.

TYPES OF GUT IRON BUTTERFLY SPREADS

There are only two types of gut iron butterfly spreads, long gut iron butterflies and short gut iron butterflies. Long gut iron butterflies are used when you have a neutral sentiment, and short gut iron butterflies are used when you have a breakout sentiment. They also differ by whether you pay an initial debit or receive an initial credit when you establish them. Because of the narrow range of strikes used in establishing gut iron butterflies, they are most appropriate for stock priced under 100.

Long Gut Iron Butterfly—Quick Overview

A long gut iron butterfly is made up of one long call at the lowest strike, one short call at the middle strike, one short put at the same middle strike, and one long put at the highest strike, with the same strike price interval between all legs. All legs should also have the same expiration month. All sides of this spread are opening transactions, and the quantity of all four legs is always the same. This strategy is actually made up of one short gut spread and one long gut spread combined together as a single strategy. This can also be viewed as being made up of one put debit spread and one call debit spread (see Figure 16.1).

At Entry The white line in Figure 16.1 represents what the strategy typically looks like at the point of entry. As expiration approaches, the curve moves toward the black lines, which illustrate the final profit and loss boundaries at expiration.

Direction Neutral

FIGURE 16.1

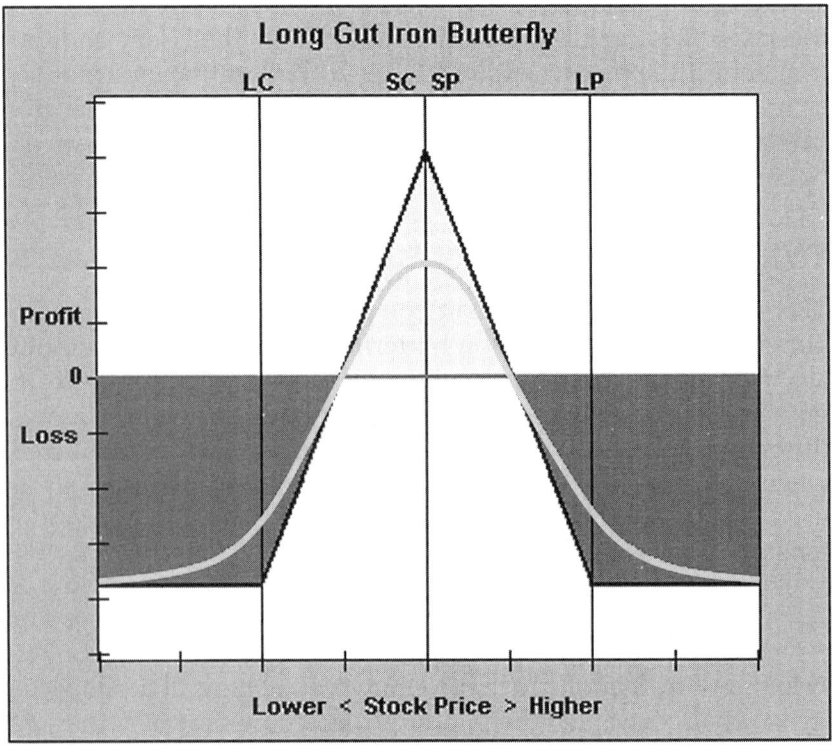

When to Use You would typically employ a long gut iron butterfly in neutral markets and would hope to profit if the underlying stock remains very flat until the expiration date of the options. Generally, the underlying stock price should be close to the middle strike price at the time of entry. If you are moderately bullish or bearish, you could use strike prices that are slightly higher or lower, respectively, but this strategy generally works best when you stay closest to the middle.

Risk vs. Reward Limited risk with limited profit potential

Volatility The effect of volatility varies depending upon the strike prices chosen. This strategy generally benefits moderately from decreases in volatility.

Time Decay The effect of time decay on this strategy varies with the underlying stock's price level in relation to the strike prices. If the stock price is between the outer strike prices, the effect is positive. If the stock price is above the upper strike price or below the lower strike price, the effect is negative.

Prior to Expiration

- Depending upon the original strike prices and the movement of the stock throughout the life of the strategy, it will often be possible to close out this spread at a loss that is less than the maximum loss at expiration or a gain that is less than the maximum gain at expiration.
  - Often the decision to do so depends upon whether or not your sentiment of the underlying stock has changed since the original position was established.
  - If the underlying stock has remained relatively unchanged but you are now expecting a possible breakout, you may want to close your positions to preserve your profits.
  - If the underlying stock has remained relatively unchanged and you still believe it will remain relatively unchanged, you may want to continue to hold your positions.
  - If the underlying stock has already broken out and you now believe it may pull back closer to where it started, you may want to continue to hold your positions.
  - If the underlying stock has already broken out and you believe it is unlikely to pull back closer to where it started, you may want to close your positions to cut your losses.

- Comparing the early close gain or loss to the maximum potential gain or loss at expiration can help you decide if holding until expiration makes sense.

At Expiration

- Below the lowest strike, all call options expire worthless, but all put options are exercised and/or assigned and max loss is sustained.
- Between the call strikes, long stock can be acquired through exercise of the long calls. The short calls options expire worthless and all put options may be exercised and/or assigned. The long stock can then be sold in the market. The trade may or may not be profitable.
- At the middle strike price, all long options can be exercised, all short options expire worthless, and max gain is achieved.
- Between the put strikes, a short stock position will be created through exercise of the long puts. The short puts expire worthless and all call options are exercised and/or assigned. The short stock position can then be closed out in the market. The trade may or may not be profitable.
- Above the highest strike, all put options expire worthless, but all call options are exercised and/or assigned and max loss is sustained.

Long Gut Iron Butterfly—Detail

When you establish a long gut iron butterfly, the combined credit from the second and third legs will be less than the combined cost of the first and fourth legs. As a result, a long gut iron butterfly is established at a net debit. This type of strategy is intended to take advantage of a stock that is moving sideways and is therefore considered a neutral strategy.

Example

Buy to open 5 XYZ Dec 65 Calls @ 5.50
Sell to open 5 XYZ Dec 70 Calls @ 1.80
Sell to open 5 XYZ Dec 70 Puts @ 1.50
Buy to open 5 XYZ Dec 75 Puts @ 5.20

Debit (DR) = 7.40 (–1st leg + 2nd leg + 3rd leg – 4th leg)
Lower Breakeven (BE) = 67.40 (middle strike – MG)
Upper Breakeven (BE) = 72.60 (middle strike + MG)
Max Gain (MG) = 2.60 points or $1,300 (difference in call strikes + difference in puts strikes – debit) (occurs at the middle strike)
Max Loss (ML) = –2.40 points or $1,200 (debit – difference in call strikes or debit – difference in puts strikes) (occurs beyond the outside strike prices)

When you set up an order like this, most order entry systems automatically calculate the market price of this 5/5/5/5 spread. To do so manually, reduce the spread by its greatest common factor of 5 to 1/1/1/1. Then multiply each leg by the market price using the ask price on the legs you are buying and the bid price on the legs you are selling:

$1 \times -5.50 = -5.50$
$1 \times +1.80 = +1.80$
$1 \times +1.50 = +1.50$
$1 \times -5.20 = -5.20$
Net = –7.40 × 5 spreads × 100 shares per contract = ($3,700) total initial debit

Figure 16.2 depicts the profit/loss zones of this example, including the breakeven points at the option expiration date.

As you can see, the maximum gain on this strategy, which occurs only at the price of 70 at expiration, is $1,300. There are two breakeven points at 67.40 and 72.60. All prices below 67.40 or above 72.60 result in a loss. The maximum loss on the upside or downside is –$1,200 and occurs below 65 or above 75. To get a better feel for the profit and loss zones, see the following sample prices at expiration.

XYZ at 65 at expiration:

Initial debit:	($3,700)
Assigned on 70 puts to buy 500 shares:	($35,000)
Exercise 75 puts to sell 500 shares:	$37,500
All call options expire worthless:	-0-
Net profit/loss:	= **($1,200)**

XYZ at 67.40 at expiration:

Initial debit:	($3,700)

FIGURE 16.2

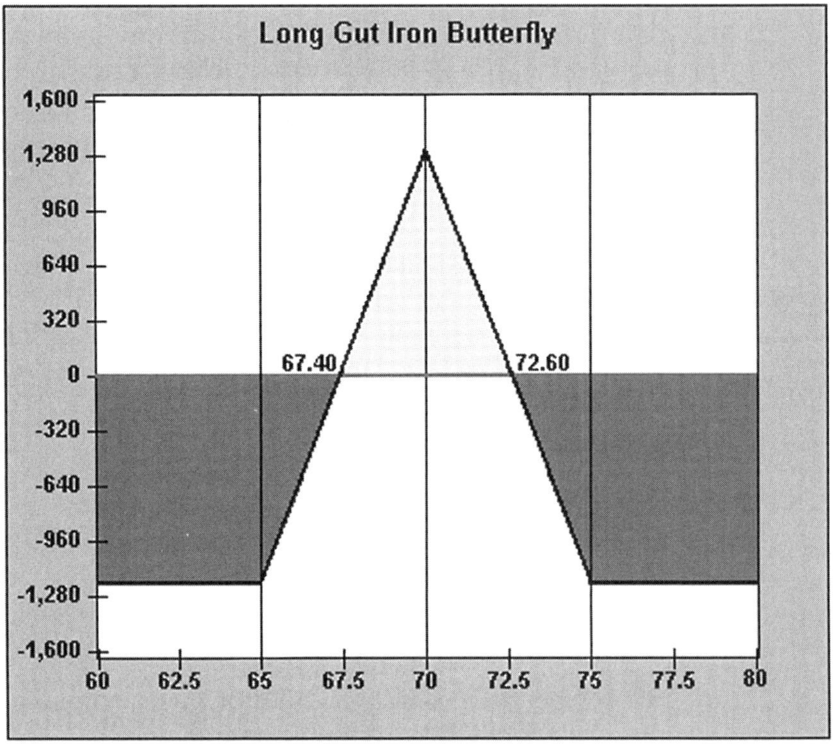

Strategy at Expiration

Assigned on 70 puts to buy 500 shares:	($35,000)
Exercise 75 puts to sell 500 shares:	$37,500
Exercise 65 calls to buy 500 shares:	($32,500)
500 shares sold @ market:	$33,700
Short call options expire worthless:	-0-
Net profit/loss:	= **$0**

XYZ at 69 at expiration:

Initial debit:	($3,700)
Assigned on 70 puts to buy 500 shares:	($35,000)
Exercise 75 puts to sell 500 shares:	$37,500
Exercise 65 calls to buy 500 shares:	($32,500)
500 shares sold @ market:	$34,500

Short call options expire worthless:	-0-
Net profit/loss:	= **$800**

XYZ at 70 at expiration:

Initial debit:	($3,700)
Exercise 75 puts to sell 500 shares:	$37,500
Exercise 65 calls to buy 500 shares:	($32,500)
Short call options expire worthless:	-0-
Short put options expire worthless:	-0-
Net profit/loss:	= **$1,300**

XYZ at 71 at expiration:

Initial debit:	($3,700)
Exercise 75 puts to sell 500 shares:	$37,500
Exercise 65 calls to buy 500 shares:	($32,500)
Assigned on 70 calls to sell 500 shares:	$35,000
500 shares bought back @ market:	($35,500)
Short put options expire worthless:	-0-
Net profit/loss:	= **$800**

XYZ at 72.60 at expiration:

Initial debit:	($3,700)
Exercise 75 puts to sell 500 shares:	$37,500
Exercise 65 calls to buy 500 shares:	($32,500)
Assigned on 70 calls to sell 500 shares:	$35,000
500 shares bought back @ market:	($36,300)
Short put options expire worthless:	-0-
Net profit/loss:	= **$0**

XYZ above 75 at expiration:

Initial debit:	($3,700)
Exercise 65 calls to buy 500 shares:	($32,500)
Assigned on 70 calls to sell 500 shares:	$35,000
All put options expire worthless:	-0-
Net profit/loss:	= **($1,200)**

As you can see, this strategy has very similar profit and loss characteristics to a long iron butterfly. Since you are required to pay a debit up front, one advantage in trading a long gut iron butterfly over a long iron butterfly is that the margin requirements are lower.

Since this strategy is made up of two debit spreads, it has no margin requirements other than the initial up-front debit, while a long iron butterfly is made up of two credit spreads and does have a margin requirement equal to the maximum loss amount.

Short Gut Iron Butterfly—Quick Overview

A short gut iron butterfly is made up of one short call at the lowest strike, one long call at the middle strike, one long put at the same middle strike, and one short put at the highest strike, with the same strike price interval between all legs. All sides of this spread are opening transactions, and the quantity of all four legs is always the same. This strategy is actually made up of one long gut spread and one short gut spread combined together as a single strategy. This can also be viewed as being made up of one credit put spread and one credit call spread (see Figure 16.3).

FIGURE 16.3

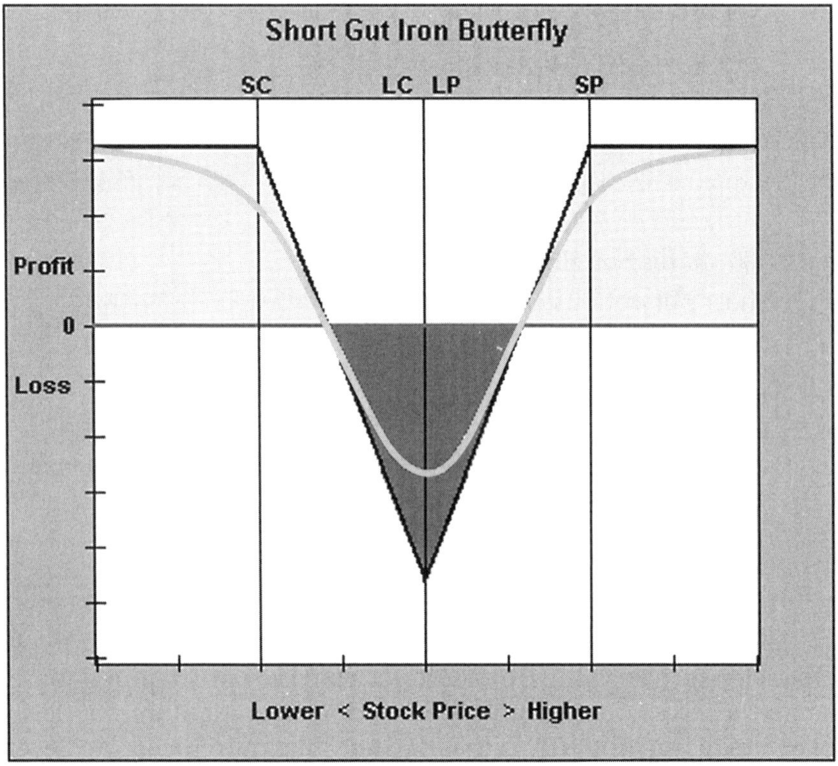

At Entry The white line in Figure 16.3 represents what the strategy typically looks like at the point of entry. As expiration approaches, the curve moves toward the black lines, which illustrate the final profit and loss boundaries at expiration.

Direction Breakout

When to Use You would typically employ a short gut iron butterfly in uncertain markets and would hope to profit if the underlying stock breaks out either higher or lower than the current price by the expiration date of the options. Generally, the underlying stock price should be near the middle strike price at the time of entry. If you are moderately bullish or bearish, you could use strike prices that are slightly higher or lower, respectively, but this strategy generally works best when you stay closest to the middle.

Risk vs. Reward Limited risk with limited profit potential

Volatility The effect of volatility varies depending upon the strike prices chosen. This strategy generally benefits moderately from volatility increases.

Time Decay The effect of time decay on this strategy varies with the underlying stock's price level in relation to the strike prices. If the stock price is between the outer strike prices, the effect is negative. If the stock price is above the upper strike price or below the lower strike price, the effect is positive.

Prior to Expiration

- Depending upon the original strike prices and the movement of the stock throughout the life of the strategy, it will often be possible to close out this spread at a loss that is less than the maximum loss at expiration or a gain that is less than the maximum gain at expiration.
  - Often the decision to do so depends upon whether or not your sentiment of the underlying stock has changed since the original position was established.
  - If the underlying stock has remained relatively unchanged but you are still expecting a breakout, you may want to continue to hold your positions.
  - If the underlying stock has already broken out and you believe a pullback closer to where it started is unlikely, you may want to continue to hold your positions.

- If the underlying stock has remained relatively unchanged and you now believe it will remain relatively unchanged, you may want to close your positions to cut your losses.
- If the underlying stock has already broken out and you now believe it may pull back closer to where it started, you may want to close your positions to preserve your profits.
- Comparing the early close gain or loss to the maximum potential gain or loss at expiration can help you decide if holding until expiration makes sense.

At Expiration

- Below the lowest strike, all call options expire worthless, but all put options are exercised and/or assigned and max gain is achieved.
- Between the two call strikes, a short stock position will be created through assignment of the short calls, the long calls expire worthless, and both put options can be exercised and/or assigned. The short stock position can then be closed out in the market. The trade may or may not be profitable.
- At the middle strike price, all short options are assigned, all long options expire worthless, and max loss is sustained.
- Between the two put strikes, long stock will be obtained through the assignment of the short puts, the long puts expire worthless, and both call options are exercised and/or assigned. The long stock position can then be sold in the market. The trade may or may not be profitable.
- Above the highest strike, all put options expire worthless, but all call options are exercised and/or assigned and max gain is achieved.

Short Gut Iron Butterfly—Detail

When you establish a short gut iron butterfly, the combined debit from the second and third legs will be less than the combined credit of the first and fourth legs. As a result, a short gut iron butterfly is usually established at a net credit. This type of strategy is intended to take advantage of a stock that is expected to move sharply in either direction and is therefore considered a breakout strategy.

Example

Sell to open 5 XYZ Jan 65 Calls @ 5.40
Buy to open 5 XYZ Jan 70 Calls @ 1.85
Buy to open 5 XYZ Jan 70 Puts @ 1.60
Sell to open 5 XYZ Jan 75 Puts @ 5.10

Credit (CR) = 7.05 (1st leg – 2nd leg – 3rd leg + 4th leg)
Lower Breakeven (BE) = 67.05 (middle strike – ML)
Upper Breakeven (BE) = 72.95 (middle strike + ML)
Max Gain (MG) = 2.05 points or $1,025 (credit – difference in call strikes or credit – difference in put strikes) (occurs beyond the outside strike prices)
Max Loss (ML) = –2.95 points or $1,475 (difference in call strikes + difference in put strikes – credit) (occurs at the middle strike)

When you set up an order like this, most order entry systems automatically calculate the market price of this 5/5/5/5 spread. To do so manually, reduce the spread by its greatest common factor of 5 to 1/1/1/1. Then multiply each leg by the market price using the ask price on the legs you are buying and the bid price on the legs you are selling:

1 × +5.40 = +5.40
1 × –1.85 = –1.85
1 × –1.60 = –1.60
1 × +5.10 = +5.10
Net = +7.05 × 5 spreads × 100 shares per contract = $3,525 total initial credit

Figure 16.4 depicts the profit/loss zones of this example, including the breakeven points at the option expiration date.

As you can see, the maximum gain on this strategy, which occurs only above or below the outer strike prices at expiration, is $1,025. There are two breakeven points at 67.05 and 72.95. All prices between 67.05 and 72.95 result in a loss. The maximum loss is –$1,475 and occurs only at the middle strike price of 70. To get a better feel for the profit and loss zones, see the following sample prices at expiration.

XYZ at or above 75 at expiration:

Initial credit:	$3,525

FIGURE 16.4

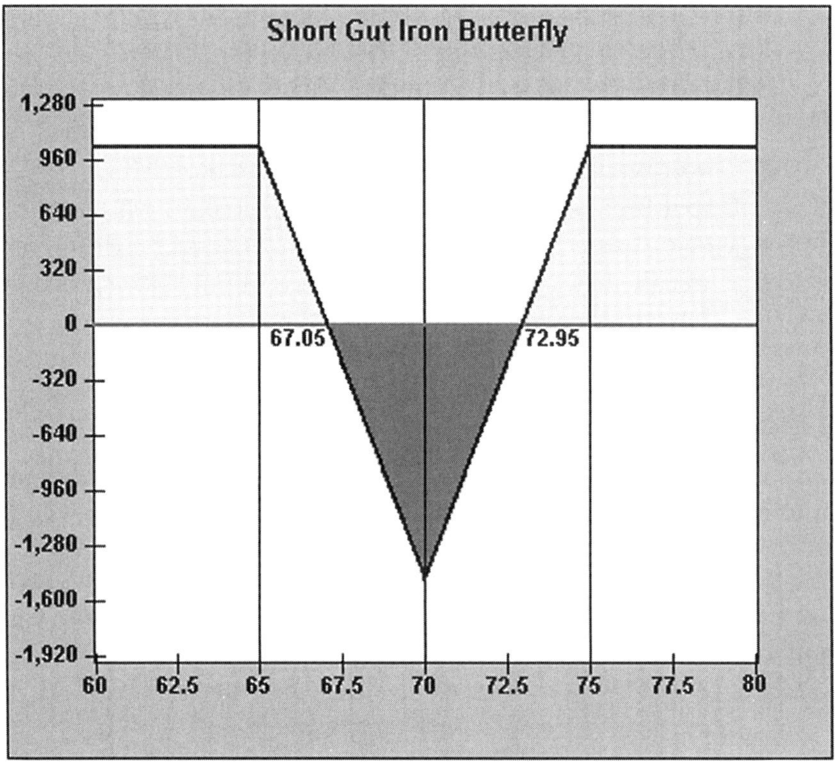

Strategy at Expiration

Long 70 calls exercised to buy 500 shares:	($35,000)
Short 65 calls assigned to sell 500 shares:	$32,500
All puts expire worthless:	-0-
Net profit/loss:	= **$1,025**

XYZ at 72.95 at expiration:

Initial credit:	$3,525
Long 70 calls exercised to buy 500 shares:	($35,000)
Short 65 calls assigned to sell 500 shares:	$32,500
Short 75 puts assigned to buy 500 shares:	($37,500)

500 shares sold @ market:	$36,475
70 puts expire worthless:	-0-
Net profit/loss:	= **$0**

XYZ at 70 at expiration:

Initial credit:	$3,525
Short 65 calls assigned to sell 500 shares:	$32,500
Short 75 puts assigned to buy 500 shares:	($37,500)
70 puts expire worthless:	-0-
70 calls expire worthless:	-0-
Net profit/loss:	= **($1,475)**

XYZ at 67.05 at expiration:

Initial credit:	$3,525
Short 65 calls assigned to sell 500 shares:	$32,500
Short 75 puts assigned to buy 500 shares:	($37,500)
Long 70 puts exercised to sell 500 shares:	$35,000
500 shares bought back @ market:	($33,525)
70 calls expire worthless:	-0-
Net profit/loss:	= **$0**

XYZ at or below 65 at expiration:

Initial credit:	$,3,525
Short 75 puts assigned to buy 500 shares:	($37,500)
Long 70 puts exercised to sell 500 shares:	$35,000
All calls expire worthless:	-0-
Net profit/loss:	= **$1,025**

As you can see, this strategy has very similar profit and loss characteristics to a short iron butterfly. Since it is made up of two credit spreads and has an initial margin requirement, one advantage of a short gut iron butterfly over a short iron butterfly is that you get to bring in a credit when the trade is established.

CHAPTER 17

Gut Iron Condor Spreads

A gut iron condor spread is very similar to an iron condor spread. The only real difference is that with an iron condor spread, the put strike prices are lower than the call strike prices. As with other gut spreads, gut iron condors are exactly the opposite. In other words, the call strikes are both lower than the put strikes for both long and short iron condor spreads. Despite this key difference, the profit and loss chart of a gut iron condor spread looks very similar to that of an iron condor spread. Like iron condors, gut iron condors involve buying and selling of both puts *and* calls at four different strike prices.

TYPES OF CONDOR SPREADS

There are only two types of gut iron condor spreads, long gut iron condors and short gut iron condors. Long gut iron condors are used when you have a neutral sentiment, and short iron condors are used when you have a breakout sentiment. They also differ by whether you pay an initial debit or receive an initial credit when you establish them. Because of the wide range of strikes used in establishing a gut iron condor, it is most appropriate for stock priced over 50.

Long Gut Iron Condor—Quick Overview

A long gut iron condor is made up of one long call at the lowest strike, one short call at the lower middle strike, one short put at the upper middle strike, and one long put at the highest strike, with the same strike price interval between all legs. All legs should also have the same expiration month. All sides of this spread are opening transactions, and the quantity of all four legs is always the same. This strategy is actually made up of one short gut spread and one long gut spread combined together as a single strategy. This can also be viewed as being made up of one put debit spread and one call debit spread (see Figure 17.1).

At Entry The white line in Figure 17.1 represents what the strategy typically looks like at the point of entry. As expiration approaches, the curve moves toward the black lines, which illustrate the final profit and loss boundaries at expiration.

Direction Neutral

When to Use You would typically employ a long gut iron condor in neutral markets and would hope to profit if the underlying

FIGURE 17.1

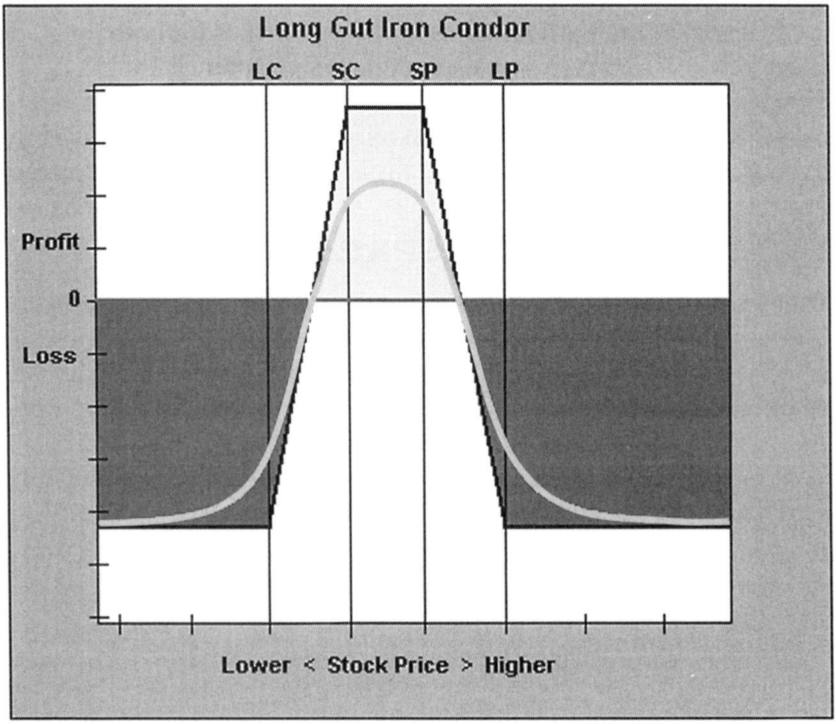

stock remains relatively flat until the expiration date of the options. Generally, the underlying stock price should be between the two middle strike prices at the time of entry. If you are moderately bullish or bearish, you could use strike prices that are slightly higher or lower, respectively, but this strategy generally works best when you stay closest to the middle.

Risk vs. Reward Limited risk with limited profit potential

Volatility The effect of volatility varies depending upon the strike prices chosen. This strategy generally benefits moderately when volatility decreases.

Time Decay The effect of time decay on this strategy varies with the underlying stock's price level in relation to the strike prices. If the stock price is between the outer strike prices, the effect is positive. If the stock price is above the upper strike price or below the lower strike price, the effect is negative.

Prior to Expiration

- Depending upon the original strike prices and the movement of the stock throughout the life of the strategy, it will often be possible to close out this spread at a loss that is less than the maximum loss at expiration or a gain that is less than the maximum gain at expiration.
  - Often the decision to do so depends upon whether or not your sentiment of the underlying stock has changed since the original position was established.
  - If the underlying stock has remained relatively unchanged but you are now expecting a possible breakout, you may want to close your positions to preserve your profits.
  - If the underlying stock has remained relatively unchanged and you still believe it will remain relatively unchanged, you may want to continue to hold your positions.
  - If the underlying stock has already broken out and you now believe it may pull back closer to where it started, you may want to continue to hold your positions.
  - If the underlying stock has already broken out and you believe it is unlikely to pull back closer to where it started, you may want to close your positions to cut your losses.

- Comparing the early close gain or loss to the maximum potential gain or loss at expiration can help you decide if holding until expiration makes sense.

At Expiration

- Below the lowest strike, all call options expire worthless, but all put options are exercised and/or assigned and max loss is sustained.
- Between the lowest and lower middle strikes, long stock will be acquired through exercise of the long calls. The short calls options expire worthless, and all put options are exercised and/or assigned. The long stock can then be sold in the market. The trade may or may not be profitable.
- Between the two middle strikes, all options are exercised and/or assigned and max gain is achieved.
- Between the upper middle and highest strikes, a short stock position will be created through exercise of the long puts. The short puts expire worthless and all call options are exercised and/or assigned. The short stock can then be closed out in the market. The trade may or may not be profitable.
- Above the highest strike, all put options expire worthless, but all call options are exercised and/or assigned and max loss is sustained.

Long Gut Iron Condor—Detail

When you establish a long gut iron condor, the combined credit from the second and third legs will be less than the combined cost of the first and fourth legs. As a result, a long gut iron condor is usually established at a net debit. This type of strategy is intended to take advantage of a stock that is moving sideways and is therefore considered a neutral strategy.

Example

Buy to open 10 XYZ Dec 85 Calls @ 9.70
Sell to open 10 XYZ Dec 90 Calls @ 5.50
Sell to open 10 XYZ Dec 95 Puts @ 3.10

Buy to open 10 XYZ Dec 100 Puts @ 6.60

Debit (DR) = 7.70 (–1st leg + 2nd leg + 3rd leg – 4th leg)

Lower Breakeven (BE) = 87.70 (2nd strike – MG)

Upper Breakeven (BE) = 97.30 (3rd strike + MG)

Max Gain (MG) = 2.30 points or $2,300 (difference in call strikes + difference in puts strikes – debit) (occurs between 2nd & 3rd strikes)

Max Loss (ML) = –2.70 points or $2,700 (debit – difference in call strikes or debit – difference in puts strikes) (occurs beyond the outside strike prices)

When you set up an order like this, most order entry systems automatically calculate the market price of this 10/10/10/10 spread. To do so manually, reduce the spread by its greatest common factor of 10 to 1/1/1/1. Then multiply each leg by the market price using the ask price on the legs you are buying and the bid price on the legs you are selling:

1 × –9.70 = –9.70

1 × +5.50 = +5.50

1 × +3.10 = +3.10

1 × –6.60 = –6.60

Net = –7.70 × 10 spreads × 100 shares per contract = ($7,700) total initial debit

Figure 17.2 depicts the profit/loss zones of this example, including the breakeven points at the option expiration date.

As you can see, the maximum gain on this strategy, which occurs between the prices of 90 and 95 at expiration, is $2,300. There are two breakeven points at 87.70 and 97.30. All prices below 87.70 or above 97.30 result in a loss. The maximum loss on the upside or downside is –$2,700. To get a better feel for the profit and loss zones, see the following sample prices at expiration.

XYZ at 85 at expiration:

Initial debit:	($7,700)
Assigned on 95 puts to buy 1,000 shares:	($95,000)
Exercise 100 puts to sell 1,000 shares:	$100,000
All call options expire worthless:	-0-
Net profit/loss:	**= ($2,700)**

FIGURE 17.2

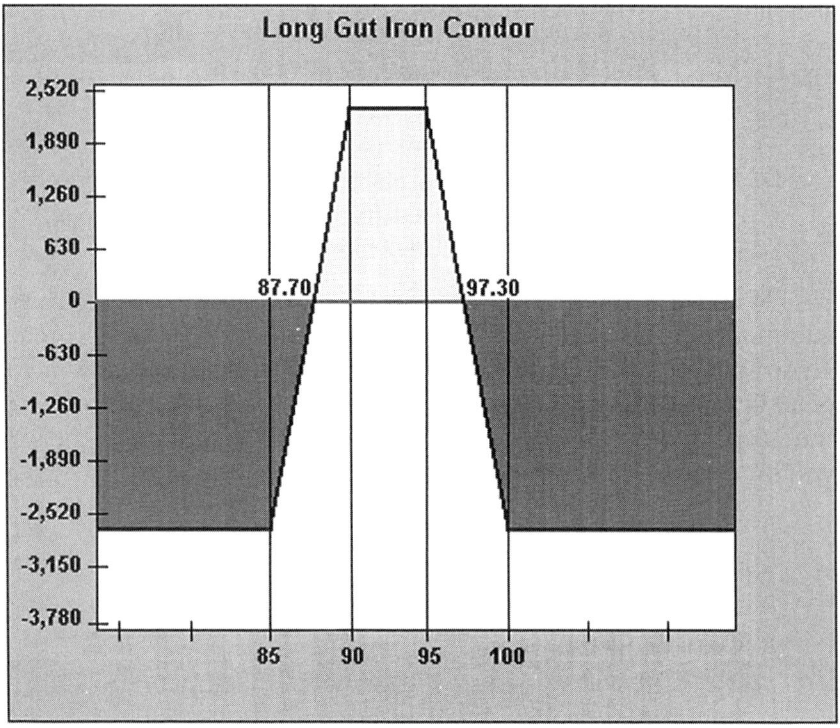

Strategy at Expiration

XYZ at 87.70 at expiration:	
Initial debit:	($7,700)
Assigned on 95 puts to buy 1,000 shares:	($95,000)
Exercise 100 puts to sell 1,000 shares:	$100,000
Exercise 85 calls to buy 1,000 shares:	($85,000)
1,000 shares sold @ market:	$87,700
Short call options expire worthless:	-0-
Net profit/loss:	= **$0**
XYZ at 90 at expiration:	
Initial debit:	($7,700)
Assigned on 95 puts to buy 1,000 shares:	($95,000)
Exercise 100 puts to sell 1,000 shares:	$100,000

Exercise 85 calls to buy 1,000 shares:	($85,000)
1,000 shares sold @ market:	$90,000
Short call options expire worthless:	-0-
Net profit/loss:	= **$2,300**

XYZ at 95 at expiration:

Initial debit:	($7,700)
Exercise 100 puts to sell 1,000 shares:	$100,000
Exercise 85 calls to buy 1,000 shares:	($85,000)
Assigned on 90 calls to sell 1,000 shares:	$90,000
1,000 shares bought back @ market:	($95,000)
Short put options expire worthless:	-0-
Net profit/loss:	= $**2,300**

XYZ at 97.30 at expiration:

Initial debit:	($7,700)
Exercise 100 puts to sell 1,000 shares:	$100,000
Exercise 85 calls to buy 1,000 shares:	($85,000)
Assigned on 90 calls to sell 1,000 shares:	$90,000
1,000 shares bought back @ market:	($97,300)
Short put options expire worthless:	-0-
Net profit/loss:	= $**0**

XYZ above 100 at expiration:

Initial debit:	($7,700)
Exercise 85 calls to buy 1,000 shares:	($85,000)
Assigned on 90 calls to sell 1,000 shares:	$90,000
All puts expire worthless:	-0-
Net profit/loss:	= **($2,700)**

As you can see, this strategy has very similar profit and loss characteristics to a long iron condor. Since you are required to pay a debit up front, one advantage in trading a long gut iron condor over a long iron condor is that the margin requirements are lower. Since this strategy is made up of two debit spreads, it has no margin requirements other than the initial up-front debit, while a long iron condor is made up of two credit spreads and does have a margin requirement equal to the maximum loss amount.

Short Gut Iron Condor—Quick Overview

A short gut iron condor is made up of one short call at the lowest strike, one long call at the lower middle strike, one long put at the upper middle strike, and one short put at the highest strike, with the same strike price interval between all legs. All sides of this spread are opening transactions, and the quantity of all four legs is always the same. This strategy is actually made up of one long gut spread and one short gut spread combined together as a single strategy. This can also be viewed as being made up of one credit put spread and one credit call spread (see Figure 17.3).

FIGURE 17.3

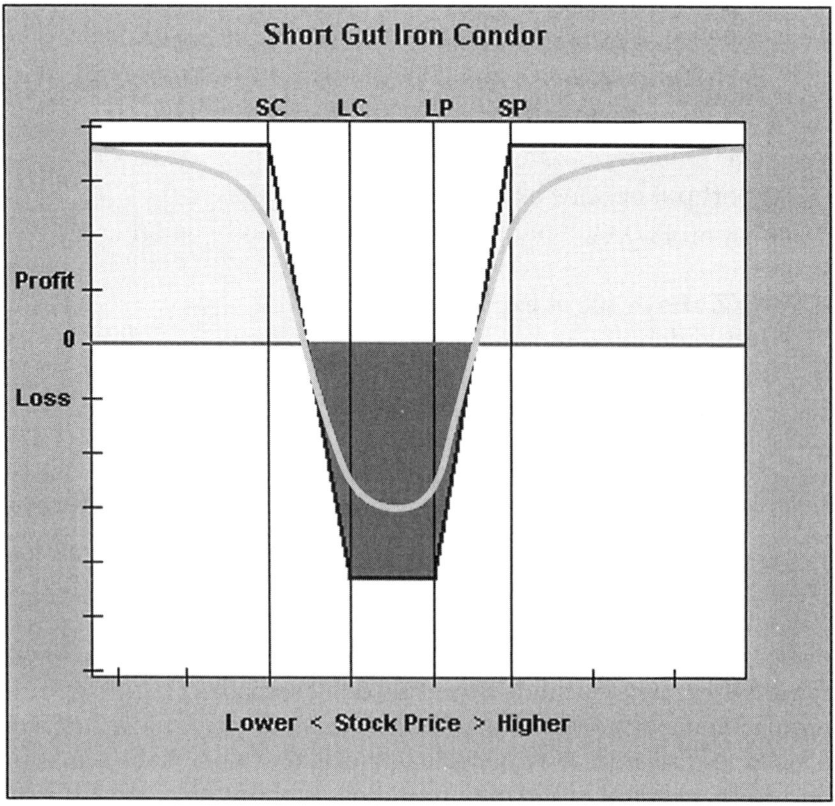

At Entry The white line in Figure 17.3 represents what the strategy typically looks like at the point of entry. As expiration approaches, the curve moves toward the black lines, which illustrate the final profit and loss boundaries at expiration.

Direction Breakout

When to Use You would typically employ a short gut iron condor in uncertain markets and would hope to profit if the underlying stock breaks out either higher or lower than the current price by the expiration date of the options. Generally, the underlying stock price should be between the two middle strike prices at the time of entry. If you are moderately bullish or bearish, you could use strike prices that are slightly higher or lower, respectively, but this strategy generally works best when you stay closest to the middle.

Risk vs. Reward Limited risk with limited profit potential

Volatility The effect of volatility varies depending upon the strike prices chosen. This strategy generally benefits moderately when volatility increases.

Time Decay The effect of time decay on this strategy varies with the underlying stock's price level in relation to the strike prices. If the stock price is between the outer strike prices, the effect is negative. If the stock price is above the upper strike price or below the lower strike price, the effect is positive.

Prior to Expiration

- Depending upon the original strike prices and the movement of the stock throughout the life of the strategy, it will often be possible to close out this spread at a loss that is less than the maximum loss at expiration or a gain that is less than the maximum gain at expiration.
  - Often the decision to do so depends upon whether or not your sentiment of the underlying stock has changed since the original position was established.
  - If the underlying stock has remained relatively unchanged but you are still expecting a breakout, you may want to continue to hold your positions.
  - If the underlying stock has already broken out and you believe a pullback closer to where it started is unlikely, you may want to continue to hold your positions.

- If the underlying stock has remained relatively unchanged and you now believe it will remain relatively unchanged, you may want to close your positions to cut your losses.
- If the underlying stock has already broken out and you now believe it may pull back closer to where it started, you may want to close your positions to preserve your profits.
- Comparing the early close gain or loss to the maximum potential gain or loss at expiration can help you decide if holding until expiration makes sense.

At Expiration

- Below the lowest strike, all call options expire worthless, but all put options are exercised and/or assigned and max gain is achieved.
- Between the lowest and lower middle strikes, a short stock position will be created through assignment of the short calls, the long calls expire worthless, and both put options are exercised and/or assigned. The short stock position can then be closed out in the market. The trade may or may not be profitable.
- Between the two middle strikes, all options are exercised and/or assigned and max loss is sustained.
- Between the upper middle and highest strikes, long stock will be obtained through the assignment of the short puts, the long puts expire worthless, and both call options are exercised and/or assigned. The long stock position can then be sold in the market. The trade may or may not be profitable.
- Above the highest strike, all put options expire worthless, but all call options are exercised and/or assigned and max gain is achieved.

Short Gut Iron Condor—Detail

When you establish a short gut iron condor, the combined debit from the second and third legs will be less than the combined credit of the first and fourth legs. As a result, a short gut iron condor is always established at a net credit. This type of strategy is intended to take advantage of a stock that is expected to move sharply in either direction and is therefore considered a breakout strategy.

Example

Sell to open 10 XYZ Jan 85 Calls @ 9.60
Buy to open 10 XYZ Jan 90 Calls @ 5.60
Buy to open 10 XYZ Jan 95 Puts @ 3.20
Sell to open 10 XYZ Jan 100 Puts @ 6.50

Credit (CR) = 7.30 (1st leg – 2nd leg – 3rd leg + 4th leg)
Lower Breakeven (BE) = 87.30 (2nd strike – ML)
Upper Breakeven (BE) = 97.70 (3rd strike + ML)
Max Gain (MG) = 2.30 points or $2,300 (credit – difference in call strikes or credit – difference in put strikes) (occurs beyond the outside strike prices)
Max Loss (ML) = –2.70 points or $2,700 (difference in call strikes + difference in put strikes – credit) (occurs between 2nd & 3rd strikes)

When you set up an order like this, most order entry systems automatically calculate the market price of this 10/10/10/10 spread. To do so manually, reduce the spread by its greatest common factor of 10 to 1/1/1/1. Then multiply each leg by the market price using the ask price on the legs you are buying and the bid price on the legs you are selling:

1 × +9.60 = +9.60
1 × –5.60 = –5.60
1 × –3.20 = –3.20
1 × +6.50 = +6.50
Net = +7.30 × 10 spreads × 100 shares per contract = $7,300 total initial credit

Figure 17.4 depicts the profit/loss zones of this example, including the breakeven points at the option expiration date.

As you can see, the maximum gain on this strategy, which occurs only above or below the outer strike prices at expiration, is $2,300. There are two breakeven points at 87.30 and 97.70. All prices between 87.30 and 97.70 result in a loss. The maximum loss is -$2,700 and occurs only between the two middle strike prices of 90 and 95. To get a better feel for the profit and loss zones, see the following sample prices at expiration.

FIGURE 17.4

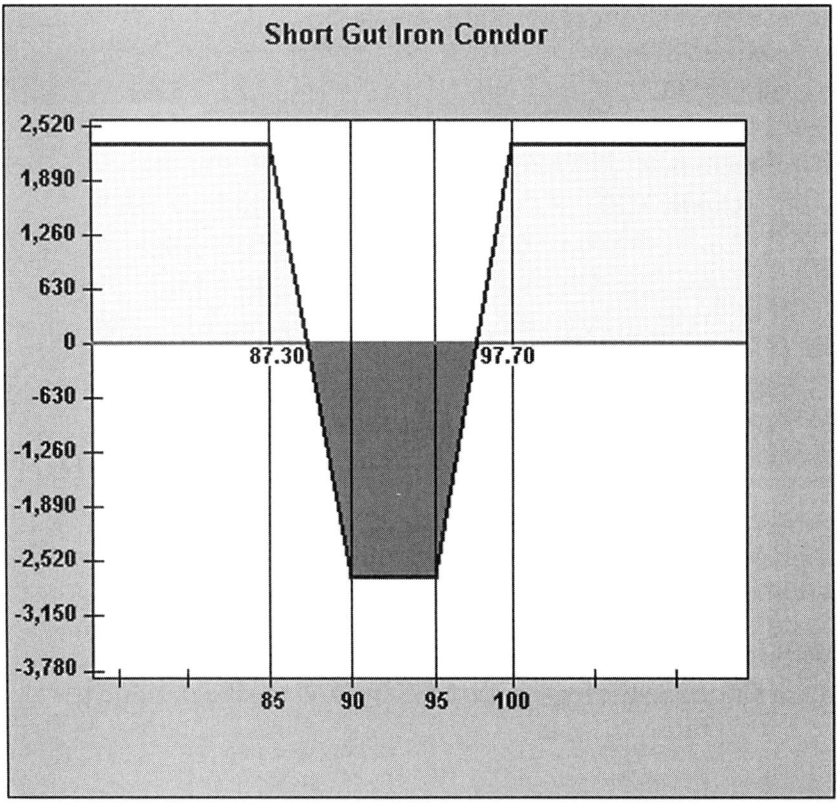

Strategy at Expiration

XYZ at or above 100 at expiration:	
Initial credit:	$7,300
Long 90 calls exercised to buy 1,000 shares:	($90,000)
Short 85 calls assigned to sell 1,000 shares:	$85,000
All puts expire worthless:	-0-
Net profit/loss:	= **$2,300**
XYZ at 97.70 at expiration:	
Initial credit:	$7,300
Long 90 calls exercised to buy 1,000 shares:	($90,000)
Short 85 calls assigned to sell 1,000 shares:	$85,000
Short 100 puts assigned to buy 1,000 shares:	($100,000)

1,000 shares sold @ market:	$97,700
Net profit/loss:	= $**0**

XYZ at 95 at expiration:

Initial credit:	$7,300
Long 90 calls exercised to buy 1,000 shares:	($90,000)
Short 85 calls assigned to sell 1,000 shares:	$85,000
Short 100 puts assigned to buy 1,000 shares:	($100,000)
1,000 shares sold @ market:	$95,000
Net profit/loss:	= **($2,700)**

XYZ at 90 at expiration:

Initial credit:	$7,300
Short 85 calls assigned to sell 1,000 shares:	$85,000
Short 100 puts assigned to buy 1,000 shares:	($100,000)
Long 95 puts exercised to sell 1,000 shares:	$95,000
Buy back 1,000 shares @ market:	($90,000)
Net profit/loss:	= **($2,700)**

XYZ at 87.30 at expiration:

Initial credit:	$7,300
Short 85 calls assigned to sell 1,000 shares:	$85,000
Short 100 puts assigned to buy 1,000 shares:	($100,000)
Long 95 puts exercised to sell 1,000 shares:	$95,000
Buy back 1,000 shares @ market:	($87,300)
Net profit/loss:	= $**0**

XYZ at or below 85 at expiration:

Initial credit:	$7,300
Short 100 puts assigned to buy 1,000 shares:	($100,000)
Long 95 puts exercised to sell 1,000 shares:	$95,000
All calls expire worthless:	-0-
Net profit/loss:	**= $2,300**

As you can see, this strategy has very similar profit and loss characteristics to a short iron condor. Since it is made up of two credit spreads and has an initial margin requirement, one advantage of a short gut iron condor over a short iron condor is that you get to bring in a credit when the trade is established.

CHAPTER 18

Gut Iron Albatross Spreads

A gut iron albatross spread is very similar to an iron albatross spread. The only real difference is that with an iron albatross spread, the put strike prices are lower than the call strike prices. As with other gut spreads, gut iron albatrosses are exactly the opposite. In other words, the call strikes are both lower than the put strikes for both long and short iron albatross spreads. Despite this key difference, the profit and loss chart of a gut iron albatross spread looks very similar to that of an iron albatross spread. Like iron albatrosses, gut iron albatrosses involve buying and selling of both puts *and* calls at four different strike prices.

TYPES OF GUT IRON ALBATROSS SPREADS

There are only two types of gut iron albatross spreads, long gut iron albatrosses and short gut iron albatrosses. Long gut iron albatrosses are used when you have a neutral sentiment, and short iron albatrosses are used when you have a breakout sentiment. They also differ by whether you pay an initial debit or receive an initial credit when you establish them. Because of the wide range of strikes used in establishing a gut iron albatross, it is most appropriate for stocks priced over 100.

Long Gut Iron Albatross—Quick Overview

A long gut iron albatross is made up of one long call at the lowest strike, one short call at the lower middle strike, one short put at the upper middle strike, and one long put at the highest strike, with the same strike price interval between the first two and the last two legs. The strike price interval between the second and third legs is larger than the interval between the first and second legs or between the third and fourth legs. All legs should also have the same expiration month. All sides of this spread are opening transactions, and the quantity of all four legs is always the same. This strategy is actually made up of one short gut spread and one long gut spread combined together as a single strategy. This can also be viewed as being made up of one put debit spread and one call debit spread (see Figure 18.1).

At Entry The white line in Figure 18.1 represents what the strategy typically looks like at the point of entry. As expiration

FIGURE 18.1

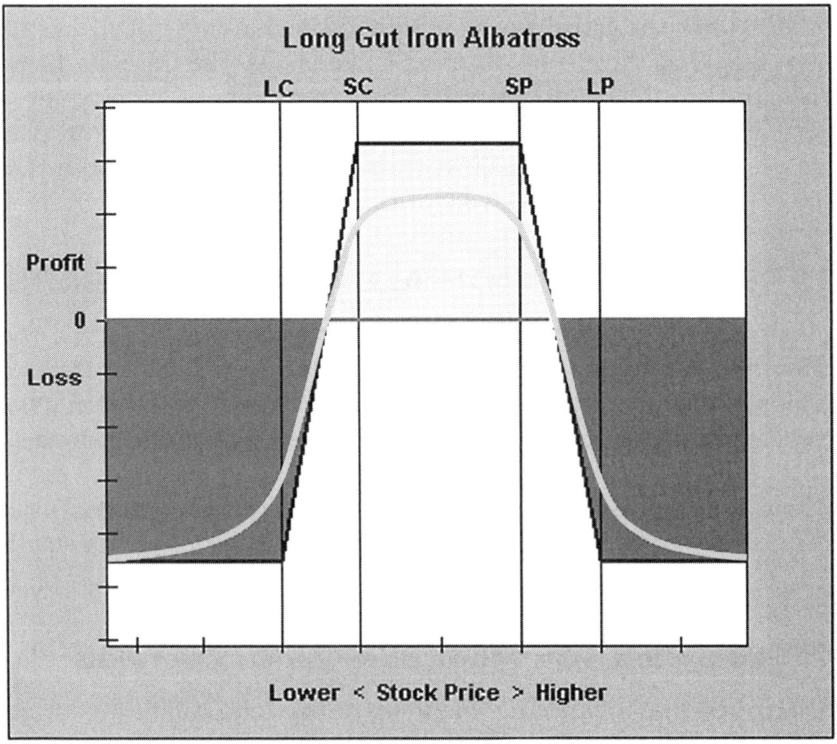

approaches, the curve moves toward the black lines, which illustrate the final profit and loss boundaries at expiration.

Direction Neutral

When to Use You would typically employ a long gut iron albatross in neutral markets and would hope to profit if the underlying stock remains relatively flat until the expiration date of the options. Generally, the underlying stock price should be between the two middle strike prices at the time of entry. If you are moderately bullish or bearish, you could use strike prices that are slightly higher or lower, respectively, but this strategy generally works best when you stay closest to the middle.

Risk vs. Reward Limited risk with limited profit potential

Volatility The effect of volatility varies depending upon the strike prices chosen. This strategy generally benefits moderately when volatility decreases.

Time Decay The effect of time decay on this strategy varies with the underlying stock's price level in relation to the strike prices. If the stock price is between the outer strike prices, the effect is positive. If the stock price is above the upper strike price or below the lower strike price, the effect is negative.

Prior to Expiration

- Depending upon the original strike prices and the movement of the stock throughout the life of the strategy, it will often be possible to close out this spread at a loss that is less than the maximum loss at expiration or a gain that is less than the maximum gain at expiration.
  - Often the decision to do so depends upon whether or not your sentiment of the underlying stock has changed since the original position was established.
  - If the underlying stock has remained relatively unchanged but you are now expecting a possible breakout, you may want to close your positions to preserve your profits.
  - If the underlying stock has remained relatively unchanged and you still believe it will remain relatively unchanged, you may want to continue to hold your positions.
  - If the underlying stock has already broken out and you now believe it may pull back closer to where it started, you may want to continue to hold your positions.

- If the underlying stock has already broken out and you believe it is unlikely to pull back closer to where it started, you may want to close your positions to cut your losses.
- Comparing the early close gain or loss to the maximum potential gain or loss at expiration can help you decide if holding until expiration makes sense.

At Expiration

- Below the lowest strike, all call options expire worthless but all put options are exercised and/or assigned and max loss is sustained.
- Between the lowest and lower middle strikes, long stock will be acquired through exercise of the long calls. The short calls options expire worthless, and all put options are exercised and/or assigned. The long stock can then be sold in the market. The trade may or may not be profitable.
- Between the two middle strikes, all options are exercised and/or assigned and max gain is achieved.
- Between the upper middle and highest strikes, a short stock position will be created through exercise of the long puts. The short puts expire worthless, and all call options are exercised and/or assigned. The short stock can then be closed out in the market. The trade may or may not be profitable.
- Above the highest strike, all put options expire worthless but all call options are exercised and/or assigned and max loss is sustained.

Long Gut Iron Albatross—Detail

When you establish a long gut iron albatross, the combined credit from the second and third legs will be less than the combined cost of the first and fourth legs. As a result, a long gut iron albatross is always established at a net debit. This type of strategy is intended to take advantage of a stock that is moving sideways and is therefore considered a neutral strategy.

Example:

Buy to open 5 XYZ Dec 115 Calls @ 10.30
Sell to open 5 XYZ Dec 120 Calls @ 6.45
Sell to open 5 XYZ Dec 130 Puts @ 7.35

Buy to open 5 XYZ Dec 135 Puts @ 11.40
Debit (DR) = 7.90 (–1st leg + 2nd leg + 3rd leg – 4th leg)
Lower Breakeven (BE) = 117.90 (2nd strike – MG)
Upper Breakeven (BE) = 132.10 (3rd strike + MG)
Max Gain (MG) = 2.10 points or $1,050 (difference in call strikes + difference in puts strikes – debit) (occurs between 2nd & 3rd strikes)
Max Loss (ML) = –2.90 points or $1,450 (debit – difference in call strikes or debit – difference in puts strikes) (occurs beyond the outside strike prices)

When you set up an order like this, most order entry systems automatically calculate the market price of this 5/5/5/5 spread. To do so manually, reduce the spread by its greatest common factor of 5 to 1/1/1/1. Then multiply each leg by the market price using the ask price on the legs you are buying and the bid price on the legs you are selling:

1 × –10.30 = –10.30
1 × +6.45 = +6.45
1 × +7.35 = +7.35
1 × –11.40 = –11.40
Net = –7.90 × 5 spreads × 100 shares per contract = ($3,950) total initial debit

Figure 18.2 depicts the profit/loss zones of this example, including the breakeven points at the option expiration date.

As you can see, the maximum gain on this strategy, which occurs between the prices of 120 and 130 at expiration, is $1,050. There are two breakeven points at 117.90 and 132.10. All prices below 117.90 or above 132.10 result in a loss. The maximum loss on the upside or downside is –$1,450. To get a better feel for the profit and loss zones, see the following sample prices at expiration.

XYZ at 115 at expiration:

Initial debit:	($3,950)
Assigned on 130 puts to buy 500 shares:	($65,000)
Exercise 135 puts to sell 500 shares:	$67,500
All call options expire worthless:	-0-
Net profit/loss:	= **($1,450)**

FIGURE 18.2

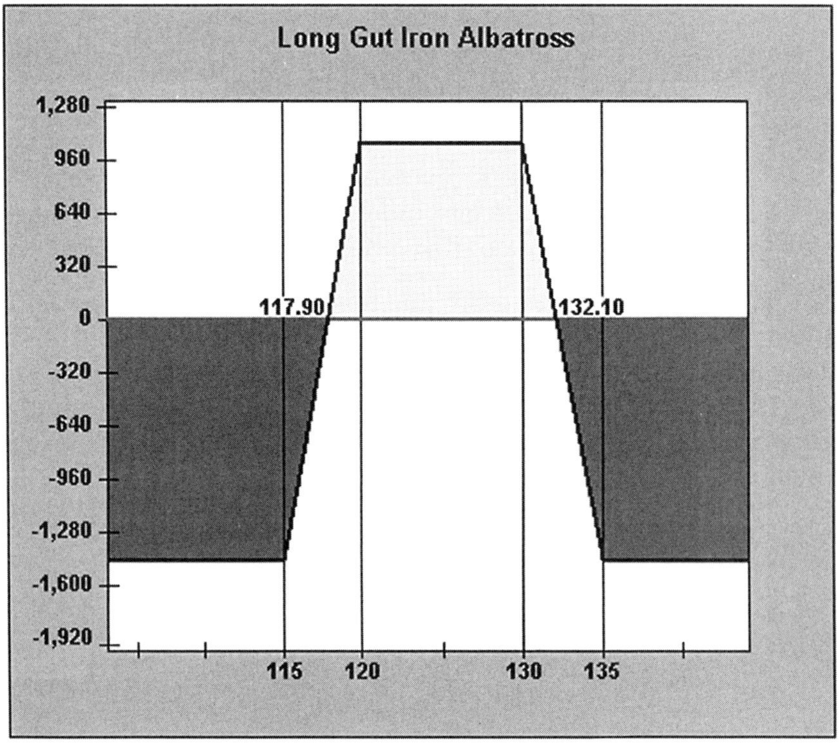

Strategy at Expiration

XYZ at 117.90 at expiration:	
Initial debit:	($3,950)
Assigned on 130 puts to buy 500 shares:	($65,000)
Exercise 135 puts to sell 500 shares:	$67,500
Exercise 115 calls to buy 500 shares:	($57,500)
500 shares sold @ market:	$58,950
Short call options expire worthless:	-0-
Net profit/loss:	= **$0**
XYZ at 120 at expiration:	
Initial debit:	($3,950)
Assigned on 130 puts to buy 500 shares:	($65,000)
Exercise 135 puts to sell 500 shares:	$67,500

Exercise 115 calls to buy 500 shares:	($57,500)
500 shares sold @ market:	$60,000
Short call options expire worthless:	-0-
Net profit/loss:	= **$1,050**

XYZ at 130 at expiration:

Initial debit:	($3,950)
Exercise 135 puts to sell 500 shares:	$67,500
Exercise 115 calls to buy 500 shares:	($57,500)
Assigned on 120 calls to sell 500 shares:	$60,000
500 shares bought back @ market:	($65,000)
Short put options expire worthless:	-0-
Net profit/loss:	= **$1,050**

XYZ at 132.10 at expiration:

Initial debit:	($3,950)
Exercise 135 puts to sell 500 shares:	$67,500
Exercise 115 calls to buy 500 shares:	($57,500)
Assigned on 120 calls to sell 500 shares:	$60,000
500 shares bought back @ market:	($66,050)
Short put options expire worthless:	-0-
Net profit/loss:	= $**0**

XYZ above 135 at expiration:

Initial debit:	($3,950)
Exercise 115 calls to buy 500 shares:	($57,500)
Assigned on 120 calls to sell 500 shares:	$60,000
All puts expire worthless:	-0-
Net profit/loss:	= **($1,450)**

As you can see, this strategy has very similar profit and loss characteristics to a long iron albatross. Since you are required to pay a debit up front, one advantage in trading a long gut iron albatross over a long iron albatross is that the margin requirements are lower. Since this strategy is made up of two debit spreads, it has no margin requirements other than the initial up-front debit, while a long iron albatross is made up of two credit spreads and does have a margin requirement equal to the maximum loss amount.

Short Gut Iron Albatross—Quick Overview

A short gut iron albatross is made up of one short call at the lowest strike, one long call at the lower middle strike, one long put at the upper middle strike, and one short put at the highest strike, with the same strike price interval between the first two and the last two legs. The strike price interval between the second and third legs is larger than the interval between the first and second legs or between the third and fourth legs. All sides of this spread are opening transactions, and the quantity of all four legs is always the same. This strategy is actually made up of one long gut spread and one short gut spread combined together as a single strategy. This can also be viewed as being made up of one credit put spread and one credit call spread (see Figure 18.3).

FIGURE 18.3

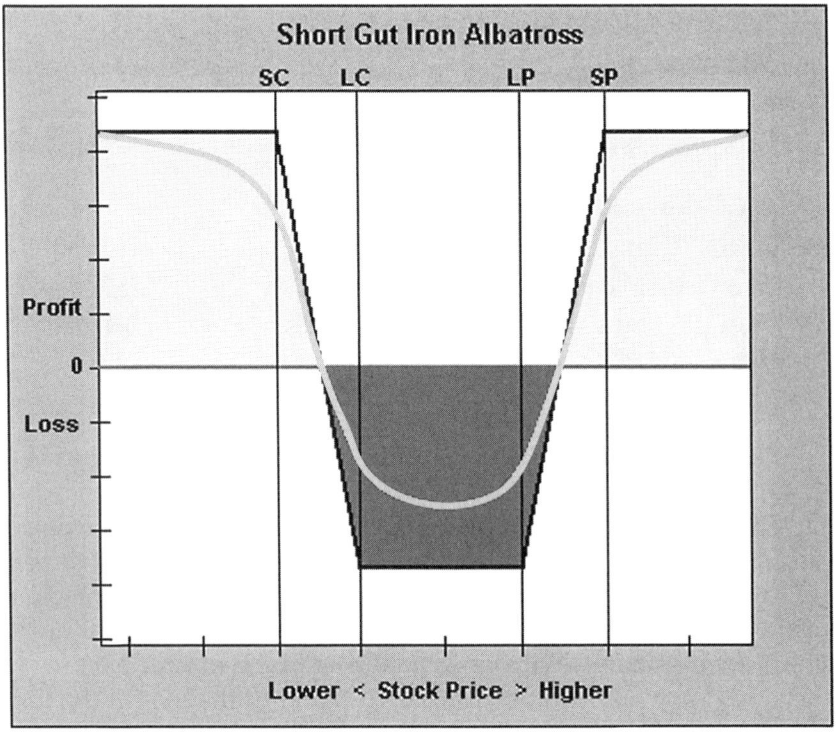

At Entry The white line in Figure 18.3 represents what the strategy typically looks like at the point of entry. As expiration approaches, the curve moves toward the black lines, which illustrate the final profit and loss boundaries at expiration.

Direction Breakout

When to Use You would typically employ a short gut iron albatross in uncertain markets and would hope to profit if the underlying stock breaks out either higher or lower than the current price by the expiration date of the options. Generally, the underlying stock price should be between the two middle strike prices at the time of entry. If you are moderately bullish or bearish, you could use strike prices that are slightly higher or lower, respectively, but this strategy generally works best when you stay closest to the middle.

Risk vs. Reward Limited risk with limited profit potential

Volatility The effect of volatility varies depending upon the strike prices chosen. This strategy generally benefits moderately when volatility increases.

Time Decay The effect of time decay on this strategy varies with the underlying stock's price level in relation to the strike prices. If the stock price is between the outer strike prices, the effect is negative. If the stock price is above the upper strike price or below the lower strike price, the effect is positive.

Prior to Expiration

- Depending upon the original strike prices and the movement of the stock throughout the life of the strategy, it will often be possible to close out this spread at a loss that is less than the maximum loss at expiration or a gain that is less than the maximum gain at expiration.
  - Often the decision to do so depends upon whether or not your sentiment of the underlying stock has changed since the original position was established.
  - If the underlying stock has remained relatively unchanged but you are still expecting a breakout, you may want to continue to hold your positions.
  - If the underlying stock has already broken out and you believe a pullback closer to where it started is unlikely, you may want to continue to hold your positions

- If the underlying stock has remained relatively unchanged and you now believe it will remain relatively unchanged, you may want to close your positions to cut your losses.
- If the underlying stock has already broken out and you now believe it may pull back closer to where it started, you may want to close your positions to preserve your profits.
- Comparing the early close gain or loss to the maximum potential gain or loss at expiration can help you decide if holding until expiration makes sense.

At Expiration

- Below the lowest strike, all call options expire worthless, but all put options are exercised and/or assigned and max gain is achieved.
- Between the lowest and lower middle strikes, a short stock position will be created through assignment of the short calls, the long calls expire worthless, and both put options are exercised and/or assigned. The short stock position can then be closed out in the market. The trade may or may not be profitable.
- Between the two middle strikes, all options are exercised and/or assigned and max loss is sustained.
- Between the upper middle and highest strikes, long stock will be obtained through the assignment of the short puts, the long puts expire worthless, and both call options are exercised and/or assigned. The long stock position can then be sold in the market. The trade may or may not be profitable.
- Above the highest strike, all put options expire worthless, but all call options are exercised and/or assigned and max gain is achieved.

Short Gut Iron Albatross—Detail

When you establish a short gut iron albatross, the combined debit from the second and third legs will be less than the combined credit of the first and fourth legs. As a result, a short gut iron albatross is usually established at a net credit. This type of strategy is intended to take advantage of a stock that is expected to move sharply in either direction and is therefore considered a breakout strategy.

Example

Sell to open 4 XYZ Jan 115 Calls @ 10.20
Buy to open 4 XYZ Jan 120 Calls @ 6.50
Buy to open 4 XYZ Jan 130 Puts @ 7.30
Sell to open 4 XYZ Jan 135 Puts @ 11.30

Credit (CR) = 7.70 (1st leg – 2nd leg – 3rd leg + 4th leg)
Lower Breakeven (BE) = 117.70 (2nd strike – ML)
Upper Breakeven (BE) = 132.30 (3rd strike + ML)
Max Gain (MG) = 2.70 points or $1,080 (credit – difference in call strikes or credit – difference in put strikes)
(occurs beyond the outside strike prices)
Max Loss (ML) = –2.30 points or $920 (difference in call strikes + difference in put strikes – credit) (occurs between 2nd & 3rd strikes)

When you set up an order like this, most order entry systems automatically calculate the market price of this 4/4/4/4 spread. To do so manually, reduce the spread by its greatest common factor of 4 to 1/1/1/1. Then multiply each leg by the market price using the ask price on the legs you are buying and the bid price on the legs you are selling:

$1 \times +10.20 = +10.20$
$1 \times -6.50 = -6.50$
$1 \times -7.30 = -7.30$
$1 \times +11.30 = +11.30$
Net = +7.70 × 4 spreads × 100 shares per contract = $3,080 total initial credit

Figure 18.4 depicts the profit/loss zones of this example, including the breakeven points at the option expiration date.

As you can see, the maximum gain on this strategy, which occurs only above or below the outer strike prices at expiration, is $1,080. There are two breakeven points at 117.70 and 132.30. All prices between 117.70 and 132.30 result in a loss. The maximum loss is –$920 and occurs only between the two middle strike prices of 120

FIGURE 18.4

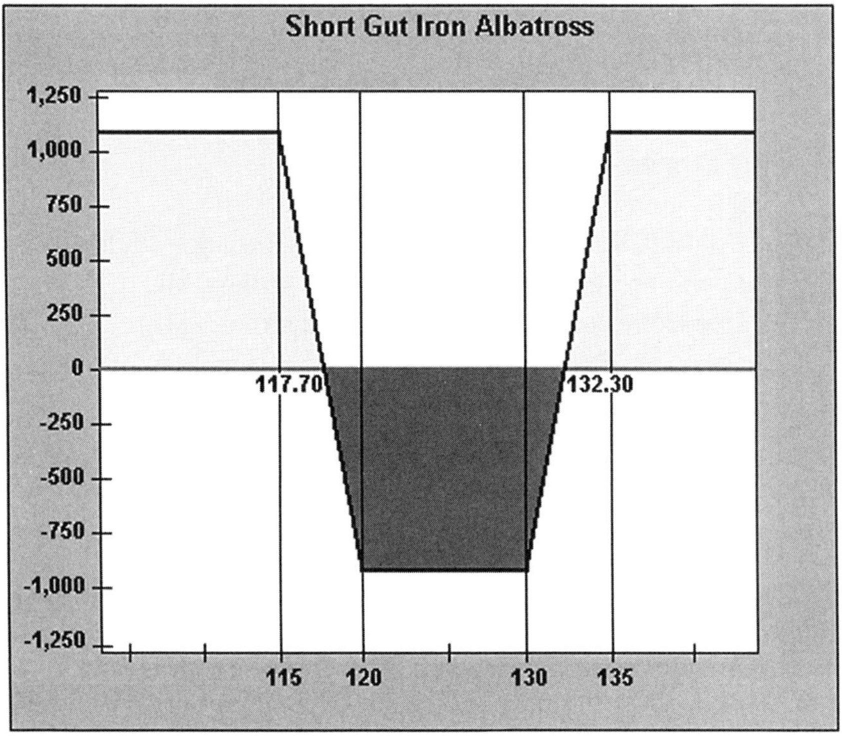

Strategy at Expiration

and 130. To get a better feel for the profit and loss zones, see the following sample prices at expiration.

XYZ at or above 135 at expiration:

Initial credit:	$3,080
Long 120 calls exercised to buy 400 shares:	($48,000)
Short 115 calls assigned to sell 400 shares:	$46,000
All puts expire worthless:	-0-
Net profit/loss:	= **$1,080**

XYZ at 132.30 at expiration:

Initial credit:	$3,080
Long 120 calls exercised to buy 400 shares:	($48,000)
Short 115 calls assigned to sell 400 shares:	$46,000

Short 135 puts assigned to buy 400 shares:	($54,000)
400 shares sold @ market:	$52,920
Net profit/loss:	= $**0**

XYZ at 130 at expiration:

Initial credit:	$3,080
Long 120 calls exercised to buy 400 shares:	($48,000)
Short 115 calls assigned to sell 400 shares:	$46,000
Short 135 puts assigned to buy 400 shares:	($54,000)
400 shares sold @ market:	$52,000
Net profit/loss:	= **($920)**

XYZ at 120 at expiration:

Initial credit:	$3,080
Long 130 puts exercised to sell 400 shares:	$52,000
Short 115 calls assigned to sell 400 shares:	$46,000
Short 135 puts assigned to buy 400 shares:	($54,000)
Buy back 400 shares @ market:	($48,000)
Net profit/loss:	= **($920)**

XYZ at 117.70 at expiration:

Initial credit:	$3,080
Short 115 calls assigned to sell 400 shares:	$46,000
Short 135 puts assigned to buy 400 shares:	($54,000)
Long 130 puts exercised to sell 400 shares:	$52,000
Buy back 400 shares @ market:	($47,080)
Net profit/loss:	= $**0**

XYZ at or below 115 at expiration:

Initial credit:	$3,080
Short 135 puts assigned to buy 400 shares:	($54,000)
Long 130 puts exercised to sell 400 shares:	$52,000
All calls expire worthless:	-0-
Net profit/loss:	**= $1,080**

As you can see, this strategy has very similar profit and loss characteristics to a short iron albatross. Since it is made up of two credit spreads, each of which has an initial margin requirement, one advantage of a short gut iron albatross over a short iron albatross is that you get to bring in a credit when the trade is established.

The idea of a gut spread is simply trading both calls and puts, where the call strike prices are lower than the put strike prices. This concept could be applied to many other types of spreads. This section is intended only to show some of the more common types. One of the important things to keep in mind is that unlike many other types of spreads, when gut spreads are established you know for certain that at expiration there will be assignments or exercises, since the strike prices of the options guarantee that some of them will always be in-the-money. Most other types of spreads have at least one price point where all options expire worthless. As a result, commissions are a very important consideration for all types of gut spreads, because you can always count on commission costs—both when establishing the positions and when closing them out, even if held until expiration.

CONCLUSION

If you buy stock, you can make money if the stock goes up. If you sell stock short, you can make money if the stock goes down. If the stock does not go up or down, you simply cannot make money (except for dividends on stocks that pay dividends). Many of the spread strategies discussed in this book can be profitable even with no movement in the underlying security.

When you own a stock, your risk is substantial if the stock goes down. If you sell stock short, your risk is potentially unlimited if the stock goes up. Many of the spread strategies discussed in this book have a limited amount of risk, and that risk can often be calculated or at least estimated before the positions are established.

Option trading can be more risky or less risky than equities trading. Option trading can be more profitable or less profitable than equities trading. Option trading can be more or less complicated, require more or less capital, and require more or less collateral. Option trading may need to be watched more or less closely than equities trading. These are all true statements when you consider the thousands upon thousands of different options strategies that can be formed.

Speaking in general terms, while spread trading tends to be a little more complicated and may need to be watched more closely in some cases, it is generally less risky, requires less capital and less collateral, and can be more profitable (from a percentage standpoint) than equities trading. Most of all, though, you must understand how the different types of spread strategies work.

There are literally thousands more spread combinations in addition to the ones discussed in this book. It would be impossible to cover them all. Hopefully the calculations, theories, characteristics, and examples contained in this book will help you analyze any spread combination you may encounter.

A.M. and P.M. Settlement: There are three distinct characteristics that classify all index options.

- They are American-style or European-style.
- They are broad-based or narrow-based.
- They stop trading on Thursday or Friday of expiration week.

Whether an index option is a.m. settled or p.m. settled depends upon the last trading day. Those that stop trading on Thursday of expiration week are a.m. settled, and those that stop trading on Friday of expiration week are p.m. settled.

While there are exceptions to these rules, in general, most American-style index options stop trading on Friday of option expiration week and are therefore p.m. settled. This simply means that the settlement value (the value that determines the amount an expired option is in-the-money or out-of-the-money) is simply the difference between the closing price on Friday of expiration week and the strike price of the option.

Adjusted Options: Adjusted options are options that existed on the original company and have been adjusted to include shares of both the original company and the new company. This ensures that holders of options prior to the spin-off retain the original value of those options. Since it is unlikely that these calculations will work out to an even amount, the options will typically include a small amount of cash in lieu of a fractional share stock. The calculations are complex and can vary widely by company. If you own options of a company prior to a spin-off or if you plan to trade options of a company that has gone through a spin-off, it is important to be aware of the contract size, multiplier, and cash in lieu (CIL) of the option. Some brokers make this information available to you, but many do not. You can typically find this information on the Web site of the option exchange(s) where the particular option trades or on the Options Clearing Corporation (OCC) Web site.

Because the number of corporate actions that can result in adjusted options are numerous and the adjustments are complex, below is a list of the most common types of adjustments to be aware of.

Cash Dividend

Symbol change?	*Strike price change?*	*Multiplier change?*	*Contract size change?*
< 10% Sometimes	Sometimes	No	No
> 10% Yes	Yes	No	No

Stock Dividend

Symbol change?	*Strike price change?*	*Multiplier change?*	*Contract size change?*
< 10% Sometimes	Sometimes	Sometimes	Sometimes
> 10% Yes	Yes	Yes	Yes

Rights Offering

Symbol change?	*Strike price change?*	*Multiplier change?*	*Contract size change?*
< 10% Sometimes	Sometimes	Sometimes	Sometimes
> 10% Yes	Yes	Yes	Yes

Stock Split

Symbol change?	*Strike price change?*	*Multiplier change?*	*Contract size change?*
2 for 1: Yes	Yes	No	No
3 for 2: Yes	Yes	Yes	Yes
3 for 1: Yes	Yes	No	No
4 for 1: Yes	Yes	No	No
4 for 3: Yes	Yes	Yes	Yes
5 for 1: Yes	Yes	No	No
5 for 4: Yes	Yes	Yes	Yes
6 for 5: Yes	Yes	Yes	Yes
7 for 5: Yes	Yes	Yes	Yes

Reverse Stock Split

Symbol change?	*Strike price change?*	*Multiplier change?*	*Contract size change?*
1 for 2: Yes	No	No	Yes
1 for 5: Yes	No	No	Yes
1 for 7: Yes	No	No	Yes

1 for 10: Yes	No	No	Yes
1 for 20: Yes	No	No	Yes
1 for 50: Yes	No	No	Yes
1 for 100: Yes	No	No	Yes

Spin-Off

Symbol change?	*Strike price change?*	*Multiplier change?*	*Contract size change?*
Yes	No	No	Yes

Merger or Acquisition

Symbol change?	*Strike price change?*	*Multiplier change?*	*Contract size change?*
Acquirer: Sometimes	No	No	No
Acquiree: Yes	No	No	Yes

LEAPS Conversion

Symbol change?	*Strike price change?*	*Multiplier change?*	*Contract size change?*
Yes	No	No	No

Stock Symbol or Company Name Change

Symbol change?	*Strike price change?*	*Multiplier change?*	*Contract size change?*
Sometimes	No	No	No

American and European Styles: American-style options can be exercised at any time prior to expiration. All equity and ETF options are American style. Some index options are American style. American-style options generally stop trading on the third Friday of the month.

European-style options can only be exercised at expiration. Most index options are European style. Many European-style options cease trading on the Thursday before the third Friday of the month.

Information regarding whether an option is European- or American-style and whether it stops trading on Thursday or Friday of expiration week can be obtained from your broker or the option exchange Web site where the option trades.

Automatic Exercise: Long option positions that expire in-the-money will be automatically exercised under the following conditions:

Equity options that expire in-the-money by .05 or more
Index options that expire in-the-money by any amount

If you wish to exercise equity options that expire in-the-money, you should always call your broker with specific exercise instructions. Do not assume that your broker will automatically exercise your equity options if they expire in-the-money. Most brokers will not automatically exercise your equity options if they expire in-the-money by less than .05, and in the absence of instructions from you, your options will be left to expire worthless. Depending upon your commission structure, it may be advantageous for you to exercise options that are in-the-money by only a few cents.

Example:

You own 50 XYZ Aug 120 calls on the third Friday in August. XYZ closes at 120.04 and you have not given your broker instructions to exercise your options. Your options would be left to expire worthless even though the intrinsic value on your entire position was $200. Even with commissions as high as $1 per contract, selling these options before they expired would have returned $150. If you neglected to sell them before market close, you could still exercise then, creating a position of 5,000 shares of XYZ stock that could be sold at market open on Monday morning. Unless XYZ opened below $120 per share, even after paying the commission to sell the 5,000 shares, you would still likely end up with some remaining value.

Typically, any time you purchase stock you are required to make a Reg T minimum deposit prior to the sale of that position. When you sell an equity position without making the Reg T deposit (or without already having the Reg T requirement in your account) it is called "free riding" and could result in your broker restricting your account to a "cash-up-front" basis. This means you would not be able to purchase stock unless sufficient funds required to meet Reg T minimums were already in the account at the time you place the trade. Option expiration is the one time you can take possession of a stock position and not be obligated to deliver funds to your broker to meet the Reg T requirement. As long as you close out your stock position on the Monday after expiration, you will generally not be obligated to deposit any funds. Keep in mind, however, that in situations where the value of the stock position you would acquire through an option exercise is significant, your broker *may* choose to close out your options on Friday of expiration week rather than allowing you to exercise. This is generally done to reduce risk, which is greatest when your options expire only slightly in-the-money. As you probably know, stocks do not always open at the same price at which they closed the prior day, and the Monday after expiration is no exception. If a stock gaps significantly, that can expose you and your broker to significant risk.

Example:

Assume you have only $4,000 worth of equity in your account (not counting your options) and you are long 500 contracts of XYZ Nov 100 Calls. It is expiration Friday, and XYZ closes at 101.

If your broker takes no action and allows the options to expire one point in-the-money, you will purchase $5,000,000 worth of stock. Unless you have the ability to deposit $2,500,000, which would be required to maintain the position (Reg T), the position would need to be liquidated on Monday at market open. The risk to you and your broker is that XYZ could gap down and begin trading at a price lower than 100 at market open Monday morning. If XYZ opened at 99 (only 2% lower) and your shares were liquidated, it would result in a $50,000 debit to your account. Your broker would then be left having to obtain the $46,000 unsecured debit from you.

To avoid this potential risk, your broker would simply place an order to close out all 500 XYZ November 100 Calls a few minutes prior to market close on the Friday before expiration. Chances are the options application you signed when you opened your account authorized your broker to take such action when considered necessary to avoid excessive risk.

Broad or Narrow Based: Index options are classified as either broad based or narrow based. Broad-based indices are typically more diversified and therefore less volatile than narrow-based indices. Because of this diversification, industry regulations allow brokerage firms to hold lower margin requirements on broad-based index options, although not all brokerage firms choose to do so. Narrow-based index options are typically treated similarly to equity options for purposes of calculating margin requirements.

Cash and Physical Settlement: As described above, equity options that are exercised involve the purchase or sale of an underlying *security*. By contrast, index options that are exercised involve a *cash* credit or debit.

Example:

XYZ is a stock. If you exercise a standard XYZ Aug 130 Call, you will pay $13,000 out of your account and you will acquire 130 shares of XYZ. The market price of XYZ stock is irrelevant, although you would typically not want to exercise your call options unless XYZ was trading above 130 per share.

Example:

XYZ is a stock. If you exercise a standard XYZ Aug 130 Put, you will receive $13,000 into your account and you will be required to deliver 130 shares of XYZ out of your account. The market price of XYZ stock is irrelevant, although you would typically not want to exercise your put options unless XYZ was trading below 130 per share.
Number of contracts (1) × option strike price (130) × option multiplier (100) = $13,000
Index options that are exercised involve a cash credit of the intrinsic value of the option.

Example:

ZYX is an index. If you exercise a ZYX Nov 550 Call with ZYX at 562, your account will be credited with $1,200.
In-the-money amount (562 - 550) × option multiplier (100) = $1,200

Example:

ZYX is an index. If you exercise a ZYX Nov 550 Put with ZYX at 538, your account will be credited with $1,200.
In-the-money amount (550 - 538) × option multiplier (100) = $1,200

Cash In Lieu (CIL): Cash in lieu (CIL) is sometimes included as part of the contract size of an option. The most common time for this to occur is when a company decides to spin off part of its business as a separate company. When a company undergoes this type of reorganization, the value of the part of the business being spun off must be calculated.

Commissions: Most brokers charge a commission when you execute option trades. Commissions can be a significant factor when implementing any options strategy. Multiple leg strategies such as spreads involve multiple commission charges. Most of the examples in this book do not include commission charges, which may be significant and will impact the profit or loss.

Contract Size, Multiplier, Cash in Lieu (CIL): The contract size, also known as the option package or the deliverable, is the underlying securities and/or cash that is delivered when the option is exercised/assigned. The contract size for most options is 100 shares of the underlying stock. However, due to mergers, spin-offs, stock splits, and other types of corporate reorganizations, the contract size could involve more than one stock, could be more or less than 100 shares, and could involve a certain amount of cash. If you trade options that have been adjusted because of a corporate reorganization, it is very important that you understand the contract size. Some brokers make this information available to you, but many do not. You can typically find information regarding contract size adjustments on the Web site of the option exchange(s) where the particular option trades or on the Options Clearing Corporation (OCC) Web site.

The multiplier is multiplied by the quoted price of an option (also known as the premium) to determine the actual cost of an option purchase or exercise. All standardized equity and index options, when newly created, start out with a multiplier of 100.

Example:

When you purchase 10 XYZ Aug 100 Calls at 5, your total cost would be $5,000. This is calculated as follows:
Number of contracts (10) × option premium (5) × option multiplier (100) = $5,000

However, just like with contract size, mergers, spin-offs, stock splits, and other types of corporate reorganizations can cause the multiplier to be adjusted during the life of the contract to a number other than 100. When this occurs, the amount you pay or receive when you trade an option will change. The most common of these is probably a 3 for 2 stock split, which will typically result in a contract size of 150 and a multiplier of 150.

Example:

You have $6,000 in cleared cash available in your account. You want to buy 10 XYZ Aug 50 Calls at 5

In most cases, with a standard multiplier of 100, this trade would cost you $5,000 (excluding commission) and you would therefore have sufficient funds in your account to enter this trade. However, if this option had previously been adjusted due to a 3 for 2 stock split, it would have a multiplier of 150 and this trade would actually cost you $7,500. It is also important to understand how this affects your ability to write covered calls against a long stock position.

Example:

Assume you own 800 shares of XYZ stock. XYZ goes through a 3 for 2 stock split and your position is adjusted to 1,200 shares. You would like to sell 12 contracts of the XYZ AUG 33.3 calls for $2. These options existed before the split and were formerly the XYZ AUG 50 calls.
Due to the split, the new multiplier is 150 and the new contract size is 150. To create a covered call position, you would only need to write 8 contracts and you would receive $2,400.
This is calculated as follows:
Number of contracts (8) × contract size (150) = covers 1,200 shares
Number of contracts (8) × option premium (2) × option multiplier (150) = $2,400

Exercise and Assignment: Although statistically about 50% of all options are closed out prior to expiration and about 30% expire worthless, you may request to exercise a long option position if you so choose. Equity options are American style and can be exercised at any time. European index options can only be exercised at expiration.

Usually option exercises occur only at specific times during the month. A common time to exercise a long call option is the day before x-dividend date. The reason you may want to do this is because you will acquire the stock at the strike price and you will also receive the dividend payment. If you were to exercise on x-date or after, you would pay the same amount for the stock but would not receive the dividend. However, an exercise such as this still only makes sense if the dividend is worth more than the time value of the option. Whenever an option is exercised, any time value remaining in the price of the option is forfeited.

Another common time to exercise a long call option is during the week of expiration. During the last week and especially during the last day, occasionally an option may trade at or below intrinsic value. If this happens, it might be better to exercise the option than to sell it. By exercising you will always receive the full intrinsic value of the option, but if the bid price of the option is below intrinsic value, you may receive less if you sell it.

A third common time to exercise a long call or a long put would be right before earnings or other significant news announcements. If you anticipate a large price movement in the equity, you may use a put option to get rid of a long position that you think might drop significantly. You might also use a long call option to acquire a stock you think will have a significant upside movement. However, you should still consider that the time value will be forfeited and you may benefit just the same by holding the option and selling it later at its increased value, which may also occur if there is significant news.

Cutoff times for exercise requests are as follows:

- All Options 4:30 p.m. Eastern time

Cutoff times for trading are as follows:

- Equities and narrow-based index options 4 p.m. Eastern time
- Broad-based index options 4:15 p.m. Eastern time

You can always exercise an American-style option even if it is out-of-the-money. However, it rarely makes sense to exercise an option unless it is in-the-money.

Expiration: The date and time after which an option no longer exists. All options have an expiration date. That date is typically fixed from the moment the option is first listed until it expires. Equity options typically stop trading on the third Friday of the month and expire on the Saturday after the third Friday. Index options may stop trading on either the third Friday of the month or the Thursday just before and expire on the Saturday after the third Friday.

In-, Out-of-, and At-the-Money: A call option is consider in-the-money when the price of the underlying security is trading higher than the strike price. If the underlying security is trading lower than the strike price, the call option is considered out-of-the-money. When the two are equal, the option is considered at-the-money.

A put is in-the-money when the price of the underlying security is trading lower than the strike price. If the underlying security is trading higher than the strike price, the put option is considered out-of-the-money. When the two are equal, the option is considered at-the-money.

Intrinsic Value and Time Value: The price of an option contract is made up of two components: intrinsic value and time value. Intrinsic value is the amount by which an option is in-the-money.

Example:

If a call option has a strike price of 30 and is trading at a price of 3.50, when the underlying stock is at a price of 33, then it is in-the-money by 3 and the intrinsic value is 3. The remaining .50 is time value. If an option is out-of-the-money, the intrinsic value is 0. The price of that option will be 100% time value.
Time value is the difference between the intrinsic value and strike price of an option when an option is in-the-money. When an option is out-of-the-money, time value equals the price of the option. The time value part of an option's price gets smaller as option expiration approaches and the deeper the option is in-the-money.

LEAPS: LEAPS were created by the CBOE in 1990 and are an acronym for Long Term Equity Anticipation Securities. LEAPS on equities typically expire in January. LEAPS on indices typically expire in June or December, although there are some exceptions to this rule. LEAPS trade in the same manner as regular options; they simply have a longer time before they expire.

Melding: You probably already know that not all stocks have options. It is equally true that not all stocks that trade options trade LEAPS. With the exception of a one-week period before the May, June, and July option expirations, stocks that trade LEAPS will typically trade two years of LEAPS at a time. Equity LEAPS will be converted into regular January options one week before January, or a later month, becomes the second cycle month for that option series. This conversion is called melding. At that same time, the next LEAP series will also be introduced. When a LEAP is melded, its symbol changes to that of a regular January option, but everything else about the option remains the same.

Example:

If a cycle 1 option has LEAPS, the closest year LEAPS will convert to regular January options on the Friday before the May expiration, and the next LEAP series of options will be introduced the same day.

Cycle 2 LEAPS convert a week before the June expiration because February becomes the second cycle month at that time. Cycle

3 LEAPS convert a week before the July expiration because March becomes the second cycle month at that time

Open Interest: Open interest is a term used to show the number of outstanding contracts that exist on an option. Liquidity on a stock is typically measured by the daily volume. Since most options trade less volume than stocks do, open interest is typically a better gauge of liquidity. An option with high open interest will typically be easier to trade in large size without significant price movement than an option with low open interest. When an opening options trade is executed, it increases open interest by 1. The opening trade could be a long call, a long put, a covered call, a covered put, a naked call, or a naked put. It could also be part of a spread or any other multi-leg option strategy. All option orders are marked as either opening or closing, and that is used to calculate open interest. The open interest is provided by the Options Clearing Corporation and is only calculated once at the end of each day.

Option Cycles: Equity options typically trade four months at a time: the current (also known as the front) month, the next month, and two farther out cycle months. All equity options are designated as either first cycle, second cycle, or third cycle. Some index options and ETFs will trade six months at a time. In addition, some securities will also trade LEAPS. To determine what cycle the options of a particular equity are on, simply find the current month in the first column and then read the months across. For example, if it is currently October and you are looking at a typical options chain quote window and you see October, November, January, and April options available (see Table BM.1), you would know that the stock is a cycle 1 stock. If you see October, November, February, and May (see Table BM.2), you would know that the stock is a cycle 2 stock, and if you see October, November, December, and March (see Table BM.3), you would know that the stock is a cycle 3 stock.

Option Premium: The option premium is simply the quoted option price. For example purposes, it will be the *ask* (or offer) price of an option being purchased and the *bid* price of an option being sold. The terms *premium* and *price* are used interchangeably throughout this book.

Pegged Options: A stock becomes *pegged* if a covered option that is in-the-money has been written against it. A peg causes the amount

TABLE BM.1

Cycle 1	Current	Next	Cycle	Cycle
Jan	Jan	Feb	Apr	Jul
Feb	Feb	Mar	Apr	Jul
Mar	Mar	Apr	Jul	Oct
Apr	Apr	May	Jul	Oct
May	May	Jun	Jul	Oct
Jun	Jun	Jul	Oct	Jan
Jul	Jul	Aug	Oct	Jan
Aug	Aug	Sep	Oct	Jan
Sep	Sep	Oct	Jan	Apr
Oct	Oct	Nov	Jan	Apr
Nov	Nov	Dec	Jan	Apr
Dec	Dec	Jan	Apr	Jul

TABLE BM.2

Cycle 2	Current	Next	Cycle	Cycle
Jan	Jan	Feb	May	Aug
Feb	Feb	Mar	May	Aug
Mar	Mar	Apr	May	Aug
Apr	Apr	May	Aug	Nov
May	May	Jun	Aug	Nov
Jun	Jun	Jul	Aug	Nov
Jul	Jul	Aug	Nov	Feb
Aug	Aug	Sep	Nov	Feb
Sep	Sep	Oct	Nov	Feb
Oct	Oct	Nov	Feb	May
Nov	Nov	Dec	Feb	May
Dec	Dec	Jan	Feb	May

TABLE BM.3

Cycle 3	Current	Next	Cycle	Cycle
Jan	Jan	Feb	Mar	Jun
Feb	Feb	Mar	Jun	Sep
Mar	Mar	Apr	Jun	Sep
Apr	Apr	May	Jun	Sep
May	May	Jun	Sep	Dec
Jun	Jun	Jul	Sep	Dec
Jul	Jul	Aug	Sep	Dec
Aug	Aug	Sep	Dec	Mar
Sep	Sep	Oct	Dec	Mar
Oct	Oct	Nov	Dec	Mar
Nov	Nov	Dec	Mar	Jun
Dec	Dec	Jan	Mar	Jun

of money that can be borrowed against a particular equity position to become fixed rather than variable as the prices change daily.

Example:

Long 100 shares of XYZ
Short 1 XYZ Jan 120 call
Current price of XYZ is 125

Though margin policies can vary from broker to broker, this stock position is pegged, and therefore you would only be able to borrow against XYZ as if it were priced at 120 and not at 125. Regardless of how high XYZ goes, you can still only borrow against it as if it were worth 120. The reason for this is because when the call option is in-the-money you are at risk of being assigned at any time. If you are assigned, you will only be paid 120 for your stock. If your broker allowed you to borrow against your stock based on the market price, your proceeds at the time you were assigned may not be sufficient to cover the amount you borrowed against the stock.

A short stock position can become pegged as well.

Example:

Short 100 shares of XYZ
Short 1 XYZ Jan 110 put
Current price of XYZ is 105

A short stock position releases more and more buying power for you to trade with as the price drops. However, in this scenario, once XYZ gets to 110, you will no longer benefit from any further downside movement. As will the long stock position, your short put obligates you to buy back your short position at a price no lower than 110. Therefore, your broker will peg your short position at 110 to ensure you can cover your margin loan if assigned.

Puts and Calls: An option is a contract that gives you the right, but not the obligation, to either buy or sell an underlying asset (usually a stock or ETF) at a specified price within a specified period of time. Despite this fact, that vast majority of the time, the contract is not used for this purpose. If you read articles and publications relating to options, you may see statistics often (mis)quoting the fact that 80% of all options expire worthless. This is completely incorrect but probably comes from the actual fact that about 80% of all options are never *exercised*. That does not mean they expire worthless. In fact, most are closed out prior to expiration by an offsetting trade, which could result in either a gain or a loss.

It is important to understand that there are three possible outcomes with an option contract, not just two. The option contract can:

1. expire worthless
2. expire in-the-money and be exercised
3. be closed out prior to expiration

Historical data from the CBOE going back to 1973 indicates that the number of options that actually expire worthless is only about 30%. About 50% are typically closed out prior to expiration, and 20% are actually exercised.

Random Allocation: European-style options can only be exercised at expiration and therefore carry no early assignment risk. Anytime you are short in-the-money, American-style put or call options, you are at risk of being assigned. Though most assignments occur at expiration, if your short options are deep in-the-money or the time value is very low, you could be assigned prior to expiration. Though most brokers will attempt to inform you when you are assigned, if you do not log on to your account daily, you may not immediately know that you have been assigned. Because short option holders are randomly selected for assignment, if you have in-the-money short options, you should check your account regularly.

Option assignments are handled by the Options Clearing Corporation (OCC) after the trading day ends, and the resulting long or short stock positions should show up in your account prior to market open the next morning. The number of early assignments will usually increase throughout the month up until the weekend of option expiration, with most of them occurring during the week of expiration.

Reg T (Regulation T): The Federal Reserve Board regulation that governs customer cash accounts and the amount of credit that brokerage firms and dealers may extend to customers for the purchase of securities. According to Regulation T, you may borrow up to 50% of the purchase price of securities that can be purchased on margin. This is known as the initial margin.

Rights vs. Obligations: If you **buy a call option,** you have the **right to buy** an asset at a specified price during a specified time period. However, you may also sell the option to close or allow the option to expire worthless.

If you **buy a put option,** you have the **right to sell** an asset at a specified price during a specified time period. However, you may also sell the option to close or allow the option to expire worthless.

If you **sell a call option,** you have the **obligation to sell** an asset at a specified price during a specified time period. However, you may also buy the option to close or wait until the option expires worthless.

If you **sell a put option,** you have the **obligation to buy** an asset at a specified price during a specified time period. However, you may also buy the option to close or wait until the option expires worthless.

Settlement Value: Most European-style index options stop trading on Thursday of option expiration week and are therefore a.m. settled. This means that the settlement value (the value that determines the amount an expired option is in-the-money or out-of-the-money) is based on the opening price of all the issues in the index on Friday morning. Typically, this value is not available until at least an hour after market open on Friday. Do not confuse the Friday a.m. settlement value with the opening price of the index on Friday. The two values can be very different, since the settlement value is theoretical and not determined until all of the issues in the index have opened for trading.

Since an index has many components (anywhere from about 10 to over 5,000), it is very unlikely that at the exact moment the market opens on Friday morning each of them will have an opening trade at the exact same time. As a result, there is often no true actual opening price for the index. Although you will see a quote as of 9:30 a.m. EST each day, the first quotes you see are based on the opening prices of the components that *have* opened and the prior day's closing prices of those that *have not* yet opened. Several minutes later, when the slower components have opened, it is possible that the earlier components will have already changed prices. The settlement value is calculated using the first price that each component traded at, and most of the time, those first prices did not actually all occur at the exact same time.

To determine the settlement value of an index that stops trading on Thursday, a special symbol is assigned to that index. Typically, you would only use this symbol on Friday of expiration week.

The following is a sample list of some settlement symbols:

Regular symbol	Settlement symbol
$SPX	$SET
$DJX	$DJS
$RUT	$RLS
$NDX	$NDS
$MID	$MIV
$XAL	$XAO

To be certain that the settlement value has been updated, you should see values for open, close, high, and low. If you do not see these values, the settlement has not yet been updated. Additional information and settlement symbols are available on the Web sites of the option exchange where the index options trade.

Strike Price: The price at which the underlying stock will be delivered in the event that the option is exercised or assigned is called the strike price. All call and put options have a strike price associated with them. The strike price of a call option is the price at which you can purchase the underlying stock if you decide to exercise your option contract. The strike price of a put option is the price at which you can sell your stock if you decide to exercise your option contract. In the case of index options, the strike price is used to determine the amount in which the option is in-the-money or out-of-the-money, which will determine the amount of the cash debit or credit to your account.

INDEX